gift
contributed by

FRIENDS OF THE LIBRARY

Valley of the Tetons Library

The Education

of an

American Dreamer

The Education

of an

American Dreamer

How a Son of Greek Immigrants
Learned His Way from a Nebraska Diner
to Washington, Wall Street, and Beyond

Peter G. Peterson

TWELVE

NEW YORK   BOSTON

Twelve
Hachette Book Group
237 Park Avenue
New York, NY 10017

Visit our Web site at www.HachetteBookGroup.com.

Twelve is an imprint of Grand Central Publishing
The Twelve name and logo are trademarks of Hachette Book Group, Inc.

Printed in the United States of America

First Edition: June 2009
10 9 8 7 6 5 4 3 2 1

Library of Congress Cataloging-in-Publication Data

Peterson, Peter G.
    The education of an American dreamer : how a son of Greek immigrants
learned his way from a Nebraska diner to Washington, Wall Street, and beyond /
Peter G. Peterson.—1st ed.
        p.   cm.
    ISBN: 978-0-446-55603-3
    1. Peterson, Peter G.   2. Greek Americans—Biography.
  3. Businessmen—United States—Biography.   4. Peterson family.   I. Title.

    CT275.P58544A3   2009
    978.2'394034—dc22
    [B]
                                                                2009003407

Dedicated with love, admiration,
and gratitude to my parents,
Georgios Petropoulos and Venetia Papapavlou,
who became George and Venet Peterson

CONTENTS

CHAPTER 1

KEARNEY

Beacon in the Night

Kearney, Nebraska, where I grew up in the 1930s, was a good-sized town by the standards of the plains. It was large enough for people to want to eat at all hours of the day and night, and the Central Cafe, my father's restaurant, was there for them. It was half a block from the Union Pacific railway station, its neon sign blinking through the night beckoning the train crews rotating off their shifts and the passengers who had arrived, for whatever reason they had come, at the absolute midpoint of the United States. Kearney was halfway between Boston and San Francisco, 1,733 miles from each, as attested by the plaque near the swimming pool at the 1733 Park where I played as a boy.

My father had worked for the railroad. He took a job no one else wanted, washing dishes in the steamy caboose that served as living quarters to a crew of laborers laying track in western Nebraska. From washing dishes he learned to cook, which he much preferred to driving railroad spikes and hauling rails and ties. But the track crews couldn't work through the Nebraska winter, so when the crew crossed paths with a traveling circus looking for someone to feed its collection of roustabouts, aerialists, and animal tamers, my father took off with the circus. This was sometime around 1917, five years after he arrived at America's golden shore from Greece, a boy of seventeen who spoke no English and had a third grade education.

1

Other cooking jobs followed, and he learned more about the restaurant business. He learned to speak English. His employers often gave him room and board, which allowed him to save much of what he earned. Finally, his experience and his savings reached the point where he was ready to start out on his own. He bought and quickly sold restaurants in Lexington, Nebraska, and in Iowa before settling on Kearney, a town with growth potential and not much competition. It had a college that he envisioned as a source of cheap, smart labor, a handful of Greek families that would make him feel at home, and a vacant lot downtown near the railway station. He bought it and built the Central Cafe, whose sign was a beacon not only to the travelers who passed through Kearney but to its townspeople as well.

"Home of Fine Foods Since 1923," read that sign in inexhaustible neon. That was the year my father opened the cafe. It stayed open twenty-four hours a day, and for twenty-five years it would literally never close. He married my mother a year later. Two years after that I came into the world, and by 1934, when I was eight, I was counting out change to my father's customers.

My biggest challenge as a boy was trying to fit in. But fitting in was really tough, because I wanted to be 100 percent American while my parents clung to their Greek customs. They pulled furiously one way, I the other. All children struggle to escape their parents so they can define themselves, but mine had roots deep in another world.

George and Venetia

My father was George Peterson, which was not the name he was born with. That was Georgios Petropoulos, the surname literally translating into "Peter's son," and often over the years he told me he deeply regretted changing it. "I wouldn't want anyone to think I wasn't proud of our race," he said. In the scheme of things, however, he kept the more important thing he brought from the Old Country, his bedrock values.

He was from a town called Vahlia, in the mountains of the Peloponnesian Peninsula in southern Greece. It was a poor town, and his family was among the poorest. His father, Peter, for whom I am named, according to the family lore preferred sleeping under an apple tree to working and would move only to find a new patch of shade when the shifting sunlight hit his eyes and woke him up. His indolence did nothing to diminish the imperial tendencies of his wife, my grandmother Nicoletta, who upon meeting new people would offer her hand to be kissed. They tried to keep a garden, but rainfall was sparse and water had to be carried in buckets from a nearby stream. They kept chickens, which provided eggs, and goats, which provided milk, and when a new baby was born in the family, a goat was slaughtered over the protests of the children, who had made pets of the animals. My father had six brothers and a sister, and they all slept on straw mattresses crowded together on the floor of the family's two-room house or, if the weather was good, outside in the yard. Regardless of the season, none of them wore shoes. The shoes their parents wore were fashioned from discarded tires. They told time by the sun since they could not afford a clock, and on cloudy days relied on guesswork.

School was an afterthought. Girls could expect six years of education. Boys might reach higher, but only if they paid a price. They would have to leave home at the beginning of each week, walk thirty miles to a larger village that had a more advanced school, and live in a hostel with other boys until the weekend when they could walk home again. This was not my father's lot. For his older brothers who went off to school, my grandmother would bake a loaf of bread and score it with a knife five times, to let them know how much—or little—they could eat each day with slices from the block of cheese she gave them from her homemade stores. At some point, they started dreaming of America.

My father's older brother Nick was the first to make the passage. By 1912, he had a job at a meatpacking plant in Milwaukee and could send money for my father's ticket. The *Titanic* sank that year, but my father's trip was uneventful in his fetid quarters deep in the ship's bowels where he longed to breathe fresh air. He entered America through Ellis Island and headed to Milwaukee to meet up with Nick as soon as he cleared the immigration hurdles. His first job, at a fruit stand, fell through because he could not understand the customers; if asked for "a couple of apples," he would heave a sackful on the counter. Soon, however, Nick got him a job at the meatpacking plant. It was the starting job from hell, feeding cattle hooves and horns into grinding machines to be processed into fertilizer, the kind of job that to this day immigrants are willing to do because their foothold in America is that precious. Choking dust rose from the machines; the men fed them with one hand and clamped damp rags over their noses with the other, which was murder on their arms and shoulders. My father almost gave up and headed home. But he stuck it out and moved up to cutting meat, learning the fine points of reducing cattle and hogs to roasts and chops with very little waste. When he moved on to the railroad job, he changed his name to Peterson, as Nick had done before him. If he was sorry for it later, he could blame the Union Pacific timekeepers who claimed they could never understand him when he said Petropoulos. And as he grew into his twenties and cooked for railroad laborers and circus folk and saved money and set his sights on building the cafe, he waited for someone to marry.

My mother, Venetia Papapavlou, lived in Niata, in southern Greece southeast of Sparta. The Papapavlous had prospered by comparison with the Petropoulos clan. Yanni Papapavlou—or Big John, as her father was known—had land and a big house. Like everyone else in the village, he had no electricity or running water. Rain supplied drinking water that was stored in big clay pots called amphorae, and there was a cistern that provided water for the garden so that no one had to haul water from a stream.

Olive, almond, fig, orange, and lemon groves, wheat fields, and vineyards dotted the landscape beyond the house. Only the olive groves qualified as a commercial operation. Big John had an olive press and used the proceeds from the oil to purchase more olive groves. He paid his workers with the very crops they harvested; the olive pickers were paid one bushel of olives for every four they picked, which he would then press into oil for them. The men who picked grapes and stamped them to make wine kept much of it for themselves and sold the rest.

My mother remembered an abundance of food prepared by her mother, Demitroula. Hungry neighbors always knew they would be fed, and her father's generosity extended to the local schoolhouse, where he would hand out small cloth bags filled with a mixture of sun-dried raisins, fruit, and almonds. On weekends this became the stuff of barter and a social life, with Big John hitching up his horses, piling his children—known collectively as Little Big Johns—into the wagon, and driving to town to trade the bags of fruits and nuts for other goods. If there were any bags left, he would give them away rather than carry them back home.

John and Demitroula had an easy, bantering relationship. His was the only horse-drawn wagon in Niata, and he always insisted that she ride in the front seat with him as he drove, a rare display of gender equality in that place and time. But he also warned her, laughingly, that if she got too big for her britches he would assign her to "live spotter" duty in front of the horses, a reference to the dangerous job of locating the land mines that littered the countryside after Greece's past wars. Of course he never did carry out his threat.

His generosity was deep. He had an old neighbor, Stavros, who depended on his donkey, called Kitso, or "helper," to gather wild berries and tsai, the Greek mountain tea also called shepherd's tea. Stavros sold some of what he had gathered for a few pennies or traded it. Returning from church one Sunday with three of his children, Big John heard a commotion as they were passing Stavros's small house. Stopping to inquire, he found Stavros berating his donkey, which had died. "Look what Kitso did to me," Stavros cried. "How could she do this to me?"

Big John agreed that Kitso was a thoughtless beast but joked that she had never done such a thing before. Stavros, not amused, ordered him off his property forever. John hustled away, bought another donkey, and returned the next day to present it as a gift from all the Papapavlou children. They were there as their father knocked on the old man's door and they saw how, still furious, he again ordered Big John off his property. Sadly, Big John explained that his children would have to give the donkey to someone else. The old man was moved to take a look at the animal and then received it with gratitude, gushing with prayers that Big John would live a long and healthy life.

"You had better pray for an even longer and healthier life for your new Kitso," said Big John.

Life in Niata had changed. The young men began to leave for better jobs. Without them Big John could not cultivate his groves, and young women like mother had fewer chances of marrying. So the day came when Big John accepted that three of his children had little choice but to emigrate and join other members of the family already in America. On a mid-September day in 1920, eight years after my father had arrived in America, my mother, Venetia, her sister Patra and brother Demetrios (James), with his new wife Adamandia, boarded a ship called the *Megali Hellas* in Piraeus bound for New York. They had nineteen days of hell, with passengers falling sick all the way before they steamed past the Statue of Liberty and docked at Ellis Island on October 4, 1920. My mother, like my father, was seventeen when she first set foot in America.

And like him, she traveled halfway across the continent. With the small group of immigrant Greeks, she boarded a train for Fremont, Nebraska, west of Omaha. It was all mapped out. She was to work as a housekeeper for her Uncle John and Aunt Vasso Petrow and nanny to their three children. John was an entrepreneur who owned a restaurant and a J. C. Penney store in Fremont. It was he who had sent the money for her passage.

Venetia quickly learned that she would pay a price for her journey to America. She cleaned house and cared for John and Vasso's children and toiled in his restaurant, too. There was no letup and she, like my father, dreamed of what now seemed like a golden past in Greece. But to return home would have been disloyal, and she forced herself to look ahead. After three and a half years, when she turned twenty-one, Uncle John decided it was time for his ward to marry. This could not have come as bad news to my mother.

The Nebraska Greek community was small and highly interwoven, and John knew where to find likely candidates for marriage to a beautiful and highly eligible young woman. One was my father, whose reputation for making a success of the Central Cafe had spread the 160 miles that separated Kearney from Fremont.

Three bachelors called simultaneously at John Petrow's house that day in late May 1924. One, to hear my mother tell it, was a version of Washington Irving's Ichabod Crane, gawky and tall, all limbs and knees and elbows. The second apparently was not memorable enough to recall. The third was my father, smelling of Aqua Velva aftershave, his jet-black hair combed straight back from his forehead and shining with a dose of

Lucky Tiger hair tonic. As the bachelors sat in the Petrow living room, no doubt appraising one another, my mother served them water and fruit drinks and thus had a chance to imagine what might lie ahead.

"Which one do you want?" her uncle asked when she returned to the kitchen with the empty tray.

She and my father were married forty days later.

The Peterson Family Begins

They were married twice, as it turned out. The first time, on July 6, they exchanged vows in the Fremont chambers of a Dodge County judge named Wintersteen. This was legal and official, but it lacked the over-arching authority of the Greek church. The church ceremony came a few days later, when the one Greek Orthodox priest for Nebraska and parts of Iowa had a break in his schedule and came out from Omaha. Uncle John Petrow had assembled his Greek friends and relatives in a roped-off section of the J. C. Penney store before it opened. Uncle John gave Venetia away, and a cousin of my father's stood up as his best man. My parents dressed for this one, my father in a rented tuxedo, my mother in a white dress and a fantastic hat made from layers of chiffon. She carried an equally fantastic spray of flowers. By all accounts the occasion was a joyous one, but the formality of the official wedding portraits seems to have overwhelmed them. Neither looks happy. They stare at the camera with grave, almost grim expressions, in my mother's case perhaps because the Greek Orthodox ceremony places the wife secondary to the husband, who is "head of his wife" in a marriage. After-ward, everyone rode out to the Petrow farm for the wedding lunch.

I imagine those early days were hard. They were two people whose only certain points of common interest were that they were Greek and had to struggle to survive. My father, the child of poverty, ascetic and hardworking; my mother, warmer and spontaneous—in a perfect world each would have complemented the other and compensated for what the other lacked. But the depth of their divisions came to light at once.

They honeymooned in Colorado. This was not a romantic choice, but a family obligation. My father's closest maternal relative in the United States, his mother's sister, lived in Colorado Springs and he wanted to show his new bride to his aunt. My mother had the idea that her honeymoon was worth recording, so she got her hands on a Brownie camera and took some photographs. Somehow this escaped my father's notice.

Back in Kearney, they set up housekeeping. My mother had the film developed and one day, when they were walking the seven blocks from the Central Cafe to their house—the family budget did not permit a car—she brought out the photographs to show my father. She must have been shocked at his reaction.

He erupted in fury, raging at her "gall" and "disrespect" for taking and developing photographs without his knowledge and consent. It was an act of disobedience, and furthermore, an unapproved expense. No bride of his could walk with her husband after committing such an act. He ordered her across the street to walk on the opposite sidewalk the rest of the way home.

What to make of this? It was not in my mother's nature or her cultural background to complain about her marriage, but it was she and not my father who told me this story many years after it had occurred. In fact, she waited until he died to tell me, although I had long since concluded that she had much more to complain about. After my father's death, her manner was completely different from the one I had known much of my life. As a widow, she found a joy I hadn't seen. She spoke with a voice that was happy and light. Cousins who had known her as a girl in Greece said she was that girl again. She was finally free of the yoke of the imperious patriarch, my father.

She always was a loving mother. That was clear to me from my earliest moments. She could anticipate my needs, which spoiled me and caused problems later in my life when others—business colleagues as well as romantic partners—could not do the same. Her doting gave me a punch line when Jewish colleagues told me stories about the fussy attentions of their mothers and their maternal pride. I'd listen to them all and say, when they were finished, "Greek mothers make Jewish mothers look criminally negligent."

The world began to open up to me when I was about three. By

then I had already been to Greece with my parents on a visit to their home villages, but I was only two and don't remember the trip. One of my first memories is of attending a movie with my mother. It was Al Jolson's *The Singing Fool*, the tale of a singer who broke the hearts of those early talking-picture audiences as he sang "Sonny Boy" to his dying son. I remember jumping up in the dark theater and shouting, "I am the Sonny Boy!" My mother shrugged off the stares and laughed and hugged me.

Soon after that, in 1929, my sister, Elaine, was born. I think this fulfilled my mother in some way that I or any son could not. My mother felt born again. Elaine would achieve the life my mother had imagined for herself. The year after Elaine was born, we were happy.

The following summer, my parents drove away—we were now the owners of a Model T Ford—to spend a weekend with the Petrows in Fremont. They had two things to celebrate—the Fourth of July and their sixth wedding anniversary two days later. They left Elaine and me in the care of one of Kearney's eight Greek families, but before the weekend was over Elaine developed a frightening, barking cough. A phone call brought my parents rushing home, but it was too late. She died at age one on their anniversary, July 6, of croup. Croup is a child's disease, a normally mild viral infection that restricts the upper airways. The worst cases occur not in the summer but in the winter and the early spring, and even in those cases it is rarely life-threatening. But this time the stars were cruelly misaligned. That Elaine died was bad enough. That her death occurred on the anniversary of a marriage that was tense at best can only have added to the pain. My father was a stoic. Of my two parents, my mother seemed to suffer far more.

A deep gloom descended over my mother and she could not escape it. Pregnant at the time of Elaine's death, two months later she went into early labor, two months premature. She called my father at the cafe to say she was having rapid contractions and needed to go to the hospital. He told her he was baking pies and couldn't leave, and sent someone else to take her. My brother, John, was born into her sadness.

And pretty baby though he was, he could not lift her spirits. Nor could I, as eager as I was to see her smile and feel her warmth again. But her life was as barren as the Nebraska winter that followed the summer of Elaine's death. "Just push me into the grave with my beloved Elaine," I heard her say once to my father. She couldn't even bear to hold my brother when he was a baby, something my brother never got over.

I had felt special, doted on, warm, secure, and all of that vanished. After Elaine's death, my mother was a different woman, cold, detached, and strange. I tried to be perfect and loving in order to please her: There we are, the two of us, in the kitchen of our house. I am standing over the register in the corner trying to catch the heat rising from the coal furnace in the basement, but my father keeps the heat low to save money and I am never warm enough, so I shiver, hug myself, hop from foot to foot. It's a little dance I do for her, hoping she will notice. She sits across the room at the table, with a heavy shawl around her shoulders, her fingers twisting the fringes at the ends, staring at nothing. Sometimes she hums, over and over, a sad tune that must have been a Greek lament. But more often she sits in utter silence. That is the worst. The silence is a clammy hand, and I try to drive it away with Mommy this, Mommy that, Mommy, Mommy, Mommy. And she responds with more silence. That is why, today, I fill a pause with words, too many, some would say. In my experience, silence is a pall.

Freudian psychologists tell us that a child's separation from the mother, when the child suddenly realizes he or she is no longer the center of the solar system, is nearly always painful. When the separation takes place at a very young age, suddenly and in the midst of tragedy or trauma, it is especially painful. As indeed I learned.

Thus, the year went by. My father, deprived of his helpmate at the restaurant, decided to try anything to get her back. This led him to bring her to the Mayo Clinic in Rochester, Minnesota, which by the early 1930s was already a major medical institution serving a wide range of conditions both physical and mental. My mother stayed there for two or three weeks, and returned with a diagnosis of "nervousness." How language changes. What was once called "melancholia" evolved into "neurasthenia," then "nervousness," and then the dire-sounding "nervous breakdown." Today she would have "clinical depression," the debilitating state memorably described by novelist William Styron as "darkness visible." The cure prescribed, in those days before effective and tolerable psychotropic drugs, was rest and counseling. She got the rest, but not the counseling.

Enter Mrs. Boulos. That Kearney, Nebraska, could be so filled with immigrants strikes me as remarkable only in retrospect. Our little neighborhood seven blocks from downtown included not only Greeks but a poor Lebanese Catholic woman. Her kitchen was always fragrant with the smell of fresh-baked pita bread. She offered a lifeline of escape from the lonely quiet imposed by our mother's need to rest and withdraw. As soon as my brother, John, was big enough to toddle, I would take him by the hand first thing on weekday mornings and lead him through backyards to Mrs. Boulos's kitchen door. Barreling into her warm kitchen, we left behind our distracted mother and received instead the indulgence of an older woman whose own children were grown. She must have liked having children around, because she fussed and served us piping hot rounds of pita bread and tousled our hair as we sat at her kitchen table with our toys.

If my own mother ever resented this turn to a substitute, I never knew it. She was probably relieved that we left her to her rest, and neither she nor my father ever worried, because the Bouloses were friends as well as neighbors. As John got older and more athletic, he tried to outrun me to Mrs. Boulos's door, but it didn't matter who got there first since she was equally warm and giving to us both.

"Economia!"

My father played a small part in this equation. As my awareness grew, he was a distracted and elusive figure who appeared mainly late at night. Sometimes, if I was up early on a weekday, around six or so, I could see him leave for work. He would rush into the kitchen fresh from shaving, his cheeks aglow, combed-back hair still neat and glistening, wearing the uniform in which he presided over the Central Cafe—dark pants and a white shirt, a tie that he stuck between the buttons of the shirt to protect from stains, black shoes, and white socks, the socks white on the theory that white was better for the feet because it retained less heat and moisture. Then he was gone. There were no hugs, kisses, or conversation, only the kitchen door banging in his wake.

Saturday night was the occasion for a family meal at the cafe, but even then my father was continually jumping up to attend to customers. On Sundays we had lunch together at home, but this was a hurried affair at around eleven-thirty in the morning so he could get back to the cafe by noon. When he came home at night, usually at nine or later, he looked exhausted, his combed-back hair unkempt, the cheeks that had been glowing in the morning now dark with stubble, the promise of his white socks replaced by the reality of fifteen painful hours on his feet and varicose veins that he wrapped in damp cloths and soaked in a tub of water laced with Epsom salts while he sat at the kitchen table with his trouser legs rolled up. He didn't talk to us, or to Mother, very much. (I never once in my lifetime saw him hug her.) There was no joshing, no sitting down with us to read, not much curiosity about how we spent our days or what we were studying in school. He never worked around the home, never mowed the grass. Yet it wasn't that he didn't care for us. It was just that he seemed able to express his love only by his utter and exhausting devotion to our livelihood and our future through his work at the cafe. He was what would later come to be called a workaholic, and this tendency to focus on work at the expense of family and personal relationships was, unfortunately, one of the legacies he passed on to me.

Elaine had died approximately eight months after the stock market crash of October 1929. I was too young to notice how things changed as a result of the widespread loss of jobs and income that came to be called the Great Depression. Farmers had been locked in a depression of their own caused by crop surpluses, drought, and mortgage debt for most of the 1920s, so maybe things didn't change that much in Kearney. Cattle and hogs continued to ride through daily on the Union Pacific, one-way passengers bound for the Omaha stockyards. I do remember that encouragements to thrift were everywhere, at the cafe and at home. Visiting the cafe's sole bathroom brought one face-to-face with the sign my father had taped to the paper towel dispenser: "Why Use Two When One Wipes Dry." It was not a question. To my father, "big spender" was a big-time insult.

But at least the customer had a choice. At home things were different. There we lived according to a set of rigid guidelines calculated to squeeze every last measure of wastefulness out of our behavior. The worst of these governed the weekly Saturday night bath. Never was a ritual designed that said more about a child's place in the pecking order. It began with a steaming tub in our one small—and in the winter frigidly cold—bathroom. My father was first into the tub, and I expect he sank into the hot water with a sigh of relief from the pain of his labors. Once he was soaped and rinsed and out, it was my mother's turn. Next, it was time for John and me. We bathed together in the twice-used, now lukewarm water, and it was never clear to me whether I was cleaner after the bath, or before.

The living room was kept cold and was sealed off during the entire winter, as was the small guest bedroom that my father had made by erecting a wall that cut the living room in half. The bedroom was opened for guests, who came frequently and often unannounced. This was a habit among Nebraska's Greek immigrants; they treated one another's houses and restaurants like wayside inns where they expected to find overnight lodgings and good food, all for free. In our house they had to endure the plastic coverings my father kept on all the furniture to protect the upholstery, another of his economizing measures. But my mother loved the company and saw these visits as great social occasions.

Other visitors stayed longer. I would arrive home from school to find that a new crop of my father's relatives from Greece had shown up, wearing odd clothes and carrying old suitcases tied up with twine, and had taken over the guest bedroom where they would stay for months while they worked at the cafe. This, I later learned, was by prearrangement: their labor in exchange for room and board and small wages that would give them footholds in America and allow them to move on, the same path my father had taken. But in contrast to the vacationers, these visitors were a burden on my mother, who had to clean up after them, do their laundry, and cook for them when they weren't eating at the cafe. My father argued that it saved money on wages.

He also saved money on the party line telephone, an antique term that piqued interest in my grandchildren until they learned that it meant a line shared by three neighbors, on which a nosy neighbor could listen to your conversations. And I remember my mother's shouted call to "Close the lights!" when someone left a room, knowing that lights left burning would bring my father's wrath. "Economia!" he hurled at her. "Economia!" Even today, when I leave a room, I need to "close the lights."

My father's economies at the cafe extended well beyond the paper towels. To keep his costs low, he would go to the markets and pick up day-old vegetables and fruit, and whatever else he could purchase at a discount. He produced some of the better restaurant meals in Kearney with this provender, and some of his most popular dishes, like meatloaf, were made from the previous day's leftovers. He did his own butchering in the restaurant kitchen. From his experience at the meatpacking plant in Milwaukee, he could look at a loin of pork and know exactly how many pork chop tenderloins he could cut from it. He could attack a quarter of beef with a meat saw and a butcher knife and reduce it to steaks, short ribs, fat and lean cuts for stew and hamburger, and bones for soup stock, with hardly any waste.

The Central Cafe's menu brimmed with this hearty fare, offered for what today seems like a song. The most popular item was probably the "Hot Beef Special," an open-face sandwich featuring a mound of roast beef on white bread slathered with mashed potatoes and gravy, a slice of pie, and coffee, all for thirty cents. The coffee, over which a customer could linger through unlimited refills, was five cents by itself. Beef stew, stewed chicken with noodles, liver and onions, ham hocks and beans, hamburgers, and the aforementioned meatloaf accounted for most of the rest of the lunchtime orders. For the evening meal, beginning at five-thirty, which in our part of Nebraska was supper (lunch was called dinner), diners favored steaks and chops, prime rib of beef, and roast pork loin. Potatoes and gravy, macaroni and cheese, green beans, presliced white bread, and simple salads were the staples on the side, followed by fruit pies, or ice cream for dessert, and the drinks of choice were coffee, milk, iced tea, and water, in that order. There were no Greek dishes on the menu. Stuffed grape leaves would have puzzled

Kearneyites; they liked their rice straight, and ground beef, too. Even my mother's glorious baklava, her butter-rich wonder of honey, nuts, and wafer-thin stacks of phyllo dough, was too exotic for the cafe's dessert case. Later, when Nebraskans followed the nation's lead and repealed Prohibition in the state in 1934, my father put beer on the menu but not wine or hard liquor. (My mother was one of Prohibition's many scofflaws, making wine from grapes she grew in our backyard and crushed in the time-honored way, by foot in a tub in our basement. Kearney's police chief was one of her prime patrons and she loved those customer relationships. No one was sure if my father knew about her cottage industry.)

For all of my father's cost cutting, the Central Cafe was the town's only white tablecloth restaurant. Its fifteen tables were "four-tops," meaning they sat four people each, and the counter that ran along one wall could accommodate another eighteen. Each of the tables was laid with a tablecloth, white cloth napkins, and heavy stainless cutlery designed to take a beating in the large sinks in the kitchen at the back. The counter, of course, had no tablecloths, but counter customers got cloth napkins like everybody else. This apparent contradiction to my father's "economia" gave the restaurant a feel of quality that set it apart in Kearney.

He changed the menu every day, depending on what he found at the markets. His first task each morning, while the early breakfast crowd was waking up to coffee, pancakes, waffles, and bacon and eggs, was to type out the dinner and supper offerings on a messy two-ply Ditto form rolled into the big square Underwood typewriter on his small desk. Hunched over the machine, he hunted and pecked with one finger until the menu was composed, then wrapped the form onto a drum on his hand-cranked Ditto machine to turn out copies on cheap paper. They came out smelling of the duplicating fluid, a smell that only people of a certain age will remember, and with purple letters that were unaligned like children's letter blocks pushed together on the floor, one high, one low, one tilted, because the typewriter was old. The flimsy, purple, oddly printed menus contrasted with the feel of the seemingly luxurious white tablecloths.

Depression Baby Businessman

I started working at the cafe when Prohibition ended in 1932. I was eight. It was my job to take cash and make change at the register at the front of the long counter, and I liked it from the start. The numbers fell in line for me. Customers squinted at the bills and coins I counted out into their hands, looking for mistakes I never made.

This success emboldened me. One of my father's pricing innovations, designed to keep the cafe filled, was a 10 percent bonus for customers who paid in advance—diners who bought a $5 meal ticket up front would get $5.50 worth of food. Many of the tickets were kept in a little box on the counter and once I took my station at the register, I made it my business to look them over to see whose were on the verge of running out. Woe to the patron who was a ten-cent slice of pie away from spending his $5.50. I would confront him at the register while he was fumbling for his change. "Would you like to renew your meal ticket? This one's almost out." Most of the time they did, without a fuss. But the Depression had reduced the number of people who could advance $5 against their future meals, even with a 10 percent return, and sometimes I ran into resistance. I responded with aggressive salesmanship, a trait I would refine and depend upon as time went on; learning early on not to take no for an answer was a valuable lesson. I sometimes hovered near tables while customers were eating. Once I chased the local haberdasher down the street (when he forgot to pay a nickel for a cup of coffee). I never questioned whether my targets thought I was pushy or obnoxious; my goal was to improve my numbers for the recognition I would gain, and, maybe, win my distant father's approval.

For many, of course, the Depression was far more serious than mustering $5 in order to save fifty cents. Millions had nothing at all. In Kearney, we saw enough to know the country was struggling, and that people had to try to take care of one another. Dozens of jobless and underfed men found their way to the Central Cafe's back door begging for food, and my father never turned a single one away. He didn't just hand out meals for free, however; sensing that their pride depended on it, he always found some chore that they could do in exchange for a heaping plate of stew. It was his version of a welfare-for-work program.

Many people never made it to the cafe's doorstep, but my parents managed to help them in other ways. The hardships that hit the Great Plains farmers in the 1920s continued into the 1930s, worsening the effects of the failed economy. There was drought and more drought. As a child in the mid-1930s, I recall dust storms that blackened the skies at noon and choked people and animals with swirling grit. Business at the cafe dropped down to nothing because nobody went out. At school, teachers turned the lights on and tried to teach, but nobody could concentrate in the black-brown darkness because you could hear the dirt peppering the window glass and the windows and doors rattling in the wind. It was scary. The sound was alive, like a rasping intruder clawing at the walls. Thick grit drifted in around the windows and under the doors and nobody could stop it. At home, even when we had some warning of an approaching storm, and Mother got John and me to help her tape cellophane or wax paper over the windows, the dirt still found its way inside. When the storms ended, we swept the dirt up and carried it outside in buckets. Worse still were the storms of grasshoppers. They, too, blackened the sky as they swooped down to devour entire fields of wheat and corn, denude home gardens, and form writhing, hopping clusters on the streets and sidewalks, where they crunched sickeningly under your feet when you walked.

The victims of these plagues—and they seemed biblical in their ferocity—were often immigrant farm families. There were kids in my school who wore the same grimy overalls for days on end and slumped at their desks looking dirty, dusty, and hungry. My parents made food baskets for such families. My mother had emerged from her depression and found busyness the best therapy to keep it from returning. So she made scarves, hats, socks, and mittens for needy children and baked bread for bake sales to benefit the poor of Kearney. Their charity also went back home to Greece in the form of the clothes my mother made and the money my father gave to benefit their villages—half his savings when the times were prosperous. It was to be a lesson I never forgot.

As a young man, I did not fully appreciate the lesson these efforts of my parents conveyed. It was as simple as could be: Give something back. Nobody gave my parents anything except the most precious gift of all—the opportunities this country offered them when they landed on its shores. For the chance to be who they could be and to be successful, they recognized civilized society's fundamental bargain—it's a two-way street—and they repaid their gift by helping those less fortunate, near and far away.

Although the dust storms and raining grasshoppers frightened me and I felt bad for the hungry men and the poor farmers, the Depression came down to something more self-centered. Two or three of Kearney's barbers ate at the cafe, and they were hard-pressed to pay for meals once their customers started skipping haircuts. My father worked out a reciprocal trade agreement, swapping food for services: Whenever my brother and I needed haircuts, our father sent us to the barber who was next in the rotation. This would have worked just fine, except that they didn't all give good haircuts. If the wrong barber came up in the rotation, I could end up with a bowl haircut that left me looking like the farm boys who (I imagined) got shorn at home by their fathers, using pruning shears or blunt scissors. I hated these haircuts, and argued with my father about getting them. But in the end, I had no choice because, as he explained, they were the only way these men had of satisfying their debts to the cafe, and he was not going to turn them into deadbeats just because his son was too vain to accept a perfectly good haircut. I usually snipped away with scissors afterward, trying to repair the damage, but it never did much good. Only later did I appreciate the thrift that the Depression enforced with a harsh hand, the lesson of never, even in the bad times, spending more than you earned. And in the good times, you saved and saved.

In our family, my father enforced the saving habit rigidly. He brought me a piggy bank from the local home savings and loan bank, but the pennies and nickels I put into it weren't for a rainy day. He wanted me to prepare for a monsoon. I was not allowed to raid the piggy bank for something I might want, like the little snapshot camera that I craved. Savings were meant to be saved. Rather, I stuffed the bank until it weighed a ton. Only then would my father unlock it and let me spill out its treasure of coins onto my bed, where the sight of them made me feel rich, but, alas, I couldn't spend them. I had to count them and stack them in wrappers to be taken to the bank to put into my passbook savings account, which slowly grew larger. My father carefully supervised this rigorous process for years. This personal savings account helped pay for college.

Eager to Please

Most of what I did as a young boy was designed to please one of my parents or the other. To my father, I wanted to prove that I was up to his taskmaster's standards. As for my mother, I simply wanted to regain her attention and make her happy. I was still young and naive enough to think I could fill the void caused by Elaine's death.

After she returned from the Mayo Clinic, on the better days of her recovery, she regained her magician's touch in the kitchen. She was a great baker, and when I arrived home from school in the afternoons I would find warm buttered toast made from her homemade bread, a big pot of hot chocolate, and Greek pastries. You couldn't stop eating her glorious baklava or her kourambiethes, almond shortbread cookies sprinkled with powdered sugar. Her theeples were equally addictive, thin triangles of dough rolled together and deep-fried and then lathered with honey, nuts, and cinnamon.

Since I considered it a high priority to please my mother, it was obviously my duty to appreciate her cooking. The way I figured it, the more I ate, the happier she would be and the more attention she would pay to me. Like a dog chasing its tail, I could never eat enough to bring back Elaine and erase her depression, but I kept trying anyway. Physically, given the butter-drenched goodies that emerged from her oven, my eager eating made me a chubby little boy. I've since conquered the worst of such temptations, but pastries obsess me to this day. My wife jokes that if I were standing by a pastry shop when a nude supermodel sashayed down the street, I'd be more interested in the shop window. (This addiction to food foiled one of my father's plans to economize. He wanted John to wear my clothes when I outgrew them, but John was slender and my clothes swallowed him, so he got new ones of his own.)

One could argue that pigging out on my mother's confections was not the hardest duty. But that was not all I did to curry favor. One year, with Mother's Day approaching, our elementary school teacher organized a craft project in which we would make papier-mâché boxes for our mothers to store their jewelry and knickknacks. That was not nearly good enough for me. Somehow I got hold of some alabaster. That was proper jewelry box material, and I set about carving it into what I was sure would be the best present ever. I worked obsessively, spending recesses and after-school hours carving while the other kids were playing. (Not being particularly athletic, I preferred this to roughhouse playground games in any case.) When I presented her the box, she smiled and hugged me and told me how sweet it was of me to think of her. Then she put the box away and I never saw her use it.

The depth of her loss was just too great for me to understand. Once I asked her why she never displayed a photograph of Elaine downstairs in the living room where she had photos of John and me in small silver frames on a side table. "Because I cannot bear to look at it," she said. "You see where it's hanging?" She kept the photo, the only one taken of Elaine before she died, on a wall in the staircase leading to the attic. "When I miss her and want to look at her, I come up here, turn on the light, talk to her, and cry."

I entered first grade at the Emerson Grade School, one of Kearney's several public elementary schools, when I was five. Private schools were unheard of; Kearney would have been offended by anyone who thought its tax-supported schools couldn't prepare its young people for whatever they decided to take on, be it farming, shopkeeping, or college. From Emerson through junior high and Longfellow High School, I felt I had to be the best-behaved and best-performing student in the school. And I was. Hard as it may be to believe, I don't ever recall any notable naughty behavior on my part. I accumulated gold stars and As with a vengeance. My only B was in biology, and that was because I couldn't draw the frogs we were studying. I started playing the clarinet in the ninth grade and I practiced obsessively. I even persuaded my father to buy a machine made by Philco that made recordings on a plastic disc so I could listen to myself and work on my mistakes. In a little over a year I had mastered—I use the term loosely—the third and fourth movements of Mendelssohn's violin concerto, held first chair in both the high school band and orchestra, and was selected as first clarinetist in the Nebraska clinic orchestra, composed of high school musicians from throughout the state.

It Wasn't That Easy Being Greek

My dedication to pleasing my parents sometimes found its limits. This was partly due to the conflict they felt at being American but nonetheless determined to remain loyal to Greece, its religion, and its customs. Kearney's Greek community was an isolated island in the American sea of Nebraska, and this insularity affected me in ways that I stopped counting. The worst of it was the clothes Mother sent me off to school in. She made, at home, bouffant, blouselike shirts with ruffles on the front. These frilly white numbers, worn with knickers and high-topped black patent leather shoes, set me worlds apart from my schoolmates. On my first day in the first grade, all the other boys in their bib overalls, denim shirts, and work boots stared at me in my Little Lord Fauntleroy outfit, first with curiosity and then giggling behind their hands while I flushed with embarrassment. I protested when I got home that afternoon, but she persisted in making me wear those clothes to school, and she did the same to John when he started the first grade. This went on only for a few years but, at the time, it seemed like forever.

Special occasions such as Easter were even worse. For these, she dolled us up in foustanellas, outfits worn for Greek folk dancing and by the king's guardians known as Evzones. These consisted of a white shirt with bloused sleeves and a skirtlike flared bottom, worn with a vest, a decorative sash at the waist, and leggings with garters at the calves. So much for fitting in.

In both cases, I later wondered if Mother was trying to reclaim Elaine by dressing us in these effeminate costumes. If so, even understanding her motive could not offset the embarrassment we felt at having to wear these ethnic red flags that looked girlish to boot. None of the other Greek boys in town had to wear such outfits. My good friends throughout my childhood, Gus Poulos and John Mitchell—John's family name was condensed from Mitchellopoulos—at least understood my discomfort, but the non-Greek majority gave my brother and me looks and snickers every time we had to go out wearing them.

Even my name seemed to conspire against me. Mother called me Petie, an innocent diminutive but one that caused confusion. I learned this my first day in junior high school, when the teacher started calling the roll and then stopped to ask, "Petie Peterson. Is that a boy or a girl?" Laughter ran around the room, and after that I insisted that my mother make sure the school system knew my name was Pete. But to her, I would always be Petie. Indeed, after Elaine's death she had hovered protectively over our every activity, forbidding John and me from playing contact sports. When we went into the water at Kearney's one public swimming pool, she insisted on being near us at the pool's edge. Once on the Fourth of July, she read the riot act to my Uncle Bill, my father's brother, after the fuse of a cherry bomb he lit spurted off and hit me in the eye. She even forbade us to climb the cherry tree in the backyard, though its limbs were not more than six feet off the ground. I was labeled a sissy by the other boys in those circumstances, and, I suppose, I was. (John escaped that dubious designation, in part because he was more into sports and also because he was a little devil with an infectiously naughty and, at times, disingenuous personality who charmed everyone he met and, in particular, my mother.)

Even innocent family customs seemed to conspire against my desire to fit in. We received regular packages of herbal teas from Mother's family in Greece. This tea, called tsai, was stored in a trunk in the cool basement to keep it fresh. There were two varieties: one my mother enticed me to drink in the mornings by calling it "brain food" and saying it would make me very smart; the other—chamomile—she drank in the evenings because it helped her go to sleep. One day in school our teacher asked what we drank with breakfast. Most of my classmates said they had milk or Ovaltine with their morning meal, but when my turn came I answered, "Tsai."

"What is tsai?" she asked.

Not knowing to call it tea, I explained that it was tsai, and that I drank it with meli—honey. I said, "It's good and it's sweet and it makes me smart. I drink it every morning so I can be smart all day."

"Does your mother drink it also?"

"No, she drinks the other kind of tsai, the kind that puts you to sleep at night."

"And where does your mother get this tsai?" the teacher continued.

"Out of the suitcase. There's a suitcase downstairs in the dark room and she goes down there and puts the tsai in a jar and keeps it in the cupboard. And then she makes it for me in the morning, and she drinks hers at night so she can go to sleep."

These mysterious doings apparently set off warning bells of stimulants and opiates and strange foreign customs, because before I knew it the teacher asked, "Why don't you have your mother visit and explain it to me, and then we can explain it to the rest of the class." It was another example of our differentness, and I felt embarrassed to be singled out.

Nor did I ever have my own birthday party, though I was permitted to go to a few parties of others. Greek tradition dictated that we celebrate my Name Day—June 29, the day in the church calendar dedicated to Saint Peter—rather than the anniversary of my birth. But Name Days were for adults, not for kids. It was another case of being different and not the American kid I wanted to be.

By the time I reached junior high school, Mother was no longer trying to make me look like a Greek folk dancer. But the Old Country still cast a long and sometimes—I felt—stultifying shadow. Junior high meant it was time to attend Greek School. The classes were held in one of our classrooms at Kearney Junior High after regular school hours. The teachers were Greek Orthodox priests who journeyed the forty or so miles from Grand Island, the closest town with an Orthodox church, to ruin the after-school lives of boys who would much rather have been playing football or basketball or shooting marbles. Their job was to teach us how to speak and write the mother tongue. The process began with subtle indoctrination: The first thing the priest/teacher of the day would do was to set up a small flag with a blue and white Greek flag upon the desk. They wore long beards and black robes, and they taught with unsmiling, rigid discipline. While we struggled to grasp the strange shapes of the twenty-four-letter Greek alphabet and connect them to words and words to comprehension, our non-Greek classmates passing in the hall would cast glances at us in the classroom with eyes that said, "How strange!"

Here again, I was driven to excel. I mastered Greek to the extent that I could write letters to our Greek relatives in their home villages and read the ones that we received. I also recited long Greek poems to my mother at home, at church, and at Name Day parties.

But as time went on, I tried harder and harder to escape. My parents' Greek habits and culture seemed like a vortex dragging me down while I wanted to break free and become more American. When I could I much preferred attending Kearney's Episcopal church, where I served as an acolyte, rather than going on the long drive in summer heat and winter snows to Grand Island for the interminable Greek Orthodox services. These could go on for three excruciating hours in rapid-fire Greek. It was trying during Lent, when the first day's bite of food, near the end of the service, was the communion bread, one small piece representing the body of Christ (oh, how I prayed for the second coming!).

There was no departing from these practices, however, since my parents believed that the Greek church was superior, indeed the source of Christianity. When they crossed themselves, their hands went from forehead to navel to the *right* chest and then to the left, and they insisted that the Roman Catholics who touched the left side of their chests first were doing it all wrong. As I rebelled against, or at least questioned, these assumptions, my father summoned various visiting Greek priests and bishops to sit down with me and set me straight. They all said the same thing: I should think of the world's religions as a tree in which the roots and the main trunk were all of Greek Orthodox origin. The Catholic and Protestant churches were mere branches.

None of their certainty about the church interfered with equally strong folk beliefs and superstitions. My mother once summoned my godmother to banish a wart from my hand. We assembled at midnight for the exorcism and my godmother, a strange-looking woman whom I barely knew, waved the branch of a particular kind of tree while she muttered incantations, and then applied some kind of homemade ointment to the wart. To my astonishment, it shrank and eventually disappeared.

Life Comes into Focus

This reliance on faith in all its forms made it hard for my parents to accept my nearsighted, color-blind eyes. By the seventh grade, I was practically sitting on the teacher's lap to see the blackboard, and plunging my face deep into books to read. Every time I attended a movie in Kearney's one theater, I headed straight for the front row. When the kids chose sides for softball, I was always picked last because I couldn't see the ball well, and on winter afternoons when I played Monopoly I had to lean over the board to see how many squares my roll of the dice had bought me. "Nonsense," my mother said when I told her there might be a problem. "Your father's and my eyes are fine."

When the school nurse finally insisted that I see an optometrist, he had me look through a succession of lenses at an eye chart that became clearer and clearer as he adjusted them. Understandably, he asked to see my current glasses, to determine the advance of my nearsightedness. He was stunned when I told him I had never had glasses, but surely not as stunned as I was when, at age thirteen, I walked out with my new glasses and saw the world in focus for the first time I could remember. I had no idea I had missed so much. The cars on the street had license plates that actually bore numbers; the signs in the store windows told of shovels for sale and discount trousers, and, even from a distance, I could read the Central Cafe's neon sign: "Home of Fine Foods Since 1923." The movie theater was a block and a half from where I stood, and I could see without running to stand under the marquee that George O'Brien was playing in something called *Painted Desert*. At home, I picked up the afternoon newspaper from the front steps and realized I could read it without holding it inches from my face. In the days to come I learned that I didn't have to squint except when the sun was bright.

But my parents were still convinced that my eyes should have been more like theirs. They were equally suspicious to learn that I was colorblind. In fact, my father insisted on taking the color perception test himself, and when he passed it he looked at me with doubtful disapproval. How could such a smart kid flunk such an easy test? Experiences like that dramatized the distance that grew between what I knew of the world, and what I saw my parents believed.

Adolescence sharpened still further the differences between the Greek world that my parents inhabited and the American world that I longed to join. Non-Greek girls brought out the worst of their prejudices. With no Greek girls my age in Kearney, I had to look elsewhere. But whenever I seemed interested in one of the American girls, my parents' comments were anything but civil. My mother was especially harsh, making some awful generalizations about *Amerikaniki* girls.

I did have one girlfriend, Jean Christman, whose father owned the town's bakery and was a regular customer at the Central Cafe. I put off telling my parents that we were going out, but I had to come clean when I wanted to take her to the high school dance. My sense is that the customer relationship softened the news just a bit, and as a result the prom came and went without too much commotion.

Outside the cafe my parents' social exposure to Americans, and certainly American girls, was at best limited. I do not recall ever being with my parents in a non-Greek home. This lack of interaction resulted far more from fear than any real distaste. Like many immigrants, past and present, my parents worried that popular culture, represented then by things like jazz and swing (they only played Greek music!) and the equivalent today of hip-hop, rap music, and suggestive advertising, would engulf their children and sweep away their values, even their respect for their customs and rules.

My father enforced with his hands the importance of respect for him and his rules. If I came home even five minutes late at night, he slapped me, always after asking if I preferred the blow *anapodi* or *dipli* –backhand or forehand. I always chose *anapodi* because the slaps seemed less hard. I quietly, but deeply, resented this extreme and bullying discipline that none of my friends had to put up with.

This cultural tug-of-war came to a head in my senior year in high school, when I led an effort to win parental support for a lighted, chaperoned dance in the school gymnasium. I had learned ballroom dancing from my Uncle Bill Peterson's American-born Greek wife, Helene, of whom my mother disapproved not just because she danced American style, but because she also favored innovations such as store-bought clothes over the home-sewn variety. I had visions of a swing band playing all-American wartime hits like Jimmy Dorsey's "Tangerine" or Glenn Miller's "Moonlight Cocktail" and chaste couples dancing on the hardwood floor, and I went all out for this, my first extracurricular crusade. The proposal went out to a vote by parents, and I was shocked and embarrassed to learn that my father, from whom I'd kept the knowledge that the whole thing was my idea, was one of only five parents to oppose it. I'm sure he wanted to reduce the chances of my involvement with a non-Greek girl. The dance happened nonetheless, in a very well lit gymnasium under the watchful eyes of our high school teacher chaperones.

Our high school dance was just a small example of the changes taking place. The day that really changed everything had happened two years earlier. I was fifteen, in the tenth grade, and that Sunday morning I had gone to the home of one of my Greek friends to listen to music on the radio. Suddenly the music stopped and a shocked announcer reported that Japanese planes had attacked the American fleet at Pearl Harbor. We listened in rapt and frightened silence as new details came in—battleships sunk, planes destroyed, soldiers firing pistols at the attacking bombers. I'm not sure either of us knew where Pearl Harbor was.

I raced home to get my mother's reaction. She never listened to the radio and had not heard the news. That night when my father came home he was grim. Though I sometimes heard him singing "God Bless America" softly to himself as he was shaving in the morning, with all his Greek attachments I had never fully realized his devotion to America. His voice shook and tears filled his eyes as he spoke of the sneak attack on "the greatest of all countries."

By the next morning, everybody knew where Pearl Harbor was. The kids at school, from the seniors down through the seventh graders— the high school and junior high shared one building complex—talked of nothing else. The teachers, too, pointing to world maps or spinning globes to show us what was going on in the Pacific. Everyone was numb. At eleven-thirty the whole school assembled in the auditorium to hear President Franklin D. Roosevelt address a joint session of Congress. Speakers were hooked up to a radio. Roosevelt came on and started a short speech with stirring words: "Yesterday, December 7, 1941—a date which will live in infamy . . ." When he finished, we weren't numb anymore, we were angry.

In the days that followed, everyone of military age, including myself, volunteered. Sadly, my advanced nearsightedness kept me out of the military. John was too young to be drafted. If not drafted, the rest of us planted Victory Gardens and shared the sacrifice of rationing butter and sugar and meat, gasoline and tires. Women took their places in the factories and we all bought war bonds to keep up the supplies of goods, arms, and ammunition.

Those last years of high school sped by. My work duties at the cafe had expanded from the cash register to the kitchen and all points in between. I washed and dried dishes, waited and bussed tables, mopped the floors, for which my father paid me a dollar a day. On weekends I worked at the Kearney Country Club, tending bar at night in exchange for golf lessons and caddying during the day, for which I collected the grand sum of fifty cents a round and sometimes a ten-cent tip. When I was a senior, the same year I organized the dance, construction crews moved into Kearney to start work on a new Army Air Force base outside town. The crews meant new business and more income for my father. One day when I was working the counter I met the foreman who was overseeing construction of the runways. He became a regular and I served him extra-large slices of pie until I worked up the nerve to ask what kind of jobs might be available.

"Come out Saturday. We'll see," he said.

He assigned me to watch a huge pile of builders' odds and ends, mostly junk, that had accumulated in one corner of the base complex. The work was anything but demanding. All I had to do was sit there and warm my hands on an open fire while I watched the junk pile to make sure there was no pilfering. At the end of that day, he told me I had qualified for weekend overtime pay and handed me a check for the astounding sum of $18.

That evening I walked into the cafe kitchen where my father was hard at work cutting up a piece of beef, his sleeves rolled up and a blood-stained apron covering his shirt front. When he saw me he pushed his hair off his forehead with his wrist and said, "Well, big shot, how does it feel to put in a real day's work for a change?" The moment I had been waiting years for had arrived at last.

"Actually, Dad, I enjoyed it a lot. And you might be interested in what they're paying me." I threw the check down on the worktable.

He was speechless. I am confident there were many days at the Central Cafe when he did not earn $18. The entire twenty-four-hour-a-day, seven-day-a-week operation took in perhaps $25,000 a year during the long years of the Depression, and that sustained our family, two cooks, four waitresses who were paid a dollar a day plus meals and tips, a dishwasher, and Jack Ryan, who for years held down the overnight shift all on his own—he, all alone, and with an unceasing smile, did it all; he cooked, served, and washed the dishes. The Central Cafe produced regular gifts of cash back to my father's family in Vahlia, and less frequent ones to my mother's village of Niata, as well as wardrobe-sized boxes of used clothing to both places. And it produced my father's promise to me that when I graduated from high school he would provide me "the best education money can buy," a promise that gained momentum when I won the New York State Regents' prize, which provided a scholarship at a New York university, scoring highest on a standardized test given to all the high school students in Buffalo County, where Kearney is situated.

The Regents prize was one clear signal that my future did not lie in Kearney. The $18 check lying on the table was another. For the first time I realized there were options out there. I didn't know what they were, but I wanted to find out. I also knew, or sensed, that I would have to seek them elsewhere. One day soon I would leave my hometown and my parents and enter a new world that I could explore on my own terms.

CHAPTER 2

LEAVING KEARNEY

Slow Train East

The day came. Once I graduated from Longfellow High School at the top of my class of about 180 in the spring of 1943, I was willing and eager to leave Kearney for a wider, less insular—and most importantly, less Greek—experience. As for ready, that was another story.

I had perversely chosen to apply for admission to Massachusetts Institute of Technology. MIT wore a halo of excellence bestowed by a long history of fine engineering education. My father's friend Dr. Herbert Cushing, the president of Nebraska State Teachers College in Kearney, who was a regular customer at the Central Cafe, told him it was the best. My parents valued Dr. Cushing's opinion because his doctorate represented an immigrant family's highest aspirations for their children. Dr. Cushing had also said I probably wouldn't be able to get in. With the war on, the school was heavily involved in military research, from radar systems to, as the world would later learn, the atomic bomb. Teaching was taking a back seat, and MIT had decided to admit only a very small freshman class so that its faculty could devote its attention to research. If my high school years had taught me anything, it was that I could prevail through sheer obsessive diligence. I could out-work and out-study almost anybody, and if that is what it took to conquer a situation, that's what I would do. That meant spending two quarters at Nebraska State Teachers College taking physics and math courses.

Finally, in the early spring of 1944, I was ready to go. So when my acceptance arrived in late 1943, I felt the smug satisfaction of "I told you so."

The choice of MIT was complicated and, in certain respects, a terrible one. On the one hand, I wanted to get far away from Kearney. The plaque by the swimming pool at the 1733 Park told me all I needed to know: If Boston was 1,733 miles from Kearney, then so was MIT. That meant a two-day train ride. School vacations were limited and transportation tight in those war years, so, if I needed it, I would have a good excuse for not returning home to the inward-looking Greek village I was leaving behind. On the other hand, I was also poor engineer material. I was at the top of my game when it came to math, but engineering required at least a modest ability to draw in those days before computers. I was hard-pressed to draw a picture of a brick that anyone would recognize, let alone something complicated like a bridge. And my mechanical IQ was in the basement. Even today, I can barely open a FedEx envelope, and "assembly required" toys and furniture are well beyond my skills. Add it all up, and I clearly should have known better than to set out for MIT.

The Union Pacific's *City of Denver* was a streamliner that went from Kearney to Chicago. It came through at night (Kearney was hardly a major stop). I packed my suitcase in the afternoon, leaving out the jacket of my one suit to wear on the train. When the time came, I clicked the suitcase shut and lugged it to the car. My father signaled me to sit in the front seat next to him and my mother climbed into the back seat alongside John. It was a short drive to the station past the neon sign of the Central Cafe, and when we got there, we all walked together to the platform and waited. I was feeling a mixture of eagerness and fear. My mother nervously picked imaginary lint off the coat I wore on that cold night, John was asking me to send him postcards, and my father pressed $200 in worn bills into my hand and told me to put it in my wallet. Some of it was my own money, from the piggy bank he had brought me long ago, ultimately transferred to my savings account. And some of the money was his: a rare gift. "That's going to have to last," he said.

Soon we heard a blast from the train's horn from the west, then its lone headlight appeared, and a moment later it slid into the station, a huge diesel engine pulling twelve cars. Kearney wasn't a long stop; the train seemed to run in place, trembling with eagerness to be on the move again. I hugged my mother and accepted the box of pastries she had made to get me through the night. I shook hands with my little brother. I was going to miss John; I both envied and admired him, for his carefree personality, his boldness in pushing the social envelope and getting away with things I never would have tried. Ever carrying the burden of the firstborn son, I told him to take good care of Mom. My father asked for the Pullman car and carried my suitcase aboard to stow above my berth, shaking off a porter who offered to assist us. I was astonished that he had paid for a place in the sleeping car, but it was no surprise that he didn't want to tip a porter. After all, the waiters at the Central Cafe rarely received tips. Then as the conductor on the platform called out, "All aboard," he placed a hand on my shoulder and looked me in the eye. "I told you I was going to get you the best education money could buy, son," he said. "And you're going to do well. I know it." It was less a prediction than an order. With that, he abruptly turned and limped down the steps onto the platform.

Far ahead, the horn sounded and the train began to move. I glanced at the platform to see my melancholy mother and brother waving and my father standing stoically. At last I was free. I was free of being Greek, free of my mother's sadness, my authoritarian father's rigidity, free to become what I so desperately wanted to be, a full-fledged American. And yet, seeing them standing on the platform, I had felt somewhat uneasy. After all, I knew I had led a very provincial life, never having been "back East," where we'd been told all those sharp "city slickers" lived and worked. I knew I could compete in Kearney, but what about Boston and New York?

I felt like a small-town hick among the train's sophisticated interstate rail travelers, but I was happy to find that none of them seemed to look down on me. My happiness lasted until my fellow passengers began to prepare themselves for bed. One minute they were wearing ordinary clothes, then they disappeared and moments later reappeared wearing pajamas and robes. It had not occurred to me that in a sleeping car people might wear their sleeping clothes. So much for young Mr.

Sophisticate from Kearney as my face flushed and seemed to shout: "Here's a hick who hasn't done much traveling."

I slept in my pants that night, restless as I considered my mistake. It troubled me to think that maybe I wasn't so smart after all. I liked knowing the angles and being on top of situations. The night passed slowly. Finally the eastbound train met the rising sun, and I rolled out of my berth eager that everyone would soon be back in their daytime attire and I'd blend in again. I splashed some water on my face and brushed my teeth. But when I patted my pockets to make sure I had everything I'd gone to bed with, I couldn't find my wallet. A wave of panic passed over me as I patted myself down again. And again. My wallet was gone!

Dark thoughts raced through my mind. Was I such a hick that one of my fellow passengers saw me as a helpless rube and lifted it from my pocket in the night? Did I lose it back in Kearney when I was getting on the train? I was less than halfway into my proud journey into a new world and already I had slept in my pants—their wrinkles advertised the fact—and lost all the money my father had said would have to last for months. What else could go wrong? I looked around until I saw my suitcase on the rack overhead. At least it was still there. But it was not an auspicious beginning.

I rushed to the end of the car where I found a porter and, stammering with embarrassment and fear, told him my story. "Don't worry, son. We'll find it," he said sympathetically. He followed me to my berth and started straightening up, and after a minute turned around and produced my wallet with a flourish and a grin. It had been stuck in a crease between the mattress and the wall. I thanked him profusely and headed with my recovered riches to the dining car for breakfast. When I sat down to look at the menu, the world outside Kearney hit me in the face yet again. The bottomless five-cent cup of coffee that was a staple of the Central Cafe was nowhere to be seen. In its place I saw a rich man's brew, a cup of coffee advertised at forty cents, eight times the price that I was used to. After the close call with my wallet, I decided that since I still had my money I should not throw it away. Sheepishly, I got up and walked out. The smell of coffee tortured me all the way.

Back in the Pullman car, I confronted my next big financial deci-

sion: what to tip the porter. I figured I owed him something. Back at the
Central Cafe, the biggest tip I ever received waiting tables was ten cents,
and raking oiled sand greens at the Kearney Country Club for a four-
some over eighteen holes of golf might also produce a ten-cent tip. By
that reckoning, I decided that twenty cents ought to be enough to give
the porter. I tendered him two dimes and he looked at them in the palm
of his hand. Then he looked up at me and smiled. "Sonny," he said
gently as he pressed the coins back into my hand, "you'd better keep this
money. Something tells me you need it more than I do."

By now the train was entering the outskirts of Chicago. I looked
out the window at junkyards and used tire stores, blocks of small shops
and wooden homes, then more substantial buildings, warehouses and
small factories, until the gray mass of the city rose up outside the windows and I had arrived at the hub of the Midwest.

Union Station was like nothing I had ever seen. There were more
people in Union Station than in all of Kearney. That was my first fleet-
ing experience with the lonely, impersonal feeling of big cities. In Kearney, I knew most of the families and cared for many of them. Here, I
knew nobody. And they all were in a hurry in the morning rush. Businessmen in suits, ties, and hats strode through the crowd, newspapers
wedged under their arms. Businesswomen, too. Like the men, they carried briefcases. In Kearney, only the lawyers—all men—carried briefcases, the streets were rarely crowded, and people moved more slowly.
This was my first glimpse of a different style and pace of life. Soldiers in
khakis clustered, smoking and laughing as they waited for trains to take
them home, or more somberly waited to go back to their bases and perhaps to Italy or the Pacific. Lugging my suitcase and comforted by the
feel of my wallet restored to my back pocket, I found a restaurant at the
station where coffee was fifteen cents and a breakfast of eggs, potatoes,
and toast could be had for another fifty cents. Sixty-five cents would buy
a much better meal in Kearney, but as I had to keep reminding myself,
I wasn't in Kearney anymore.

The comfortable part of my trip was over, my father having decided that after the Pullman to Chicago I could complete the ride in
coach. I made my way to the coach section of my Boston-bound train
and found the cars jammed with passengers and bags. Some travelers

had claimed a patch of floor or space in the vestibules between the cars. The rest of us didn't have that luxury and had to stand. I wedged myself into a notch between some piled-high luggage and the vestibule door at the end of one car. Knots of servicemen formed around card and dice games, and I saw bottles being passed around. The car was thick with smoke.

After Cleveland, my throat grew sore and I started having trouble swallowing. I thought it was the smoke, so I found an open window and sucked fresh air but instead of getting better, it got worse. By the time the train crossed through Pennsylvania into New York state, I had a rising fever. This, too, got worse until I was nearly reeling in the aisle. When we reached western Massachusetts, I finally found a seat on the floor and curled up for the last leg of my journey. A few hours later I stumbled off the train in Boston, a sad vestige of the boy who had abandoned Kearney for the larger world just two days earlier.

In those days there were chaperones to meet the incoming students, at least those who had been solicited by fraternities as I had been. After ascertaining that I was indeed Pete Peterson, my chaperone from the Theta Chi fraternity took a hard look at me and said, "We have to get you to a hospital." Within hours of arriving at my new stomping grounds, I was undergoing an emergency tonsillectomy. What an entry to my new and longed-for world!

MIT

A few days after my tonsillectomy, when I was getting settled in the fraternity house, my chaperone, Chris, came around and asked to take a look at my wardrobe. I opened the small closet to show him my suit, the few shirts, sweaters, and trousers I had brought, and my other pair of shoes. He nodded thoughtfully and after a minute said, "You know what, Pete? You need a new suit. Get one where the jacket can double as a sport coat. If you do that, you'll have two outfits right there." Spending the money was more easily said than done given my slim budget, but I found a place that advertised year-round suits for less than $50 and bought one in navy blue. I spent an extra few dollars on two ties, another of my chaperone's suggestions. Later, on those occasions when a suit or a sport coat was required, I was glad I'd found a way.

But Chris failed to convince his fraternity brothers that he could make a New England sophisticate out of a Nebraska rustic, and the Theta Chi chapter decided I was not for them. Another fraternity, Phi Mu Delta, stepped in. My new brothers began a new phase of my education. Their lessons were painful in the short run, but over time would prove immensely practical. They taught me that persuasion was often the difference between failure and success.

Anyone who has been initiated into a college fraternity, particularly in those days, knows the path to membership runs through a dark forest of humiliation. The prospective member, or pledge, in order to satisfy the brothers that he is worthy of entering their ranks, endured a trial period of menial tasks, verbal abuse, and corporal punishment. A pledge who was too slow delivering the asked-for cup of coffee was routinely ordered to "assume the position." This meant dropping your pants and bending over for a whaling with a paddle, often drilled with holes for extra sting. But these arbitrary punishments were easily endured compared with the more creative forms of hazing. That was how I crossed paths with Sally Keith.

Queen of the Tassel Tossers

Sally "Queen of the Tassel Tossers" Keith was Boston's leading stripper. She won her nickname honestly, having developed the ability to twirl the tassels attached to the pasties on her ample breasts in opposite directions. This feat of musculature drew patrons from married couples to college students to Boston's Scollay Square where the bars and burlesque houses were. Sally performed in the venerable Crawford House, which had a supper club offering "3 Sparkling Floor Shows Nightly." Between shows the wives were said to try to emulate her in the ladies' room—without success. It was here that I was sent one night on a particularly fiendish fraternity assignment. I was to bring back one of Sally's G-strings.

To make it interesting, the brothers sent me out without a penny in my pocket. I hitched a ride partway to the theater and walked the rest. When I got there I told the guard at the stage door I had come to ask Sally for one of her G-strings. He shook his head as if he had heard it all before. "What are you, kid, some kind of pervert?" he growled.

I explained my predicament, and said I was in for a paddling that would result in more welts on my behind if I didn't deliver the goods. "They'll do it, too. Here, I'll show you," I said, and started fumbling with my belt.

"Hold on, hold on," he said, and he let me in with a warning that if I wasn't back in ten minutes he was coming to get me.

The old theater's backstage area was a labyrinth of corridors and tiny rooms, with curtains and ropes dangling from the ceiling. I found the door marked "Miss Keith" and knocked timidly. "Come in," called a Boston-laced voice from inside. I edged the door open, stepped timidly inside, and found myself face-to-face with the platinum blond burlesque queen. All about the small dressing room were costumes—robes, embroidered satin shorts and abbreviated tops, tall hats with feathers, boots, lots of high-heeled shoes. She was wearing a bright silk robe just draped over her shoulders, exposing massive cleavage contained in a flimsy brassiere that I had to struggle to keep from staring at. She wore heavy makeup under which she looked older than advertised—she was supposed to be in her late twenties—but she had a warm and sympathetic openness about her. I remembered reading that she visited wounded veterans at the VA hospital. When I told her of my plight she smiled, opened a drawer, and produced a G-string. "Here y'are," she said with total nonchalance, dangling the wisp of fabric from her outstretched hand. I stammered out my gratitude and turned to leave when she added, "Come see the show. And bring your friends. All I see are married men and Harvard boys. I'd like to meet some engineers." It was not an invitation we could resist. My knowing Sally turned out to be quite a status symbol.

As dizzy as I was from these various distractions, I wondered as I left what my parents would have thought about these very un-Greek, un-Kearney highjinks. I was confident it wasn't what my father had in mind when he sent me off for "the best education money can buy."

If obtaining Sally Keith's G-string turned out to be a pretty nice experience, my next assignment was anything but. I was to steal the phone from the main desk of the Boston Sheraton Hotel and return it to the fraternity house within the hour. On the one hand, theft and vandalism were involved. But, on the other hand, I was motivated, since the punishment for failure was going to be twenty-five "assume the positions" that would surely leave me unable to sit down for days. Again I started penniless. After wangling the loan of a metal file from a local repair shop, I made my way to the hotel and engaged the clerk at the desk. I told him my big family was coming to Boston and I needed to know all the options. Then I sent him off on various tasks, such as retrieving pictures of the rooms. Each time he left, I managed a few strokes of the file on the telephone wire. Wire-cutting pliers would have done the job a whole lot better, but my mechanical IQ wasn't up to figuring that out. Snorts of barely concealed laughter sounded from across the lobby, and I turned to see two of the brothers sitting in club chairs and smoking as they watched me saw away. Finally, after enough of the clerk's absences, I was able to part the wire and run out with the phone to more laughter from my torturers. Later, when my conscience bothered me—what must the poor desk clerk have told his boss about my outrageous prank?—my fraternity mates flatly refused to let me return the phone to the hotel, on the grounds of avoiding self-incrimination.

On another occasion, knowing I didn't smoke and hated the smell of burning tobacco, they stuck me in a small closet with a cigar that must have been a foot long that I was required to smoke down to a one-inch nub. It took what seemed like hours before I burst out, red-eyed and gasping for air, convinced that I would never be able to stop coughing.

None of this foolishness had any great high purpose or significance, unless you count my lifelong aversion to cigars and cigarettes. It was simply part of a young man's introduction to the world beyond his family's protections and his hometown's inhibitions, a seamy side of my coming-out party. It included what were, in those days, the routine temptations of booze and girls. I knew very little about either. I might have had a beer or two in my Longfellow High School days, but what sex I had experienced was entirely imaginary. It opened my eyes to realize that my fraternity house at MIT combined aspects of a saloon and a (free) brothel. Our parties featured a heavily spiked fruit punch that disguised cheap grain alcohol. It lowered inhibitions and eventually eyelids among the Radcliffe and Wellesley girls who attended, and a lot of them woke up in the upstairs bedrooms to find themselves in various states of undress. If there were complaints, we never heard them, and the administration, preoccupied as it was with the school's wartime research, never called us down.

My MIT friends and I had debated whether it made more sense to date Wellesley girls or Radcliffe girls, those two private women's colleges being the prime segments of the local dating market. Our research determined that Radcliffe, which was affiliated with Harvard, was physically closer and therefore more convenient, and the women there were very, very smart. On the other side was anecdotal evidence that the Cliffies were less attractive than the girls from Wellesley. But the kicker was that the men from Harvard monopolized the Radcliffe market. This market analysis led us to focus our sales efforts on Wellesley. Harvard controlled a large share of the market there as well, so our first task was to get the girls' attention. We decided to play to our comparative advantage, a capacity (not true in my case) for technical ingenuity. One of our more gifted MIT colleagues rigged up a friend's car so that it could be controlled by a remote device operated from the floor. We hung signs on the car proclaiming "The World's First Driverless Car" and headed to Wellesley. During class breaks, we tooled around the campus with no one in the driver's seat, grinning and waving while one of us—we took turns—hunkered on the floor and manipulated the wheel and pedals according to instructions from above. This stunt attracted surprisingly large crowds.

Now that we had our market's attention, we decided to pretend we were from Harvard and developed a song that we hoped would cast effete aspersions:

Peaches and cream. Peaches and cream.
We are the men of the Harvard team.
We are not rough and we are not tough,
But mercy, are we determined!

Consequently, I met and dated a smart and attractive Wellesley woman. But beyond the immediate gratification lay a connection I had yet to make. Studying markets, analyzing what you learn, and drawing up a set of actions in response was a powerful tool. Done right, it could change behavior, with results that ranged from the As I would get to possibilities that remained in my as yet unimagined future.

Indeed, with the war raging there was a sense of living for the moment. It was easy to believe, despite the headlines and newsreels that told us America and the Allies were advancing against the enemy, that tomorrow might never come and we had to experience life before it was too late.

A Different World

I turned eighteen that summer. A day later, on June 6, 1944, the D-Day invasion gave hope that Hitler's days were numbered, a hope that increased with each Allied thrust against the Nazis as the summer deepened. I survived the hazing of the Phi Mu Delta brothers and was initiated into the fraternity. I had seen the brilliance of MIT and its quirky geniuses. One day in calculus class the professor, Jan Strick, was filling the blackboard with a complex equation when a short, plump, bearded man shuffled into the room. He walked to the blackboard, erased a section and, mumbling, wrote down some numbers and symbols while Strick and the rest of us watched quizzically. Then he walked out and left the building, wearing only a short-sleeved cotton shirt on a bitterly cold and windy day. It was the famously absentminded Professor Norbert Wiener, who was developing equations to aim antiaircraft guns that would save American ships late in the war; he would later lead in creating the field of cybernetics. Such mental feats were beyond me, but I had at least survived the academic competition with students who were far better trained than I was, graduates of such private schools as Andover, Exeter, St. Paul's, and Choate. My singular academic failure was my own fault, not that of the public schools of Kearney. In a course called Descriptive Geometry, the professor expected us to visualize what an object would look like from several angles and set it down on paper. After I submitted my work, he called me into his office to explain that I had achieved a unique distinction—the lowest score he had given in his twenty-seven years of teaching the class. He wondered how I could ever have picked engineering as my field of study. Increasingly, the same question had occurred to me.

I had also met a lifelong friend. Gene Pope was also a child of immigrants: His parents were Italian. We both, in a way, were passing; Pete Peterson was a name people assumed was Scandinavian, and I was happy to let them think so. Gene Pope sounded squarely in the American mainstream, but his actual name was Generoso, after his father. All I knew was he seemed like a great guy, and when he asked me to spend a school break with him and his family in New York that summer, I quickly accepted. I was attending summer classes, and the short breaks between quarters made the long ride home to Kearney out of the question. My parents, to whom I wrote long letters in Greek and made brief phone calls to avoid running up long-distance bills, were happy when I told them I was visiting someone with similar origins. Waiting with Gene at Boston's South Station for the train to New York, I assumed I would be spending a few days with a humble but warm family that depended on a grocery store or other small business for a living. My friend had given me no reason to think otherwise.

When the train was announced, I headed for the coach section with the crowd hoping to grab a seat before they were all taken, but Gene stopped me. "Hold on, Pete," he called, "we're down here." He led the way to the club car, where a conductor looked at the tickets he presented and showed us to a pair of reserved seats. I knew these were not only expensive, but hard to get at any price during those war years when the nation's transportation networks were stretched beyond capacity. I wondered how Gene could manage to afford them, but I suppressed curiosity as the train pulled out of Boston and I settled into my luxurious seat. We talked about the exams we'd just finished and our plans for the summer and the Wellesley girls we hoped to meet. Before long I forgot entirely our special place on the train.

New York's Grand Central Station was even busier than Union Station in Chicago. On our way to the street, I had to pause in the soaring central lobby to gaze in awe at the dusty shafts of sunlight streaming through high windows and the arched ceiling painted with the constellations. When we reached the street, a limousine was waiting for us. The driver, whom Gene introduced as Tony, greeted him warmly, and I told myself that they were personal friends and Tony, an Italian, was doing Gene a favor.

The reality got through to me after we arrived at our destination. It was an apartment building at 1040 Fifth Avenue, at 85th Street across from Central Park. Jackie Kennedy lived there for a while. A doorman wearing white gloves and a uniform hurried from the canopied entrance to open the door of the limousine. "Mr. Pope," he said to Gene, "how good to see you." Gene introduced us and the doorman said, "Welcome, Mr. Peterson. Let me know if there's anything you need." A light finally turned on: My friend Gene Pope was rich.

Walking into his family's apartment, I ogled at the huge living room two stories tall with walls done in red silk, elegant furniture, the book-lined library, the gigantic dining room. A marble staircase swooped up to a second floor, with a series of bedrooms, each with its own bathroom. I had thought such unbelievable luxury existed in the palaces and the mansions of the rich, but not in apartments inside other buildings. Then when a butler in formal clothes carried my suitcase into "my" bedroom and opened the door to show me "my" bathroom, I thought I had wandered onto a movie set. Back in Kearney, my mother had never had help of any kind, let alone butlers and maids in uniform. Gene's own closet revealed riches unimaginable to me. It contained eight or ten suits and half a dozen sport jackets. I had never seen him wear those fancy clothes at MIT or heard him say anything about his family's wealth.

It turned out that Gene's father—Generoso Pope Sr.—had worked, like my father, as a railroad laborer. But Mr. Pope had gone on to much bigger things. He had then worked for a construction company called Colonial Sand and Stone, and later bought it out and made it into a major building materials supplier. He later bought *Il Progresso Italo-Americano*, the leading Italian-language daily in the United States, and a weekly called *Il Corriere d'America*. I later heard that he was the first

Italian-American millionaire. I was to learn he was also very powerful politically.

Dinners at the Popes' were my first adventures into purposeful social conversation, where I observed people pursuing serious goals and having fun at the same time. Governors, mayors, secretaries of state, all frequented their table. The food was extraordinary. At one of my first dinners, someone passed a shallow silver tray that contained, swaddled in exquisite linen, a pile of thin brown pencil shapes. I had never seen anything like them. I glanced up and down the table and could not catch anybody else eating one, so finally I asked. That was how I made my acquaintance with the breadstick.

Mrs. Pope was a lovely woman, a brunette with black eyes who looked directly at you when she spoke. She was Italian, too, like her husband, but she spoke perfect, unaccented English, and she ran the Pope household with the gracious manner of a perfect hostess. She asked me what I hadn't seen and what I wished to see while I was in New York. The answer was everything. And on that visit and every time I returned with Gene, the Popes displayed the generosity of true hosts and an enthusiasm for the city, over time providing prime seats to *La Bohème* at the Met and the Rockettes at Radio City Music Hall, tickets to the great Rodgers and Hammerstein musical *Carousel*, views of Central Park from the roof of the St. Regis Hotel, and much more. On all of these excursions I heard "Mr. Pope, Mr. Pope," spoken reverently by doormen, coat check girls, and maître d's, and I calculated that the tips he handed out during one night on the town easily exceeded a whole day's revenue back home at the Central Cafe.

Any prominent Italian-American in those days was often linked with the Mafia, whether the association was true or not. Mr. Pope was said to have ties to Frank Costello, who at the time was known for his relationship to Lucky Luciano and as a fixer who bridged the divide between the criminal world and the legitimate world of business and politics as represented by the Pope family and their friends. But none of this affected our friendship. We were inseparable at MIT, and whenever our paths crossed thereafter, we totally trusted each other.

Roy Cohn

Gene and I would remain close friends, but my academic status would radically change before that freshman year was over. One of Gene's New York friends was a kid named Roy Cohn, who was a year younger than we were. He would later become notorious, as Senator Joseph McCarthy's right-hand man during McCarthy's Communist witch hunts in the 1950s, and then as a high-powered lawyer who employed suspect methods on behalf of his clients. At the time, he was an undergraduate at Columbia College in New York, but his relentless attraction to important people was already clear. That summer, we attended a dance at the Westchester Country Club in Rye, New York, north of the city. Gene and I spent the evening chasing girls around the dance floor, but Roy was chatting up the power figures at Mr. Pope's table. (The world would later learn that he was a deeply closeted homosexual; he died of AIDS in 1986.) Roy was clearly brilliant. And that brilliance had produced a term paper that he was more than happy to share with Gene and me.

Term papers were practically a commodity at MIT. The fraternity had a file drawer full of them that members routinely copied and submitted word for word. Words like plagiarism or, God forbid, cheating, never occurred to anyone. But we were all inclined to rationalize. The world was at war, after all, and if we were going to make a difference it was going to be through engineering some new weapon or a better way of detecting Nazi submarines, not with an original term paper. I was fast becoming a man of the world in the newfound and exhilarating social life I was enjoying in the Popes' circle in New York, and that seemed to be a more important education.

I had never cheated in school. My parents had strict standards when it came to honesty and they passed them on to me. I had never needed to cheat, but I knew what cheating was. One of my techno-wizard classmates might photograph and reduce to tiny palm-sized crib sheets the formulas for chemistry and calculus that might be needed on a test. *That* was cheating, I figured, but substantially revising someone else's term paper as the basis for one of my own was altogether different.

Long story short, I made some additions—considerable additions, actually—to one of Roy's papers and turned it in. The subject was *casus belli*, loosely translated as "case for war," the various justifications nations may use for making war and the process by which they arrive at those justifications. Gene submitted Cohn's paper untouched, but he was in a different class. I have no idea what my professor saw in my paper that raised his suspicions, but soon afterward I received a notice to report to the dean of the school. I arrived at his office without a clue about the reason for my summons. But when I saw that the dean was holding my paper between two fingers like a dirty diaper, with my professor by his side, understanding hit me with a chill. Perhaps Cohn's paper had eventually shown up in classes other than just mine and Gene's. I confessed that I had used another's paper as my starting point but argued that I had done a lot of my own work, too. It was pure rationalization. I thought the worst that could happen was that I would fail the course. But the administration must finally have seen the extent of the "borrowing" that was going on, and decided that an example needed to be made. A letter from the dean's office arrived in my fraternity house mailbox a few days later informing me that I had been expelled. It was the fall of 1944.

Interim

Mortified does not begin to describe the way I felt. How could I explain to my rigidly honest parents that I had been kicked out of MIT for cheating? Neither of them would have understood it. They had spent thousands of exhausting Central Cafe hours working and saving to get me "the best education money could buy," and my grateful "thank you" to them was to cheat my way out of that educational opportunity. My father was so unpracticed at deception that on those occasions when he sat in on the quarter-limit poker game at Kearney's Elks Club, he nearly always lost because he couldn't keep a poker face. I couldn't even explain it to myself. But there was one small glimmer of hope. My expulsion wasn't final. If I got a job and restored my honor, the administration said I could return. I dreaded the conversation with my parents and decided to postpone it until I had a better script.

Gene was as mortified as I was, maybe more so, since he got away clean. As I thought about it, I began to view my misstep as unintentionally prophetic, a perverse example of dumb luck. I had decided by then that I was not an engineer. No matter how good the education being offered, my genetic limitations—my mechanical klutziness, my inability to draw—were at war with my true interests. My skill at mathematics was a waste as I was trying to apply it to engineering, which placed me at a profound disadvantage compared to the talented engineers-to-be around me. I hadn't yet articulated the career principle of playing to my strengths. I just knew I needed to find a place where I could put numbers and data to use in human or business situations, not in structures and machines.

But in order to go anywhere I had first to erase the blot on my record, so I told my parents in a phone call I was applying for a position in the purchasing department of MIT's Radiation Laboratory. I had no idea that what went on there was of vital significance to the war effort. The war had reached a point where the Allies had the upper hand in Europe, but in the Pacific the Japanese were fighting to the last man for every blood-soaked island. The hunt was intensified for some kind of knockout blow, to develop a superweapon before the enemies could. I got the job, which enabled me to stay on at the Phi Mu Delta house and retain my active social life. Instead of attending classes, though, I was sent out to procure components for the Radiation Lab.

Oddly, I seemed to be no ordinary traveler but one with superpowers, a lowly eighteen-year-old clerk who bumped other passengers off sold-out planes. The parts I found and arranged for shipping back to Cambridge were not always uncommon. They were often things like piping and gaskets that the war had rendered hard to find, and I always understood that there was no time to waste, that the lab needed them "right now." I also knew my credentials simply said "Manhattan," but I had no idea what it meant.

It was only after the Japanese finally surrendered on August 14 that details emerged about the Manhattan Project and that the Radiation Lab had played a role. I suddenly realized that I had been tracking down components, some of which went directly into developing the atomic bomb. My parents were simply delighted I was contributing to the war effort.

With the war's end, I returned to Kearney for the first time in eighteen months. I expected to return to MIT that fall while I surveyed my other options. As it turned out, I was able to bypass that step when Nebraska State's Dr. Cushing wrote a strong letter of recommendation that highlighted my service to the Radiation Lab during the temporary suspension of my student status. The letter went to Northwestern University with my application, and I was accepted for the fall of 1945, to my everlasting gratitude. Luckily, the dean of the Business School apparently had some difficulties of his own with MIT and told me he was very sympathetic to my case.

Northwestern

Some people called Northwestern the "Country Club of the Midwest." This implied that it was in the top rank of party schools, although it was a stretch to believe that any university could approach the levels of boozing and debauchery I'd seen at MIT. And in fact, Northwestern didn't come close. This was partly because of its location. The school stood on the shores of Lake Michigan in Evanston, Illinois, a northern suburb of Chicago that was also the home of the Woman's Christian Temperance Union. The WCTU had lost the national battle against Prohibition a dozen years earlier, in 1933, but it still reigned in its hometown. Alcohol sales were prohibited throughout Evanston, and while that didn't mean that drinking was illegal, it certainly put a damper on it, especially where the fraternity houses were concerned.

Northwestern was pretty buttoned-up about sex, too. In contrast to MIT's far more liberal policies (or the absence of any policies at all), Northwestern decreed that women in the school's fraternity houses could venture no farther than the first floor living rooms—and those had to be well lit.

I arrived at Northwestern in the fall of 1945 and quickly fell in love with the school. It was a perfect fit for me. After the fraternity highjinks and dubious behavior at MIT, I embraced Northwestern's wholesome social life, with its enthusiasm for Big Ten football and wide range of student activities. The girls were far better-looking, too! I remembered, or thought I did, that most of the few coeds at MIT had a kind of pinched intensity. Not that the male students were very nice to them, referring to them as "murgatroids." By contrast, the girls at Northwestern were open, fresh, and unassuming. They were all apple cheeks and flowing hair and easy smiles. My friend Gene came out for Homecoming that year, and as the parade floats passed with various "queens" and "sweethearts" waving from on high, he pronounced each one more beautiful than the last. The fraternity and sorority balls we attended were equally dazzling in their arrays of stunning girls.

Phi Mu Delta had a chapter at Northwestern that was about to merge with the older, larger, and more well established Alpha Tau Omega, so my fraternity and social life went on uninterrupted. It was ironic, looking back, that I embraced so eagerly the faux Greek life of college fraternities and sororities as my main source of highly American friendships and social contacts while turning away from the practices of my Greek immigrant parents. More ironic still was the fact that I was one of the few, maybe the only, fraternity man who could actually speak and write the language of the society after which the campus Greeks were supposedly modeled.

The small allowance my father sent from home didn't cover all Northwestern's social possibilities, but I found a way to stretch it soon after I arrived. The Delta Delta Delta sorority had an opening for a waiter at its house dining hall. This was a job I knew well, having spent years in training at the Central Cafe. I could carry three plates of food on one arm, right up to the elbow, and bus tables with equal proficiency. It paid only board, but by saving the cost of my meals I had more left for taking dates to concerts, movies, and dances. The Tri Delts were a mirror of the coed population as a whole, in that they were uncommonly attractive, and an added bonus of the job was that I got to meet a lot of girls. Some of them I took to performances of the Chicago Symphony Orchestra with the two inexpensive season tickets—the seats were in the rafters—I bought with some of my newly freed-up money.

With all this, my social confidence seemed to grow. The tentative-ness I had felt at MIT and on my first visits to New York with Gene was now behind me. I blossomed into a bit of a prime mover at Northwestern, on and off Greek Row. In 1946, I was asked to be the advertising manager of the yearbook, the *Syllabus*, an important job because ad sales helped support the publication. That fall, a Northwestern administrator named Joe Miller asked me to co-chair the 1947 Waa-Mu show. This was an all-student musical revue that had a long tradition. The unusual name came from the groups that first put it on in 1929, the Women's Athletic Association and the Men's Union. Production had been suspended during the war. Cloris Leachman had starred in the first show after it resumed, in 1946, and there was plenty of talent that was bursting to take the stage again in this original extravaganza. The show was presented in the spring, after months of writing and rehearsals. I helped the producers assemble writers, singers, and dancers, gearing up advertising and promotion—the whole range of things that go on behind the scenes to create a successful show before the curtain rises. It was a lot of work, because Waa-Mu had a reputation to live up to. But what fun it was! I got to work with some great talents, including comedian Paul Lynde and actress Charlotte Rae, who starred in that 1947 show, and Sheldon Harnick, who wrote the lyrics for *Fiddler on the Roof* and *Fiorello!*, for which he shared the 1960 Pulitzer Prize.

It was a time of shaping and forming values. If my friend Gene Pope and his family had shown me the world of wealth and power, my three years at Northwestern helped teach me what I could accomplish on my own. I found out that I was good at what later would be called multitasking, and that I liked it; I was restless in my interests, and got bored doing just one thing. I didn't know it at the time, but I was setting a pattern I would follow for the rest of my life. In addition to co-chairing Waa-Mu, I became the president of my fraternity, by then Alpha Tau Omega as the merger was completed. I also encountered disappointment. I ran for student body president and finished as the runner-up, but that was small compared to a more disturbing letdown. I had a close black friend who was as involved in campus activities as I was, and who was also a great student. I put him up for membership in ATΩ, but when the box was passed and the brothers anonymously entered their white or black marbles to indicate acceptance or rejection, I was shocked when the box was opened to see quite a few "blackballs." This sobered me and gave me insights into the social mores of the time. Nevertheless, I was still happy there in the heart of the Midwest to let people assume that Pete Peterson, despite my dark hair, came from hearty Nordic stock in someplace like Sweden.

I wondered if I would have enjoyed the same level of acceptance had I been known not as Scandinavian but Greek. After all, we Greeks were not immune from small-mindedness and discrimination. My father had told me that when he opened the Central Cafe in 1923, the local Ku Klux Klan, lacking any black citizens to terrorize in all-white Kearney, picketed the restaurant with signs reading, "Don't Eat with the Greek." When he recounted this, he never failed to add, "These are not the real Americans."

Breaking the Code

For all of my busy social life, I managed to maintain high grades. This was a subject of curiosity among my fraternity brothers. Some of them assumed that sheer brilliance accounted for my regular appearance on the Dean's List. Not so. My secret was that I had learned to read an academic code.

It was clear to me that most professors were intellectual evangelists who let their conviction show. If you paid close attention, you could see the extra animation in their gestures and hear the passion in their voices when they talked about their favorite themes. In other words, I learned how to listen not just to the lyrics of the lecture, but also to the music that surrounded it.

I started marking my lecture notes accordingly. When examinations came around, I would study my notes with the highlighted passages in mind, poring over them until I had them memorized, and then write into my answers as many of these themes as I could. No matter what the question, I would find a way to play the professors' passions back to them. It was flattery, and I suppose it was cynical, but what I got in return for these manipulations were As and A-pluses.

The grades, though, were not the most valuable outcome, but I don't think I knew it at the time. What I was learning, in addition to a straight path to the Dean's List, was to listen and, from what I learned, read people. This was something that would shape the early days of my career.

Near Death

That future was suddenly in peril in my senior year at Northwestern. I normally possessed a high degree of physical and mental energy, enough to keep all of my academic, social, and extracurricular balls up in the air. But in the winter before I was to graduate, I was suddenly overcome with lethargy. I found myself falling asleep in classes, movies, while I was reading or reviewing notes, even nodding during the pauses after meals. What with Waa-Mu, the presidency of the fraternity, all my classes, and continuing to wait tables at the TriDelt house, I thought I had simply not been getting enough sleep. But after a couple of weeks, when I suddenly developed a high fever, I checked in at the student health service. The nurses there decided to put me into the hospital for observation. This produced no conclusions but one additional symptom, a sharp back pain that a young intern blamed on the rubber mats on the hospital bed! I was released after a few days, but my constant drowsiness persisted.

This uncommon lassitude caused concern among my fraternity brothers. One urged me to go see his father, an Evanston urologist. Dr. Corbus listened as I described my "sleeping sickness" and asked if I had had any other symptoms. When I told him about my back pain, he frowned and said, "Let me get this straight, Pete. You had drowsiness, a high fever, and a sharp back pain?" I said I had.

Within minutes, he was injecting my veins with dye to perform an X-ray of my urinary tract. The result must have been impressive, because when the film came out I heard him saying to his oldest son, with whom he shared the practice, "Holy shit, Bud, take a look at this."

I was let in on the secret moments later. It was my left kidney that had brought his exclamation. It had swollen to the size of a large balloon. "You have uremic poisoning," he told me. "You'll die if you don't have surgery." Within hours I was in the hospital, and the next day a nurse wheeled me into an operating room and Dr. Corbus removed a stray blood vessel that was blocking the flow of urine from the kidney to my bladder. Unable to reach the bladder, it had leaked throughout my body, poisoning me and putting me to sleep.

The operation, which lasted several hours, saved my life and restored my energy. I graduated summa cum laude that August 1947, ready at last to put my newfound skills to work and join the American mainstream.

My Brilliant Career in Retailing

The marriage part I had already planned out. Since my junior year I had been dating an attractive journalism major from Twin Falls, Idaho, named Kris Krengel. Kris belonged to a sorority, Alpha Chi Omega, and we met at one of their mixers where dance records were stacked one atop another on the record player. We were both good dancers, and had a great time together as the tunes played deep into the evening. That first night led to others. Kris, then a sophomore, helped edit *The Daily Northwestern*, the student-run paper that served the university and surrounding Evanston, and her classmates and fellow editors held her in high regard. We dated regularly during my senior year. I gave her my fraternity pin, a ritual that among campus Greeks often precedes an engagement. We were, to use a term that admittedly lacks passion, "suitable" for one another. Before I graduated, we agreed that we would get married when she completed Northwestern the following year.

Looking back at those years so close on the heels of World War II, it is clear that we were doing the expected thing in planning a wedding soon after her graduation. In those days, men and women married much younger than now; once you were out of school, you were supposed to get on with life, which meant a job, a wife, and children. Such a so-called normal life was much to be desired after the twin traumas of the Depression and the war. The pressure was especially hard on women, who risked being thought of as old maids if they didn't land a husband within a year or so of graduation. I suppose Kris saw in me a good provider, given my degree with honors, and she wanted to follow the path of her sorority sisters who had also gotten married. I just wanted to marry a "suitable" non-Greek girl to cement my wholly American status. I knew my parents would hate my making such a statement, so I waited to tell them until just before the wedding in the summer of 1948.

While we waited for Kris to graduate with the class of '48, I cast about for the first real job of my career. My degree from Northwestern was in retailing. I suppose I had picked it because my father was a retailer of sorts. It was rather like a vocational school curriculum, with practical courses like retail inventory control, sales promotion, and so forth. Armed with my degree and a promise from Kris's uncle, who had ties in Portland, Oregon, to help me find a job, I headed west in September 1947.

It was raining when I stepped off the train in Portland, and it kept raining during the next few days as I found a small, cheap room and started a series of job interviews arranged by Kris's uncle. Before long, I landed a job at Roberts Brothers, one of Portland's department stores, in the toy department. The job didn't have a title; it was completely open-ended, but as the fall deepened, bringing more rain, and the Christmas shopping season approached, it had more and more to do with knowing what toys we had and what kids wanted. I quickly learned that nobody really knew what the company's warehouses contained. In those pre-computer days, the only way to find out was to go look and count. I spent many hours walking the aisles of dusty, cold, damp warehouses, counting boxes of toys and cataloguing them in lined notebooks, with my raincoat buttoned up around my neck to fend off the Northwest chill.

On nights and weekends, I would work in the Roberts Brothers toy department listening to unhappy and demanding children scream out their preferences for toys. Of course, some of them couldn't make up their minds. Others believed Santa's bag (or their parents' pocketbooks) were bottomless. "I went to college for this menagerie?" I asked myself.

I made notes, and passed on my recommendations for toy orders, and our merchandise was pretty much on target. After Christmas, Bill

Roberts, one of the store's owners, offered me a promotion to assistant buyer in another department.

But by then I had decided that retailing was not for me. This, of course, defied conventional career-planning logic. Tradition stated that you were supposed to pick your field, presumably your college major, and work your way up. That assistant buyer job could have led to another promotion. Maybe I would have ended up as the head buyer for men's suits. Eventually another, larger retailer might have hired me away. I could have made a slow climb through bigger offices, more important titles, and higher salaries. That was the way it was typically done. But I just couldn't see following that path. Even then, I knew that my interests and passions were elsewhere. I liked analyzing market trends and building the right inventory. But I was not a glad-handing person who enjoyed give-and-take with strangers. I had a short fuse for co-workers who didn't quickly grasp what I wanted and why (often holding them up against my mother, who had an instinctive understanding of my thoughts and needs). I was not, in short, a gregarious retail salesman, and a retailer who's not a salesman has made a bad career choice. In a reversal of Adam Smith's wisdom, I was applying some of my comparative *dis*advantages. So as soon as the after-Christmas sales were underway, I quit my job at Roberts and headed back to Chicago. I had been in Portland just four months, and I don't think I saw the sun during the entire time.

CHAPTER 3

CHICAGO, ROUND ONE

Starter Job

Back in Chicago, three of my fraternity brothers from Northwestern were trying to make ends meet in starter jobs. They shared a two-bedroom, single-bath apartment in Evanston. Splitting the rent four ways instead of three appealed to everybody, so I moved in and started looking for work. After a few weeks, steered by recommendations from some of my professors at Northwestern, I landed a job at a very small market research firm with an office in the heart of downtown Chicago at 39 South La Salle Street. The pay was meager, $50 a week or $2,600 a year—about $22,000 in 2009 dollars. None of my roommates was making much either. To save money, we cooked for ourselves a lot of terrible meals in that apartment. There was only one car among us, and it wasn't mine, so I had to beg and borrow if I needed to get somewhere the commuter trains or buses didn't go. But I enjoyed my job. It was a good match for my skills and temperament, and I threw myself into it, joining the hordes of commuters who rode into Chicago each day.

The name of the firm was Market Facts. It performed research on a wide range of products, from personal items like toothpaste, soaps, cosmetics, beer, and whiskey to hard goods such as ranges, lawn mowers, farm equipment, appliances, and autos. As the firm's "junior professional," another name for a still wet behind the ears new guy, one of my jobs was conducting pilot interviews. These were aimed at getting a

55

rough picture of how different people viewed different products. My interviews would then be used to write survey questions that would refine and quantify the picture with a much larger sample of respondents, as we called the interviewees.

The people I interviewed had often been selected from lists of residential street addresses. I would knock on doors along dark halls in tenement buildings filled with cooking smells and broken toys and watch the shadow come over the peephole in the door as the occupants studied the bespectacled, harmless-looking young man outside. Wherever I went, I tried to dress to fit the neighborhood—open shirt and khakis in the poorer ones, a suit and tie when I was visiting houses in rich areas. It took the full range of persuasion to get past some of these doors and, when I had to, I fell back on sympathy, telling my subjects that my boss would dock my pay if I didn't get the interview.

My wardrobe was very limited. I had just one suit, the one I wore when I went into upscale areas. Naturally, the day came when my assistant dropped a lit cigarette that burned a big hole in the pants. Buying a new suit was out of the question on my salary. I went to a tailor to see if the damage could be mended, and I got a rude shock at the price he quoted for reweaving. My next stop was an establishment on Wabash Avenue in the shadow of the Chicago el. Ben's Match Your Pants was an inspired business model for dealing with hand-me-downs and cast-offs. Its proprietor was a small, bearded man who had a yarmulke and a Yiddish accent. He watched with growing exasperation as I laboriously shifted through the piles of pants looking for the perfect match—a task not aided by my color blindness. Finally he spoke in a loud voice over the rumble of a passing train.

"Hey, sonny?" he said. "You hear that el train?"

I looked up at him quizzically.

"What color was it?" he wanted to know.

I had no idea. "I don't remember," I said.

"And you think someone is going to notice if your fucking pants don't match exactly?"

There was a lesson to remember. One's self-centeredness is hardly ever shared by others. Nobody else I met was going to care nearly as much about my pants as I did. I picked a pair I had been obsessing over, turning the fabric to catch every angle of the light, before Ben questioned me about the color of the el. I think I paid $5. In any case, I wore those pants steadily, and nobody ever mentioned that they didn't quite match my suit coat. Over the years since then, I have attended a great many events that called for a tuxedo. I often saved time and trouble going directly from work in a dark navy suit, a regular white shirt, and a black bow tie and cummerbund I carried with me. I don't think anyone has ever noticed, or if a few did, they didn't care.

What market researchers especially wanted to know in those days was: Why do consumers really follow certain purchase patterns? This motivational research, as it was called, was the part of the market research business that engaged me the most.

Packaged cake mixes from General Mills and Pillsbury had recently come on the market. They were not the slam-dunk sales success their makers had expected. Why? Motivational research revealed an interesting conflict in the minds of homemakers: They liked spending less time sifting flour and stirring batter, yet they weren't comfortable if the job became *too* easy. In the postwar world of working dads and stay-at-home moms, their cooking and baking skills formed an important part of their identity, and using a cake mix that only needed to be put in a pan and popped into the oven diminished that sense of self-worth. To make the new cake mixes psychologically attractive required counterintuition: Add back some work. When a homemaker had to stir a fresh egg into the mix, the extra step allowed her to feel that it was "her" cake.

Automatic washing machine sales suffered from a similar need to preserve the homemaker's identity. We researched a new automatic washing machine from Maytag and learned that many women felt some unease about a way of washing clothes that seemed too easy. In this case we tried to interpret the product in terms of their broader values. The Maytag automatic washer had devices that saved soap and hot water, and we recommended that the company emphasize this in its advertising. A housewife using Maytag's washer would therefore be thrifty, a positive value that offset the negative—I'm being lazy!

The Ford Motor Company hired Market Facts to look at car-buying psychology. Part of my job in this assignment was to spend time in showrooms watching how car buyers shopped. An old saw held that consumers liked to "kick the tires" as a way of judging a car's worth. I found that no one really did that. What many did instead was slam the doors, deciding from the sound whether or not they thought the car was solid. A solid car meant a safe car, and consumers were interested in safety.

Ford's reputation, however, was for power. It had pioneered the V-8 engine, and while this was attractive to some buyers, for others the image of the old Tin Lizzie dominated and made them think Fords were flimsy and unsafe. Motivational research offered proof. We asked Ford, as well as Chevrolet and Plymouth, owners to quickly complete the following sentence: "In an emergency, a car must have . . ." We needed the respondents to answer without taking time to think about it—free association—because a quick answer was most likely to reveal their underlying feelings. Chevy and Plymouth owners came back with "brakes" most of the time, but the Ford owners were more likely to say "power."

We also applied a thematic apperception test, in which the subject views an ambiguous picture and supplies a story. Viewing a picture of a serious crash in which the car could not be identified, far more people than not imagined that the twisted metal was a Ford. When our research was completed, we recommended that Ford pay more attention in its future product design and marketing to emphasizing safety, stressing the quality of its brakes, and making its car doors close with a solid "thunk." I found this research and the conclusions it stimulated utterly absorbing. It was everything that retailing had not been for me, and every day gave me a new reason to be engaged and happy in my work. It also verified the whole principle of focusing on one's comparative advantages.

Kris graduated on schedule in the spring of 1948, and we planned a modest wedding ceremony at her parents' home in Twin Falls, located in south-central Idaho midway between Boise and Pocatello. Despite my waiting until the last minute to inform my mother and father, they and John traveled from Kearney that summer for the wedding. My brother was delighted that I was setting the pace and marrying a "real American girl." My parents, as I had expected, were extremely unhappy about my marrying a non-Greek, but they tried not to let it show. Kris's parents were good hosts. They were sensitive to my parents' discomfort, and kept the civil ceremony and the reception afterward small and quiet.

I noticed signs of aging in my parents, my father especially, when we were together on that visit. He was fifty-three, and his lifetime of long days on his feet had taken its toll, installing a permanent ache and varicose veins in his legs, salting his black hair with gray, and creasing his forehead and the corners of his eyes. But there were positives as well. With the Depression long over, the wartime boom that the air base had brought to Kearney, and the farmers regaining some of their prosperity, the Central Cafe was thriving. The restaurant's income meant that my parents were able to be ever more giving to the villages and people they had left behind in Greece.

It was partly to advance this generosity that my father was planning a sea change in their lives, he told me proudly when we were gathered in Twin Falls. Jack Ryan, after years of watching the day break over downtown Kearney at the end of his regular graveyard shift, had told him he no longer wanted to work nights. He did, however, want to stay on at the restaurant. That made Dad think, and he seized the opportunity. "Twenty-four hours a day, three hundred and sixty-five days a year, it's too much," he said. "No more." He was promoting Jack to manager and changing the hours. The cafe would now open from six in the morning to nine at night. Making Jack manager would allow my parents the freedom to travel, and they intended to return to Greece as often as they could. Now they could afford it. My mother was already accumulating travel brochures and mapping their first trip while she awaited the switch to the new hours. (When the day finally came, at the end of 1948, my father ran into a complication. The first time he went to close up for the night, he fished in his pocket and suddenly realized that he had no key. In the twenty-five years since he had opened up, the Central Cafe had never been closed, its door never locked. He had to roust one of his customers, a locksmith, who hurriedly fashioned a key to fit the lock. It was another week before he remembered to turn off the neon sign at night.)

Kris and I spent a one-night honeymoon, all we could afford, in the Idaho resort town of Sun Valley. Back in Chicago, we moved into a single bedroom that was part of a larger house in the Chicago suburb of Park Ridge, west of the city. With her degree in journalism, she landed a public relations job with the American Medical Association, and for a time we lived the life of a two-income couple with (a little) money to spare. But I spent much more time at my job than she did at hers, and more and more Kris came to feel that I was neglecting her. I would not have wanted to admit it, but I was my father's son. Pursuing my work and achievement, I was replaying his obsessive devotion to the Central Cafe neglecting my mother.

Then I made a decision that kept me away from home, and my attention away from Kris, even more. The marriage would take care of itself.

Night School

By now it was 1950, and I was seeing with each passing day that my retailing BS degree wasn't doing me much good. I continued to find market research the key to an amazing variety of commercial decisions, but I needed a broader business education. I needed an MBA.

My original plan had been to go back to Northwestern, but the graduate business school was a long way off. I was pondering what to do when I happened to glance up one day as I walked on South La Salle Street a few doors from the Market Facts office. The sign that caught my eye at 19 South La Salle read: The University of Chicago Graduate School of Business.

I knew nothing about this school's program, but it was a one-minute commute from my office. That alone made it worth investigating. As I asked around, the opinions that came back to me were "very intellectual," "research-oriented," "theoretical," "quantitative," this last meaning that the professors stressed analysis based upon large data sets. The most telling comment was that the program was "very academic and not very practical." That was the clincher. I had had experience with a "practical education." Thus began a breathtaking roller-coaster ride of intellectual stimulation, challenging thought, and relentless analysis that shaped me, my politics, my friendships, my career, and my approach to life more than anything before or since.

I didn't actually know much about business at that point, but from the moment I set foot in the unprepossessing building down La Salle Street, I had to rethink everything I thought I knew. I also took on a new view of my own talents. Summa cum laude at Northwestern, and a Big Man on Campus to boot, and coming into the Chicago GSB as a cocky young man of twenty-four, I thought I was pretty damn smart. But when I heard teachers such as Milton Friedman and George Stigler—both in their late thirties and developing the thinking in economics that would later win them Nobel Prizes—expounding their theories in front of rapt classrooms, I realized there was smart, and then there was *really* smart.

Friedman was physically diminutive in contrast with his huge intellect. He was all of five feet four inches, and his eyes behind his glasses sparkled with rare insights and zest for life. He could be intimidating, because his self-assurance was formidable, and he always said exactly what was on his mind. He liked to say, in looking at the markets, "I may sometimes be wrong on timing but never on direction." Free markets were his mantra. He spoke of their immense power, of how they work best when kept open and unhampered by interference and Keynesian manipulations. Later in Washington, I was to experience firsthand the political economy, or what some would call the real economy. More recently, I have observed the devastation unfettered capital markets have inflicted on all of us. If Milton were alive today, I would be inclined to say, "Milton, I must say to you that today's real economies may be more complicated than you would seem to suggest." Still, at the head of a class, Milton treated ideas like a cat with a toy, swatting them this way and that to see what they would do, seemingly for the pure joy of it.

Stigler was another character who leavened his brilliance with insightful humor. Advertising was climbing to prominence, and thus new criticism, in American business life. Stigler took issue with those who blamed advertising for its influence on buyers, saying that was "like blaming the waiter for obesity." He had also done some classic studies of the dangers of overregulation and how bureaucrats often became the captives of the very industries they were assigned to regulate. Stigler also taught us not to obsess about alternatives that don't exist.

They were both enormously persuasive. I was shaped by their basic principles from then to now. They have stuck with me and proven far more practical than my Northwestern courses in retail inventory control and retail sales promotion. I often think of how different my life would have been had the University of Chicago Graduate School of Business not been so close to my Market Facts office. Dumb luck played a big role, as it did in my escape from MIT, and I tip my hat to chance.

My goal was to obtain my MBA in five quarters of night classes while continuing to work at my day job at Market Facts. It normally took six quarters on a regular day schedule. Three nights a week, for three hours, I took classes after work. When they were over, I rushed to catch the train to Park Ridge and if I was lucky I might make it home by eleven o'clock, in time to fall into bed exhausted. I spent weekends doing homework because I told myself I had to get straight As. What was more, I committed myself to writing a thesis. This was not a requirement, but it would get me special honors, and I was the only one of the students in my class who took on this added task. I did ease my path a bit by choosing a topic I could research easily: Market Facts shared a law firm with the Morton Salt Company, which had recently been taken to court by the Federal Trade Commission on antitrust grounds. I wrote about the company's pricing and trade practices, and our mutual law firm allowed me to do my research in their offices.

All this took its toll on Kris. I was repeating my father's pattern and treating my wife much as he had treated my mother. It was a pattern with multiple mistakes. My father had tried to build a secure life that he assumed would give her pleasure in the absence of attention and affection. I had believed that I could win my mother's love with material gifts, as with the alabaster box I made for her, and with my achievements. I was reliving not just my father's errors, but my own. My MBA and my growing career at Market Facts would be my gift to Kris.

Alas, this was not the gift Kris wanted. One day late in 1950, she told me she wanted a divorce. I hadn't seen it coming. Perhaps this in itself was a sign of my preoccupation and insensitivity, but I was shocked to tears. My brother, John, was at Northwestern then, and when I told him and one of my best friends I broke down crying. More telling as a measure of my obsession with career and school was that my recuperation period was short. The breakup was clearly my fault. I acknowledged responsibility for neglecting the marriage, agreed to the divorce, and moved back into the postgraduate fraternity life, sharing an apartment with several former Alpha Tau Omega brothers, all of us dating and partying and having the best time we'd had since we were at Northwestern.

A year after I had been awarded my MBA in 1951, the Graduate School of Business made me an astonishing offer—an associate professorship focusing on marketing. It was unheard of for a non–Ph.D. to teach at the graduate level, especially in a highly regarded program like the University of Chicago GSB with its resident geniuses. The offer was flattering, but I turned it down. For one thing, it paid less than half of what I was making at Market Facts, and I wanted to stay in the practical world, where I could apply what I had learned in the academic. Market research and its potential applications remained fascinating for me. I did, however, agree for a few years to teach one course a quarter at the GSB at night.

I think one reason the GSB approached me, beyond my thesis and good grades—one B, the rest As—was that my work had started to gain attention outside Market Facts. I wasn't content to simply know what I knew, or thought I knew. I wanted to write about it, speak about it, even teach others. Although I was only in my mid-twenties, I had begun to accumulate a dossier of contacts with corporate practitioners of market research that would widen my world beyond a small Chicago market research firm. I kept these contacts on cards in a growing, if small, Rolodex.

By then I was dating again. Sally Hornbogen was a warm, attractive, fun-loving Northwestern junior from Marquette, Michigan. She had been engaged to one of my younger fraternity brothers when the army sent him to Germany, and our attraction flowered in his absence.

We shared at least two things in common. We both loved classical music, and she was a very good piano player. I still had the season tickets in the upper balcony of the Chicago Symphony, so hardly a week went by without our going to these concerts. We also loved to dance. My Aunt Helene's early dance lessons in Kearney really paid off.

"I Like Ike"

I had first voted in the 1948 election, the first after I turned twenty-one, which was then the voting age. I cast my ballot for Republican Thomas Dewey, who was running against President Harry Truman. He lost by a hair. As the 1952 presidential race approached, I developed an interest in politics that was far more intense than any I had experienced before.

I have tried to reflect on why I voted for Dewey. One reason was that I was trying to establish my credentials as a young businessman, and virtually every business executive I knew was Republican. Perhaps I also bought the popular stereotype that Truman was a failed Kansas City haberdasher and a poor president. His favorable ratings were down in the twenties, rather like George W. Bush's at the end of his administration. How wrong I was! As I read David McCullough's great book on Truman, I was reminded that he had probably made more right, tough, and courageous big decisions than any president I could recall.

My uremic poisoning and the surgery that followed led to a draft deferment that kept me from serving in Korea, but that war, so soon after World War II, was an enormous trauma. Once again, America's young men were called to fight an enemy ideology, not Fascism this time but Communism in which the North Koreans were proxies for the Soviet Union and Red China. As the Soviets supplied MiG jet fighters and Chinese troops reinforced the North Koreans, it was the first hot salvo of the Cold War. And it stretched on, with mounting deaths and no apparent end, even after the two sides settled into an unofficial stalemate along a line that divided the Korean peninsula north of Seoul.

The Korean standoff continued into 1952. By then, the country had had twenty years of Democratic presidents, Truman for one elected term and the better part of another, when he had succeeded Franklin Delano Roosevelt on his death early in his fourth term in 1945. Truman's list of accomplishments was impressive, especially on the international front; he had supported enduring global institutions such as the United Nations, the World Bank, and the International Monetary Fund. He was also responsible for the Marshall Plan, which rebuilt the war-ravaged nations of Europe as a bulwark against Communism, and his own Point Four program, aimed at modernizing developing nations by supplying them with U.S. skills, knowledge, and equipment. It was also courageous of him to fire General Douglas MacArthur, an enormously popular man who, among others, needed a strong reminder that in America, the civilians were in charge.

The market-oriented fiscal conservatives who dominated the faculty at the University of Chicago GSB were overwhelmingly Republican. I respected their thinking, and as I looked at the potential candidates, I decided to join the impressive list of people who hoped to draft General of the Army Dwight D. Eisenhower as a candidate for the party's nomination. Eisenhower's chief opponent was the old-line Senator Robert A. Taft of Ohio. He was a clear favorite of the Republican establishment.

I believed Eisenhower transcended ordinary politicians. Having led American forces to victory in World War II and served as Supreme Allied Commander thereafter, he was a conquering general. But there was nothing fierce or warriorlike about him. With his warm and genuine smile, his balding head, and the straight talk that grew from his Kansas roots, he had the persona of a beloved and trusted father figure.

My entry into the Eisenhower camp started in 1951 with a phone call from George Fry. Fry was leading the Eisenhower recruitment effort in Illinois, but he was calling for another reason. I had collaborated with his management consulting firm on a few market research projects, and he was trying to recruit me. I demurred on the job offer, but I took the opportunity to tell him of my attraction to Ike and my preliminary views of how to sell him to the public. Fry was intrigued, and he authorized me to do some pro bono research to back up my gut reactions. I persuaded W. Lloyd Warner, the great sociologist from the University of Chicago who had done seminal research into American views on social class, to join me as an unpaid volunteer. We started talking to people using some of the latest interview and motivational research techniques. In each interview, we would eventually put the questionnaire aside and talk informally, and these sessions, when people thought the interview was over and relaxed, revealed far more than their answers to specific questions.

"I just like Ike," they said. "I don't know why, but I really trust this man. He just seems like the kind of leader you can trust to do the right thing."

Fry relayed these findings to Republican senator James H. Duff of Pennsylvania, who was managing the recruit-Eisenhower campaign nationally. Soon I was sending memos to the national headquarters, reporting the general's advantage in being a charismatic father figure people liked and trusted to make the right decisions on the issues. We recommended that he should not descend into traditional politics and the negative campaigning that went with it. By the fall of 1951, "I Like Ike" was appearing on buttons and other paraphernalia. I never knew what specific influence our work had, but I felt it was correct to focus on Ike's persona of likability and trust more than his specific views on the Taft-Hartley Labor Act, for example.

"I Like Ike" became one of the most successful slogans in American presidential politics. Eisenhower had the advantage of not having to campaign in the Republican caucuses and primaries. He remained in France as the head of NATO forces and only returned to the United States on June 1, 1952. Four days later, he announced his candidacy, and six weeks after that, at the Republican convention in Chicago, he won the nomination on the first ballot over Taft. How sweet and simple the nominating process was in that election!

Warmth and trust remained Eisenhower's trump card in the general election. His opponent was Illinois's Democratic governor, Adlai Stevenson, a sophisticated man who had won nomination partly on the strength of his brilliant keynote speech at his party's convention. But voters struggled to define him, as we learned in our continued interviews. He was "decent," a "thinker," a "bit complicated," yet there was little spontaneity in these responses. Mentioning Ike, on the other hand, made our subjects light up and start to talk with feeling. Voters didn't have to sift through the issues to decide if he was right for them; they just liked him and believed he would do what was right for them. I was so sure of what our interviews revealed that I bet some of my business colleagues $500, which was more than I could afford to lose, that Ike would beat Stevenson in Illinois.

I watched the election returns on November 4 on a black-and-white television set at the Eisenhower headquarters in Chicago. Eisenhower won decisively, and earned me $500 by outpolling Stevenson in Illinois

by over 400,000 votes. It convinced me more than ever of the validity—
and importance—of well-targeted research.

When the campaign invited me to Ike's inauguration, I jumped at
the opportunity. Sally came with me, though we were not yet married.
We rode the train to Washington and stayed at the apartment of Uncle
John Petrow's daughter Helen, one of the children my mother had nan-
nied when she first came to America from Greece. Helen had grown up
to marry a prominent Washington lawyer named George Vournas, and
in the Greek tradition they welcomed us into their home. Ike was sworn
in on January 20, 1953, amid a swirl of festivities that included the traditional parade, several balls, concerts, a star-studded show with Hollywood and Broadway stars, and various other fetes and parties. I wore
a rented tuxedo and Sally and I jostled with the celebrating crowds, sipping cocktails and eating from sumptuous buffets. The thought occurred
to me, "Wow! I'm a long way from Kearney, Nebraska."

A Step Up

Kearney was in my rearview mirror and disappearing fast. All of it, that
is, but those troublesome traits that I was dragging along with me, like
my perfectionism and obsessive devotion to work.

I hoped these traits wouldn't cripple my new marriage, but in all
honesty I can't say I really took this to heart, at least over the longer
term.

Sally and I had tied the knot at her family's home in Marquette, on
the north shore of Michigan's Upper Peninsula, in June 1953. The
winds blowing off Lake Superior still had an icy feel that was matched
by her father's sharp watch on the proceedings. Dr. Daniel Hornbogen's
reputation across the Midwest as a crack ophthalmologist was exceeded,
in my eyes, only by his forbidding, austere character.

My parents were absent this time. They didn't know about the
wedding, because I hadn't told them. My brother and I had talked at
length about their strong disapproval of their boys marrying outside the

Greek community. I was doing this now for the second time, and we decided that having them at the wedding would be too awkward. So John stood up as my best man, and I phoned my parents afterward to give them the news. (John, always enormously popular, went on to be a serial best man, performing the duty for no fewer than twenty-one of his friends.) My parents were upset at the time, but a year later, with the birth of our first son, they softened.

We named our firstborn John, after my brother and my mother's father. His birth highlighted the same workaholic tendencies that had led to my breakup with Kris. Sally was due in a week, and I thought I could squeeze in a last business trip, and that was a very bad mistake. I was in Baltimore when she went into labor, and although I rushed back, I missed Johnny's birth by about eight hours. Sally was not pleased as I entered her hospital room, but she didn't stay angry when she saw my delight at holding our first child. The birth of John greatly warmed Sally's and my relationship with my parents. Sally was no longer the *vromitsa*, non-Greek girl. She was the loving mother of their beloved first grandchild. My parents also loved Sally's warm embrace of them.

By then I had been executive vice president of Market Facts, the firm's number two position, for a year. My boss, Bill O'Dell, was teaching me a lot. He advised me on how not to wear out my welcome with my colleagues. Just as I had at my first job in Portland, I was too quick to criticize them, often not in a particularly constructive vein. When they failed to grasp a point I was making or a result I wanted, I sometimes turned on them with a quiet disparagement. Part of this, I think, was feeling that I was a young man in a big hurry. Word about my work in market research and analysis was getting around, and new invitations to speak about it to business and academic groups were arriving more frequently than I would ever have expected. I enjoyed the public recognition that came from these appearances almost as much as I enjoyed doing the work.

My salary had quintupled, from the $50 a week I started at to almost $250. At $12,000 a year, I could afford more than one good suit. I was now shopping at Brooks Brothers, the fashion citadel of the White Anglo-Saxon Protestants, particularly the Eastern ones, that I then hoped to emulate.

One day in the spring of 1953 my secretary buzzed me and said that Sid Wells was on the phone. Sidney A. Wells managed the Chicago office of the large international advertising agency McCann-Erickson. He said he had called to compliment me on some of our newer market research techniques, and I gathered he had attended or at least heard of one of my speeches. Then he stunned me with an offer out of the blue.

Would I be interested in coming to work for McCann-Erickson as director of marketing services of the Chicago office? He would double my pay, to a mind-numbing $25,000, and put me in line to become a vice president within a year, which he said would make me the youngest VP at a major advertising agency. I had been itching to move beyond research into a field closer to the action, and these were numbers and opportunities that my dear friend Bill O'Dell simply could not match. So I changed careers again and entered the wonderful, crazy business of advertising.

As director of marketing services, I was responsible for research, media, and sales promotion. I knew nothing about the last two. But my first days were such a blast I had no time to focus on what I didn't know. I was plunged into a swirl that took me to the best clubs and restaurants. I enjoyed (but didn't personally indulge in) the well-lubricated camaraderie of the infamous "three-martini lunch," attended new product introductions under glaring TV lights and popping flashbulbs, and ate shrimp and filet mignon at launch parties for new television shows for which network executives were trying to land sponsors.

But I had not been at my new job for very long before I learned the truth of the old adage: "If it sounds too good to be true, it probably is." I began to understand why McCann-Erickson had made such a generous offer to bring me on board.

I learned that 80 percent of McCann-Erickson's Chicago income came from only one account. That was Standard Oil of Indiana. But the account was in peril owing to an antitrust ruling that was forcing the national family of regional Standard Oil companies to break up into competing companies. With the prospect of competition among the oil companies that were descended from John D. Rockefeller's original Standard Oil Trust, the implications for McCann-Erickson were clear. The advertising would be splintered like the companies themselves, because they would not want to share the same agencies and their confidential advertising plans with their new competitors.

Still, trying to hang on to the Standard Oil of Indiana account was crucial. That brought me to the door of Alonzo W. Peake, the chairman and CEO. He was a man of the old school, having risen from the oilfields to the executive suite, and he still preferred a high, stiff collar that matched his personality. Moments after I entered his office, I noticed a rounded brass container on the floor beside his desk. I wondered what it was until he leaned over and directed a stream of tobacco juice from the chaw in his mouth into the spittoon (a name I learned later). It landed with a resounding "ping," and as I proceeded with my presentation, the "pings" of tobacco juice on brass interrupted my points with unnerving regularity.

I was talking to Peake about their Standard Oil (Indiana) motor oil called Permalube. To me, its potential claim to fame from an advertising standpoint was that it was one of the first motor oils to contain detergents. Our research showed that car owners worried that dirt and sludge in motor oil could damage their cars' engines. We thought the best way to sell Permalube was to tell drivers it cleaned their engines as they drove.

I laid out my case with charts and graphs and a lot of information from the latest techniques in market research we had applied. Peake, impatiently, I thought, kept leaning to one side and spitting into the spittoon, and finally he lodged his chaw in one cheek and interrupted me with a look that bordered on disdain. "Listen, sonny," he said, "isn't Permalube the best motor oil money can buy?"

"Oh, yes sir, Mr. Peake," I hastily agreed.

"Then why in hell don't you just say it?"

So much for sophisticated market research. We ran the campaign Peake wanted, keyed with the tired cliché just as he stated it: "Permalube: the best motor oil money can buy." A few weeks later we got word we were losing the account, and the McCann-Erickson Chicago office went into shock.

If I had been brought on board to help save this account, I had failed and, for a while, felt terrible about it. I even worried for a bit that

I might get fired. But I came to understand from our New York colleagues that the Standard Oil decision was made at the highest levels due to the recent Supreme Court antitrust decisions: It had nothing to do with how good or bad a given product campaign was.

My job now was to help land some new clients. I reviewed how McCann-Erickson had sold itself to clients in the past, and quickly concluded that it had not gone about this very cleverly for a business that was supposed to be creative. Every pitch had focused too much on McCann-Erickson—the terrific ads it had done, the awards it had won—and not enough on the client. Other ad agencies could also trot out impressive spots and shelves full of plaques and trophies. I determined that we could stand apart by focusing on our potential clients and their consumers and what we could do for *them*. This meant researching a company's and its consumers' needs *before* we made our presentation. We would have to invest some time without a guaranteed return, but if we landed the account we were ahead of the game.

We started researching our new business prospects—their products, their distribution, their image, their customers. From this research we would try to come up with an array of creative suggestions—not just advertising ideas but thoughts on new products, packaging, and promotions.

This kind of attention amounted to high flattery. We then enhanced this flattery by stressing that no matter how it appeared, we really didn't know nearly enough about their companies and wanted to learn much more. *They* were the experts. We had spent only a few weeks looking at the businesses to which they had devoted their entire working lives. We could make informed suggestions, but the final answers lay with them. The executives we pitched seemed impressed, and they liked the idea of working with advertising people who offered more than jingles and ad copy.

Slowly our client list grew, replacing at least part of the lost Standard Oil of Indiana business. It looked as if the Chicago office of McCann-Erickson would be saved, and my job with it. I was feeling relieved, and even a little cocky, but not so cocky as to anticipate what happened next.

Ascending

The man who headed McCann-Erickson's worldwide operations from a sumptuous office high above Lexington Avenue in New York City was Marion Harper. He had worked his way from McCann-Erickson's mailroom and the research department to the presidency, which he achieved in 1948 at the age of thirty-two. I had dealt with him several times since I had joined the agency. He was tall and balding, brilliant and highly articulate, all in all a commanding figure with a fondness for analysis that contrasted with other leading advertising men of the time. Leo Burnett, whose Chicago agency bore his name, and Bill Bernbach of Doyle Dane Bernbach in New York, were advertising legends and great talents who believed that research often got in the way of creative thinking. They thought the right ideas would pop up out of nowhere, like rubbing Aladdin's lamp. Marion, on the other hand, believed that certain structural elements had to be in place before you could devise an ad; his was a formulaic approach. I stood somewhere between Marion and the legends. The optimal results, I thought, would come from giving our creative people insights about the customers we were trying to reach. While I was always a bit doubtful about Marion's genuine feel for great ads, he could really communicate with corporate CEOs. He talked about "moving your goods" and "building shareholder value," suggestive of a deeper partnership than that offered by the average agency.

I had no reason to suspect anything more than a routine business call that spring day in 1954 when my secretary told me Marion was on the line. I expected him to tell me about a new prospect needing research. Instead, he came on the line and without preliminaries said, "Pete, I have good news. We're making you head of the Chicago office."

"My God, Marion, why would you do that?" I blurted. I had been at McCann-Erickson for a little more than two years, was just twenty-seven, and he was asking me to run an office that employed some two hundred people.

He responded with a tone of droll complacency: "Since you asked, we figured that since we lost the Standard Oil account, what else have we got to lose?"

With that resounding vote of confidence, I became a McCann-Erickson vice president in charge of the Chicago office. This was a stunning development, and a little hard to come to terms with. Incredulity kept popping into my thoughts—"Just think, this Greek kid a vice president of a major advertising agency at only twenty-seven." Finally, I mustered the courage to ask a veteran of the business what it meant to be the vice president of a major advertising agency. His comment brought me down to earth. "Don't take the title too seriously," he said. "There are hundreds of them, so it's not what *being* a vice president means. It's what *not being* a vice president means."

My first vice presidential decision was to add more creative depth. I found the answer in McCann-Erickson's New York office. Chester L. Posey was working in the shadow of his father, Chester A. Posey, a senior vice president and one of the senior creative people. When I asked Chet if he was willing to move to Chicago as *the* creative director of our office, he jumped at the chance. He was about three years older than I was and had served as a navy lieutenant in the Pacific during World War II. He shared my view that the creative side should work hand-in-glove with market research.

Chet and I went after the Rival dog food account using our research-driven pitch. We were struck by the way dog owners identified with their dogs. The next question was: What aspects of their own lives did the owners project onto their pets?

We learned that many urban dog owners were uneasy about being overweight and not getting enough exercise. Our research showed that they worried that their pets were too fat and sedentary, too, so we pitched Rival as "a modern dog food for city dogs that don't get enough exercise."

Chet came up with creative commercials that showed a portly, pipe-smoking couch potato watching television, with his equally portly dog dozing at his feet. But the dog is dreaming, and in his dream the scene dissolves from the city living room to the outdoors where an obviously leaner, healthier dog is running joyously through fields and jumping over fences.

To make the ads work, we told the Rival people we thought they should put more protein and less fat into their product. We also suggested tweaking the presentation with a bit of red food coloring, and a touch more meat so they could justifiably claim Rival was "meatier." The company took our advice. The effect was electric! Rival's market share zoomed from 12 percent to 17 percent in a very crowded dog food market.

We delved deeper into the mysteries of human personalities in the peanut butter wars. Peter Pan was sold in a jar with a vacuum lid to prove nobody else had opened it, but Skippy had no special seal on a wide-mouthed jar. We concluded that the different containers appealed to different people, defined in psychological terms as anal compulsives and oral impulsives. Anal compulsives are the kind of people who walk into a room and want to straighten the pictures on the wall and empty the ash trays. Neatness and cleanliness are their priorities. They went for the Peter Pan jar. Oral impulsives just want to dig in, and hence Skippy was their choice; and the Peter Pan vacuum seal sometimes bent on opening so it didn't close correctly, exposing the peanut butter to air that dried it out.

Could we come up with a peanut butter jar that appealed to both personality types? We did, urging Peter Pan to adopt the wide-mouthed jar for the orals but a paper "purity" seal to appeal to the anals. Peter Pan made the changes, and sales increased.

We even engaged in a little child psychology. Working for Swiss Meats for Babies, we watched mothers feeding their babies and noticed that often, without thinking, they'd pull a face as they tasted the food themselves first. We didn't have to interview the babies to conclude that their fussy reaction to the food was because they'd subliminally copied the mothers. We suggested making the baby food tastier for adults, for example, ham with a raisin sauce that would not be too spicy for a baby. Once again, the clients saw sales increase.

The Chicago office had previously been considered a backwater outpost. Now we would sometimes sign up more significant new business clients than even the giant New York office. In one year our small-ish operation got about three-fourths of all McCann-Erickson's new business in its sixteen U.S. offices. Marion Harper decided to come out to see how we were doing it. He sat in on a pitch we were making for the Tums antacid account that a lot of major agencies were drooling for because Tums advertised so heavily. We gave the Tums executives ideas for introducing flavored Tums and creating special packages for frequent users in a presentation designed to show we knew the product and its customers very well. The management team we pitched took the almost unprecedented step of awarding us the account—a very big one—on the spot, minutes after we wrapped up. Marion was a hard man to impress, but this example of rainmaking got his attention.

The ascending fortunes of the Chicago office matched my own. Looking back, I have to say (immodestly) that I was probably better at this advertising business than anything else I have done in my career, before or since. The combination of relentless analysis and creativity seemed to fit me, and it was paying off. I was making a salary of $50,000.

Jim, our second child, was born in 1956. This time I managed to attend. Sally and I had been living in a two-bedroom apartment in North Evanston since our marriage. With Jim on the way, we had gone house hunting and settled on a suburb a bit farther north, Kenilworth, Illinois, with its highly regarded Joseph Sears public elementary school. The four-bedroom, three-bath home we bought even had a small maid's bedroom with a bath, and it seemed like a palace. What was more, the backyard had enough room to play touch football, with a small side area that could be turned into a hockey rink. Sally and I made a ritual of strolling along the quiet streets pushing the boys in an open carriage and they both, but Johnny especially, loved those walks. He was always finding something to look at in the sky. Birds, planes, and clouds all attracted his attention. A second ritual was my weekend golf games. I was becoming addicted to the sport and, looking back, I spent too much time on the links and too little at home with Sally and our little family.

I'd seen little of my mother and father in these hectic years. My father was spending less time in his restaurant. He'd followed through on a promise that they'd visit Greece, and they did. His charity to Vahlia was assuming serious dimensions, like paying to pave the roads and install water systems. Our new, spacious Kenilworth house allowed me to host my parents in my own home for the first time. They'd stay for several days, spoiling their grandchildren, who called them YiaYia and Papou. (I am now a "papa" to my nine grandchildren!) My father appeared to have abandoned his strict "economia," so far as the grandchildren were concerned, but he was still strict and formal with my mother. Sally's rather cold, Germanic parents were of a different stripe. They never stayed for long, pausing for a few hours on their journeys to and from the exclusive Hobe Sound resort on the east coast of Florida.

Creative Minds at Play

My McCann-Erickson colleagues and I were young, successful, on top of the world. You can't be in this field without having fun with words and images; it's a playful business even while it's deadly serious, and it attracts playful and imaginative people. At McCann-Erickson's Chicago office, some of us tried to best our colleagues in long-running games of one-upmanship that took the form of increasingly elaborate practical jokes.

Elmer Rich, whose family owned the Simoniz car wax business, had become a good friend when we still lived in Evanston. Chet Posey and I were making a pitch for the Simoniz account, so I scheduled a dinner for the Riches at our home. Typically, I obsessed about every detail of the dinner. I made an elaborate checklist of every liqueur I thought the Riches might expect to find in a household as worldly and sophisticated as their own, a level of sophistication to which I only pretended. I went to the local liquor store and purchased a variety of cordials and brandies. Returning home with bagsful of bottles that included every kind of fruit, nut, and creme liqueur I could lay my hands on, I was confident that I could meet the most exotic wishes of our guests.

The big night came. Dinner went beautifully. The Poseys and the Riches enjoyed the food and each other. As the dessert plates were being cleared, I began taking orders for after-dinner drinks.

"Hmmm," Chet said, his eyes dancing with mischief. "I think I'll have a shot of grappa." He gave me a big smile.

"Grappa?" I said.

"Yes, grappa," he replied. "You do know what it is, Pete. Don't you?"

"Of course," I said, although I didn't.

"As you know, the Italians distill it from what's left over after they make wine. The French call it *marc*. Nectar of the gods. That's what I'll have. Just a shot, thanks." He held his fingers up an inch apart.

I would have bet the house that Chet had found grappa in a wine and spirits dictionary. He didn't know about it any more than I did. But he had me, because among all my bottles there was no grappa. I learned later he'd discovered this gap in my alcoholic armory during a secret inspection of my liquor cabinet earlier that evening. Now he feigned surprise and disappointment. Acting the martyr, he refused to have anything at all when I offered one of my better cognacs as a substitute. "No. No," he said in a voice that suggested that one of his good friends had died. "That was all I really wanted."

We never landed the Simoniz account, but Chet and Elmer became good friends who shared a wicked sense of humor.

One Christmas morning I opened my front door to get the newspaper and found a huge box tied with a red ribbon. I tried to pick it up but couldn't move it. Shivering in my bathrobe and pajamas, I untied the ribbon, lifted a corner, and took a peek inside. It was dark in there and I pried the top another inch or two until I saw what looked like fur. When I finally got the package fully open, I gaped at the sight of a large, bloody, and very dead black bear.

I smelled Chet Posey's and Elmer Rich's handiwork. My first thought was to get rid of it before Elmer, who was now our neighbor, dropped by with his wife, Patty, and their kids for Christmas eggnog. I knew he'd pretend to be curious about the big box on my doorstep and express all kinds of spurious wonderment about who could possibly have presented me with such a gift. Of course, he'd ask what it was and then play the violin strings of sympathy that I'd been the butt of such a joke. My first call was to the Kenilworth police. I thought they could dispatch someone to come pick it up.

"That won't be possible, Mr. Peterson," said the officer on duty. "I have to warn you that any large dead animal is a health hazard," he said. "You'll have to dispose of it promptly."

"How am I supposed to do that? It's Christmas Day," I said.

"I don't know," he said. "Maybe you can bury it."

I thought about spending the rest of Christmas morning digging a hole deep enough in the frozen ground for this big—and now very stiff—bear and realized that was just what Chet and Elmer would have wanted.

One of the axioms of the advertising business is that sometimes you have to make lemons into lemonade. This bloody bear was a very big lemon. But then what could be the lemonade? And then—Eureka! Bear rug, I thought. If I could turn the bear into a rug, I would have some lemonade.

I looked up the nearest taxidermist, dialed the phone, and told him what I wanted. Yes, he said, he could make the bear into a bear rug, but he wasn't going to start on Christmas Day. I pleaded and begged and explained my predicament with the police. Finally, he yielded. John and Jim, who were then eight and six, and a neighbor who had made the mistake of asking what was in the box helped me wrestle it to my Chrysler sedan and heave it into the trunk for the drive to the taxidermist.

A cardinal rule in practical jokes is that the victim must never let the perpetrator know that he is suffering, concerned, or in fact even aware that a joke has been performed. We said nothing when Elmer and his family came around later.

Some weeks later, the taxidermist called and I picked up my bear rug. It was a classic of the form, complete with beady glass eyes and toothy jaws open in a permanent snarl. I put it in the living room and waited.

A few days later, we were having a Sunday brunch with Elmer and his family at their home. One of their older sons took me aside and said, "Mr. Peterson, you are driving my father crazy. Whatever happened to that bloody bear?" Aha, I thought. Suspicions confirmed. The boy continued, "Dad and Mr. Posey spent all kinds of time and money. They had to hire a hunter to kill the bear. They had to ship the bear from northern Wisconsin. Dad had to beg the head of the Evanston hospital to keep the bear in its morgue until Christmas Eve. Then they had to wrap it up and bring it over here in the middle of the night. They're so curious and disappointed that they haven't heard from you."

How sweet it was! I organized another dinner party with Messrs. Rich and Posey high on the guest list. When the party was assembled I casually led the guests into the living room where the bear rug snarled before the fireplace. "I want to make a toast," I said, raising a glass. "I don't know who I'm toasting, but I'm enormously grateful. Somebody gave us this bear, and I have always desperately wanted a bear rug. I just wish I could thank whoever was this extraordinarily generous."

"You son of a bitch!" Chet and Elmer screamed in unison. The bear was center stage for the rest of the night.

Practical jokes seem to be a thing of the past, and I often wonder why.

An Ethical Dilemma Leads to a Fork in the Road

I was still short of my thirtieth birthday one day in 1956 when I received another significant phone call from Marion Harper in New York. He was reorganizing McCann-Erickson again, and he wanted me to become one of his two new high-level assistants. I was to coordinate the regional offices in the Midwest, Southwest, and West, and also serve on the five-member board of directors. I would remain headquartered in Chicago, which was better situated to travel among the offices for which I was responsible, but I would also have a large office in New York. The other assistant to the president was to monitor the Eastern offices.

I marveled yet again that I had hit the big time for certain. But the higher I rose in the advertising business the more my life seemed to be defined by one client crisis or another. It seemed I was always in the air, or on my way to or from an airport, to help others with presentations, some of them all-night sessions before the clients arrived in the morning. I kept a suitcase packed, and there were many days when, homeward bound at last, I wondered if my children would recognize me when I got there.

But it was finally not the workload that got to me. It was my doubts about Marion Harper's leadership, indeed, his honesty and his integrity.

It is hard to overstate the extent to which he dominated McCann-Erickson as its CEO. In 1957, the company's profits were down across the agency, to the point where we executives started flying coach rather than first-class, and we were forced into some serious layoffs. Advertising is a business that depends on people, and handing out pink slips to employees, some of whom had been around for years, was painful. Yet in the midst of this retrenchment and cost cutting, Marion unilaterally committed McCann-Erickson to buy a plane.

And not just any plane, but a Douglas DC-7, a four-engine commercial airliner. The propeller-driven DC-7 could carry up to 110 passengers, but Marion had it outfitted as an executive plane, largely for his own use. I was genuinely disturbed that he would spend the company's money this way, and I said so one day when I was having lunch with Pat Patterson, the CEO of United Air Lines. When you have Pete Peterson and Pat Patterson at lunch, it sounds like there might be a punch line right around the corner. What Pat told me, however, wasn't funny. The rap on the DC-7, which United had been flying for several years, was that it burned so much fuel that it couldn't turn a profit even at high passenger loads. "That plane is a big money-loser, Pete," he said.

Marion followed the DC-7 purchase with another act of financial misfeasance. This one was much worse than an inefficient airplane; it struck at the company's promises to its employees. McCann-Erickson had a profit-sharing retirement trust fund that was the only retirement plan for most of its employees. The funds were invested in a conservative and balanced portfolio of stocks and bonds whose aim was preserving and slowly growing the capital that would produce the income that McCann-Erickson's retirees would depend upon. There is the "prudent man" rule in the investment of such pension or retirement funds. It seemed obvious to me, although I was years from retirement, that prudence was the only appropriate approach. My days as both a student and a teacher at the University of Chicago's Graduate School of Business had taught me the importance of fiduciary responsibility and, where retirement monies were concerned, the avoidance of unnecessary risk. I suppose my father's "economia" and memories of the Depression played a role as well.

But Marion had some grand ambitions. He envisioned McCann-Erickson as a broadly diversified communications empire, and to that end he was eying some acquisitions in public relations and specialty advertising that I thought were highly questionable. To raise the money to pursue them, he sprang a proposal on the board that the profit-sharing fund sell most of its investments and put the money into newly issued McCann-Erickson stock. There were several things seriously wrong with this idea. Advertising by its nature is a volatile and risky business. It is good or bad depending on the economic cycles as well as the fortunes of clients who rely, at least in part, on advertising to promote those fortunes. And, of course, investing in the stock of a single company is not a way to balance risk. When I spoke up at the board meeting and asked who would control the vote of the shares in this plan, Marion announced that he intended to act as the fund's trustee.

McCann-Erickson was not a public company with the accompanying board oversight requirements. I told the board that I had serious questions about what he wanted to do. It put our employees' savings at risk and gave Marion a double-barreled coup—cash to pursue his expansion adventures, and an uncommon and unwarranted degree of control over the agency. I was the sole dissenting vote.

Several months later, following my pattern of speaking and writing to explore the boundaries of my work, I wrote a paper outlining my thoughts about the future of the advertising business, and what I thought McCann-Erickson's place in it should be. I saw an increasingly consumer-driven market economy, in which ad agencies needed to grow far beyond writing copy and producing TV commercials and get into things like product development, package design, and sales promotion.

I supplied numerous examples in the piece, and sent copies around to my colleagues. The reviews were positive, and my premise was acknowledged to be true. As a matter of courtesy, I also sent a copy to Marion's office for his comments.

I thought he might want to put it out under his own name. He was the boss, after all, and it was his role to define the mission of the enterprise, as this piece tried to do. I was also prepared for the possibility that he disagreed with it, and that would be the end of it.

But I was not prepared for what did happen. I called Marion's office several times to get his reaction, but never heard from him. I began to believe he rejected the thinking in the piece, and just didn't want to hurt my feelings. Then one day several months later, I picked up a copy of *Advertising Age*, the industry's trade journal. There, in the opinion section, prominently displayed under Marion Harper's byline, was my piece word for word. Even the title was unchanged. An editor's note said that it would run in its entirety over the next few issues.

I was appalled. To have him do this without the candor or courtesy of discussing it with me beforehand was simply unacceptable. Marion Harper was a brilliant man, but I was convinced now that he lacked integrity. I knew I could never trust him again.

I had no choice but to move on. I discussed with Sally my anguish and this clash of values with Marion, and she understood. "You'll land on your feet," she said. "In the meantime, we have money in the bank and one thing I don't worry about is your ability to earn a good living."

My lack of trust in Marion was clearly one important reason I knew I had to leave McCann-Erickson, but there was another. My life was being consumed by the constant and, at times, hysterical planning and traveling for meetings.

When I returned one night from still another trip, my son Jimmy, aged eighteen months, looked up surprised. It was as though he was thinking, "Who is this man?" That did it.

I shared my feelings with Chet Posey. I got word to Marion, too. My intentions reached him about the time of McCann-Erickson's global management meeting; the company was now operating in more than a dozen countries, and all of the managers would be there. I flew in from Chicago, and when I reached the office on Lexington Avenue, Marion asked to see me privately. I expected him to apologize at last for the *Advertising Age* betrayal, but he never mentioned it. Instead, he talked as if I had never told him I was leaving. He plied me with effusive rhetoric about all the great things I had achieved and said that he was going to make an announcement at the meeting: I was to be named president of the entire agency, and he would move up to chairman and continue as the CEO. We would achieve great things together. But I had made up my mind, and nothing, not even the best offer in the advertising world, was going to change it. Marion Harper and I were not going to be partners.

I told him clearly and firmly, thank you but no. He seemed stunned. Did I understand that I was to be president of one of the world's largest advertising agencies at thirty-one years old? Yes, I did. The answer was still no.

The meeting convened. I gathered with my management colleagues and Marion kicked it off. He spoke of the growing demands of our global business, and said there was one person who could best help him guide the firm in the trying days ahead. I laughed to myself, thinking that he had had another Pete Peterson in the wings all along. But no. The person who would help guide McCann-Erickson into the future was none other than—Pete Peterson. He said my name, beaming as if our earlier talk had never happened. My colleagues greeted the announcement with what felt like rousing applause. He even made me stand up and take a bow.

Maybe he thought his force of personality would rule the day, or that I could not possibly turn down such an extraordinary offer at my age. But I thought that his announcement displayed a fundamental character deficiency yet again. His ego was so great that he could not imagine failing to get what he wanted. When the meeting broke up I told him again that I would not be staying, and kept repeating it until I finally broke through his incredulity.

Several weeks later, after wrapping up loose ends, I walked out of McCann-Erickson for the last time. I was thirty-one, married with two kids, and unemployed, but I had made up my mind that I'd never again work for a boss I did not both trust and admire, and with whom I did not share fundamental values.

CHAPTER 4

LESSONS IN
MANUFACTURING

When I decided to leave McCann-Erickson early in 1958, I had visions of spending time with Sally and the boys that had been lost because of my hectic travel schedule. My mother, however, had plenty of ideas. She saw me jobless and in need of the comforts and support of home. Now was the time to give up the rat race and come back to Kearney. She said that my father, after almost thirty-five years of overseeing the Central Cafe, would welcome me into the business. The community would welcome me back, too. My reputation as a good student would open doors. It was not inconceivable that with my MBA and my teaching record at the Chicago GSB I might even succeed my father's old friend Dr. Cushing as head of Nebraska State Teachers College. These were admirable aims, but it was clear to me that Kearney was in my past and was going to stay there.

I was still working out my notice when I got a call from Chuck Percy. He was also an Eisenhower man. We met during the movement to draft Eisenhower in 1951 and had frequently discussed my research on Ike's likability. Now we lived two blocks apart in Kenilworth and had become friends, playing tennis together. He was only about ten years older than I, but he had already been running the Bell & Howell Corporation for eight years as its board chairman, president, and CEO. To my mind, he was a legend.

Bell & Howell was an old-line maker of movie equipment, microfilm products, and audiovisual sound projectors used in education. It had adapted its cameras for military use in World War II, and since then had moved aggressively to expand its line of consumer products. I was familiar with the company since McCann-Erickson handled its advertising. Now and then, between sets of tennis at Chuck's house, we had talked about the product development and marketing challenges he faced as the head of a company whose photographic and audiovisual equipment occupied the high end of the market. Just before I resigned from McCann-Erickson, I had made a presentation to Bell & Howell executives addressing ways they could gain ground on their major competitor, Kodak.

Our other point of common ground was the Chicago GSB. Chuck was a University of Chicago graduate and a trustee, and had heard of my teaching of marketing.

"Pete," he said into the phone, "I have something I want to talk to you about. It's important, and I'd like to get together right away. I'll send a helicopter to pick you up." In less than thirty minutes I was being landed on the beach in front of Chuck's lakefront home in Kenilworth, blowing up a cloud of sand. I doubt it was a legal landing, but it was sure a fast and exciting ride, taking less than fifteen minutes. Chuck, a master salesman, knew how to impress me. He came out onto the beach to greet me and wasted no time with small talk as we walked back to his house. He said that he had been impressed with the marketing work I had done on the Bell & Howell advertising account. One of my suggestions was that Bell & Howell should focus on the network of hugely important, big camera dealers that preferred to sell higher-margin, high-end products like Bell & Howell's, rather than Kodak's lower-price, lower-margin products. The kinds of dealer promotions, salesman incentives, and product displays I recommended were far less costly than a major advertising program that Bell & Howell could not afford anyway.

Then, without further preliminaries, he offered me a job as Bell & Howell's second executive vice president, a seat on the board, a ten percent salary increase, and, thankfully, a lot of stock options that turned out to be much more valuable than my cash income.

I was stunned. I knew I was good at advertising. I believed my next offer would come from one of McCann-Erickson's competitors. But Chuck argued against my continuing in advertising. It was only then I told Chuck I was thinking of leaving McCann-Erickson. He said I was right to do so because I was "too serious and broad-gauged" a guy to stay in a business that was inherently limited. I smarted a little bit at his description, because he was essentially saying that down deep advertising was a shallow business compared with running a company that actually made and sold quality products. I had to admit that those of us in advertising did spend an awful lot of time and effort making a great deal out of little or sometimes nothing.

Chuck's offer both frightened and intrigued me. I worried that I would leave a place of comparative advantage, a field I had more or less mastered, for one where I needed to climb a steep learning curve. But Chuck's perception of my capabilities was something of a revelation. He made me believe it wasn't such a stretch. And the idea of working with Chuck excited me. He was already a highly respected national figure, admired not only for his business achievements but also for his forward-looking views on social policies. Bell & Howell, I knew, had become a national leader in minority hiring at a time when the civil rights movement was barely a blip on the radar. It was a board seat that would bring me in regular contact with some of Chicago's biggest business luminaries, including the CEOs of United Air Lines, Sears, Roebuck, and Inland Steel, among others.

I discussed it with Sally but we really did not have to think too long. I joined Bell & Howell in the spring of 1958.

Zooming In

The first thing my new boss did was to send me on vacation.

"Pete, I know you've been working hard," Chuck said. "Why don't you take some time off?" So I spent my first three weeks on the Bell & Howell payroll on the beach in Bermuda with Sally and the boys. We had just gotten word that Sally was pregnant with our third child, and I took the time to play with Johnny and Jim, rest, and look ahead.

I had a great time playing with the boys on the beach. John was strangely obsessed with the waves. We were later to understand why. Jim, a natural athlete, loved football on the beach.

When I reported for work on May 21, tanned and ready, I arrived at a far different workplace than the McCann-Erickson offices downtown. Bell & Howell occupied a plain old two-story building near the northern city limits, where Chicago met Evanston. The executive offices were spartan with a single window looking out on a parking area. There was a little room with a linoleum tile floor and aluminum window blinds where the executives ate lunch. The offices adjoined a huge manufacturing plant that Chuck recently had built, where several thousand workers put together Bell & Howell's movie and audiovisual equipment. This was a 1.5 million square feet facility, and it was immediately clear to me why "a broader approach to marketing" was needed—it was to keep that huge facility operating at peak efficiency.

I was the company's number three executive. Chuck acted as CEO, president, and chairman. Number two was the first executive vice president, William Roberts, a friend of Chuck's and, like him, a Christian Scientist. I reported to Roberts, but awkwardly. His brother-in-law, Carl Schreyer, who was the vice president for marketing, reported to me.

I once heard the theologian Paul Tillich say that "the problem of twentieth century man is to be comfortable with ambiguity." At Bell & Howell, I had to be comfortable not just with ambiguity but what felt, in the beginning, like my total ignorance. My first job as an executive vice president was to act as the senior marketing officer. That was within my expertise. But I was soon to take over the consumer photographic and audiovisual businesses, which accounted for the majority of the company's revenues. Manufacturing was totally new to me. The process of creating quality products and producing them en masse seemed to require an interminable number of steps that I knew nothing about.

Bell & Howell's engineers probably had the most misgivings about me. They patiently walked me through many product demonstrations to familiarize me with what the company was selling. They must have seen my hapless mechanical ineptitude, but in a way, this was an advantage. I was the canary in the mineshaft, a kind of early warning signal. If I had trouble using a Bell & Howell camera, the designers knew they had to

work extra hard to create a version that the average, nonmechanical consumer could manipulate easily.

To this end, I took all of Bell & Howell's advanced photo equipment home and tried it out. Taking decent motion pictures was particularly complicated. For one thing, the 8mm movie camera we sold to
home users often incorporated a lens turret with three lenses of different
focal lengths. It was a weird-looking thing, with the triangular turret
jutting out. If your subject got too close or too far away, you had to stop
shooting and rotate the turret to a different lens and a different distance.
I was expressing my frustration about this one day when the engineers
showed me a zoom lens that eliminated the lens-rotating hassle. I loved
it! Not only was it easy to use, it gave the cinematographer an entirely
new level of freedom. Instead of worrying that the kids were running
too far out of range while you fumbled with the lens turret, you could
follow them with the zoom.

At home, where I used my neighbors and guests as guinea pigs, the
response was equally enthusiastic. I called it the "Wow!" factor. They
would sight through the camera, turn the lens ring to zoom in or out,
and immediately exclaim, "Wow!"

I wondered why such a lens was available only to our professional
customers. I called our chief optical engineer and asked, "Why don't we
have the zoom lens in our mass market consumer cameras?"

His reply was condescending. "Why, Pete," he said, "a zoom lens
like this would be far too costly for the consumer market."

"I understand that," I told him. "But what could we do to make it
far less costly?"

Reducing the range of the zoom at both ends, giving up some
close-up capability and some distance magnification, still resulted in an
exciting consumer product unlike any on the market.

At the same time, other advances were taking place in the new
world of video. Television, and in particular sports television, was a
growing fascination at the end of the 1950s, as I could see from my own
viewing experiences at home and from my conversations with other
sports enthusiasts.

Here another concept in product development took hold. I called
it "inventing the question." Market research had taught me that the

right question was often helpful in creating the right product, so I asked our product design people if there were any sports television techniques we could incorporate. Before long, one of the engineers came back to me and said, "What would you think about slow motion?"

Now I was the one who said, "Wow!" How great it would have been to be able to see my children's first steps, slowed down to each precarious component. How much fun, or at least instructive, to look at my golf swing in slow motion so that I could break it down in hopes of reducing my high incidence of hooks and slices. I gave him the go-ahead.

The result was a beautiful camera that we called the Zoomatic. It was a sensation, though it later figured in one of America's great trage-dies. Abraham Zapruder used one to film his famous—and in-focus—footage of John F. Kennedy's assassination, which in turn made the Zoomatic one of the most studied and analyzed cameras in history.

These technical innovations gave us a very attractive product line, but we needed to increase sales in other ways, too. As I studied the num-bers, I was struck by how large the fixed costs were—such as tooling, sales organization, building, and utilities—that couldn't be reduced much whether we sold ten thousand cameras and projectors or a million.

I saw an opening here. How could we persuade dealers to sell Bell & Howell products at levels that substantially exceeded our fixed costs and current sales levels? We explained our cost structure to important dealers and told them they would have a share in the higher profits from sales above our planned sales levels. Dealers who exceeded the previous year's sales would earn bonuses in the form of Bell & Howell stock. As stockholders, they would be personally invested in the company's profit-ability and its future. We called the program "Partners in Profits."

It worked beautifully. Sales soared across consumer product lines in 1958. Despite an already high price-earnings ratio, Bell & Howell stock rose along with sales. Wall Street called us a growth company, a real achievement in a tough economic atmosphere.

We still were competing against a giant. Our share of the home movie market equaled Eastman Kodak's, but Kodak outspent us on ad-vertising by thirty to one—their $30 million to our $1 million. This was possible because Kodak enjoyed a near-monopoly in the highly profit-able film market. Ninety-five percent of the color film sold in the United

States was Kodak film. It was Kodak film that rolled through Bell & Howell's movie cameras. Like Gillette, which sold razor blades as well as razors to improve its bottom line, Kodak made its money selling very profitable film and could easily subsidize or lose money on its movie camera equipment.

We, alas, had only equipment to sell.

Increasing Exposure

One Saturday morning at the end of 1958, I was sitting in the bedroom with Jim, who was then two, changing television channels to find his favorite cartoon. As I turned the dial—this was before remote controls—I noticed that one of the channels was showing a documentary and I stopped. Jim yowled, but I was fascinated. *The Face of Red China* was the first television look at China since the Maoist revolution of 1948, and I wondered why CBS was airing it during Saturday morning cartoon time when few adults would be watching.

I remembered that a couple of months earlier Edward R. Murrow of CBS had delivered a rousing criticism of television networks relegating important news programming to an "intellectual ghetto" on weekends. His own *See It Now* public affairs series, famous for discrediting Senator Joe McCarthy's anti-Communist witch hunts, had lost its time slot to *The $64,000 Question* after Alcoa had dropped its sponsorship. Congress had called hearings and I had an idea. Perhaps Bell & Howell could step in? Our tiny advertising budget allowed us to run spots only on cowboy and detective shows, whereas Kodak had its name tied to major shows like the Walt Disney series. When Chuck picked me up on the first workday after the holidays, I canvassed the idea.

"What if we were to make this proposition to one of the networks? 'Gentlemen, you have a problem and we have a problem. You are in growing trouble in Washington about not meeting your public service responsibility. We have a small budget and big dreams. Suppose we sponsored public service programming in prime time. We would share in the production costs and give you total editorial freedom, both of which you don't have now. You choose the subjects—civil rights, abortion, you name it. But it has to air in prime time and be called *Bell & Howell Close-up.*'"

Chuck mused for a moment and said, "You're assuming this would generate a lot of favorable publicity beyond just the exposure."

"That's my theory," I said. "But keep in mind, it's just a theory."

A few minutes after arriving at work, Chuck had Frank Stanton on the phone, the president of CBS, whose sparkling reputation had led to the nickname "the Tiffany network." This made CBS the right choice for us.

Before long, Chuck and I were on a plane to New York for a meeting at CBS headquarters on Madison Avenue at 52nd Street. I laid out the concept to Stanton and the network president, James Aubrey. They had obviously done some thinking about it, too, because when I was finished Stanton said, "We like the idea, but with one exception. We'd have to call it *CBS Reports, Presented by Bell & Howell.*"

That was a tough point to concede, but we didn't have a better alternative. And Stanton persisted in pinning us down on the other question that dominated his concerns: "Are you two gentlemen really serious about us having total freedom on subject matter and content?"

We assured him that we were.

"Trust me, you guys are one of a kind," he said.

I have always been a so-called Rockefeller Republican, a rapidly vanishing species. I joke that there are only two of us left, David Rockefeller and myself. We think of ourselves as being conservative on fiscal matters and moderate or liberal on social issues. Fortunately, Chuck Percy and I had very similar views. Unlike the vast majority of CEOs, he was also receptive to our taking on controversial issues such as civil rights and right to life versus choice.

Thus *CBS Reports*, hosted by Edward R. Murrow, produced by Fred Friendly, and *Presented by Bell & Howell*, debuted on October 27, 1959. Its first show, in those days of the heated space race with the Soviets, was the biography of a rocket designed to carry a satellite into orbit, from its early construction stages to its launch. It featured Murrow interviewing Dr. Wernher von Braun, the German rocket scientist who was now working for NASA, the National Aeronautics and Space

Administration. When the rocket failed seconds after launch and crashed to earth, viewers got both high drama and insight into the challenges of rocket engineering.

Other early shows were far more controversial. A debate on abortion between Father Ted Hesburgh of Notre Dame and Bishop James Pike of the Episcopal Church in San Francisco caused a firestorm. I came to rather appreciate the firestorms. Hate mail flooded into the network and to us. The show's other sponsor, B. F. Goodrich, pulled out, which generated more publicity and made Bell & Howell look noble by comparison.

The accolades far outweighed the criticism. My favorite editorial, which ran in the *Chicago Daily News*, bore the headline, "Love Letter to a Sponsor." Awards filled our trophy case. Most importantly, our brand awareness, image, and market share all rose.

We had committed to sponsor nine shows. That was all we could afford, and the occasional nature of the documentaries contributed to the feeling that they were indeed special, not part of the regular television lineup. Then one day I got a call from James Aubrey, the network president. He requested a meeting on my next trip to New York.

When I got to La Guardia, a driver ushered me to a super-long stretch limousine where Aubrey was waiting in the back seat. (I've always hated those cars; they may be fine for kids looking to show off on prom night, but for business I think they're ostentatious and pretentious, and besides, they cost too much.) I guess I was supposed to be impressed, but it got my back up. It wasn't long into our conversation, which started in the car, that I learned why Aubrey was known as "The Snake" in television circles.

"Pete," he said, "*CBS Reports* has been a spectacular success. The public loves it, so does Washington, and the bottom line is we want to do many more of them. In fact, we're going to have thirty-nine of them next year, one for every week of the television season in prime time. We assume you will join us."

My initial shock quickly turned to anger. We had given him all the shows our budget could cover, and they knew nine shows was the limit. That had been clearly understood. Now he wanted us to more than quadruple our commitment, to $4.5 million.

"That's not what we agreed to," I said. "You knew nine was what we could afford." I told him flatly that I considered this a betrayal of the spirit of our original agreement, and that we could not go forward.

"Don't you have to check this with Chuck Percy?" he asked me.

"No, I don't," I said. "He knows our budget just as well as I do, and he knows we can't begin to spend that kind of money."

When word got out that Bell & Howell was not on board, Aubrey's play backfired. The Snake could not find a single other sponsor, and since they'd announced the expansion, CBS had to swallow all the costs of the thirty-nine-show series. *CBS Reports* went on to deserved accolades thanks to Murrow and Friendly, but our advertising exposure, without a vehicle, was back to square one.

We did not stay there for long. An alternative had come our way on the wings of the dumb luck that has animated my life from time to time. Ollie Treyz, the president of ABC, had called me before the news broke that we and CBS were parting company. ABC was a weak third network in those early days when CBS and NBC were dominant. ABC apparently had seen the strength of documentaries in attracting critical acclaim, viewers, and the kind attention of the FCC and Congress. Ollie made it clear his network simply had to move in this direction.

"Pete, I hate to beg," he said, "but I must come out to see you. We're in deep trouble in Washington. I know you're tied in to *CBS Reports*, but I want to persuade you to join us as a sponsor."

I told Ollie I would listen. He came to Chicago and presented an extraordinary proposal: ABC would run twenty-nine documentaries under the *Bell & Howell Close-up* title. Further, we would be the sponsor of record on a series dramatizing Winston Churchill's six-part history of the Second World War, hosted by the great Richard Burton. All this was ours for a mere $600,000. Ollie was thrilled when I accepted. So was I.

We sponsored dozens of *Bell & Howell Close-up* shows in prime time, and ABC operated with total editorial freedom. The shows dealt with sensitive topics both domestic and international. *Walk in My Shoes* dramatized what it was like to be black in America, and won numerous top prizes. *Yankee No!* and *Ninety Miles to Communism* reminded Americans of the Soviet menace in Cuba near our southern shores. *The Red and the Black* documented the growing Soviet influence in Africa.

Some of the shows drew negative public reactions, as similar subjects had at CBS. Images of whites throwing rocks, picketing, and cursing a black family that had moved into a white neighborhood in Louisiana prompted the state legislature to ban the purchase of Bell & Howell products by state agencies. But our sales continued to grow. We had been able to do well by doing good, and it was a great feeling.

The Mailman Cometh

Our forays into documentary sponsorship with CBS and ABC happened at about the same time as I embraced another experiment in marketing. For years, Bell & Howell had assumed that the home movie market would expand substantially, almost exponentially. Instead, we were seeing early signs of stagnation, and the expensive 1.5 million square foot plant Chuck had built in Lincolnwood was significantly underutilized.

My waking hours (and sometimes my sleeping ones as well) were filled with thoughts about how to keep boosting sales. I was increasingly frustrated.

One day at a photographic convention, I was approached—or perhaps I should say accosted—by a man with a complaint. "Mr. Peterson, your marketing people won't listen to me," he said. "Maybe you will."

"I'm listening," I said, resisting the impulse to look at my watch and make up a meeting I had to rush off to.

"Direct mail," he said. This only increased my desire to find an excuse and rush away. But he had me by the elbow and I had to admit it was something I hadn't thought of. So I listened.

The idea was to sell complete motion picture packages by direct mail. These would include a camera, a projector, and a screen, along with a film splicer and cartoons. "Free" movie film would be thrown in. The man—I wish I could remember his name—said he had sold several hundred thousand power tool kits by direct mail, and he couldn't see why Bell & Howell shouldn't adopt the same technique for movie equipment. He would help define the makeup of the packages and help us get the best mailing lists in exchange for a commission on each package sold.

I had seen how effective retail dealers could be in selling our movie cameras to consumers. Indeed, based on long experience, Bell & Howell believed that customers shopping for home movie gear wanted and *needed* to see, touch, and handle the equipment, and also to be shown how to operate it by someone they perceived as an expert, before they would commit to purchasing. The business school graduates on our marketing staff strongly pushed this point of view. Hands-on selling was the only way to peddle motion picture cameras and projectors.

"That's what people told me about power tools," the fellow said. He put on an exaggerated voice. " 'You've got to *feel* a power drill. You've got to *handle* a circular saw.' It ain't so. You ought to give it a try. Besides, you can try various packages and do only what pays off." This, he reminded us, was not true of most marketing and advertising programs where you make a full commitment up front without knowing the results.

Back at the office, our team plunged into discussions. These went on for weeks, then months, and they were not only prolonged but contentious. Finally, I realized that we were paying a high opportunity cost for all this wrangling. Sometimes you spend so much time debating one thing that you give up the opportunity to do something else that could help you. At that point, we got back to the direct mail man and, more out of frustration than anything else, made him a proposition: How about partnering with us and simply testing the idea with one particular package of equipment? If he was so confident, he could share fifty-fifty in the cost of the test. He agreed.

We targeted households that were likely markets for home movie packages—middle-class families with children—and offered the packages for less than $200. To entice them further, we included a moneyback guarantee. But to keep returns to a minimum, we added a caveat. Customers could get a full refund, but only if they returned not only the equipment but also the now used film that came with the package. This worked, because those films were precious. They captured moments in the lives of families and children that would never be repeated, and very few people wanted to return them.

To our astonishment, the sales from this targeted campaign took off. At the height of the direct mail campaign in 1961, the packages we were selling through the mail amounted to nearly 20 percent of the entire market. At this level of sales, we became worried about the reaction of our dealers. We need not have. They came to believe that people introduced to film making by our simpler, lower-focused models would graduate to the more sophisticated (and expensive) movie cameras they sold in their stores. And, in our relentless search for new revenues, we started applying our direct mail knowledge selling products other than movie equipment.

Young President

One day in the spring of 1961, when we were garnering kudos (and the occasional brickbat) from the *Bell & Howell Close-ups* on ABC and pushing the limits of the home movie market with our direct mail offering, Chuck came into my small office and closed the door. Our discussions weren't usually private, and I couldn't imagine what was up. "Pete," he said, "I've made a decision.

"I'm stepping down as the company's president," he continued. "I'm going to stay on as chairman and CEO, but I want you to be the president." He paused briefly. "What do you think?"

"I'm a little shocked," I said. I was not yet thirty-five, I had been there only about three years, and I felt very unprepared. I knew Chuck must have a long-range plan for the company, but I didn't know what the hurry was.

I was soon to find out. Chuck was an inspiring and charismatic leader, an optimist who could draw people into his vision of the future. He was a natural for public service. In fact, President Eisenhower had appointed him to head a task force looking at America's goals. Although I didn't know it at the time, public service and politics were what Chuck wanted to pursue. He had chosen this time to begin freeing himself for a run for elective office. In the meantime, by staying on as CEO, he wanted to reassure himself that he had named the right person to shepherd the company he had run for twelve years, since he was twenty-nine.

Bill Roberts, a Bell & Howell lifer who most people (including Bill and myself) would have identified as Chuck's heir apparent, was the immediate casualty of my promotion. I suspect Bill got the word from Chuck before I did, because he resigned shortly afterward to become the CEO of Ampex, a maker of audio and videotapes and recorders.

In the meantime, the board agreed to my appointment, the press release was duly written and distributed, and suddenly I was, for a few hours, a darling of the media. Reporters called all day, and when I got home to Kenilworth, I found a photographer who had staked out my house to get a picture of the man who, according to the release, was at thirty-four the youngest president of one of America's Fortune 300 companies. My mother was with us for a visit at the time. She watched all the commotion, the flashes blinking, me being directed to strike this pose and that for the camera. As soon as the photographer and reporter left, she offered her priceless reaction to the whole affair. She said, "Petie, I don't understand you. Why do you put up with all these crazy things when you could be in Kearney owning your own business?" By which she meant, of course, the Central Cafe.

George Stigler, my friend and old professor at the University of Chicago Graduate School of Business, was also very amusing. At a University of Chicago business function, he welcomed me with these brief words: "I would now like to introduce the new president of what *used* to be characterized as a growth company."

George's tongue-in-cheek humor masked a brutal truth. Little yellow boxes of movie film were piling up on closet shelves. Our own projector case was gathering dust. We had not pulled out the screen in months and now it stood in a corner of the garage behind some brooms and mops. Making home movies had been a novelty at first, but the novelty had faded. We rarely viewed our old home movies, partly because each roll of film provided only two or three minutes' viewing, and to edit and splice them was beyond my meager mechanical abilities. Others were having the same experience. Every time we visited friends, I included them in my informal consumer survey and found that they, too, had little yellow boxes and film projection gear stuck away in storage areas, unused.

Chuck, ever the optimist, assured me that I was just a worrywart. The home movie market was going to grow year after year, he said, and justify that 1.5 million square foot plant investment. It was no time to be losing faith. It's true that I tended toward pessimism, but I was also analytical. We decided to hire the A. C. Nielsen market research firm to track our market share performance, and the total market. The answer was a pessimist's nightmare.

The home movie market was indeed shrinking. Worse still, lower cost and very skilled Japanese companies like Canon, that already had taken the lion's share of the upscale still camera market, were now entering the home movie business.

We had no choice but to reach out to the Japanese. We formed a joint venture with Canon; they would manufacture certain models that complemented our line and we would market them, some as Canon products and some much needed still-motion cameras under the label Bell & Howell Canon. This produced a short-term uptick in both sales and market share. But Canon would not need to piggyback on our brand for very long. I could see that they had longer-run ambitions of doing their own marketing to American consumers across all their product lines. (And indeed they have.)

Being president of Bell & Howell did buy me its share of kudos. For one, the Junior Chamber of Commerce ("the Jaycees") named me one of America's Ten Outstanding Young Men for 1961. As gratifying as this was, the honor paled next to the one my parents received two years later. I've mentioned their generosity to their hometowns and relatives in Greece, with Mother sending boxes the size of refrigerators full of her handmade clothes back to Niata, the town of her birth, and my father paying for the paving of the main street in the Peloponnesian mountain town of Vahlia, where he had come from. And so in 1963, the Greek embassy in Washington sent word that Vahlia's main street was to be renamed. It would be known as George and Venetia Petropoulos Street; and further, my parents were to receive a First Class Gold Medal. King Paul of Greece, in the last full year of his reign before his death, presented it to them on one of their visits. One Greek citizen referred to my father as a "one man Marshall Plan." I was truly proud and inspired.

That same year, two years into my presidency, as I contended with the increasingly dire market trends in the home movie camera industry, Chuck dropped the other shoe. He was going to run for governor of

Illinois in 1964. And I, at the age of thirty-six, was to take over his CEO responsibilities at Bell & Howell.

The company now had some fifteen thousand employees, for whom I was suddenly responsible. I had to make decisions that would preserve their jobs, maintain the company's stock price, and pay dividends at levels shareholders would approve, all in a market where our largest business, home movies, was in ever steeper decline.

I concluded that the only way to survive this riptide was to try to sail around it by adding new products. Which is why you can thank me—I confess, and beg your mercy—for inspiring the invention of the boom box. That is correct: the late and unlamented boom box.

Some background: It turned out that we could build tape recorders just as well as cameras at our big and underused Lincolnwood plant. I worked feverishly with our product development engineers to come up with easy-to-use tape recorders. My role was that of the thick-fingered mechanical klutz ever in need of the most basic levels of simplicity. I would invent some questions or consumer needs and they would invent the answers. The engineers actually seemed to like this creative partnership, and so did I.

Audiotape, in those days before cassettes were developed, had to be manipulated through a recorder's audio heads. Threading it was hard because the tape was thin, flexible, and extremely light. Early on in my product development education, one of our engineers had told me that a basic premise of their profession was to try to take advantage of a material's qualities rather than fighting to overcome its deficits. How can we do this with audiotape? I asked the engineers. In a few days, they came up with a simple fan that would blow the tape through the audio heads automatically, eliminating the need for hand threading. Bell & Howell later used the same technology to develop the first in-flight motion picture system, using film before the development of videocassettes.

So on to the boom box. I had observed that young people riding around in cars liked to play music at peak volume, often to the point that you could feel the bass through the soles of your shoes. I asked our engineers if they could develop a portable device that would give kids some of that same "boom" feeling when they weren't in their cars. They quickly produced a union between cassette recorder/player and speakers, giving the user a portable music player with the potential to crank up the volume. We called it the Bell & Howell Boom-Box. The rest is history, or at least a loud footnote to history.

Of course, the boom box led to other innovations in listening, such as lightweight, portable earphones, which mostly returned to the public at large the freedom it deserves from other people's music choices.

I was the final check on our products' consumer friendliness, the dreaded "Peterson Test." Precisely because I was so mechanically hopeless, I gave our terrified engineers a real-life look at the most dire things that could befall their products. They would fearfully watch me fumbling around, trying to figure out a phase of the operation, and guide me to a page of the instruction book: "But Pete, that's covered on page 38."

"But fellas, people don't carry around instruction books," I'd tell them. "Why can't we make it clear on the product itself?"

They'd sigh, and go back to the drawing board. And they would almost always produce an easier way of operating a function. Long after my stint at Bell & Howell, I remain convinced that many companies could use a Peterson Test for their consumer products. At least one of the companies that sells hard-to-open airline cracker packages could use one—that is, if airlines are still handing out crackers to their passengers by the time you read this.

CHAPTER 5

CHICAGO, ROUND THREE

John

Our third son, David, was born in December 1958, during my first year with Bell & Howell. He was an adorable baby, and we were captivated with him from the start. John was almost four then. Jim was only two, but it was hard not to notice the differences between them. Jim was rattling off complete sentences and displaying insights that showed a growing knowledge of the world around him. Sally and I congratulated ourselves on how bright Jim was.

What defined John was his loving nature. He was a sweet, kind, and gentle child who took enormous delight in his physical surroundings. On our weekend strolls through Kenilworth with him in the baby carriage, he pointed and clapped his hands at birds, dog, cats, and airplanes flying overhead, his handsome, dark eyes shining. His delight never seemed to progress to curiosity, but not until Jim came along did we have clear benchmarks for John's development. Like any parents, I suppose we were not inclined to look for faults. The province of parenthood lies in the kingdom of hope, and it did not occur to us at first that Jim sparkled by comparison because John's capacities were far from what they should have been. But gradually, the contrast between the two boys sobered us and forced us to seek a professional assessment of why John was developing so much more slowly.

We first consulted John's pediatrician. The doctor recommended an "expert" who gave him some tests and confirmed our fears: John suffered some cognitive impairment. But it was mild, he said, and John would most likely be able to graduate from high school. We accepted this prognosis and did not seek special help. But the difference between his capabilities and those of Jim and other children his age whose parents were our friends grew more and more striking. Our growing agony warred against our shrinking hope. Late at night, when the boys were all asleep, we lay awake and talked in the dim light of our bedside lamps. Sometimes we couldn't keep from crying. Finally, these painful and heart-wrenching discussions led us to face the truth: We had to help him.

The chief neurologist at the University of Chicago hospital performed a battery of tests and gave us a surprisingly benign report. But we now accepted that John was, at best, quite slow. In response, we began to search the world of child development for techniques that might help him maximize his capabilities. Our research led us to Philadelphia and the Institutes for the Achievement of Human Potential.

By now it was 1960, and the institutes' two founders, Glenn Doman and Carl Delacato, had published an article in *JAMA*, the *Journal of the American Medical Association*, that described their evolution-based theory for helping retarded children. It was basically to send them back to square one, in evolutionary terms, and "re-pattern" their development. That is, to take them through a series of creeping and crawling procedures as if they were still babies, indeed, as if they were still evolving up the ladder from fish to reptile to mammal to human. This was supposed to give them a second chance to get right the developmental pathways through which the rest of us living beings emerge.

The *JAMA* article produced a storm of publicity for the institutes and also generated much controversy. Doman was a physical therapist and Delacato an educational psychologist, and traditional neurologists disputed their theory. But when we read about it sometime after the article was published, it sounded plausible. We were still so full of hope. If this were a key that might unlock our sweet and lovely son's hidden potential, we wanted to try it. We took John to Philadelphia and met Doman and Delacato, who evangelized about their program and gave him yet another examination. This, we were told, involved taking a picture of his brain with a modified Polaroid Land Camera. Led on by our hope, we ignored the preposterous notion that this amateur camera could be a sophisticated diagnostic tool. When the two pronounced John a good candidate for their treatment—as, we later learned, they did every child, no matter how damaged—we walked into their arms.

For two years, we followed the most grueling regimen I could have possibly imagined. At this time, John could walk normally, but "patterning" was still required. The "patterning" was a matter of moving John's limbs through motions that resembled swimming, creeping, and crawling. It required repetition in order to reprogram his brain, at least that was the theory. And so several times a day, in our carpeted living room, four people, one for each of his limbs, manipulated his arms and legs in the required way. Sally took the lead in these sessions. She was also caring for the other boys and performing the duties of a corporate wife. Coordinating friends and hired staff to provide John his day-long dose of "patterning" gave her a mammoth scheduling load to handle. I helped when I could, typically on weekends and at night. Then the process moved from the living room to the basement, where we had linoleum installed to create a smooth and nonabrasive surface for him to crawl on. This was my job more than it was hers. I scuttled around the basement floor on my hands and knees, guiding John's motions, to the point of sore elbows and knees, and exhausted spirits.

How Sally lived through this two-year trial is beyond me. I at least had the demands of business and the compulsions of the relentless workaholic to distract me. If there was any benefit at all, it was in John's social development. He soaked up the attention, and repaid all that love with happiness. His sunny, cheery disposition made the sessions with him much easier to endure, even when we were all tapped out emotionally and physically.

But he made no progress. And so, one afternoon in John's ninth year, we finally consulted a real expert. This child psychologist worked in Evanston, Illinois, and specialized in developmental problems. He spent two hours with John while Sally and I waited nervously in an outer office, leafing through old magazines and sipping machine coffee. Now and then we would catch each other's eye and then glance away, afraid to speak for fear we'd send vibrations of hope that would be dashed or pessimism that would shame us. At last the psychologist emerged. "Come in," he said quietly with a sympathetic nod. We entered his office while John waited happily in an adjacent room. The diagnosis was unambiguous. John was retarded, as they called it in those days, with an IQ of between 60 and 70, the intellectual equivalent of a six-year-old, and would never improve. This psychologist was the first, oddly enough, to have given John an IQ test.

Even if you expect bad news, you can still be shattered by it. The doctor recognized that we needed to react in private and showed us to a terrace outside his office, where we held each other and sobbed. When we stopped crying, we collected John and drove home in a daze, not speaking. There were no words to describe our feelings, but if there was a bright side it was that John was as happy as ever but quieter, as if he sensed that we were troubled. We tried to put on a good face for Jim and David and especially John over the evening meal. Finally, when the boys were all in bed and we had some time to ourselves, the crying started again as we faced the reality that this was a tragedy that would last a lifetime.

One aspect of our situation was encouraging. Many learning disabled children, as they are now called, have behavior problems, up to and including violence that they can't control and which naturally gets worse as they grow older and bigger. John was blessed with the sweetest of dispositions and a curiosity that will always be childlike. He has never been violent.

Our first step, now that we finally had a diagnosis that we trusted, was to look at schooling and living situations that would be right for John and for the rest of us. Chicago's public schools had no place for a child like John. We cared for him at home while we looked for a residential facility where he would be safe and happy.

The Amazing Dr. Land

While we went through the difficult exercise of finding the right school for John, the pressure at the office continued at a high pitch. At work at the time, I was desperately trying to find the right direction for Bell & Howell. With the movie equipment market shrinking fast, I ordered never-ending rounds of cost cutting and downsizing. I brought in McKinsey, the management consulting firm, to look at new product line possibilities and ways to increase production at the increasingly underutilized and costly Lincolnwood plant. But I kept my eyes open too. One day in 1967, I saw a news item that contained a surprising piece of information: The Polaroid Company did not manufacture *any* of its own camera equipment. This was a revelation. I quickly realized that the key to dealing with Polaroid was its legendary founder and resident genius, Dr. Edwin Herbert "Din" Land, whose cameras bore his name.

So, ever the compulsive analyst, I gave myself a crash course in all things Land. Although he was commonly referred to as "Dr." Land, he did not have a Ph.D., having dropped out of Harvard to develop the polarizing lenses and film that would later make him famous—and rich. He was the quintessential inventor-entrepreneur, with over five hundred patents, a record of invention second only to Thomas Edison. He established the Polaroid Corporation in the 1930s and in 1947 showed the world the first instant camera and film (it actually took about sixty seconds for the film to develop). The Land Camera was on the market two years later, and it was an instant sensation. Its various models were all elegant creations of steel and imitation leather, with a bellows-style lens mechanism that pulled out of its case for use and nestled back into a slim, flat package for storage. Land's instant camera grew in popularity through the 1950s and into the 1960s despite generally retailing for over—sometimes well over—$100. I read in research reports that he wanted, at some point, to attack the huge market for point-and-shoot snapshot cameras that had long been dominated by the Kodak Brownie. Bell & Howell could build a camera like that at our Lincolnwood plant.

Before I approached Dr. Land, I did some consumer research. I wanted to be able to speculate with him on the philosophical or psychological underpinnings of Polaroid's extraordinary appeal. I used some of the thematic apperception motivational research techniques I had learned back in my early days at Market Facts. I had two sets of pictures taken. One set showed another person roaming a party taking pictures with a 35mm still camera, while the other showed a partygoer shooting with a Polaroid. Pictures in hand, we assembled a focus group and asked it to tell us stories about what was going on. Most of them saw the

35mm photographer as somewhat of a self-absorbed geek who was interrupting the party and bringing it down by making people stop to pose. But the focus group liked the Polaroid user; it saw him as joining in the fun of the party and adding to it by showing pictures of everyone having a good time and even sharing the pictures. So, the Polaroid user was a social enhancer, while the 35mm photographer was a social interrupter.

I called Land at his office in Cambridge, Massachusetts, saying I had some research I thought would interest him. He invited me to come see him.

The Polaroid Corporation's offices were just a few blocks from MIT. It was my first trip back since my checkered days there, in school and in the purchasing department of the Radiation Lab. Dr. Land's office was small and unpretentious, in an old building that looked as if it might have been a warehouse. He reminded me a little of myself, physically at least— stocky, with broad brows and a shock of thick, dark hair. Beyond that, I found him elegant, and a bit of a Renaissance man, and I liked him right away. He was instantly engaging and intellectually alive, curious about almost everything and able to talk about a broad range of topics. I showed him the pictures and talked about the reactions of the focus group. He loved the implications, and we discussed them at length. And I was right in thinking he had an eye on the Kodak Brownie market.

He called about a week later to say he thought we might be good partners for Polaroid's new, high-volume Swinger, a Brownie-style black-and-white camera that would bring instant photography to the mass market with a sale price of under $20. He told me he expected to sell three million of them a year. "Would Bell & Howell be interested in manufacturing them?" he asked.

"We certainly would," I said.

Soon I was back in Cambridge at his invitation, looking over a prototype he had assembled of the Swinger. Another part of my preparation to meet the inventor of the Polaroid had been to spend some time with his cameras, becoming familiar with their strengths and weaknesses. The shortcomings included the need to focus very carefully in order to avoid a blurry photograph. Indeed, some of the earlier models carried step-by-step instructions that included this advice, printed on a card that could be held inside the back of the camera.

After I had played around with the working model he showed me, lining up shots as I looked through the eyepiece, he asked me what I thought. It seemed to me easy for a user to forget about the need to focus, and I told him—reluctantly and with some fear about how he would react—that I thought this could be a problem with the Swinger.

He nodded and looked thoughtful, then took the camera from my hands and excused himself. "Please wait right here," he said. Minutes passed. I began to worry that my frankness had irritated him, and that I had blown the deal.

After about half an hour, he returned with a smile on his face. "Mr. Peterson, tell me what you think," he said. I looked through the viewfinder to learn that he had incorporated a "periscope," as he called it. Actually, it was only a mirror that showed the distance setting on the lens as you looked through the viewfinder; it reminded the photographer to focus. I was amazed. Land was said to believe that intense concentration on a problem often produced innovation. He sometimes worked nonstop for days as he fought to find the solution to a sticking point. Here he had concentrated for half an hour and produced a result that confirmed his reputation.

He seemed delighted, both to have had the problem pointed out and to have been able to arrive at a solution so quickly. "Mr. Peterson," he said, "you and I can work together."

From those first meetings grew a beautiful and very profitable friendship. As I recall, making the Swinger added about $20 million in sales at a time when we desperately needed both the sales and the production. I learned over time that Land and I shared important values. He had broken the gender barrier, hiring and training many women to work as research scientists, and later committing Polaroid to affirmative action in hiring African-American scientists and workers. From time to time, as we spent hours and days together advancing our business partnership, it took on the same symbiotic quality of our first meeting on the Swinger. I helped invent the consumer need or problem. He took on the much more difficult task: He invented the solution.

Some misgivings nagged at me as we worked together. I assumed and, frankly, feared that Land might be applying his formidable inventive powers to a motion picture system. Which, indeed, he was. Similar to Polaroid's still cameras, this would take movies and develop the film instantly, on the spot. Land finally took me into his confidence about this super-secret project.

I was always ready to fly to Cambridge on short notice when Land had something he wanted to discuss. The call I received at six A.M. one day in 1970 was short notice indeed. Din, as I called him by then, had been working all night, as he often did, and he wanted me to fly to see him that very morning. I found him disheveled from his nonstop labors—no time to change clothes—and he proudly showed me a working prototype for an instant motion picture system. It was astonishing. Unlike the Polaroid still camera system that created a positive print, the motion picture system produced a negative like any movie, but instantly, and it could then be threaded into a special projector and shown without being sent off to be developed.

"What do you think?" he asked. "Be frank. You always are."

I considered that a command. His basic technical achievement in photochemistry was extraordinary. To be able to go more or less instantly from camera to projector was an incredible feat. But I remembered that my role in the process of invention was to stand in for the end user. I was supposed to use my own technical or mechanical ineptitude on behalf of all consumers to help produce a product that the mechanically challenged could use without mishap or hair-pulling frustration. I took a breath and gambled that our relationship was strong enough to send him back to the drawing board.

"Din, it's remarkable," I said. "But I see a problem."

"Please, what is it?" That was why he was so remarkable. He never took this kind of a response as a put-down or a value judgment, only as a problem to be solved.

I told him that the photochemistry itself was unbelievably elegant. The mechanics of getting the film into the camera and later the projector, on the other hand, were not only inelegant but rather cumbersome. It was a departure from the value that consumers had come to expect from Polaroid, that sense of instant gratification. I wondered if the process could be incorporated into a cartridge, something modular along the lines of an audiotape cassette that could go straight from the camera to the projector, allowing users to go easily from taking movies to viewing them. Din was already thinking about the question when I left for the airport that afternoon.

Back in Chicago, Bell & Howell's engineers shook their heads and said he'd never make such a cartridge work. Too much complex chemistry in too small a space, they said. We should forget the whole idea of gearing up to manufacture such a thing.

Two weeks later, I received another early phone call from Din Land. He sounded exhausted, but excited. Could I come to Cambridge that morning?

When I got there, he handed me a cartridge, fully operational. After our previous meeting, he had gone home, showered, shaved, and changed his clothes and returned to the office where he worked for two weeks straight, sleeping on the couch again as he pondered the problem. The cartridge became the core of what he called the Polavision system.

It was an incredible achievement, but it had come too late. Like Land, Polavision and, indeed, Bell & Howell were being outstripped by new technology. We did manufacture the Polavision system. But videotape and videotape cameras were already beginning to render it obsolete by the time it went into production. The original video cameras were expensive, but they offered sound, color, instant playback, and other features such as the ability to reuse the tape. This was the leading edge of the electronic revolution that would accelerate in the years to come, ending up with the low-cost, high-quality, and ever more compact video equipment that we see today.

There is no mystery or secret to this story. The new always overwhelms the old in the mass consumer market. The advance of technology from electromechanical devices and films to electronics was the fundamental cause of the problems I faced at Bell & Howell and Din Land faced at Polaroid. Every old-line photographic company faced the same decision: Change or die. Creative destruction takes its toll, elevates the innovators, and forces business leaders to look for new solutions. Polaroid slogged on for another thirty years. Without Land, who died in 1991, it finally went bankrupt in 2001.

Desperate Measures (Slogging On)

On December 21, 1964, ten years and five days after John came into the world, Sally bore our fourth child and first girl. When I saw her at the hospital for the first time, all the noise in my busy world receded. It shrank away and left, for a little while at least. She was the most beautiful baby I have ever seen. And she remains beautiful today.

At the hospital, we fussed and cooed and called her Amy, the name we had decided on. We brought her home on Christmas day. Wreaths and sprays of greenery hung everywhere, at the hospital, and the shopping areas we passed. The decorations sent a message. Such a blessing as our little girl would have to reflect the holiday when she arrived, so we changed course and named her Holly.

By this time, we had found some placement possibilities for John. The prime prospect was about an hour outside Chicago. It was a Catholic institution called the Kennedy School, and it housed about one hundred retarded children to whom it offered classes, sports, and field trips. We took John to visit, and he seemed to like the staff and they liked him. We loved John very much but accepted the idea that his life would be enhanced by living at a nearby place that could give him the attention he needed. He moved to Kennedy around the time he was twelve, returning home on weekends.

As much as we tried not to let it, this changed the family dynamic and created problems. Jim and David rarely complained, but it was unfair to expect them to spend every weekend watching us attend to John and his needs and, in the process, miss many of theirs.

The rare exception was a backyard football game in which John and I played Jim and David. At the time of those family football games, my guess is that Jim and David came to appreciate John's momentary distractions from the game—as John stopped in the middle of a play to observe a plane in flight. These distractions led to some of their football victories. To be sure, there would be moments of embarrassment in their young lives as their young friends looked and wondered at John's slowness. However, Jim, David, Holly, and then Michael (our fifth child, born in 1969) were unfailingly kind to John. And that was not at all difficult given that John was and is one of the gentlest and kindest souls I have ever known.

More disturbing at the time was the fact that John grew increasingly reluctant to leave home and return to the Kennedy School. He whimpered and showed other signs of fear when we put him in a car to be driven to school on Monday mornings. Only after several months would he tell us what was troubling him. He said one of the priests at the school treated him cruelly and had even slapped him. We knew John was not a discipline problem—and slapping a retarded child was an inappropriate disciplinary move in any case. We complained to the school. Things got better for a while, but then got worse again, or at least John could never put his fear behind him.

Our own lives in the Peterson family experienced subtraction, and addition. John became increasingly fearful of returning to the Kennedy School after his weekends at home. By now he was well into his teens, but he had only the vocabulary and emotions of a six-year-old. It pained us to see him try to gather his courage as he left us each Monday morning, and it was also painful to see the extent of his relief when he returned to us on Friday afternoons. After a few weeks of this ordeal, for John and for us, Sally and I realized that we simply had to find a better placement, not only for John and us, but for Jim and David, who found him increasingly distracting from their own growing interests.

After a search of several months, we settled on a place that had better weather and a staff whose skills better fit John's needs. Cedars of Marin was located in Ross, California, a short distance north of the Golden Gate Bridge. The first time we took John there, he loved the beautiful surroundings and the range of activities that included music and art, sports, and nature, especially the waves of the Pacific Ocean. Even today, he writes letters that go on about how high the waves are and the lovely weather and temperatures. We were sad to leave him there, but he liked it so much and I think he was only half-sad to see us go. We began a routine of frequent visits with him.

Today, I am proud and delighted at my children's warm, close, and continuing relationship with John. Whenever any of the other four kids are in Northern California, they go to visit with John. Jim even makes special trips to California to be with John. When John comes to New

York for his annual summer and Christmas trips, all of the children happily invite him to their homes for a few days, take him bowling, to sports events, and, of course, to the airport where he can watch the planes. John loves nothing more than spending the day at the airport counting the number of planes landing and taking off.

At the end of the decade, our family grew yet again. Michael, our fifth child, was born on October 23, 1969. Michael was affectionately called Mighty Mouse. Before long, we could see he was far more than that. Even at an early age, we knew he was a wise soul.

I tried to be a good father. In fact, I think I was a better father than husband. The high point of the boys' week was the Bears game at Wrigley Field, hardly a modern closed stadium. We would bundle the boys up with multiple layers of long johns, sweaters, wool scarves, and wool stocking hats. Even so, the cold Chicago winds were so brutal that the kids sat there shivering. I once asked what they enjoyed. One reason was the opportunity to see their heroes. Jim's was the tight end Mike Ditka, David's was Johnny Morris, John's was the legendary tailback Gale Sayers. In their more honest moments, they admitted their real treat was stopping at the then new McDonald's, whose French fries were legendary. We didn't know or care about transfats in those days.

John has been at Cedars about thirty-five years now, and still loves it. Fortunately, I was in a position to contribute enough to Cedars for them to build John Peterson Hall, an on-campus residential building. The family and I attended its inauguration in 2006. John was thrilled with the attention and is beloved by all. Around Ross, he is affectionately referred to as "the Mayor."

The End of the 1960s

My friend Chuck Percy realized his dream of elective office in 1966. He secured the Republican Senate nomination easily enough, and launched a strong campaign against the craggy, white-haired, and legendary Democrat Paul Douglas, who had represented Illinois since 1949 and was running for his fourth term. Chuck won the race and became a U.S. senator, but his victory was marred by a devastating personal tragedy.

One of Chuck's most energetic campaign aides was his twenty-one-year-old daughter, Valerie, one of identical twins. It was still dark on the early morning of September 18 when the phone rang in our bedroom in Winnetka, a suburb to the north of Kenilworth where we had moved the year before. A distraught neighbor of Chuck's was calling to say that someone had broken into the Percys' house and murdered Valerie in her own bed. I threw on some clothes and rushed the few blocks to Chuck's house, where I found Chuck, his wife, Lorraine, Valerie's twin, Sharon, and their thirteen-year-old daughter, Gail, sitting around a table holding hands, their heads bowed in prayer. Their two sons were away, Roger at college and Mark at camp. They were all devout Christian Scientists. It emerged that the murderer had used a glass cutter to enter the house, had beaten and stabbed Valerie, and had run away after being surprised by Lorraine, who had heard Valerie moaning and gotten up to investigate.

I was the first one to arrive. Teary-eyed, I gave Lonnie and Chuck a desperate hug. The police briefly escorted me to Valerie's bedroom. From the door, I could see her bloodied body. My thoughts turned to John, Holly, Jim, and David. Valerie was a favorite baby-sitter. How would I tell my children without terrifying them?

In the coming days and weeks, Chuck handled this tragedy with extraordinary dignity, equanimity, and courage. Indeed, it was a mark of those more civil times that Paul Douglas suspended his own campaign when Chuck stopped electioneering for the remainder of September. When the race resumed, many analysts felt that Chuck's courageous response to the murder was a prime factor in his ultimate upset over Douglas. After months and years without leads in the case, suspicion finally focused on a member of a gang of high-end housebreakers in Chicago. But the man had died in 1967, and Valerie Percy's murder was never conclusively solved.

Meanwhile, Bell & Howell's problems deepened. The total annual number of sales for amateur movie cameras fell from 1.2 million units to about 500,000. We had brought as much new manufacturing business to the Lincolnwood plant as I could find. We had cut costs, laid off workers, and improved productivity in our non-union labor force. Our profit-sharing retirement plan for employees included Bell & Howell stock as its most important stock holding, so I could easily refer to Bell & Howell employees as partners. (I would decide, as I observed when I was first at McCann-Erickson, that it could be a bad idea to have too much of a company's stock in its employees' retirement plan.) At the time we were still eking out increasing profits every year, which kept our stock price high. But the long-term decline in our core movie equipment business and relentless competition from abroad meant that no cost-saving measures or efficiency gains would sustain us. We had to become less dependent on home movie equipment, a process that meant diversifying into other—but complementary—fields.

Several years later, I was tempted when Din Land asked me to take on the presidency of Polaroid. It would have been fun and stimulating to work with him. But Polaroid had many of the same problems as we faced, and I was determined that I was going to fix Bell & Howell before I moved on to any other company. For one thing, I owed it to Chuck Percy.

Chuck, while still the CEO, had begun to remake Bell & Howell into a diversified conglomerate. One of his acquisitions had been the Ditto company, which made the messy duplicating machines that produced purple copies smelling of methyl alcohol like the one my father used to reproduce the daily menus at the Central Cafe.

I thought that, in theory, the most promising of the companies Chuck brought under the Bell & Howell wing was the Consolidated Electrodynamics Corporation. CEC was a Pasadena, California, company that made aviation control systems and electronic instruments, largely for the space program. One of these products was an instrumentation tape recorder that had the potential to develop into a video recorder. To me, this was one of the company's most appealing aspects. I figured that if a low-cost video recorder could be developed at consumer level prices, it would revolutionize the home movie field. And if Bell & Howell did not have such a camera, it could devastate Bell & Howell's conventional business.

Video cameras and recorders ultimately did devastate the home movie business, but CEC turned out not to be the answer. CEC did lots of work for the space program, and its space age culture stressed tough specifications and zero defects, with costs almost irrelevant. The video recorder it developed was far too expensive for the consumer market.

While our product lines were under pressure everywhere, the information explosion made me look to grow the company in two areas: microfilm systems to tackle the paper avalanche, and education. I was interested in not just hardware, but content that in some cases would be an essential part of a hardware educational system—that is, hardware plus content.

In 1966 we purchased the DeVry Technical Institute, which operated schools that trained students in a variety of technical fields from movies to electronics, and renamed it Bell & Howell Schools. The DeVry acquisition turned out to be a particularly good one, given our increasingly technological world and the need for trained technicians. The next year, we acquired the Charles E. Merrill Publishing Company, which was to produce content for our hardware instructional systems.

By then, I was also beginning to feel some fatigue from my corporate responsibilities. The fatigue was not physical but mental, and I suspect it resulted from exhausting boredom at the repetition and narrowness of many of the daunting business issues that I faced. I also reached the point where I wondered how many more gut-wrenching divisional and cost cutting budget reviews I could tolerate. The challenges I faced at Bell & Howell were serious and they required informed and vigorous, intensive focus. Simply studying the competition, the main Japanese camera makers, was giving me valuable insights about international trade, exchange rates, and manufacturing practices, while our joint venture with Canon had been a crash course in negotiating with tough but principled partners. I thought my plate had room for larger issues, too, and I was drawn to be involved in some of them.

The world outside the company was literally exploding. The civil rights movement, the war in Vietnam, the assassinations of Dr. Martin Luther King Jr. and Robert Kennedy, the tumultuous Democratic convention that same 1968 summer in Chicago—all these events cried out for good and concerned people to seek paths of reconciliation. My parents had taught me through their own example that I could not stand back, but there is a difference in this life between believing something and doing something about it. And so I did the latter.

CHAPTER 6

A RANDOM WALK
TOWARD WASHINGTON

Project: Good Neighbor

It was hard to avoid the racism that existed in those days in Chicago. I got an early taste of it in 1964, when a professor at Chicago's Loyola University, who chaired a Chicago-area civil rights commission, called me with some news. A black family, he told me, was moving into Kenilworth.

"Why, that's good news," I said.

"Your neighbors may not think so," he warned me.

I was not very involved in local social or community affairs, and knew little about how the people in my community thought about minorities. I learned the family's name—they were the Calhouns—and called them to welcome them. But within days of their moving in, a cross was burned on their lawn, and though this horrid act was the work of teenagers, I suddenly began to appreciate the real extent of separation between the races. There were no black students in my children's schools. There were no black members in most of the social clubs. Blacks—the term African-Americans didn't enter the vernacular until much later—were virtually barred from the better restaurants—not with "Whites Only" signs as in the South but by policies of icy courtesy that bordered on disdain and imposed extraordinarily long waits.

I then came to learn, to my surprise, that Kenilworth had been founded for "Caucasians only." That policy was later relaxed to allow for

live-in maids and nannies, but the Calhouns were the first black home-
owners. And Caucasians-only also meant no Jews. Jewish people knew
this even if I didn't. A Jewish friend told me, "Pete, do you know that
some Jews express their distaste for Kenilworth's anti-Semitism by
dropping their cigarette or cigar butts or ashes on the road through your
town?"

Appalled, I did my own little check of whether there were any Jews
in Kenilworth. There had been once. The mail-order Spiegel family
apparently lived there in the 1920s. Another Jewish family had lived
there more recently. "Surely you know about the Gimbel family, Pete,"
was the standard response to my inquiries. In fact, they had moved out
about a year before.

The reasons for the Calhouns' move to Kenilworth remained a
mystery. We ourselves moved from Kenilworth a year later, in 1965.
The $120,000 house in Winnetka, which adjoined Kenilworth to the
north, was on the lakefront, with beautiful views. But beyond all that
was the discomfort I had begun to feel as I learned about Kenilworth's
history. I could not profess strong disapproval about the extent of racism in Chicago at large and still live in a Kenilworth that, tacitly if unof-
ficially, discriminated. (Happily, I recently learned that Kenilworth has
become a far more open community.)

Chicago's racism bothered me on two levels. The racism itself was
bad enough, but what was worse, few seemed to care. There was a blithe
lack of concern—or was it a purposeful blind spot?—that what I was
observing was a vigorous, albeit informal, enforcement of racial separation. I don't know exactly what awakened me to the moral awfulness of
all this racism, both active and passive. Perhaps the occasional or perceived slights about my Greek origins sensitized me to how much
sharper the sting must be for blacks.

A campaign called the Chicago Freedom Movement brought Dr.
Martin Luther King Jr. and the Southern Christian Leadership Conference (SCLC) north to Chicago in 1966 to work and march with local
community activists. King called Chicago the most segregated city in the
North, and he moved into a slum apartment to make his point. Blacks
made up 25 percent of metropolitan Chicago's population, and in many
places they obviously suffered far more hostility and discrimination than

the genteel brand practiced in the fancy North Shore suburbs like Kenil-worth. In all-white towns like Cicero, the descendants of Southern and Eastern European immigrants expressed their racism viciously and of-ten violently, while on the segregated South Side, many blacks lived in ghettolike conditions in massive, neglected housing projects.

The Chicago Leadership Council sprang up in 1966 after Dr. King's protests revealed the extent of racism and threw a spotlight on the city's closed, all-white neighborhoods and the real estate practices that kept them that way. Officially named the Leadership Council for Metropolitan Open Communities, it included leaders from virtually ev-ery sector of the city, including government, labor, media, religion, and half a dozen CEOs.

Going back to my father's experience with the Ku Klux Klan in Kearney, my high school debating team's focus on civil rights, my expe-rience at Northwestern with my fraternity's blackballing of my black friend, my occasional and depressing rides through the totally segre-gated South Side of Chicago, and oh so many other daily reminders of the moral awfulness of it all, I felt I was very much up to speed on the subject of racism. The frustration I was feeling was that I wasn't really doing anything about it. So, when the call came in to join this civil rights effort, my answer was a quick and enthusiastic yes.

In no time at all, I got a bitter taste of the racial hatred that blacks experienced every day. I was chosen to chair a Leadership Council com-mittee on open housing. The announcement made the news and within days the phone rang late one night after Sally and I had gone to bed. Sally answered, then after a minute she shouted, "Who is this?"

"What?" I said, turning on my bedside light.

She stared at me, still holding the phone. Her face was pale.

"What is it?" I said again, suddenly concerned.

She slowly repeated the caller's message: "Tell your nigger-loving son of a bitch husband, we're going to get him."

I called the police department right away, but the calls continued. We changed to a new, unlisted number. I thought often of my father in those days, imagining his feelings as he watched the hooded Klans-men brandishing their signs outside the cafe. Was he fearful, outraged, or did he pity their smallness and their intolerance? I felt all those things, and with them a surging determination that I had to try to make a difference.

The Leadership Council looked at a wide range of proposals for addressing Chicago's segregated housing patterns, making physical improvements but also defusing the simmering anger on both sides. So far, black demonstrations for fair housing, and white protests against fair housing marchers in their neighborhoods, had been contained with only minor violence, but the situation had the potential to explode. We didn't want Chicago to go the way of Los Angeles, where the Watts riots of 1965 resulted in the death of thirty-four people, most of them black, a thousand injured, and $40 million in property damage.

We decided to launch an initiative called Project: Good Neighbor. Its aim was to press the issue of open and fair housing. One of its first components was an ad campaign. I called the heads of several agencies I had competed with in my McCann-Erickson days and that were now enthusiastically volunteering their pro bono services to the Council, and gave them the germ of an idea. My thesis—drawn from American history and personal experience—was that all ethnic groups had faced discrimination at one point or another in America, and therefore knew its sting. African-Americans, or Negroes, as polite people called them in those days, were simply the latest group seeking integration through the American melting pot. Why not remind our fellow Chicagoans that we were all in the same boat, or had been at one time?

A week later, the Leadership Council's advertising team reported it had come up with a powerful idea. Maybe, they warned me, it was a little too powerful. I was consumed with curiosity.

The team came to my house that weekend to make a presentation. They readied the living room for their pitch, and the setup was just as I remembered it from my days at McCann-Erickson. My focus was directed to a central easel where a blank sheet now covered the copy that would be the animating force of the campaign. After some preliminary remarks, mainly about how I shouldn't make a hasty judgment about what I was about to see, the presenter whipped off the cover sheet.

I gasped at what I saw. "Let's Get Rid of the Niggers," shouted a headline in bold type. Beside it was a large asterisk, referring to prominent copy below. This read, "and while we're at it, let's get rid of the

Dagos, Wops, Kikes, Micks, Polacks . . ." The list of ethnic slurs went on. It was a smorgasbord of nasty reminders. Every epithet for every nationality was there, putting most Chicagoans on the receiving end of racist taunts. (Oddly enough, there was no pejorative catchword for Greeks. As the impact of what I was seeing started to sink in, I joked that "goddamned Greek" was about as strong a racial slur as I could remember hearing.)

I loved it, but the ad was too provocative for me to approve on my own. I had to review it with the entire Leadership Council, which numbered about twenty, and I was prepared to abandon it if more than a few of the members objected. When we were all gathered, I unveiled the layout and heard gasps echoing the one I had made when I first saw it. But there was only one objection. This came from the head of the Chicago chapter of B'nai B'rith, the old-line Jewish service organization. "This is a brilliant concept, Pete," he said. "But there's one word that many people will find unbearably offensive."

He meant "Kike," of course. But deferring to one group's sensitivities would unravel the entire concept.

Then John Cardinal Cody, the Irish head of the Catholic Archdiocese in Chicago, spoke up. He smiled as he said, "Pete, I don't like it either when people refer to we Irishmen as 'Micks.' But I'm with you. We're none of us exempt. I say we run the ad."

We took a vote, and it came out nineteen to one in favor. I loved the cardinal ever afterward for his helpful intervention in that moment. We ran the newspaper ad. Its aims were to encourage open housing and trigger some discussion about race. And I think it did some good.

Project: Good Neighbor included Mayor Richard Daley and the city of Chicago. It was a vigorous citywide commitment to change, reaching all the way down to the level of individual neighborhoods and streets. The Chicago media were enormously supportive and generous, offering free advertising space and airtime. The *Chicago Daily News* praised our effort as "an idea whose time has come." I believe this initiative may have helped prompt Dr. King to call off further demonstrations and declare the Chicago Freedom Movement over in 1967. He called our effort "a most creative act." The issue of race in our town was on the table, no longer a topic of benign, or perhaps malignant neglect.

I was fortunate to meet Dr. King when Project: Good Neighbor was announced. He and I stood on the same platform that day, and I remember thinking to myself, "What a giant of a man in such a tiny body." He was barely five and a half feet tall, the size of a typical thirteen-year-old. Less than a year later, in April 1968, he was killed in Memphis. I attended his funeral in Atlanta, and as I viewed that same tiny body in its casket I was convinced beyond all doubt that he was both a giant and a martyr to a cause that has made America a better country.

Brookings

In 1967, at the same time as I was involved with Project: Good Neighbor in Chicago, I received word from Douglas Dillon that I had been nominated to the board of trustees of the Brookings Institution, one of Washington's oldest and best respected think tanks. This came as a bit of a surprise. I had made no secret of my extra-corporate interests, but it was one thing to promote open housing in Chicago and quite another to take on the kinds of policy issues that Brookings dealt with. It was like a marvelous intellectual shopping mall in contrast with the often repetitive and often dreary business matters I dealt with day in and day out at Bell & Howell. A Midwesterner like me, eager to expand and deepen his interests, was ripe for the picking, and the fact that I was a Republican would help balance Brookings's left-of-center image.

The trustee meetings were an ideal place to learn about the latest projects ranging from foreign and national security policy to economic and social policy. Brookings had the stature to attract senior cabinet officials to give special briefings. Secretary of Defense Robert McNamara, serving in the administration of Lyndon Johnson, provided the most memorable of these. He came to Brookings in the midst of the heated—and getting hotter—controversy over the war in Vietnam. Later I came to know him well, and I consider him someone with a great deal to admire over his lifetime, particularly his service as president of the World Bank, which he approached with great passion. Still, he would agree that the Vietnam War was a low point, and his briefing on that war gave me a valuable lesson on how *not* to make decisions.

McNamara came to us armed with statistics. This was his reputation—he would shovel numbers on his critics until they buckled under the sheer weight. At Brookings, he used numbers to make the case that the United States was winning the war in Vietnam. He displayed a computer-generated analysis of all previous insurgent wars. This "proved," he said, that when the number of regular troops exceeded the number of insurgency fighters by a certain ratio, the regular troops had always won.

This numerical analysis was flawed in at least two respects. First, it ignored differences in the mentality of the insurgents. Those we were fighting in Vietnam were several cuts above the rebels the United States had fought in the Philippines sixty years earlier. France had already been defeated in Vietnam by the insurgents, who, at all levels, had an incredible will to sacrifice, fight, and die for their cause. (This came home to me most vividly years later, when David Rockefeller and I took a group from the Council on Foreign Relations to then peaceful Vietnam. Our hosts showed us hidden tunnels where, according to the CIA, roughly seven thousand secret Vietcong fighters had lived under the most severe circumstances, evading American efforts to sniff them out with dogs by sprinkling a dog repellent powder around the bushes that covered up the tunnel entrances. David, Katharine Graham, a principal owner of *The Washington Post*, and I managed to crawl down into the tunnels. When we finally made it through, David, always properly dressed, came out looking more than a bit soiled and bedraggled. As for Kay, as Katharine was known, she came out looking like something less than the most powerful woman in America. We were shocked—and impressed—that human beings could live in such conditions for extended periods of time.)

The second problem with Bob McNamara's analysis was, ironically, quantitative. He assumed he had given the computer an accurate number of insurgents, but he had no real way of knowing whether it was right. No one could have really known how many insurgents we were fighting, a fact confirmed when we learned about those thousands of fighters hiding in the tunnels.

So, it was a case of "garbage in/garbage out" and oversimplifying it at that. The lesson to me—in business and in life—was not to rely on numbers alone. In making decisions, qualitative factors like motivation can be even more important, particularly as those numbers in a database may well be wrong.

My term on the Brookings board brought me into ongoing contact with many interesting and powerful people. One was Doug Dillon, who had come onto the Brookings board the year before I did, and the year afterward became its chairman. Doug was an elegant man who, for all his wealth and power, was also gentle and considerate. He was older than me by sixteen years, but we shared many of the same concerns. As I was to learn later, Doug Dillon's addition to my Rolodex was a very valuable one.

The Establishment Calls

In the aftermath of Valerie Percy's terrible murder in September 1966, we had grown closer than ever to the Percy family and especially the surviving twin, Sharon, who had also been one of our regular baby-sitters. She had gone on to graduate from Stanford and then worked for John Lindsay in his Washington congressional office before he was elected mayor of New York City. While she was in Washington in 1965, she met John D. Rockefeller IV, known to everyone as Jay, who was working as an assistant to the director of the Peace Corps. The rest is a love story that united two powerful families across party lines; Jay, the great-grandson of the founder of the Standard Oil Company and the University of Chicago, now represents West Virginia in the U.S. Senate as a Democrat. Sharon and Jay announced their engagement early in 1967 and planned a wedding for that spring. Sally and I gave the bridal dinner party the night before the wedding.

The wedding attracted more than a thousand guests "from politics, business, and the social world," as *The New York Times* put it in a front-page story. The ceremony, appropriately enough, was held in the University of Chicago's Rockefeller Chapel on a rainy April 1, and it was magnificent. Our son David, a member of the bridal party at age eight, exemplified its heights of style in his dark blue velvet coat and knickers. He wore this outfit uncomplainingly despite my fear that we were forcing him into the equivalent of the dreaded Greek foustanellas my mother had made me and my brother wear for Greek ceremonial occasions when I was his age.

Amid all the festivities, I had a good opportunity to get to know Jay's parents. Blanchette, his mother, was truly warm and elegant, a model of dignity. Her husband, John D. Rockefeller III, then the dean of the family's philanthropic affairs, was a model of dignity as well. He was tall and made himself taller with a ramrod-straight carriage. He dressed impeccably and was infallibly courteous in a formal sort of way, given to reserve rather than spontaneity. For example, Sharon told me that when they spent weekends at the Rockefellers' weekend house at Pocantico Hills north of New York City, he would schedule meetings with her in the library at a designated time. All in all, he was the model of propriety you might expect of a man dedicated to maintaining one of America's premier legacies and converting family wealth to public good. I would learn in time that he had indeed been a forward thinker and a prime mover in establishing a number of major nonprofit institutions that are thriving today, including the Japan Society, the Asia Society, the Population Council, and Lincoln Center for the Performing Arts. But as a modest man, he shied away from taking credit for these contributions.

I already knew John's younger brother David through Chuck Percy and the Bell & Howell and Chase bank relationship. I had enjoyed his company enormously, and this purely social occasion merely confirmed my original impression that David was a special person with whom I might develop a deep and lasting friendship. He seemed to have met every famous person in the world, and he spoke of global political and economic matters with great command diffused by a low-key manner. His wife, Peggy, a gregarious woman with a streak of mischief, was the life of the wedding. Laughter seemed to follow her around the party.

More than eighteen months after the wedding, around the end of 1968, John D. III called me at my office. He addressed me formally as "Mr. Peterson," as he always would, and asked if I would come to the Pocantico Hills estate to discuss "something of major significance."

I had traveled far enough from my roots by then to no longer instantly give in to the "Wow, you're a long way from Kearney" impulse. But I was still enough of a Midwestern country boy to want to see how this legendary family lived. If John D. Rockefeller III thought something was "of major significance" and wanted to talk to me about it, I wanted to know what was on his mind.

Pocantico Hills was in the Hudson River Valley near the village of North Tarrytown, close enough to Sleepy Hollow to evoke Washington Irving's legends of Rip Van Winkle and the Headless Horseman. The family's large but understated Colonial Revival mansion was the centerpiece of the huge estate, named Kykuit. (Mr. Rockefeller's city home, I would learn, was a beautiful but in no way ostentatious apartment on Sutton Place with a view of the East River.) When I arrived in the car he sent to meet me at La Guardia Airport, Mr. Rockefeller greeted me wearing a dark suit, white shirt, and dark tie, even though it was a Saturday at his country house. He dispensed with small talk, and got right down to business. He was concerned about the erosion of public understanding and support for charitable foundations in America, of which the Rockefeller Foundation was among the largest. And he was not alone; John J. McCloy, then chairman of Chase Manhattan Bank, and Doug Dillon, chairman of Brookings, had also seen political storm clouds gathering over the foundations. These three powerful movers and shakers believed reforms were needed, and had decided that a major commission should study the situation and suggest changes. Would I consider heading it?

At this, I was the Greek country boy again. I was familiar with the corporate world. I knew some things about how money worked, how companies were bought, sold, and sustained in rough times, the ins and outs of global competition. But any look at American foundations necessarily involved the inner sanctums of what was then the American establishment. Indeed, Jack McCloy, who had been part of the World Bank and special American envoy to Berlin during some of the tense Berlin Airlift days, was widely proclaimed by people in the know in corporate boardrooms, the business press, and the lush apartments on New York's Park and Fifth Avenues to be the unofficial chairman of the Establishment, of this network of elite Northeasterners. Doug Dillon was certainly on its executive committee, as were the Rockefellers. This establishment had great entrée to the corridors of power and used their access and control with quiet discretion and great effectiveness. Their grip on America's major philanthropic institutions was particularly strong. To call upon a forty-two-year-old Midwestern outsider indicated that they saw a serious problem, one that required a set of fresh eyes from outside the Eastern establishment.

Mr. Rockefeller said he would finance the commission's work, provide the staff, and suggest some commission members. It sounded, and was, generous. But as usual when something sounds too good to be true, I called to mind the caution that it usually is. Before accepting, I decided to visit Washington to learn more about the politics and issues involved.

It was an eye-opening trip. Richard Nixon had just been inaugurated, and his new treasury secretary was an old Chicago friend, David Kennedy, the former CEO of the Continental Bank of Chicago. In one long day, I met with him, Senate Finance Committee chairman Russell Long, and House Ways and Means Committee chairman Wilbur Mills. From these Washington insiders, I learned that Rockefeller, McCloy, and Dillon had greatly underestimated the scale and intensity of the problem. The foundation world faced deep political peril.

Tax reform proposals circulating in Congress included a stiff 46 percent tax on foundations' income. Other bills proposed that no foundation be allowed to exist for more than ten years. Such draconian measures reflected deep resentment. It was so strong that I saw foundations being legislated out of existence unless they changed their high-handed ways.

A number of forces were to blame. On the surface, the foundations were targets of populist resentment. A senior Treasury Department official, Stanley Surrey, had stirred some of these feelings by accusing millionaires of not paying taxes and funding foundations as a tax dodge, implying that they were little more than loopholes for the rich. Longtime Texas congressman Wright Patman, a demagogue, was continuing his history of populist rabble-rousing by spinning anecdotes about various philanthropic gambits designed to cheat the taxpayers, including self-dealing in ways such as contributing dry oil and gas wells.

They weren't all off-base. A report by the Treasury Department in 1965 had revealed that a woman had taken a $39,500 tax deduction for jewelry she donated to her husband's foundation, which kept the baubles in a safe deposit box to be loaned back to her free to wear anytime she wanted.

Less obvious—but far more worrisome to Congress—were matters that had nothing to do with foundations' tax deductions, and everything to do with politics and the causes that they funded. Vernon Jordan, James Farmer, and other committed African-Americans were heading Southern voter registration drives in those days of the civil rights movement. The Ford Foundation and others were helping to fund those drives, and lawmakers, who saw any increase in black votes as dangerous to their political health, placed quiet blame on the foundations.

Nor did the foundations help themselves. Their arrogance could seem egregious. McGeorge Bundy, the Boston patrician who had been one of the architects of the Vietnam War as the national security advisor to Presidents Kennedy and Johnson, had left the government in 1966 to head the Ford Foundation. He practically sneered at congressional Southerners when he testified that he and the board controlled the foundation's agenda and that the foundation was free to pursue whatever liberal political causes—such as voter registration—they might choose. When the foundation took some of Bobby Kennedy's aides under its wing, after his death in 1968, the perception grew ever stronger that the Ford Foundation had become increasingly political and a hotbed of liberal initiatives.

With this sobering information in hand, I journeyed to New York for a meeting with Messrs. Rockefeller, Dillon, and McCloy.

We met at the famed Rockefeller offices on the fifty-sixth floor of 30 Rockefeller Center. True to the form I was coming to expect from the old-money elite, these offices were spare and unobtrusive. (This kind of modesty is a practice that David Rockefeller, the current family patriarch, follows to this day in both his personal and business lives. He occupies the smallest office I have ever seen among major executives. And his personal thriftiness is legendary. The fixtures and appliances in his home on East 65th Street in New York haven't changed in the thirty-five years that I've been going there. And there's a story, one of my favorite all-true tales, George Ball tells that he swears is true about a trip he made to Rome with David. The two of them stopped at Gucci on the Via Condotti to browse the top-quality leather goods. They both found briefcases they liked and George pulled out his credit card, but David hesitated and decided against buying. When they left the store, David asked a passerby if there were another shop nearby that sold fine leather goods for a bit less money. "Of course," said the person sympathetically as he pointed down the street. "Only a Rockefeller could afford to buy at Gucci.")

I told them I was deeply flattered by what they wanted me to do, but I felt the problem foundations face went far deeper than they might have imagined. A commission on foundation reform, supported by foundation money and foundation staff, would have no credibility. If I were to chair the body they envisioned, it would have to raise its own, nonfoundation money, hire its own staff, and not include members from the foundation world. Total independence was a must.

I saw John D. blanch as I spelled out these requirements. I don't know if it shook him to hear how badly the foundations were viewed in Washington, or to hear me insist on an independent commission. He probably thought he had made a mistake to propose this brash young Midwesterner, that I was presumptuous to look his gift horse of a well-intended offer in the mouth. To that point, Jack McCloy had sat quietly, listening to what I had to say. I had met him only in passing, and didn't know him well, but quickly saw that although he was smaller physically than Dillon he was an equally commanding figure. He exuded energy and power, and despite being in his seventies gave the impression of muscles rippling under his beautifully cut suit. Now he cleared his throat and spoke into the resulting silence. "John, I have to admit frankly I'm embarrassed," he said thoughtfully. "I believe this young fellow is proposing the wise course. I should have thought of these concerns myself."

"Do you really think so, Jack?" John D. asked.

"Yes, I certainly do."

Doug Dillon quickly weighed in with Jack McCloy, and John D. then made it unanimous. We set about to name our organization: The Commission on Foundations and Private Philanthropy. We raised the money from private sources and hired our own staff. Our commission's first surprise was how little was known about what foundations did with their money. Many foundations held the view that what they did with their money was nobody else's business. We felt this was politically naive since this informational void was filled with tall tales and innuendo that demagogues were using to attack them.

So, we launched the first nationwide survey of foundations that cast a very different light. We learned, for example, that over 99 percent of foundation grants went to conventional, or so called Triple A, charities such as universities, hospitals, and churches. Less than 0.1 percent funded causes that might be viewed as the much feared "political" grants, such as voter registration.

But we also learned that many foundations gave very little to charity. This was particularly true of many company-controlled foundations. We proposed an obvious reform. To be able to keep the tax advantages, we recommended that foundations should be required to make minimum payouts each year in amounts that would still leave their principal intact. Our figures showed that this would substantially increase the flow of foundation funds to charities.

Soon before our commission was to make this proposal public, the business systems innovator John Diebold gave a dinner at his apartment in New York. It was intended as a forum for me to discuss what the commission was doing, pro and con. McGeorge Bundy of the Ford Foundation objected vehemently—and, I thought, arrogantly—to the idea of a minimum payout. Other conversation stopped as Bundy, his voice rising, demanded, "Who are you, indeed, who is anybody, to be telling us (he meant foundations) how much of our money to contribute?"

"The tax deductions you get for charitable contributions come with certain public expectations," I explained. "The U.S. taxpayer assumes that in exchange for receiving less tax income, society is going to reap a compensating benefit. And the benefit to society in alleviating social problems, especially current social problems, should be seen as more equal to the reward for the contributor. Right now your reward seems much greater than society's benefit."

I don't think he heard me. And I really don't think he appreciated what the stakes were—that converging forces were about to lay waste to the foundation world.

Around the same time, I received a tense visit by the CEO of Kellogg, who was accompanied by "his" Kellogg Foundation executive director. The CEO complained that if our minimum payout was put into effect, because their stock dividend was quite low, the foundation would have to sell shares and they might lose control of the Kellogg Corporation.

I made the argument that I, too, as CEO of Bell & Howell, would like ironclad protection against a hostile takeover. I assumed that many corporate executives felt the same. However, that was an antitrust matter that had nothing to do with charitable giving. Were only the rich to get protection against takeovers?

"So, how can a high payout possibly harm you, and indeed, why wouldn't it help you?" I asked the foundation executive director. He uncomfortably demurred.

By now we were well into 1969. John D. Rockefeller III called me every Sunday morning at nine-thirty for progress reports on the commission's work. In the U.S. Senate, Finance Committee chairman Russell Long had come to believe that the commission and I were truly independent. I had faithfully kept in touch with him and Wilbur Mills, offering to meet with them each time I came to Washington to bring them up to date. Senator Long had been particularly responsive. That October, he gave us several hours to lay out our proposals to the Finance Committee. Seeing him as the decisive voice on the subject, I was able to schedule a long one-on-one meeting with him.

We met in his Senate office one afternoon, late enough that the sun was over the yardarm, as far as the senator was concerned. The Louisianan, son of the flamboyant Huey Long, welcomed me and sat down behind his desk next to a side table set with a tray, glasses, an ice bucket, and a large bottle of bourbon. He offered me a drink. I declined. He poured one for himself, and we started talking. Long was very smart, and colorful and voluble when he was stone cold sober; with a few drinks, he reached new heights—or some might say depths—of language. I wanted to finish my presentation before he had one too many. In the meantime he was laying it on the foundations. In referring to foundations, I heard him use versions of the F-word as a verb, a noun, and an adjective in a single sentence!

I quickly gave him a rundown on the patterns of foundation giving in Louisiana. They followed national trends; the huge bulk of money went to classic, popular institutions like Louisiana State and Tulane universities, the Catholic Church, and the like and very little for foundation voter registration efforts that so frightened our political representatives. Under the congressional proposals, I explained, these Louisiana institutions would get substantially less money. But if our minimum payout plan went into force, their contributions would go up substantially. I gave him an estimate of how much Louisiana charities would benefit.

Senator Long sat back, took a sip of his frequently replenished bourbon, and a benign smile lit up his face. "Pete," he said, "you tellin' me I can fuck the bad guys and help the good guys, all at the same time."

"Your words, Senator, not mine. But if you put it that way, yes," I said.

Not long after our meeting, Senator Long took the Senate floor to say he was withdrawing the heavy tax he had proposed for the foundations, to be replaced with our minimum payout proposal, along with some of our proposals to deal with self-dealing by foundations. It passed and went into effect soon afterward.

Finding My Throw Weight

In 1969, Jack McCloy encouraged President Nixon to appoint me to serve on the General Advisory Committee to the U.S. Arms Control and Disarmament Agency.

This committee operated within the State Department. Jack chaired it, and its members included Doug Dillon, former secretary of state Dean Rusk, Pennsylvania governor Bill Scranton, and former army secretary and deputy secretary of defense Cyrus Vance. We were charged with making recommendations to the president that might reduce the threat of nuclear war. Everything we did bore a "top secret" label. The issues had an intellectual density that fascinated me. I read everything I was given. When the time came to discuss the issues, I felt I was able to hold up my end.

One day, a three-star air force general who reminded me a bit of General Curtis LeMay, lampooned in the savagely satirical Stanley Kubrick movie *Dr. Strangelove*, met with the committee to discuss his notion of a "limited first strike." This was a Cold War term that was supposed to define a level of nuclear missile firing that would stop short of an all-out nuclear war. The general told the committee that instead of using our full complement of nuclear delivery capabilities, the United States would only "lob" as few as twenty-five nuclear weapons at the Soviets, but not at Moscow.

I asked him how he thought the Soviet air force would interpret such a "limited strike."

"Sir, those bastards know they deserve a spanking," he replied.

"And, General, thinking of the Soviet air force radar operators spotting the twenty-five or so missiles on their way, how exactly would they tell this was a 'lob,' as you put it, instead of, to use another tennis term, a 'smash'?"

He mumbled some meaningless response that put me in mind of the mad General Jack D. Ripper, bent on nuclear war. And I had thought he was a fictional character, not an air force general with his finger near the nuclear trigger. He reminded me of Abraham Lincoln's comment about one of his generals: "His headquarters were where his hindquarters ought to be."

But there was nothing to laugh about in dealing with these issues. Both the United States and the Soviet Union were developing the capability to launch multiple nuclear bombs out of a single missile and to guide these bombs independently to separate targets. They were called MIRVs, or multiple independently targeted vehicles. Our committee concluded that *even testing* these MIRVs would trigger a new round in the nuclear arms race. This was because neither side, looking down on the other from sophisticated satellites, could tell which missile-launching silos held MIRVs and which did not. We and the Soviets alike would use worst-case scenarios and determine that we had to build many more missiles, including MIRVs.

We decided that the best way to avoid such a massive escalation of the arms race was to negotiate a MIRV test ban treaty.

We had not made that decision public when classified information reached the committee revealing that the United States was planning a MIRV test within the next few months. Jack McCloy hurriedly arranged a meeting with President Nixon to press our unanimous recommendation that the United States immediately approach the Soviets to negotiate a test ban treaty. The military apparently got wind of our intentions and pushed its MIRV test forward, before we could meet with the president. The Soviets then launched a full-scale MIRV program of their own, and the arms race was blasting off again.

That result was most disappointing, but I still felt my work with the committee served me well. I gained invaluable knowledge and also expanded my roster of important connections in foreign policy circles. This was an area where I wanted to learn more and become more involved. I suspect my heart was on my sleeve because some of the Advisory Committee members apparently were dropping hints to the White House that I might be ready to take a leave from corporate life. Indeed, Gerard C. Smith, director of the Arms Control and Disarmament Agency, offered me a job as his number two. The job tempted me but ultimately seemed too limited. But these trial balloons and hints eventually led to actual discussions.

Daniel Patrick Moynihan, then serving in his third successive presidential administration, arranged for me in 1970 to have lunch with another of President Nixon's advisors, John Ehrlichman. We were joined by an old friend, George Shultz. He and I had kept in touch since we first met when I taught part-time at the University of Chicago Graduate School of Business. George was then Nixon's head of the Office of Management and Budget. Ehrlichman, the president's top domestic affairs advisor, had told George he wanted to know more about the proposals the foundation reform commission was recommending.

We ate in the smaller of the two White House mess rooms. It was reserved for senior staff, who could hold sensitive talks there without fear of information leaking out. We also talked about the challenges the nation faced abroad and at home—the Cold War and the war in Vietnam, the trade balance and foreign competition. I heard allusions that they might be interested in my joining the administration, but the matter went no further.

Around that time, near the end of 1970, *The Wall Street Journal* ran an item saying that I was being considered as deputy secretary of state. I assumed my friends McCloy, Dillon, and Cy Vance were behind that suggestion. But I had already asked George Shultz what he thought about my becoming the arms control deputy. He had said, "Pete, if and when we ask you to come to Washington, it will be for a more important job than that."

CHAPTER 7

WASHINGTON, ROUND ONE

Presidential Summons

The feeler from Washington came during the year-end holidays of
1970. George Shultz called to tell me the president planned to create a
new council on international economic policy and he wanted me to run
it. "He wants to talk it over with you," George said. "How soon can you
come to Washington?"

I arrived in the capital soon after the New Year and spent a night
with George and his wife, Obie. She was a delightful woman whom
George had met during the Second World War, while he served as a
marine in Hawaii and she was a nurse lieutenant; her odd first name was
really a nickname, a contraction of her maiden name, O'Brien. The next
morning George took me to the White House and escorted me to the
Oval Office for my one-on-one meeting with the president.

When we met early in January 1971, Nixon had occupied the presidency for almost two years. The world was changing at a dizzying pace,
capped by the Apollo 11 moon landing in July 1969. The exception was
the peace talks designed to end the war in Vietnam. Those had been
dragging on in Paris since 1968, despite Nixon's implying during the
campaign that he had a "secret plan" to end the war. But the stalemate
over Vietnam had not stopped him from embarking on new initiatives
in foreign policy. This, and bringing economic considerations into play
in charting U.S. foreign policy, was what he wanted to discuss.

An aide announced me from the door to the Oval Office: "Mr. President, Mr. Peterson is here." Nixon rose from the seat behind his desk and offered his hand and a smile of greeting. His clothes radiated businesslike formality; he rarely deviated from the white shirt, dark suit, conservative tie, and the highly polished black shoes he was wearing that morning. With the American flag pin in his lapel, a visual cue to the conservative voters below the Mason-Dixon Line who were the targets of his "Southern strategy," his outfit was complete. He motioned me to a chair and sat down across from me.

I was nervous at first. The president was relaxed. He began to speak in what quickly emerged as a world tour, and I gradually unwound and found myself more and more impressed with his thinking and grasp of the issues.

Nixon laid out his geopolitical and geo-economic views brilliantly. The U.S.-Soviet relationship would continue to be a major priority, he said, but new paradigms were emerging in the rest of the world that demanded our attention. Europe and Japan were no longer the devastated economic cripples that had emerged from World War II. Rather (with the help of the U.S. Marshall Plan), they had gotten their feet under them and were becoming major economic competitors to the United States. From now on, economics would play a far more important role in America's foreign policy. Indeed, Nixon was envisioning the interconnected geo-economic world globalists talk about today.

He felt that this vision had not been integrated into our diplomacy, that our foreign policy operated independently of our economic policy when they should operate in concert. Why that was, he wasn't sure, but he hoped that I could help, and laid out the job he had in mind for me.

Litton Industries founder and CEO Roy L. Ash had recently headed the President's Advisory Council on Executive Reorganization. Commonly known as the Ash Council, it was tasked to find ways to make the government work better. One of its recommendations (along with the creation of the Environmental Protection Agency) was that an international economic policy council be formed along the lines of the National Security Council. This Council on International Economic Policy would be chaired by the president, and include the secretaries of state, defense, the treasury, agriculture, commerce, and labor, the director of the Office of Management and Budget, the chair of the Council of Economic Advisors, the assistant to the president for national security affairs (commonly known as the national security advisor), the executive director of the domestic council, and the special representative for trade negotiations. It was a top-level group, clearly designed to elevate the importance of foreign economic policy and bring it in line with the new realities. Nixon said he wanted me to be its executive director.

I was flattered. But at the ripe old age of forty-four my tendency to analyze a situation thoroughly was, if anything, stronger than ever. I asked the president why, given the links between economic policy and national security, the National Security Council could not perform the function he envisioned. His reply shone a spotlight onto his complex relationship with Henry Kissinger, who as his national security advisor had far eclipsed Secretary of State William Rogers in guiding foreign policy. (I would learn that Nixon had great respect for Kissinger, but that he held his own foreign policy bona fides in high esteem as well, and obviously did not want Kissinger to outshine him.) The relationship reflected a profound ambivalence, one that would be heightened a year later when they shared *Time* magazine's 1972 "Men of the Year" designation, even though Nixon had been the sole designee in 1971.

"Henry doesn't know a damn thing about economics," he said. "What's worse, he doesn't know what he doesn't know."

I told the president I was very tempted by his offer. The opportunity to work with treasury secretary David Kennedy, an old Chicago friend who had been chief executive of the Continental Bank, was just one of the temptations, a point of contact in the cabinet whom I knew and trusted. But I had a reservation. One of my likely successors at Bell & Howell, Everett Wagner, had just suffered a serious heart attack, and I didn't want to leave the company without a leader. I felt responsible for the more than ten thousand employees and many friends who needed a strong hand at the helm.

Nixon dismissed my concerns. This job, he said, was too important. "Who chairs the Bell & Howell executive committee?" he asked me on the spot. I told him it was Charlie Mortimer, the CEO of General Foods, who was vacationing at the Cotton Bay Club on out-of-the-way Eleuthera Island in the Bahamas. The president quickly demonstrated that remoteness was no barrier to the White House switchboard. Within a few minutes, he had Charlie on the phone, no doubt wondering what pranksters were disturbing his vacation by insisting the president of the United States was calling.

"I have Pete Peterson here with me in the Oval Office," said the president. "He tells me there are succession issues at Bell & Howell. I hope you can take care of them because I want him to come to work for me."

Next Nixon probed to find out if my reluctance was a smoke screen, a way of hinting that what I really wanted was a bigger, more prestigious job in Washington. I could have a cabinet post if that was what I wanted. "You know, big limousines, big offices, and all," he said. But that, he added, was not the way it was. In his administration, "You have to decide if you simply want to *be* somebody, or if you really want to *do* something," he said. Under Nixon, the power doers were the senior members of his staff, the so-called Palace Guard, not the members of his cabinet. I quietly wondered if the cabinet officers had been told or understood this distinction. Two years into the administration, if the Kissinger-Rogers dichotomy was any clue, I doubted that Bill Rogers had actually been told where the power really lay.

"Mr. President, I'm very flattered by your offer," I told him as we parted at the end of our hour-long meeting. "I can't give you an answer on the spot. I need to think about my other obligations, but I'll let you know very soon."

The truth was, I didn't have to think very long. I was hardly out of the Oval Office before I found myself dreading the endless and debilitating budget reviews—and inevitable budget cuts—at Bell & Howell. I had many friends and a long history there, and I felt a burden of responsibility at the company I had come to love. But I didn't love the repetition of the tasks, those concrete, incremental jobs that it takes to run a business well and competitively day in and day out, and I did love my forays into public policy. I wanted something larger, the macro, the big abstract picture where conceptual changes took place. But truth to tell, I knew the time had come for me to move on. And aside from my own wishes, I had the best motivator in the world—a request to serve the country from the most powerful man in the world.

Sally wasn't wild about the idea, coming as it did in the middle of the school year; David and Holly were at opposite ends of their elementary school experience at Winnetka's Samuel S. Greeley School, but they both were happy there, and Jim had a circle of friends at New Trier High School he didn't want to leave. But Sally wasn't adamantly opposed, either. She said she was "okay with it," as I recall. I sweetened the pot by taking her to Saks Fifth Avenue and helping her shop for three gowns, telling her we were sure to be attending a lot of glittering fancy dinners. She gradually warmed to the thought that we would be closer to the action, where things were decided that ended up filtering down and affecting us out in Chicago and beyond.

Although later in my life I became appalled at my father's self-centeredness and concentration on his work at the expense of my mother's needs and feelings, by 1971 my own marriage had become rather like theirs. My focus on work and achievement provided material comforts but not a close relationship, and too little room for discussion when I decided to take on new challenges, no matter how time-consuming or disruptive. In such an old-fashioned marriage, the breadwinner had the first, and final, word.

My parents applauded the move. When I talked to my father, I explained that I would be giving up a few million dollars in salary and stock options for a job that paid $42,500 a year. "It doesn't matter," he said. "That's not important. You can't say no to the president of the United States even if he pays you nothing." I couldn't argue with him, nor did I want to.

I called George Shultz to say I would accept, on one condition. Henry Kissinger headed the National Security Council and was assistant to the president for national security affairs (the national security advisor). John Ehrlichman ran the Domestic Council and was assistant to the president for domestic affairs. I could already see that my success partly depended on having equal status. Washington was full of councils, commissions, study groups, and task forces, all of which could easily be downgraded, ignored, or bypassed if they weren't within the presidential orbit. I told George I wanted to be assistant to the president for international economic affairs. The president quickly agreed, and I started making plans to move to Washington.

Report Card

The Bell & Howell executive committee accepted my resignation grace-fully, and selected as my successor Donald Frey, a board member and former Ford executive known for developing the Mustang. Don was a logical choice to lead the company through the difficult days that still lay ahead. The company's top two hundred or so executives bade me goodbye at a smashing, but very sentimental, party at the Skokie Coun-try Club, where they showered me with gifts and toasts, laughter and memories, long into the night. The theme of the roasts was my being pictured as a puppet with Richard Nixon pulling the strings. I referred to those Bell & Howell memories as the best years of our lives.

As I departed Bell & Howell, I mentally wrote a report card on myself as CEO.

Looking only at the numbers, one would assume I graded my eight years pretty highly. Sales doubled and earnings quadrupled while I was in charge. But the real story was more mixed.

I gave myself an A for the relentless drive to reduce costs and, by introducing new products, maintaining market share and profits in a rapidly declining industry. But I could only claim a C for steering the company toward the future. I did not get Bell & Howell into the next big thing, which was the electronics world: cameras, recorders, every-thing. Din Land made the same mistake. Bell & Howell soldiered on, and did reasonably well for some years after I left, but eventually merged with a German company leaving another company to license the Bell & Howell name for other products including electric shavers. One lesson I learned was this, from a report by the Stanford Research Institute: "Growth companies tend to be in growth industries." And, they could have added: "Declining companies tend to be in declining industries." Oh, how I wish I could have operated in a growth industry. No one today, to my knowledge, is making *any* amateur motion picture film cameras and projectors. That business is all digital, and the all-but-exclusive property of the Sonys, the Canons, the Samsungs, the Pana-sonics, and their brethren.

When I now think of what these new digital systems can do—instant pictures, sound, color, erasability, sharpness, length of playing time, and ease of projection, I wonder how we sold any of the old amateur film movie systems. But even with all their flaws, they were what was possible at the time, and with them people made what they still make with today's more advanced equipment—they make memories, and I'm proud to have contributed to those films of the first steps of babies who are now parents and grandparents, with the old film hopefully dubbed over to videotape or digital discs in permanent family memory banks.

What general lesson did I learn from my Bell & Howell experience? I am haunted by this basic question: Why didn't Bell & Howell and Polaroid respond differently to the video and electronic threat?

At the national level, we have now seen a dramatic increase in creative destruction taking place as our global competitors rapidly develop their technological and human infrastructure. To take China and the rest of Asia as an example, by 2010, they are projected to account for 90 percent of the world's scientists and engineers. After being a leader for years in the annual numbers of students going to college, the United States is now fifth. America's fifteen-year-olds ranked 25th out of 30 in math, and 21st in science. Patents, one indicator of the pace of technological innovation, have trended downward for each of the last eleven years.

While America has the most advanced entrepreneurial spirit and structure in the world, the sheer weight and force of these global trends should capture our sustained attention.

So, why did we at Bell & Howell and Polaroid not directly confront either the specific technological threats to our business or the new opportunities that emerging video technologies represented? For one thing, our core technological competence was elsewhere—electromechanical (Bell & Howell) or photochemistry (Polaroid)—very different technologies from electronics. And if one's knowledge is not at the cutting edge of one of those technologies, one is unlikely to have a really good idea of the future possibilities.

Then there is the defensiveness too many of us have about our own core competence. We may find it difficult to accept that some newcomers to "our" industry could overwhelm our solid and historical industry that has been around for years.

Furthermore, to "merge" with a company that has the new electronic competences might, in fact, involve being taken over by the electronics firm, and many managements' enthusiasm for being taken over is pretty restrained. In my case, I was so concerned about the trends in the motion picture industry I would have welcomed it. However, the Sonys and Panasonics didn't need Bell & Howell. They already had a brand and the expertise in video products and their marketing.

Also, to build a wholly new technological competence from scratch can be a costly, arduous, and risky venture.

Should we in the industry have tried harder to get a merger or build the technology? Considering the eventual outcome, the answer is an obvious yes, we should have.

The foreign manufacturing cost-competitive threat was also in its early stages. Bell & Howell's labor costs were about $1.75/hour. Our Japanese plant's labor costs were $0.25/hour. The yen was 360 to the dollar (today it is about a third of that).

But then, in those days, there were also important disadvantages in making products abroad. At that time, very few of the foreign managers and virtually none of the workers spoke English or had technical backgrounds. And translation into foreign languages was also complicated. Today, most of the managers speak English. Communication was far more time-consuming and costly then. There were no faxes, e-mails, or videoconferences. Critically necessary blueprints and drawings needed to be shipped and transportation was far slower and costlier. Today, GE's CEO, Jeff Immelt, told me that GE can now manufacture the first generation of their most advanced products abroad. This would have been unthinkable in my time.

This leaves a related question that haunts many about American industry: Whither manufacturing? Many who ask that question start with a premise that manufacturing in the United States has already withered.

Actually, the share of manufacturing in total U.S. output has leveled off at 18 percent to 20 percent of GDP since about 1980. Contrary to popular mythology, manufacturing is not a rapidly declining sector, though it has obviously reached a modest share of the total economy as we become dominated by services (nor, I might say, has Japan taken over the world, as was widely predicted). Manufacturing employment has continued to decline steadily and now provides less than 12 percent of all American jobs. This is largely due to productivity growth in manufacturing, which has been much greater than in the rest of the economy. We produce more and more manufactured goods with fewer and fewer workers. A standard analogy is the long-term evolution of agriculture where a share of the workforce went from over one-half of the workforce a century ago to about one percent, with steadily growing output throughout the period.

International trade certainly has a role in all this because over one-third of our manufactured output is now exported and at least another one-third competes with imports. A critical variable that has much effect on international manufacturing competitiveness is the exchange rate of the dollar, thus "the decline of manufacturing" has accelerated when the dollar has become overvalued as in the first half of the 1980s and again in the first half of this decade and recouped significantly after the dollar fell.

I certainly do not downplay the competitive pressures notably on American manufacturing jobs but on American business as well. I think too much emphasis is placed on manufacturing cost-competitiveness and too little on the real ballpark of competition: technological innovation. At the very least, that will require us to foster America's entrepreneurial spirit and the human technological infrastructure. The all-important requirement is that we invest much more heavily and effectively in research and development, on math and science, education and intensely developing our technological human capital. But that is another book.

So, overall, I gave myself a B as a corporate executive, a step down, perhaps, from my rating in the market research and advertising business. But in January 1971, when President Nixon introduced me as assistant to the president for international economic affairs and head of the new Council on International Economic Policy, he called me "the greatest CEO of his generation." It was the surest sign so far that I had left the area of quantifiable data and entered the Washington realm of hyperbole and spin.

Warning Signs

I shall never forget the first morning of my White House job. Sally and the kids were still in Chicago until we could find a house and private schools, and I was living in a Howard Johnson hotel in the meantime. Since I was alone, I decided to have breakfast in the White House mess. A group of young men sat together sharing a big round table and I asked if I could join them. They were fresh-faced, probably still in their twenties, conservatively dressed, and full of energy. They made a place and welcomed me aboard. All of them were working for H. R. "Bob" Haldeman, the president's formidable chief of staff whose White House nickname was "the Brush," a reference to his flattop crew cut hairstyle.

As the new guy on the block, and curious about these young men at the epicenter of American politics and government, I asked them how they felt about their White House jobs. Several of them answered, almost in a chorus, that it was the best job they had ever had. At first I thought they simply meant the psychic income they received from the sense of public service. But no. It turned out that in most cases they were also referring to what they were being paid. They had never made so much money in their lives.

This was a bit of a shock. Of course I had taken a very large pay cut in order to work at the White House. I knew every staffer could not have come from the ranks of senior corporate management, but I did think some of them might have had substantial careers and life experiences they had put on hold to serve the country. Few, however, seemed to have advanced beyond very junior and low-paying jobs. Dwight Chapin, for example, had held a junior position at an advertising agency. Some of the others had been advance workers in Nixon's campaign, arranging photo opportunities and doing scheduling as Haldeman himself had done for Nixon back in the 1950s in his vice presidential campaigns and his unsuccessful 1960 presidential run against John Kennedy.

I was further surprised by their lack of previous public policy experience. They had come to the White House without portfolios. What was most clear, as we talked that morning and later as I came to know them better, was their total dependence on Bob Haldeman, and their intense loyalty to him.

This violated an observation I once heard: It is important to "travel light" in life. In this case, it meant that one carries baggage in one's work life—obligations to superiors, for example—and that if that baggage grows too heavy, you should lighten up and move on. As I became more familiar with life inside the White House, I saw that these young staffers were most certainly not traveling light, and the heavy baggage they were carrying was not their own. They were not only loyal and beholden to Haldeman, but also, I suspected, afraid of him. The chief of staff's crew cut was not just a fashion preference; it signified a marine-like iron discipline, and it created in his underlings an eagerness to please that led them, later during the Watergate scandal, to discard ethics and legalities and landed some of them in jail. But traveling light, they might have been able to escape the undercurrents dragging down the White House and themselves.

But I also saw the seductions that preyed on these young aides. It was terribly easy for anyone, not just the young and impressionable, to be overwhelmed by the sheer majesty of the White House and the presidency itself. Nixon contributed to this mood. His every move, and his anticipated mood shifts, trickled down to the staff, who speculated where he would go, what he would do, what he would say, and how he was feeling. I myself, in one of my first days in the White House, was taken unaware by a presidential approach and nearly got trampled by four or five Secret Service agents who surrounded him as he walked the short distance from the guarded and gated White House grounds to his favorite haunt in the Old Executive Office Building.

Rising Star

My first weeks in my new job appealed to my forte—analysis. Following my instructions from the president, I met with the various cabinet officers who were on the Council on International Economic Policy. I asked them what I thought were obvious questions: How did they assess the position and role of the United States in the world economy? What did they think of America's foreign economic policies, and how would they change them if at all? Did they think those policies were being effectively coordinated with our overall foreign policy? And if not, why not? Were our foreign and economic policies aimed at reaching the same goals? And so on. I was stunned at the range of views I got. These cabinet members appeared to be looking at the economic ebb and flow from different planets, and not seeing what was happening on the far side of the earth.

William Rogers and the State Department, for example, saw the United States maintaining its status as the world's dominant economic superpower far into the future. Standing atop our economic Mount Olympus, we could afford to make substantial trade and economic concessions as a means of promoting global harmony and our overall national interests. Our position in global economic matters should be benign and generous. Henry Kissinger of the National Security Council and the State Department stood together on these views when it came, as Henry once put it, to these "minor" commercial issues. I was getting to know—and like—Henry quite well by then and I told him, "Henry, for you to refer to 'these minor commercial issues' is a redundancy. You think *all* commercial matters are 'minor.'"

Maurice Stans and the Commerce Department held a completely different view. In their eyes, the U.S. manufacturing sector was increasingly, even desperately, uncompetitive. Unless we took strong action—which to them often meant protective tariffs and restrictions—we would soon become a nonmanufacturing economy that supplied no goods but only services.

Also, the lack of agreement on our strengths and weaknesses and priorities in foreign economic matters meant there was almost no coordination between policies. The idea of fixing problems hung up on differences over what the problems were, or indeed if there even were problems. How could we implement coherent solutions if there was not agreement on the problem?

I laid this out to Nixon in a series of memos. At first, he reacted with his lawyer's shorthand, sending back my reports with handwritten notes such as, "Proceed," "Very interesting," or "Explain further."

Back at my headquarters in the Old Executive Office Building, I and my staff of six men assigned to me by various departments sifted through vast economic data sources. Once we had some real figures, we put together an overall analysis. It covered all the major countries of the industrial world and looked at productivity growth, unit labor costs, market share, trade trends, exchange rates, and on and on. This data gave a picture that no one in the administration had seen before. It showed that the economic changes since World War II had been profound. The dominance of the U.S. economy, placed against the performance of its major trading partners, had definitely declined even as the volume of international trade was building to what we today call the global economy.

These changes, however, had not been matched by trade policy and exchange rate alterations. Both the United States and its major trading partners maintained policies that had been in place since the days when most of the developed world was still digging out of the ashes left by World War II. To use just one example, the Japanese yen had sat at 360 to the dollar for a quarter-century. Clearly, if that was the right exchange rate in 1946, it certainly wasn't the right one in 1971. But the Japanese liked it that way. A weak yen kept Japanese goods cheap for American consumers, who were snapping up low-priced Japanese cars, cameras, copiers, televisions, textiles, and other consumer goods. As a result, Japanese industries were increasing their penetration of the American market and providing more export jobs. Back here at home, we didn't fare so well. Many goods manufactured in the United States were too expensive for Japanese consumers even if the Japanese had not put up protectionist walls, and so exports to Japan provided few jobs for American workers.

Before long my conclusions, as a film distributor might put it, were ready to "go wide." With the president's encouragement, I decided to do a major report that I called "The Changing Role of the U.S. in the World Economy." We laid out the data in color slides and charts to make it more accessible. By now it was April 1971, but for some reason the White House was still in a black-and-white world when it came to the tools of bureaucratic persuasion. Thus what would be called the Peterson Color Slide Show—show biz breaches the gray walls of bureaucracy!—became something of a sensation.

The president and the entire Council on International Economic

Policy attended the meeting at which I first gave the presentation. John Ehrlichman reported afterward that Nixon had been "rhapsodic." Word got out virtually overnight about the president's enthusiasm for my report. He asked me to speak to groups across the spectrum—labor unions, business CEOs, the press. He even hosted a meeting with senior congressional leaders in the White House and sat through the report a second time.

Soon I was on the cover of magazines like *Business Week* and in constant demand for media interviews. Later in the year, after the president decided that the report should be made public, the Government Printing Office reported that it had sold over ten thousand copies, a best-seller by government standards. *The New York Times* ran a front-page story on the paradigm shift in the White House approach to foreign economic policy. Inside, where the story continued, the entire second page sprinkled a number of my charts on balance of payments, hourly wages, U.S. imports, and the like by way of illustrating why Nixon was leading the charge to reform. A short profile that appeared with my picture reported that I was known in Washington as the "economic Kissinger" whose "influence and authority in international trade and finance is roughly equivalent to that of Presidential Assistant Henry A. Kissinger in foreign policy."

This was heady stuff. It got all the more so when Bob Haldeman told me one day that the president wanted to move me into the White House, the West Wing, closer to the Oval Office. My office in the EOB—Washington shorthand for the Executive Office Building—was a large one, with an adjoining meeting room. It was spacious, even elegant, and the White House was literally only a stone's throw away. But in political Washington, as in real estate, location is everything. An office in the West Wing of the White House was a key indicator of status and power.

The West Wing offices were full, Haldeman said. He would have to work it out, meaning that someone currently in the West Wing would have to move. I awaited results. Ultimately, Haldeman reported to me that the occupant of the office to be vacated for me was, as he put it, "very upset." That occupant was the director of the White House Office of Economic Opportunity. His name was Donald Rumsfeld.

I knew Don Rumsfeld and considered him a friend. He had been my congressman in Chicago before leaving two years earlier to take the White House job. He had been something of a boy wonder at the time, but by 1971 the enthusiasm for him had diminished among the senior White House staff and—rumor had it—the president as well. Nevertheless, he was considered one of the toughest and most effective bureaucratic infighters in Washington. And he was using every move in his playbook to stay on in the West Wing.

I didn't have a playbook. My reactions were based on what I considered decency and friendship. If Don was that upset, why, I was quite willing to stay on in the EOB. Staying there wouldn't make any real difference to my work, only my immediate access to the president. The way I saw things, Nixon's enthusiasm for shaking up the old paradigms of global economics would obviate my need to be down the hall from the Oval Office. So I folded. I told Haldeman to let Don have his way.

Kissinger, who was the only equal I ever saw to Rumsfeld when it came to bureaucratic infighting, told me later it was the worst mistake I ever made.

The Connally Tsunami

There was little time to dwell on what might have been, however. I soon faced a nemesis whose stature and long shadow darkened my role in international economic policy while his star rose.

Shortly after I came on board, my friend David Kennedy resigned as secretary of the treasury—actually, he was shoved aside—to become Nixon's ambassador-at-large for trade matters. He had been my principal point of contact in the cabinet, and my enthusiasm for working with him was among the main reasons I had left Bell & Howell for public service. When Nixon announced Democrat John Connally, the former secretary of the navy and Texas governor, as his replacement, I was taken by surprise. I would have thought, as a key advisor on international economic matters, that I would have been consulted, or at least informed. But I ultimately rationalized that Nixon needed to keep the appointment confidential before announcing it. And I naively assumed that Connally would be supportive of my work, as Kennedy had been, because he had been a member of the Ash Council that recommended the creation of the Council on International Economic Policy in the first place.

And at the outset, he seemed enthusiastic about my report. "A breath of fresh air," he called it. "Finally, Washington might get the new economic realities."

But those realities, I quickly learned, would be interpreted by him and him alone. He was a big fish in the Washington pond from day one, whereas I was a relatively small one, and about to be smaller. For one thing, Nixon needed him, a Democrat, in the cabinet to be able to work with Democrats in Congress, who held majorities in both houses after the 1970 elections. And Connally himself brooked no staff intermediaries. He was the exception to the Nixonian system of concentrating power and access in his White House aides because he simply refused to deal with the Palace Guard, of which he considered me a member. He would not send memos on international economics to the president through me or anyone else, and if he ever factored into his decisions my suggestions to him about economic policy, I never saw the evidence of it. His not being situated in the West Wing was no deterrent, either. The Treasury flanked the White House on the east as the EOB did on the west, and when he needed the president's view on something, he simply marched the few hundred feet from the Treasury and went to the Oval Office.

This all contributed to a persona that was larger than life. Connally was tall, ruddy, charismatic, and distinguished looking. He wore his full head of gray hair like a crown, and he was one of those people who, unlike Nixon, looked natural and comfortable in a dark pinstriped suit, white shirt, and conservative tie, as if he'd been born wearing them. When he walked into a room, he radiated ambition, self-esteem, and power. Attention swung to his full and spontaneous smile, his booming voice, the big cigar, the firm handshake, the virile and commanding presence that signaled to everyone present—as he himself assumed—that the room was his.

His relationship with Nixon was special, even peculiar. When Connally walked into the Cabinet Room or Oval Office, Richard Nixon's eyes and spirit would seem to light up. If John Connally had been a woman, one would have assumed it was a love affair. And indeed, it was a love affair of a very different kind. The two men were psychological opposites, and these particular opposites attracted. Had Connally been president, I suspect that he would have looked into the mirror and said to himself, "Of course. And I deserve it." Nixon, I think, had quite different feelings looking in the mirror. I believe he felt self-doubt, and perhaps even a bit of self-loathing.

Through this force of personality and Nixon's own insecurities, Connally was able on a few occasions to talk the president into taking actions that were totally inconsistent with Nixon's basic philosophy. On most domestic issues, I always found Nixon moderate or centrist, as in his creation of the Environmental Protection Agency, his support of civil rights and school desegregation (despite appealing to white voters through his "Southern Strategy"), and his adoption of revenue sharing, in which federal dollars were spent by state and local governments as they saw fit. But he went totally against the grain when—at Connally's behest—he imposed wage and price controls in August 1971, and earlier that year when he used federal dollars to bail out reeling defense contractors.

It took me a while—longer than it should have—to realize that the position I held posed a threat to Connally's ego and ambitions. Word reached me through the White House grapevine that he would rant to others that he was not going to be "coordinated" by Peterson or the Council on International Economic Policy. That was not his deal with the president. Why, then, had he been so enthusiastic in proposing the Council, and later, why his enthusiasm for the Peterson Color Slide Show? My unfortunate tendency to be overly logical, innocent, and at times naive at last gave way to the reality. This was not about rational organizational structure or previous recommendations. It was about egos and power politics. As Connally himself once put it to Kissinger in a conversation, "You will be measured in this town by the enemies you destroy. The bigger they are, the bigger you will be."

Sidelined in my naïveté by the force of the Connally tsunami, the best I could do was tread water and hope to survive while I weighed my options. These came down to two—stay, or leave. In the fall of 1971, my old friend Frank Stanton of CBS tempted me with word they were considering asking me to become the network's president. It was a titillating prospect given my advertising and corporate experience. But it seemed wrong to go to Washington with all this fanfare and then leave a few months later, uprooting Sally and the kids again. I also understood payback—the seeds the White House could plant in the media about those who were disloyal or otherwise fell out of favor. So I decided to gut it out and hope for a change in the weather that might come with some life-saving assignment, or John Connally's unlikely fall from grace.

Trade War?

When the cavalry rode in, the assignment was in the unlikely form of textile policy. Nixon's narrow election over Hubert Humphrey in 1968 was accomplished in part by massive support from the textile industry. Indeed, his margin had been provided by a few textile states. The industry's financial contributions had come with the expectation of a quid pro quo—that Nixon would deliver an import quota to shore up domestic textile companies.

Three years later, he still had not delivered. It was not that he hadn't tried. Commerce Secretary Stans and Peter Flanagan, an assistant to the president, had attempted without success to negotiate quotas with the Japanese. Now, halfway through 1971, with the 1972 election looming, the textile industry had made it clear that without a quota or some other action to ease the pressure on them, the president could not count on their support.

That was where things stood when the president called to ask me to launch a new effort. "Pete, you're supposed to be a good negotiator," he said. "I want this damn textile problem solved before next year and the election. I don't give a damn what it takes. You do whatever it requires. Do you understand?"

I did, and I knew it wouldn't be easy. I was not by nature a protectionist, but at the same time did think we needed to get tougher with the Japanese. Japan's exports of manufactured goods had increased by 400 percent between 1960 and 1970; ours had risen just 110 percent.

Every comparison told a similar story. Yet endless delegations of top Japanese business leaders had told me the same sad tale, dampened with crocodile tears. "We have read your report, Mr. Peterson. But you must understand that we are a humble little country without resources trying desperately to emerge in a very competitive world economy, rather like a developing country. You must make allowances in trade and in your foreign economic policies. We humbly seek your understanding and support."

I knew this was nonsense. I had, after all, fought Japanese competition at Bell & Howell and thus encountered firsthand that country's rising economic clout. So I decided to confront them with evidence that their pleadings about "a humble little country without resources" were disingenuous and totally self-serving.

Japanese Prime Minister Eisaku Sato, a good friend of Nixon's, sent a delegation to see me from Keidanren, the major Japanese business organization. It included the heads of huge companies such as Nippon Steel and Panasonic. I greeted each of them with reminders and specific recitations of their company's competitive strengths. "Ah, Mr. Nagano," I told the man from Nippon Steel. "You are the head of the largest steel company in the world. I warmly congratulate you, sir. You have the highest labor productivity in the world in steel, the lowest unit labor costs, the most advanced automated equipment . . ."

I asked my staff to look for some added leverage in what I knew would be tough textile negotiations. After some research, one of my senior staffers, Don Webster, reported that he had good news and bad news.

"Give me the good news first," I said. "There hasn't been a lot of it."

He told me there was an obscure provision in a banking act passed in the 1930s that allowed the president to impose quotas under a simple condition. All he had to do was declare a balance of payments emergency.

"What's the bad news?"

"The provision is in an amendment to the Trading with the Enemy Act of 1918."

"Dear God," I thought, weighing the rhetorical and political impact, "do we have to call our closest ally in the Far East an enemy in order to impose textile quotas?" How would that affect Nixon's friendship with Japan and Prime Minister Sato? Still, the president had ordered me to do what it took to solve the problem.

Early in August 1971, Nixon called his top economic hands to a meeting at Camp David, the presidential retreat. I knew history was going to be made, and it was thrilling to be part of it. Once again, I gave the president and the group the good news–bad news scenario on textiles, and then spelled out a negotiating plan. He already intended to announce, on August 15, a policy change that would free the United States of its obligation to settle foreign transactions in gold—what was known as the gold standard. This was a step toward flexible exchange rates that would allow the dollar to float against foreign currencies. I suggested that when he made the announcement, he should also declare a balance of payments emergency. I would then call the Japanese ambassador and apply the leverage of that declaration to try to move beyond the fruitless discussions we had had so far. I told the president that without a deadline, the process would undoubtedly drag on and corrode relations even further. I suggested an October 15 deadline for reaching "voluntary" textile quotas, and he agreed.

The morning after the president's August 15 address on national television, I called the Japanese ambassador and relayed the message.

"Oh, Mr. Peterson, I can't believe your president would ever use the Trading with the Enemy Act against one of your closest allies," he said.

"He would certainly like not to," I replied, going over a script I had been playing in my head. "But we have been trying for years to resolve this textile issue. The president has decided it must be resolved this year. We would much prefer to do this voluntarily. In that case, you would accept voluntary restraints in some fifteen textile product categories that allow for some level of growth. Otherwise, the president will have no choice but to impose a quota with zero growth. Frankly, that is what our domestic manufacturers strongly prefer, but the president recognizes the value of our friendship with Japan."

Attorney General John Mitchell, the dour face of Nixon's law-and-order stance and his senior political lieutenant, increased the pressure when he reminded me that the textile states had been decisive in the close 1968 election and would be again in 1972. He failed to mention to me the $2 million in campaign cash that had apparently been promised in exchange for quotas. But he did mention that he would invoke the Constitution to install quotas if he had to. This was possible under the National Security clause of the Constitution.

Invoking the Trading with the Enemy Act was bad enough. Under Mitchell's tortured logic, one of twelve manufacturing jobs in the United States was in textiles. Without quotas, these jobs would be lost, endangering our economic security, which would in turn endanger our national security. It was pure protectionism, and I feared severe economic and political fallout. And it flew in the face of what I had believed was Nixon's commitment to free and open trade, making him seem hypocritical. If we could cry, "The sky is falling!" over textiles, why not set quotas on automobiles and steel as well?

I discussed these issues at length with the attorney general. When I told him we'd be laughed at on the late night shows if we imposed quotas on women's panties and brassieres on national security grounds, it brought a rare smile to his long face. "I can hear them now," I said: "'Is this really about national security, or personal security?'"

Mitchell finally relented, to my great relief. But his interest told me how tough this matter was. My plan needed to work. Otherwise, one of the other so-called solutions could create problems that would dwarf those we faced over textile imports and trade deficits.

For the next sixty days, the Japanese complained and fought, fought and complained, and complained and fought some more. In fairness, they were reeling from a triple-whammy of developments that had turned their understanding of our economic and diplomatic relationship upside down. The October 15 deadline was the third installment. Earlier, on July 15, Kissinger had visited China, signaling a new American attitude toward Japan's traditional enemy. Nixon's August 15 statement that we were closing the gold window had forced Japan to think of an upward-valued yen that would make their exports more expensive. Now, the approach of October 15 was making them contemplate restraining the exports of textiles to a 4 percent growth rate, or face zero growth quotas. These changes rocked a quarter-century of complacency, and their diplomats in Washington weren't happy. They voiced their unhappiness through the State Department. State, miffed because it had been excluded from the Camp David meeting where I laid out the quota ultimatum, took the Japanese position. I smiled when I read electronic intercepts of secret messages sent from the Japanese embassy back to Tokyo reporting the State Department's view that the president would never implement the strategy of that economic "animal," Peterson. I simply passed on these intercepts to Haldeman and asked if my instructions from the president were still the same. He always answered back, "Proceed."

October 15 dawned without word whether the Japanese would accept voluntary quotas, or force the president to use the Trading with the Enemy Act. The clock ticked through the morning and closed in on the noon deadline. Finally, at ten-thirty, the Japanese signed the voluntary restraint agreement and sent it to the White House. Nixon called me to the Oval Office shortly afterward to congratulate me. He was obviously elated. He would be able to lean on his textile manufacturer donors for contributions for the next campaign, and I was resuscitated within the White House, at least for a moment. As it turned out, it was a very brief moment.

CHAPTER 8

WASHINGTON,
ROUND TWO

Getting to Know Dr. K.

The levels of infighting and intrigue would have been unbearable had it
not been for some of the more pleasant aspects of life in Washington.
We were living in a big house with a sauna and a pool near Rock Creek
Park in the northwest section of the district. Jim, David, and Holly were
all attending Georgetown Day School, Michael was still a toddler with
an in-home nanny, and Sally and I had joined a social circuit that was
worlds apart from the partisan mind-set of the White House and its
drill-sergeant enforcer, Haldeman.

Much of this was due to my growing friendship with Henry
Kissinger. Henry had greeted me cautiously when I arrived in the White
House. As he wrote later in his memoir, *White House Years*, my job technically represented a diminution of his power. But we quickly developed
a partnership based on mutual respect and, I think, substantial affection.
And, in the end, he proved an apt student of international economics,
particularly when it intersected with critical foreign policy relationships
and issues. He eventually embraced enthusiastically the potential for integrating economic policy with foreign policy for maximum effect.

It was not inevitable that a friendship would grow out of such a relationship. But Henry's appetite for a broad range of people and opinion
matched my own. He moved easily among the pillars of the Georgetown
social circuit, named for the area of elegant old homes on the Potomac

River where many of its members lived. Henry and I were the only members of the White House staff who traveled this circuit, where we mingled with the likes of Katharine (Kay) Graham, James "Scotty" Reston of *The New York Times*, columnist brothers Stewart and Joseph Alsop, Bobby Kennedy's widow, Ethel, Washington hostess Polly Fritchey and her pundit husband, Clayton, and Joan and Tom Braden, whose careers were in the news and opinion business since Tom had left his life of intrigue in the CIA.

There were others, and most of them were Democrats. None of this mattered; Henry and his dates and Sally and I enjoyed their company; their knowledge was extensive, their opinions strong, their companionship stimulating, and we could temporarily escape the suffocating partisan and paranoid environment that Richard Nixon had created at the White House. Even at the White House, Henry moved with great confidence and verve, as on the morning he walked into the press room to ask, "Does anyone have any questions for my answers?" He was referring to the insistence on the part of some of the White House politicos that we always present the approved sound bites or talking points that made up our message of the day whether anyone had asked about it or not.

In the parlors of Georgetown and beyond, the wine and conversation flowed and we usually went home at the end of an evening feeling we knew more about the "real world" than when we arrived.

Not all of Washington was like this enlightened group. At the far end of the spectrum was the party Sally and I attended one night at the suburban Maryland home of a senior White House staffer. After dinner, the guests were all invited down to the basement recreation room. There, along with a pool table and a wet bar, our host had on proud display a dartboard whose bull's-eye contained an image of Adam Clayton Powell, the activist African-American congressman from New York. Sally, who was developing her inner bohemian after life in the Chicago suburbs and also expressing anti-establishment rebellion in Washington on several fronts, reacted furiously to this display of bigotry. "That's the *real* Southern Strategy, throw darts at blacks," she hissed. She was mad enough to walk right out. I was quietly angry and deeply embarrassed. We made our excuses and both of us left early.

On social policies, Henry and I were the odd ducks in the White

House. I found with Henry the kind of youthful rapport and friendship I had experienced in Chicago, the kind that encouraged pointed banter and took no prisoners. It was only our high level of mutual respect that let the barbs flow back and forth without drawing blood, but sometimes witnesses didn't understand that we were joking.

Henry was especially vulnerable, in my view, when it came to his reputation as a ladies' man. Between 1964, when he divorced his first wife, and 1974, when he married Nancy Maginnes, he dated many high-profile stars and starlets including Jill St. John. We often ate lunch together in the White House mess on Saturdays, and sometimes his current flame would join us. Not one to let his conquests—if indeed that's what they were—go unnoticed, he would invariably put me next to the latest bouffant, long-limbed beauty and say at some propitious moment in that gravelly, German-flavored voice that conveyed irony between the lines, "Eat your heart out, Peterson."

I liked to suggest that there might be a gap between his rhetoric and his performance. When I did, he would look at me with those baby blue eyes of his twinkling with mischief and say, "Peterson, what you would have no way of knowing, no reason to understand, is that power is the ultimate aphrodisiac." This was to become one of Henry's most enduring one-liners.

Henry wasn't the stereotypical ladies' man. He wasn't tall, dark, or handsome, and certainly not a chiseled graduate of the Charles Atlas bodybuilding school. But he was commanding, and enormously funny (and still is). He made women laugh, and when he got serious they hung on his every word, because they knew he steered the fates of nations. His use of power with women caused envy among his friends and also made him the butt of my attempts at humor. Sometimes they came off, and sometimes not.

I was the speaker at the annual black tie dinner of the Japan Society in the spring of 1972 when I tried to give Henry a little public roasting. Public speakers in the U.S. always like to lead off with a joke. I learned that night that it's a good idea to assess your audience as well.

I began with a deadpan declaration: "I am here tonight to charge the national security advisor of the United States, Dr. Henry Kissinger, with a serious abuse of power." Pause for effect. "I remind you of the

Kissinger we knew *before* he joined the Nixon administration. Did anyone ever confuse this portly, bespectacled academic with a Lothario or a Don Juan? The answer is obvious—of course not.

"Yet today, he publicly parades a bevy of Hollywood starlets like Jill St. John around the corridors of Washington. She is only one of many. What is his secret? He is obviously using the power of his office to attract them. And I believe it is time to call this what it is—I repeat: a serious abuse of power."

By now the Americans in the audience had caught on and were chuckling. The Japanese, however, were aghast. Used to deference and conformity, conditioned to avoid confrontation, they sat there fearfully stone-faced, believing that their guest speaker, this damn fool Peterson, was misusing the prestigious venue of the Japan Society to launch an attack that suggested deep divisions within the Nixon administration.

I went on. "Now, everyone knows that Henry doesn't do anything with these women." (I knew that would kill him.) Recalling that Sherman Adams, Eisenhower's chief of staff, had been fired for accepting the gift of a vicuña coat from a friend who wanted government favors for his textile business, I added, "But then, nobody ever asked if Sherman Adams had actually *worn* that vicuña coat."

Again, loud laughter from the Americans, and stony, fearful silence from the Japanese. Only when I turned to the trade topics that were the main subject of my speech did they relax in the realization that I did not intend to bring down the republic after all.

The next day, to my amazement, *The Washington Post* reprinted the toast. I dropped by Henry's office in the White House that morning, knowing that I had enhanced his reputation as a celebrity squire to the stars. He had cut out the *Post* piece and had it posted by his telephone, presumably to savor it. He got up smiling when I walked in and said, "Peterson, I didn't bring you to Washington to be your straight man." (In fact, I knew Henry loved the attention.)

Of course, Henry usually got the best of these roastings. I vividly remember once when I thought I had finally gotten the better of him. I had accepted an invitation to a special dinner and was told by the hostess that Ingrid Bergman was to be the guest of honor and I would be seated to her right. It is a fact of life that true glamour and Hollywood star power put even corporate wealth and political power in the shade. The unforgettable *For Whom the Bell Tolls*, featuring Miss Bergman and Gary Cooper against the backdrop of the Spanish Civil War, had come out when I was an impressionable seventeen and remained one of my favorite movies. I would bask in her reflected starshine. Added to the thrill was the thought, "I finally got Kissinger." I walked into his office after learning of the seating chart and said, somewhat smugly, "Well, Henry, I guess I'll be seeing you tomorrow night. By the way, where will you be sitting?"

He raised his eyebrows and gave me a look of elaborate innocence. "Why do you ask?"

"Well, I'm going to be sitting next to Ingrid and I didn't know if you were going to be at the same table or somewhere else. Maybe in another room."

He did his best to look offended. "Peterson," he said, "I'm leaving for Acapulco later on today. Why else do you think you're sitting next to Ingrid Bergman?"

I once told of Henry declining to travel because of a religious holiday. I pored over the calendars at my disposal and could not find the holiday in question. Was it Rosh Hashanah? Yom Kippur? Mystified, I finally asked him. That was when Henry told me he religiously celebrates Casanova's birthday.

We laughed a lot, and it reinforced my belief that Henry's sense of humor was and remains a rare gift. Furthermore, a shared sense of humor is clearly a great strength in a relationship.

The Connally Tsunami: Aftershock

Nixon announced temporary wage and price controls in August 1971. This was an idea the president had considered before and quickly rejected as an inflation-fighting measure, but that was before John Connally became his secretary of the treasury. I was at the Camp David meeting where Connally promoted these controls. It was about as non-market-oriented, non-Republican an idea as I could imagine. Most of us were shocked when Nixon signed on. I managed to salvage at least something from that meeting, though. My contribution was a temporary import surtax of 10 percent, aimed at moving the developed countries that were our trading partners to raise their seriously undervalued currencies and renew trade talks. The temporary surtax was the stick, the promise of removing it, the carrot. Nixon announced the surtax in the same address as the wage and price controls and the closing of the gold window. He explained that he would drop the surtax as soon as our trading partners adjusted their currencies to realistic levels and engaged in serious trade talks. This would be the first major step from fixed to floating exchange rates, a dream George Shultz and I shared with my old professor, Milton Friedman.

Milton had strong feelings about this. He had expressed them when I asked him if he thought I should take the White House job. "Absolutely not," Milton said with his usual directness. "With fixed exchange rates, that job is impossible. With floating exchange rates, it is unnecessary. At your age and stage of life, Pete, you should not take a job that is either impossible or unnecessary."

At an Oval Office meeting a few months after announcing the controls and the "temporary" import surtax, with the Vietnam War taking a toll on Nixon's popularity, Connally started talking about how well the surtax was "playing in Peoria." He argued for arbitrarily extending it during an economic policy meeting in the Oval Office, attended by the president, Connally, George Shultz, Arthur Burns, chairman of the Federal Reserve, and Paul McCracken, chairman of the president's council of economic advisors. Ordinary Americans, he said, saw it as taxing the Japanese and Germans as a way of finally getting tough with them on trade. Since it played so well politically, Connally advocated leaving the surtax in place through the 1972 election year, a year later. I was aghast. This was unabashed, unilateral protectionism, driven by pure politics. And I did not consider it a minor matter that the president would be violating what he had promised in his August 15 televised speech.

I admired Richard Nixon for his genuine intellectual curiosity and his well-trained and analytical mind. When I came on board, he told me to give him the various options we faced in a given situation and the advantages and disadvantages, costs and risks of each. He also wanted to know what critics might say about the options chosen. This time, in the face of Connally's political clout and the ease with which he could twist Nixon to his will, I decided to take the president at his word and take a stand, whatever its effects on my Washington future. It was one of those defining moments.

"Mr. President," I said, "I believe your political interests, not to mention your legacy as president, will depend heavily on your role as a global peacemaker, not as a unilateralist. The secretary's proposal suggests you violate what you said publicly last August. But setting that aside, I don't have to remind you that you are also about to build some historic new bridges to our former enemies in the form of summit meetings with China and the Soviet Union."

There was silence in the room as I continued. "What is being proposed here by Secretary Connally is, in effect, to burn bridges to our best friends while you build them to our erstwhile enemies. I believe our allies and best friends will adamantly oppose this act of unilateralism. It takes very little imagination to see how they might retaliate. They could easily impose tariffs on some of our most important exports." To my disappointment and surprise, none of my friends, with perhaps more prudence and better timing, chose to say anything.

Connally held his tongue while I spoke, but his face grew flushed with anger. The meeting ended abruptly, and Connally walked with Nixon into the Rose Garden, speaking urgently into his ear. I imagined that he was lobbying the president to fire me. I grabbed Arthur Burns, the chairman of the Federal Reserve, who shared my views, and said, "Arthur, I know what your view is, and oh, how I wish you had expressed it. But right now we have to go see Henry Kissinger." I knew Henry respected Arthur, and that his presence would give extra weight to what I had to say.

We went down the hall and found Henry in his office. I sketched Connally's proposal, and stressed that keeping the surtax for nearly another year, until after the November election, could seriously compromise the China and Soviet summits. If the summits were conducted in the context of trade wars with our allies, the president's image as a global peacemaker would suffer. I told Henry he must intervene. Arthur nodded in agreement.

I reminded Henry that a few weeks earlier, a senior deputy to

French president Georges Pompidou had come to me with a secret message. Jean Béliard, who was a friend and served in the French government, had told me that Pompidou understood our concerns about the exchange rate imbalance and was prepared to negotiate. The French might revalue the franc by 15 percent against the dollar, but only under a compromise in which they pushed the franc up by 7.5 percent and we devalued the dollar by the same percentage. I asked my friend why they didn't simply revalue the franc by 15 percent, which would produce the same result. *Mais non*, this was not about logic, but about politics, French-style. Some "political burden sharing" was required, said Béliard, because the United States was less fiscally responsible than it should have been. (When I reported this contact to Connally, his response was explicit: "Fucking French!" He said it then—and often thereafter—almost as one word.) Nevertheless, the French proposal would give the president a rationale to drop the surtax and, of course, get the major currency revaluation that we all wanted.

The scenario that I urged on Henry had its drawbacks. The president would be legally required, for example, to go to Congress for any devaluation of the dollar, which could be embarrassing domestically, which of course was part of what the French referred to as "political burden sharing." Critics would ask, "Why is the mighty dollar not that strong anymore?" Nevertheless, it was an opening that might accomplish two things—adjust the dollar against the undervalued franc and other currencies, and allow the president to keep his promise that the surtax would be temporary in order to start badly needed trade talks. I told Henry that negotiating a deal with the French was a critical step in the overall negotiation with our world trading partners and he had to move in the unaccustomed waters of exchange rates.

Within weeks, before Nixon headed off to Beijing (then Peking) for his week-long summit with Chairman Mao Tse-tung and Premier Chou En-lai, Henry had made a deal. Miraculously, it had Connally's "concurrence." Meeting with Pompidou in the Azores, Henry brokered a 16 percent French revaluation, 7.5 percent on the French side and 8.5 percent on the American. This would allow the import surtax to be lifted.

I won that battle with Connally, but he still wanted me fired. Fortunately, the election cycle provided an escape route. Early in 1972,

Commerce Secretary Maurice Stans resigned to head the finance committee for Nixon's reelection effort. Now Nixon had an out. Appointing me to Stans's old job would take me out of Connally's orbit and preserve the president's credibility with the business community, which still seemed to hold me in some regard.

Demotion by Promotion

The president did not exactly distinguish himself with grace in inviting me to join his cabinet. On February 29, the morning after he returned from his triumphant summit in China, he put it to me with all the enthusiasm of a sea captain inviting a rat to climb aboard his ship. (Even Bob Haldeman, not renowned as a master in this area, wrote in *The Haldeman Diaries* that the president's invitation was "graceless.")

The coolness of the invitation may have been Connally's influence or maybe my Georgetown "cocktail party set" connections, which I later found out bothered Nixon. He seemed almost happy to hear that the Senate confirmed me unanimously, with no debate, although my swearing-in was equally graceless—but memorable, in retrospect—for a hilarious collision of styles.

The early phone call told me the swearing-in was set for ten o'clock that morning in the Oval Office. I would have expected a little more notice before being sworn into the cabinet, which for most people is an important occasion with protocol and fanfare that you want to share with family and friends. A couple of hours doesn't cut it. The kids were already at school when the call came. I called Sally, who went rushing off to Georgetown Day School to pick up Jim, David, and Holly. Jim was fourteen then, David twelve. They both wore the long hair and grungy clothes that were the liberal fashion of the early 1970s. The same look was a virtual uniform among the protesters against the seemingly endless war in Vietnam. (My concession to that hirsute age was a daring set of sideburns that stopped at my earlobes.)

When the door to the Oval Office finally opened and Sally and the kids were ushered in, it was as if Nixon had opened the White House to a miniature delegation of his Vietnam critics. The crew-cut Haldeman took one look at the boys' long hair and had to keep himself from sneering. His look said it all: "These are not our kind of people." It turned out he was right.

The boys only looked like opponents of the administration, but Sally was another story. Her rebellious phase was in full flower. She had a different dress code than the other cabinet wives, preferring tight Pucci pants and platform shoes to matronly, knee-hiding dresses. And she plucked another page out of the antiwar stylebook by wearing her hair like the actress Jane Fonda (who that summer would make the trip to North Vietnam that gave her the nickname Hanoi Jane). Sally was also more earthy and contemporary than the other cabinet wives. These women knew it, too, as they demonstrated at a luncheon at Blair House. The hot gossip making the rounds that day was of a recent spat between Frank Sinatra and *The Washington Post*'s brassy society columnist, Maxine Cheshire. Sinatra reportedly had called her an unkind four-letter word starting with a "c." The reference was a mystery to the other cabinet wives, because they all descended on Sally as soon as she arrived to ask her what the "c" word was.

Finally, and most importantly, Sally was not reluctant to express her views of Richard Nixon. And these views were strikingly negative. Her oft-expressed contempt, which admittedly was shared by many of our friends, was, more than I realized, potential poison to my career in an administration that had more than its share of paranoid tendencies. I was to find out later that reports of her often indelicate comments filtered back to the White House from parties and dinners we attended. These reports raised questions about me and my loyalty.

Loyalty—or rather, political loyalty—was considered a prime asset in the Nixon administration. Politics drove the agenda, often at the expense of policy. Early on, when I was still an assistant to the president and technically a member of the Palace Guard, I reported every morning to the eight A.M. senior staff meeting chaired by Haldeman in the Roosevelt Room, next door to the Oval Office. The same people always sat in the same places. Henry Kissinger, George Shultz, and I lined up on one side of the table. Ehrlichman, the domestic policy advisor, press secretary Ron Ziegler, and Charles "Chuck" Colson, the president's chief counsel, sat across from us. Their titles aside, these men along with Haldeman, other than Henry, George, and me, were all political animals. They had all served as campaign advance men or other sorts of Nixon political operatives. None had much expertise, or even any history of interest, in public policy. Their priorities spoke to the great divide between winning an election and governing the country, and as the 1972 election played out, to the danger of political operatives having a monopoly on power and on the president's trust.

Haldeman had a linear, literal mind unburdened by nuance or subtlety. If Kissinger, Shultz, or I strayed too deeply into a policy discussion at one of these morning meetings, he would sometimes cut us off impatiently: "That is a matter of substance. I am not interested in that."

Ehrlichman at least had some policy interests. He was also less arrogant than Haldeman, and I felt, as Watergate unfolded, that he had been led into its lies and deceptions by others who were far more devious. But his head was undoubtedly also enmeshed in politics, as he had worked on all three of Nixon's campaigns since 1960.

Ziegler, who somewhat escaped the web of Watergate, was politically driven and fiercely loyal to Nixon, but he was not a schemer.

Among these men, Chuck Colson was in a special class. Some have called him Karl Rove's spiritual godfather, but he was actually far more of a devil than that. He was a smart and experienced lawyer and a creative and devious political operator, expert in creating and carrying out the nastiest of dirty tricks. I was always anxious about his frequent contacts with the president, because I thought Colson brought out the worst in him. Nixon had a healthy dose of deviousness himself that made him—and his paranoia—vulnerable to Colson's inspired malice.

Colson, to use an infelicitous phrase, was a "scab puller." He would get Nixon to fix on an old wound, a slight or an attack or some vulnerability. Then he would pull off the scab, producing an open, bloody wound that would need to be redressed through the use of Colson's ingenious, malicious talents of revenge and sabotage. I believe Colson was a prime co-conspirator in many of the dirty tricks that helped get Nixon in deep trouble, including organizing the White House burglary team under E. Howard Hunt infamously known as the Plumbers. Colson apparently inspired the Plumbers' caper, in which they broke into the offices of

Daniel Ellsberg's psychiatrist looking for ways to tar Ellsberg for leaking the Pentagon Papers, and later the break-in of Democratic National Committee headquarters at the Watergate complex, which led to the cover-up and ultimately to Nixon's downfall. Apparently, Colson also proposed firebombing the Brookings Institution over its criticism of Nixon, helped compose the notorious "Enemies List," and engineered the disgraceful impugning of Senator Edmund Muskie's wife that derailed Muskie's presidential campaign when he cried defending her.

Outside the scope of Watergate, but offensive nonetheless, was what he did to Arthur Burns after Arthur failed to go along with an interest rate cut the White House wanted. Arthur had recommended that the pay level for his job chairing the Federal Reserve be raised to the level of cabinet officers, not while he served but when the next Fed chair took over. Colson leaked the lie that Arthur wanted the pay raise for himself, and the newspaper coverage made Arthur look like a small person, which he certainly was not.

Colson also leaked a report that Kissinger had improperly "tilted" toward Pakistan in some diplomatic maneuvering. Henry discovered that Colson was responsible, but in discussing the leak at one of our morning meetings, Colson told Henry, "I'm standing behind you."

"I've never been so terrified in my life," Henry joked as he and I left the meeting.

"Yes," I said, "some of these guys are colleagues in the special sense that Brutus was a colleague of Caesar's."

If moving to the cabinet as Nixon's secretary of commerce removed me from the Palace Guard it also removed me from that poisonous crucible. My new position was, in their eyes, a demotion by promotion.

I left it with the impression of how few friends Nixon really had, and how the friendships he did have sometimes created complicated situations both within and outside his close circle of advisors. Once in 1971, Henry and I were working together at the Western White House in San Clemente, California. We were interrupted by a summons for me to meet with the president. Nixon was still determined to convince the Japanese to raise the value of the yen substantially. "There's a lot of pressure on us about this damn yen revaluation," Nixon told me when I reached his office. "How big a revaluation do you think we can expect?"

This was subject to ongoing negotiations, but the range was a closely held secret. Were the financial markets or currency traders to know ahead of time how much the yen might rise against the dollar, billions of dollars would be made. When the president asked the question, I noticed there was a stranger in the room.

"That's a long discussion, Mr. President," I said, using the informal code for a discussion that was, in fact, top secret. "Maybe we can pursue it at a later time when you don't have a guest."

"No, no. Go on," the president insisted without introducing his guest. It was his call, so I told him that although the Japanese had upped the yen by about 6 percent, our goal was an eventual revaluation of at least 17.5 percent. This figure was the key to pushing up the French franc and other currencies against which the dollar was overvalued.

"Who was that guy?" I asked Henry when I returned to our working session.

"Oh, that's the president's best friend, Bebe Rebozo," Henry told me, adding that Rebozo sat in on a lot of top secret discussions at the president's insistence. I thought it was odd, given the security clearance hoops we all had to jump through. I never had reason to believe Rebozo used any of this information. But it reminded us of the lack of Nixon's friendships. I think he was, at heart, a misanthrope—a rarity among politicians. He also didn't like small talk.

Bernie Sahlins had the view that Nixon was a very choreographed and un-spontaneous man. Bernie was the director of Chicago's famous Second City, the improvisational comedy sketch club that was the home of such comedic talents as Mike Nichols, Elaine May, Paul Lynde, and Charlotte Rae. I knew Second City well and Bernie was a friend.

He once told me that he had noticed that Nixon's smile seemed strangely out of sync.

To test his thesis, he compared films of people, including Nixon, telling jokes. Virtually all the others started to smile as they *began* to tell their jokes. In other words, they were anticipating the humor and enjoying it a bit themselves first. Nixon only smiled *after* he told the joke. It was as though he had to remind himself, "Oh, I told a joke. It must be time to smile." Such a lack of spontaneity, Bernie contended, was the mark of an extremely guarded person, ill at ease with himself.

Herbert Hoover, Watch Over Me

I may have been demoted in the eyes of the Palace Guard. But I was happy to put some distance between myself and the increasingly paranoid and soon to be besieged White House. If I felt slighted by being pushed out of the White House, I could respond with self-deprecating humor.

Most of us commerce secretaries have been laughably obscure, but I liked to kick off speeches by appearing to protest the notion that I had been consigned to Washington oblivion. "My predecessors," I declared, "occupied the pantheon of 'public heroes' and 'great Americans.'" Then I rattled off some of their names: William C. Redfield, Joshua W. Alexander, William F. Whiting, Charles W. Sawyer, Frederick H. Mueller. "Who can forget their stories from our history books?"

When it sank in that no one had heard of any of them, I added, "Well, we actually did have one well-known secretary of commerce in the history of America. Whether it was what he did here or afterward that made him famous I leave up to you, but here at Commerce we still refer to him as Secretary Herbert Hoover."

Outside the Washington Beltway, of course, most people considered being part of the cabinet a pretty big deal. My father was one of them. He would stop perfect strangers on the streets of Kearney and say, "My name is George Peterson. My son Peter is the first Greek cabinet officer in history. God bless America." I forgave him the small sin of selective recall in ignoring the fact that a fellow Greek, Spiro Agnew, was not only vice president but, as such, a member of the cabinet.

My new job came with some grand perquisites. I had my own chef, whose cooking was a far cry from the indifferent food offered by the White House mess. I had a limousine and driver, and Sally had a car and driver, too. And I had an office in the Commerce Building that was, by all reports, among the largest in all of official Washington. Among the first challenges I faced was where to put my desk. Maurice Stans had operated at one end, forcing his visitors to make a trek from the office door that was so long it reminded me of the Charlie Chaplin character lost and dwarfed in the grandiose surroundings of *The Great Dictator*.

To spare my visitors the extra mileage on their shoes, and psyches,

I had the desk moved to the center of the room. This, too, had its draw-backs. It was now situated near a huge and impressive fireplace where, from over the mantel, the portrait of the nation's most famous commerce secretary, Herbert Hoover, would stare down on my activities.

Hoover actually had distinguished himself in the job, and before that in getting food aid to war-torn Europe in the aftermath of World War I. But his fame, such as it was, was due to his failure as president to solve the challenge of the Great Depression of the 1930s. Working with Hoover looking over my shoulder made me shudder slightly. It reminded me how far and fast stars can fall, and I thought that might be a useful thing to remember as I went to work.

Dolphins and Baby Seals

I started out in my Commerce job by doing what any corporate CEO would do. I tried to understand the "portfolio" of the place. I quickly learned that in corporate terms, the Commerce Department is a hodge-podge, a conglomerate of many incoherent parts. It embraces the Bureau of the Census, the National Weather Service, the Bureau of Standards, the Patent and Trademark Office, the Federal Maritime Commission. Among these disparate parts was the National Oceanic and Atmospheric Administration, which concerned itself not only with the sky and sea but, as I was to soon discover, some of the creatures within. My portfolio included the regulation of matters affecting dolphins and baby seals.

This I learned on my first day on the job, when I asked my chief of staff what my first priorities should be, what issues demanded my top and urgent focus. I expected him to reel off a list including U.S. productivity in an ever more competitive world, new trade negotiations, policies on research and development. No. He told me I needed to deal with porpoises and dolphins that were getting caught in tuna fishing nets, and the practice of clubbing baby seals.

Dear God, I thought as my jaw dropped, aren't those matters for the Department of the Interior?

Alas, that was a logical thought, and logic had often not applied when the bureaucracy was pieced together. It seemed that secretaries of commerce and the interior had, over time, negotiated pieces of their respective fiefdoms. Interior got whales and other animals while dolphins and seals had gone to Commerce. Organizational coherence was not the issue. The issue was the size of one's portfolio. But now, I learned, the plights of dolphins and baby seals were generating tens of thousands of letters and phone calls to the department and the White House from Congress and activist groups. The chief of staff told me that if I didn't solve these problems I would never be able to focus on anything else.

One thing I had learned from my White House experience was a lesson that a lot of us corporate executives don't get when they take a cabinet job, and this explains why a substantial number aren't particularly successful. The politicos who worked for Nixon knew the value of photo opportunities and sound bites. The right picture and turn of phrase are powerful tools. They can dramatize and simplify the points you want to make.

And lest this be viewed as cynical, I also knew that it was important to show we understood our critics' points of view—in this case, the concern of many for the dolphins.

The problem arose when tuna fishermen discovered that tuna, porpoises, and bottlenose dolphins swam together. All they had to do was find a school of dolphins, which swim near the surface because they are air-breathing mammals, and surround them with huge purse seines to get at the tuna that swam below the surface. Untold numbers of dolphins were dying every year, drowning when they were caught and dragged in the tuna nets. (To split hairs, they didn't actually drown since their blowholes do not open underwater; rather, they asphyxiated.) Maurice Stans, unfortunately, had demonstrated only that he understood the need to improve our balance of trade by exporting more tuna. But the dolphins that were the victims of this fish harvesting had a larger political constituency that included my daughter, Holly, then seven. She thought that tuna fishermen were very mean. Whether that was true or not, the toll on the dolphins—and the political fallout—was horrendous.

Many dolphin sympathizers wanted to ban tuna fishing altogether. This was not an alternative my predecessor had considered. Nor could I, owing to our large volume of tuna exports and their contribution to the positive side of our trade balance, to say nothing of the need of tuna fishermen to make a living. But there had to be some middle ground. I asked the Bureau of Standards if anyone had ever proposed making a safer tuna net. Not recently, they said, and I asked them to investigate the possibilities. Soon, they reported several promising approaches that were underway. With that, I asked where Flipper lived.

Flipper, of course, was the lovable bottlenose dolphin made famous in a 1963 movie starring Chuck Connors and later in a television series. The image of Flipper as a sentient mammal and a friend of human beings to boot was the heart of the tuna fishing uproar. Flipper (he was actually a she, named Mitzi) lived at Sea World in San Diego, which ironically was also the home of the U.S. tuna fishing industry. Soon, I was on my way across the country for a face-to-face with the world's most famous dolphin, at which I would announce the Commerce Department's re-search program into safer tuna nets. We invited the advocacy groups and the media, and photographers couldn't get enough of the commerce sec-retary petting Flipper. Flipper did her part by dazzling them with that peculiar dolphin smile. Soon our letters and calls had flipped from nega-tive to positive, with the majority commending us for taking constructive action. What also helped was a picture shown nationwide of this capitalist Republican commerce secretary, of all people, petting Flipper. The Flip-per crisis was over for the moment, and safer nets with smaller mesh as well as safer fishing methods were eventually adopted by the industry. Today a "Dolphin Safe" label on American canned tuna signifies that the tuna were caught without harming dolphins.

That left baby seals. Here, too, my predecessor had taken a strictly commercial approach: The fur industry prized the skins of baby seals, and fur exports from the Aleutian islands of Alaska also made a positive con-tribution to our trade balance. If that meant clubbing and killing baby seals, so be it. There was also the fact that hunting seals was a traditional source of income for the island natives. But animal lovers around the world, horrified by photographs of the bloody carnage of the hunt and the sad sweet faces of the seals with their dark, appealing eyes, were outraged.

What was to be done? The hunters clubbed the seals to avoid damaging their fur. Was there, for example, a more humane way of kill-ing them?

My research into my Commerce portfolio had included briefings on the environmental movement. Rather than simply focusing on individual species, environmentalists were beginning to study ecosystems in which plants and animals coexisted and contributed to—or detracted from—one another's survival. Some environmentalists, as they looked at the maritime ecosystem, believed that feeding seals were driving certain fish species to extinction. Recalling this, I had an idea that would at least balance the carnage, and not unimportantly, take some political pressure off me.

Endangered fish versus murdered seals. I proposed a controlled five-year experiment to be monitored by a top-flight environmental advisory board. On two islands, we would prohibit the seal hunts. On two others, we would continue to issue permits to the Native American seal hunters. We enlisted the very environmental groups that were most concerned about the seals to join in the planning and monitoring of this ecosystem study during its five years.

When a junior staffer suggested that I wouldn't be at Commerce in five years, I smiled at the implied criticism. As it has turned out, international campaigns against wearing fur all but eliminated the market for sealskins. The last commercial hunt in the Aleutians took place in 1985, and today the islanders are permitted to harvest seals under controlled conditions for their meat and to use some pelts for handicrafts.

Clothes on Fire

My chief of staff had suggested a third issue that also demanded priority attention. This was the serious problem of children's clothing made from fabrics that could easily catch fire. The issue had been building since the 1940s, when there was an epidemic of serious burns to children caused by the ignition of pajamas and Gene Autry cowboy suits. Thirty years later, children were still dying when their pajamas caught fire. Several television shows in the 1960s and early 1970s dramatized these stories of tragedy and loss. Outraged consumer activists demanded a halt to sales of children's clothing made from flammable cloth.

The problem was that no one had developed fabrics that were entirely nonflammable. And the politically powerful textile industry didn't want to be told it had to lose sales or spend additional money on long-term research to guarantee a greater measure of fire safety in its clothing. The White House politicos reminded me daily of the need to keep the textile dollars rolling in to the Nixon campaign coffers. Maurice Stans had supported the domestic textile lobby, to the point that a large segment of the public believed the administration favored textile jobs over saving children's lives.

I assumed that the technology to produce more fire-resistant children's sleepwear was within reach. In the meantime, when I asked the Bureau of Standards if it had ever investigated whether there was a practical home solution to the problem that could save lives or avoid harm from burns in the short term, I was told that no one had ever asked. "I'm asking now," I said.

A staff member called me a few weeks later with exciting news. Washing clothes in a solution of borax, a common laundry product found in many homes, could render fabric impervious to fires, if only temporarily. At least I could suggest it as a stopgap while the textile industry was moving toward a permanent fix.

We now had an interesting photo opportunity. And who might best convey the impact of this story? Why not a child? Why not my own child? What could be more persuasive than a picture of Holly bravely allowing a match to be touched to her favorite doll?

"Holly, dear, how would you like to go on national television?" I asked that night when we were all around the dinner table.

"Oh, Daddy, I'd love it!"

"What is your favorite doll?"

"My Raggedy Ann doll, Daddy."

"Raggedy Ann can go on television, too," I said, but I told Holly she would have to put a lighted match to a nightgown she had put on her doll.

"Oh, Daddy, I couldn't do that."

I explained that we were going to wash Raggedy Ann in a solution that would leave her looking just the same. After the wash, Raggedy Ann wouldn't burn. And if anything did happen, I would replace her doll with *two* new ones. That bit of assurance and bribery, plus the lure of appearing on national television, won the day.

Soon we assembled at the Commerce Building in front of about a hundred reporters and photographers from the national press. Holly and I went through our drill. I explained that the Bureau of Standards had identified a washing solution that would make fabrics fire-resistant in the short term. "My daughter Holly will demonstrate with her favorite doll," I said as I struck a match and handed it to her.

The audience gasped when she held the burning match against Raggedy Ann. The flame danced against the fabric of the doll—and went out. There was a palpable sigh of relief from the crowd. The story made the national network news that night, and most major papers the next day. The attention served notice on the textile industry that it could no longer put off developing fire-resistant fabrics, and at the same time, it got me out of my political hot spot. Later that year, the Consumer Product Safety Commission adopted minimum flammability standards for children's sleepwear that reduced the number of burning deaths from an average of sixty a year to fewer than four.

The Watergate Mind

The move to Commerce from the White House had put some distance between me and the Palace Guard. I welcomed this distance, but I quickly learned that the White House politicos expected cabinet officers to be obedient to their commands. As the 1972 campaign geared up, Chuck Colson was the most demanding, often because he had played to the president's paranoia.

I had not been at Commerce long before I received a typical Colson phone call. He told me he was sending a network television crew to tape me, and a sound bite he wanted me to use: "George Meany ought to know about dictatorships. He runs one of the biggest dictatorships in the world."

George Meany was the longtime head of the AFL-CIO, the umbrella organization of the nation's largest labor unions. He was a powerful force, and most presidents, if they did not court Meany, at least tried to give the impression they would work with him. I wondered why Colson wanted the administration to throw down the gauntlet, and asked him what could justify my making such a toxic comment.

Surely I knew that Meany had called the president a dictator, he said.

I had heard nothing of the kind. Neither had my deputy, Jim Lynn. Further, Meany was vice chairman of the Commission on Productivity, which I chaired. I desperately needed labor's help on a broad range of issues, and I wasn't about to insult Meany based on hearsay from Chuck Colson. I knew how he operated.

Colson said Meany had called Nixon a dictator in testimony at a congressional hearing. I told Colson I would call him back. Jim Lynn and I sat down to review the transcript. We quickly discovered that what Meany had actually said was that some dictators in South America had at one time or another installed wage and price controls. Many pages later, he pointed out that Nixon had installed wage and price controls. Only by the most tortured inference had he suggested Nixon was a dictator.

I called Colson back and told him it was foolhardy to insult Meany on such flimsy grounds, and that I wasn't going to do it.

He snapped back in his most arrogant voice, "Do you understand that the president of the United States is ordering you to make this statement?"

"No, Colson," I responded, "all I understand is that you are telling me the president is ordering me. I would be happy to talk with the president right now about why this is such a bad idea, and certainly not in his, or my, best interest."

The president never called.

Months later, I was to discover that Colson had been a leading co-conspirator in pushing me out of the Nixon administration. What an unforeseen blessing that turned out to be . . .

To my complete surprise, he recently wrote me a generous letter commending the work of my new foundation.

CHAPTER 9

WASHINGTON,
ROUND THREE

Negotiating to Negotiate

After Nixon returned from his groundbreaking trip to China, he turned his attention to the upcoming Moscow summit, scheduled for the end of May 1972. Few presidents manage one major summit in a year; Nixon was looking to complete two within four months. He badly wanted the Moscow meeting to be perceived as a success, knowing that it would be a big boost in his campaign for reelection.

The stakes were high. The United States and the Soviet Union had glared at each other across a great divide for over a quarter of a century, since World War II ended, and with it their alliance of necessity against Nazi Germany and Imperial Japan. Since then, they had been rattling nuclear sabers at each other. No American president had visited the Soviet Union in that time. We were still faced off in Southeast Asia, where the Soviets were selling weapons to North Vietnam, and over the vassal states of Eastern Europe, cowering unhappily in the Soviet shadow.

But the world had come a long way since Nikita Khrushchev had said to the West, "We will bury you." Now both sides were beginning to see the limits of Cold War confrontation, and thinking of a framework for cooperation that might slow down the arms race.

Commercial ties could be a big part of any movement to normalize relations. So for me, the summit represented an opportunity to link economic and foreign policy on a grand scale. If commerce could be used in the service of limiting nuclear weapons and ratcheting down the threat of the Cold War, what an accomplishment that would be!

But first, I had to get invited to the party, and two eight-hundred-pound gorillas were in line ahead of me. John Connally, at Treasury, and Bill Rogers, at State, headed much higher-profile departments and had the inside track to lead the economic negotiations.

I knew that Connally was considering stepping down to chair Democrats for Nixon, a prelude to his own future presidential bid (as a Republican). Later, when Agnew was forced to resign, word around the White House was that Nixon favored appointing Connally to replace him as vice president, but it wasn't possible politically. In any case, Connally's prospective move to the campaign would open the door to a new Treasury appointment, and that would be George Shultz. I felt my old friend George might applaud my appointment as a chief U.S.-Soviet economic negotiator. And whether that scenario played out or not, I knew Henry Kissinger would resist Connally's throwing his weight around in Henry's Russian china shop, and Henry might have the clout to bring about my appointment.

Bill Rogers was a different story. He was an old, favored, and faithful Nixon friend going back to the days of the candidate's 1952 "Checkers" speech, which saved Nixon's place on the ticket with Eisenhower after he was accused of misspending campaign funds. Bill was a decent man with good judgment, but he lacked Henry's intensity and depth of knowledge. Henry felt competitive with Bill, as do many national security advisors with their secretaries of state, but he needn't have bothered. Henry's office was close to the Oval Office, and he and Nixon usually spoke several times a day. The result was that the two of them had driven the diplomacy leading to the China summit, and were doing the same in the run-up to the Soviet summit, leaving Bill Rogers pacing on the sidelines.

These tangled plot lines gave me the opening that I wanted.

As the summit approached, Nixon came under pressure from various domestic interests to persuade the Soviets to buy more U.S. exports. This would mean offering them export subsidies and financing designed to increase agricultural exports. But this scenario was based on favorable assumptions about Soviet economic strength that I wasn't at all sure were true. I decided to look hard at the USSR's economic strengths, needs, and vulnerabilities in a study similar to the original Peterson White House Report.

The results were startling, and contrarian. Conventional wisdom, driven in part by industrial interests vested in military spending, said that the USSR was an economic powerhouse. But my figures exposed a Soviet economy that was deeply troubled, and destined to sink further in the competitive global economy that was emerging. The evidence was overwhelming and consistent. In thirty-five industrial categories, they were competitive in only one—heavy equipment. Manufactured goods that they did export went to their captive states in Eastern Europe, which had no money and no real choice except to "buy Soviet." And in agriculture, the inherent inefficiencies of collective farming left them with massive shortfalls in their food production.

The Soviet Union did have some comparative advantages. They had huge raw material and energy resources, particularly oil and gas. But they faced roadblocks here as well. Developing these often remote resources took money and expertise, and the Soviets were short on both when it came to things like drilling in the frozen tundra of Siberia and building the infrastructure to pipe the oil out.

The bottom line was that we did not need to subsidize exports to the Soviets. Quite the contrary. They needed us far more than we needed them. Additionally, our potential trade with the Soviets was virtually petty cash against the overall size of the U.S. economy.

Nixon loved this kind of strategic and contrarian analysis. So, importantly, did Henry Kissinger. I may have been exiled from the White House to Commerce and photo ops with Flipper, but Henry wanted me back on his team to explore the use of economic policy to achieve diplomatic goals. Knowing that the Soviet economy was uncompetitive and needed U.S. exports gave us a lever for pressuring the Soviets to cooperate on major issues such as the Strategic Arms Limitation Talks (SALT) and Vietnam. The concept was called "linkage," and "mutual vested interests." We knew, of course, that the linkage would have to be implicit. Allowing the Soviets to maintain the illusion of economic parity would keep them from feeling blackmailed and reacting out of humiliation. But as a practical matter, it would be clear that sustainable progress on the economic front would need to be matched by diplomatic progress.

I discussed these matters with Nixon in a rare private meeting in his EOB offices. The media were expecting a commercial deal to emerge from the president's Vietnam summit talks with Leonid Brezhnev, who as general secretary of the Communist Party was the de facto Soviet leader, but the three of us knew better. Rather, the president and Kissinger needed to make progress in the arms limitation talks. A comprehensive trade agreement was part of that linkage, all feeding an improvement in general bilateral relations and a softening of hostilities that would mean the beginnings of détente, a word that had not yet made the leap from diplomatic lexicon to the front page.

After we met, Henry called to say that Nixon had decided to place me at the head of the U.S. delegation of the U.S.-Soviet Joint Commercial Commission. I was elated. The Commerce Department, normally considered a second-tier player in the cabinet, would have a chance to help build the first real economic ties between the Cold War enemies.

First Steps with the Soviets

Talks began in advance of the summit on the off chance we could quickly hammer out something that would benefit both sides. My counterpart was Nikolai S. Patolichev, the Soviet minister of foreign trade. He came to Washington with a delegation and we prepared to lay out our talking points. But first, with the help of Jack Valenti, head of the Motion Picture Association of America, our delegation joined the Soviet side at a private viewing of *The Russians Are Coming,* a good-hearted comedy about a Soviet submarine beached off the New England coast. I wanted to create a friendly atmosphere to show our guests we were serious about détente.

In the same vein, I invited Patolichev and the Soviet ambassador to Washington, Anatoly Dobrynin, and their wives to a dinner at our home. We were all supposed to meet with the president the next day.

But before the night was over, I worried the Soviets were going to give Nixon the cold shoulder and maybe even call off the summit. Late that afternoon, Kissinger called me to the White House to share a piece of top secret information. The United States believed the flow of Soviet weapons and matériel to the North Vietnamese was one of the main reasons the Vietnam War was stretching on with no end in sight. To cut off that arms flow, Nixon, with John Connally's strong support, had decided to mine the North Vietnamese harbor at Haiphong, which was the port of entry for these shipments. The president was going on television to announce the move at nine o'clock that night.

That would not make the after-dinner cognac go down well, I thought. How was I going to handle this bombshell? I decided to do it directly, in keeping with the cordial but direct relationship I was developing with Patolichev in our brief time together. We were in the middle of dinner when I told him and Dobrynin I had learned some surprising news, and that I wanted them to hear it at the same time as the American public. Then I brought a TV set to the dining table.

The two men sat stone-faced as they watched the president. The dinner broke up soon afterward, and they disappeared in a limousine I assumed was heading to the Soviet embassy where Moscow would tell them what to do. Kissinger arrived at my house after they left. "What did they say? How did they react?" he asked, more anxious than I had ever seen him. "They were like statues. It was impossible to tell," I said.

Henry was still anxious the next morning. He started calling almost an hour before the scheduled ten o'clock meeting with the president to see if I had heard anything from Patolichev. Finally, about nine-forty, the phone rang with news that Patolichev and Dobrynin were in a car and headed for my office. They arrived, and I escorted them to the White House, where the meeting with Nixon, Kissinger, and myself went on as scheduled. As did Nixon's Moscow summit.

By design, no trade agreement emerged from Nixon's week in Moscow. But the U.S.-Soviet Joint Commercial Commission was announced as the summit was winding down on May 26. It signaled a determination on both sides to forge a new commercial relationship. But it was dwarfed by more important news: the signing by Nixon and Brezhnev of the first strategic arms limitation agreement between the two powers. The press coverage suggested the Soviets were disappointed not to have signed a trade agreement at the summit, but the complex and hard-nosed talks to come proved the benefit of working with time on our side.

Preparations

The Joint Commercial Commission was to convene in Moscow in late July. As the time approached, I had the advantage of being assisted by a negotiating dream team. It included my deputy at Commerce, Jim Lynn, and Helmut "Hal" Sonnenfeldt, one of Henry Kissinger's top aides.

It seemed to me that we were moving from confronting our most powerful adversary to building a framework for cooperation. But commercial conflicts were inevitable, and no process existed for resolving them. The Soviet Union, since it imagined it was leading a worldwide alternative to Western-style democratic capitalism, did not participate in any of the conventional multilateral institutions by which other nations had agreed on how to settle arguments among themselves. I saw my first job as creating an agreed international arbitration structure.

Once we hammered together this vital arbitration structure, I hoped to find agreement on all the other elements of a constructive economic relationship. The trade agreement needed to be comprehensive. That was the only way we would avoid a breakdown over single issues. The commercial issues facing us were many: Most Favored Nation status giving the Soviets the same tariff advantages as our other trading partners; export-import credits to help finance sales; maritime agreements governing whose ships could carry goods between our nations and even who could load and unload them; and patent and copyright agreements that protected intellectual property (mostly ours) from theft. At the heart of all of this, and potentially the biggest sticking point, was an issue left over from World War II, when the United States had helped our allies, including the Soviet Union, with billions of dollars' worth of food and war supplies under the Lend-Lease Act. Our other allies had made payments against these lease loans, but the Soviets had paid nothing.

Well before we left for Moscow, we received stark evidence that the Soviets were able negotiators. Nor were they above employing devious tactics to achieve their goals. Bad weather and their systemic agricultural inefficiency had left them with a desperate shortage of wheat and other grains. We were the only country with the grain reserves large enough to fill their needs. It was a seller's market, which should have resulted in a good and profitable deal for the United States even with the export subsidies that helped finance sales of some U.S. grain to foreign buyers. Indeed, the Soviet contact who approached me said they needed an amount of grain that was well within the export credit budget set aside for subsidies.

The problem was, the Soviet grain buyers were secretly talking to a variety of U.S. grain suppliers. Their real requirement was four times the figure we in the Commerce Department had been given, and the only Americans who knew the real requirement were in the Department of Agriculture under Earl Butz. Butz had apparently decided a really big deal that was good for the farm states would also be good for Nixon's reelection prospects. The result was a $750 million deal that sent a quarter of the U.S. wheat crop and additional tons of other grains to the Soviet Union but busted the export credit budget. It came to be known as the "Great Grain Robbery," and sent American grain prices sky-high for the next two years. In other words, we were paying the Soviets many millions of dollars to take grain they could not get anywhere else.

I managed to salvage one aspect of the grain deal. Maritime practice required that one-third of any shipments must be made by U.S. union crews, including the loading and off-loading. When Ron Carey, the reformist head of the anti-Communist Longshoreman's Union, asked what help I needed with the "Cummies," as he pronounced it, I made a marriage of convenience. With the longshoremen poised to strike against "Cummy" trade, I told the Soviets we had no intention of piling government shipping subsidies on top of the excessive grain export subsidies. In fact, their shipping rates would be at a premium, 10 percent above the market rate.

Dobrynin ran screaming to Kissinger with their complaints. But I had already warned Henry of the dangers of being seen as chumps. Fair play to both sides had to be a byword of our Soviet negotiations. Otherwise, the large contingent of foreign policy conservatives in the

Democratically controlled Congress, led by Washington state's Henry "Scoop" Jackson in the Senate, would wreak vengeance on the president's grand plans.

Nixon announced the grain deal on July 8, 1972, two weeks before our delegation departed for Moscow.

Before we left, he summoned me to the Western White House in San Clemente for further instructions. The first was that we keep "the sensitive stuff" within the delegation leadership, meaning Jim Lynn, Hal Sonnenfeldt, and myself, and we were to communicate only through CIA back channels directly to him and Kissinger. This meant keeping the State Department—"You know, Pete, the types that send all those damn memos to Rogers," was the way the president put it—out of the loop of the real negotiations. This was an exclusion Rogers did not deserve. We would also be treating our State and Treasury Department colleagues on the Moscow trip shabbily, making excuses as we sneaked off to make secure communications or have "important" secret meetings among just the three of us.

The president also asked that I not announce or confirm any new commercial deals of any kind while I was in Moscow, saying that to do so would be "premature." This was to be part of our strategy in any case, but it also made sense that the president and Kissinger be allowed to release the good news as positive political developments took place and, of course, to use the economic leverage to achieve foreign policy goals.

Finally—and this he left to Kissinger to convey to me—we were to pander to the Cuban exile lobby per Nixon's pal Bebe Rebozo. No Soviet ships that had stopped in Cuba could be used to ship grain to Russia. "But Henry," I said, "obviously the Soviets want to be efficient. They expect to drop off exports to Cuba and then come to the United States to pick up the grain in those same ships." I was incredulous that we would ask them to send empty ships back across the Atlantic from Cuba, passing other empty ships coming here to pick up grain.

"You're not hearing me, Pete," he said. "This is a presidential order."

It was with this added baggage that I left for Moscow on July 19, 1972.

Wedding day photo in 1923
of Georgios Petropoulos
(George Peterson)
and Venetia Papapavlou
(Venet Paul).
My parents were married
for sixty-three years.
Peter G. Peterson

My parents on their honeymoon
in Colorado.
Peter G. Peterson

"Little Petie" in 1927.
(Those hose and shoes
were traditional Greek dress.)
Peter G. Peterson

With my baby sister, Elaine, whose
sudden death at age one
caused so much heartache.
Peter G. Peterson

Can you fault my lack of
enthusiasm for wearing
this traditional Greek outfit?
My brother, John, is on the left.
Peter G. Peterson

On the occasion of my eightieth birthday. How is it that all of my nine grand-
children (Jack, Xander, Beau, Drew, Steven, Peter Cary, Alexandra, Eliza and
Chloe) turned out to be so good looking?
Peter G. Peterson

My golfing sons and I attempt—and fail—to master Augusta National.
Peter G. Peterson

Introducing my daughter to
China on a Council on
Foreign Relations trip
in 1993.
Peter G. Peterson

My son John:
by unanimous vote,
the mayor of Cedars School.
Peter G. Peterson

My mother, during the happy times, with her two sons.
Peter G. Peterson

My wife Joan Ganz Cooney and two of her friends, Elmo and Grover.
Peter G. Peterson

The Junior Chamber of Commerce in 1961 with the ten outstanding men
under the age of thirty-five. I shared the stage with Ted Sorensen,
President Kennedy's gifted assistant and speechwriter; Harold Brown,
former Secretary of Defense; and astronaut Gus Grissom.
United States Junior Chamber

The president seems to be listening.
Official White House Photo

The president meets the Peterson hippies at my swearing-in as
Secretary of Commerce in 1972.
Sunday World-Herald Magazine of the Midlands (May 14, 1972)

Flipper: I was happy to find a dolphin rock star while swimming with the Nixon Palace Guard sharks.

Peter G. Peterson

Communist Trade Minister Patolichev and the American capitalist Commerce Secretary enjoying Czarist elegance.

Nation's Business (November 1972)

General Secretary Leonid Brezhnev listens to the Peterson Version
of the new U.S.-Soviet relationship.
Council on Foreign Relations

Camp David, August 15, 1971: The meeting that changed the dollar
forever—and closed the gold window.
Official White House Photo

Was I avoiding a handshake with Yasir Arafat?
Council on Foreign Relations

Fidel: Not a man of few words!
Council on Foreign Relations

Nelson Rockefeller and me in Kazak dress, with President Nazarbayev
of Kazakhstan in 1997.
Council on Foreign Relations

A small step forward, but the Berlin Wall and Mr. Gorbachev
were still standing.
Council on Foreign Relations

Kicking off The Concord Coalition in 1992, with former senators
Warren Rudman and Paul Tsongas.
Council on Foreign Relations

In the White House in 1986. Even though I shared with him
my concerns about growing budget and trade deficits,
he was charming.
Official White House Photo

Literally building the Council on Foreign Relations with the Kofi Annans,
Les Gelb, Henry Kissinger, David Rockefeller, and Cyrus Vance.
Council on Foreign Relations

I personify obsession.
Peter G. Peterson

He can be a good listener too.
Peter G. Peterson

At a White House dinner in 2006: the Bushes, Kofi Annans,
and the Petersons.
Official White House Photo

After a serious talk about Third World debt, Bono and Peterson
decide to have a little fun.
Peter G. Peterson

How can you not look up to Paul Volcker?
Peter G. Peterson

Christmas 2007: CEO Steve Schwarzman mentoring Blackstone's version of a Santa Claus.
Peter G. Peterson

The Manipulative Armand Hammer

Sally and the kids had preceded me across the ocean. They were in Marrakech, Morocco, gaining from that ancient and exotic city an introduction to the charms and rich culture of North Africa and the Middle East. I was due to stop there and spend a few hours with them. Then Sally and I were to head on to Moscow while the kids returned home with our cousin Anastasia.

But the prospect of a pleasant family interlude went out the window as soon as my plane landed in Marrakech. A diplomatic messenger told me that Armand Hammer, the CEO of Occidental Petroleum, was flying from London to Morocco expressly to see me. Hammer, the son of a Russian immigrant, was then seventy-four, a global deal maker and art collector who was legendary for his relationships with Soviet leaders dating back to Lenin. He knew his way around the Soviet system, having gone to Russia as a young man in 1920 to deal with his father's business, a chemical and drug company. He was widely rumored to have been a Communist, and he certainly used whatever ties he had to further Occidental's business, whether those ties were in the Kremlin or the White House.

I interrupted a reception with the senior Moroccan ministers to meet with Hammer. I took Jim Lynn and Hal Sonnenfeldt along as witnesses since another of the rumors about Hammer was that he was not to be trusted. Money and flamboyance gave him his access to power, not a dedication to the public good.

He had wispy hair, a hawkish face, and wary eyes, but what he told us seemed innocuous. He was going to be meeting with the press in London to announce that he was negotiating with the Soviets on a phosphate deal. This wasn't news; other private companies were also conferring with the Soviets on deals. I wondered why he had come all this way to impart what amounted to trivia. According to one theory, it was possible that he just wanted to confirm his status as a world traveler with White House clout.

Our delegation left for Moscow soon afterward. When we arrived we were greeted with all the bells and whistles. A military band played "The Star-Spangled Banner," a red carpet awaited us as we stepped off the stairs from the presidential airplane painted with the Stars-and-Stripes, and Patolichev and other high-level officials were on hand. It was a scene that would have made my parents proud; I could almost hear my father quietly singing "God Bless America." The press *was* there, and their first questions were not about our expectations for the U.S.-Soviet trade talks but about the huge "$20 billion phosphate deal" Armand Hammer had just announced in London. Suddenly, I understood the disingenuous purpose of Hammer's urgent trip; namely, to get me to publicly support his so-called deal. He never told us of this London announcement.

Nixon's words echoed in my ears: "No new deals. It is premature." I told the press that I understood that Hammer was negotiating, but it would be "premature to consider this a commercial deal. It is an understanding to explore the possibility of doing a variety of deals." This took the reporters by complete surprise.

The trip from Sheremetyevo Airport to the U.S. embassy in Moscow took less than an hour, but when we got there I was greeted with the news that Occidental's stock had taken a 20 percent hit, with volume so heavy that trading had to be halted.

It turned out that Hammer had been using the phosphate negotiation to talk the stock up for several days. After it fell, Hammer rushed to the White House to rant to the president about the millions of dollars in shareholder value I had recklessly destroyed. Only later, during the Watergate investigation, did I learn that Hammer had made an illegal $54,000 contribution to Nixon's reelection campaign. Nixon didn't tell Hammer that I had been following his precise personal orders not to confirm reports of any Soviet commercial deals. In the words of one of my White House colleagues, "Pete, I hope you are not overly surprised or disappointed. It's not the president's style to support a staff member if a big political contribution might be at stake."

Moscow Moments

The days in Moscow were fascinating, tough, and revealing of the Soviets' deep strain of paranoia. Hal Sonnenfeldt had told us that we should assume that everything outside the secure communications area at the embassy was being recorded on audio or video or both.

I decided to use this information to engineer some relief from the heavy, sausage-laden Russian breakfasts that, combined with a lack of exercise, were not treating me kindly. I was already at 220 pounds, and I didn't want to leave Russia looking like a taller version of Nikita Khrushchev.

One morning at a dacha outside Moscow, I said to Jim Lynn, enunciating clearly for the hidden microphones, "I don't know about you, but I'd just love a bowl of fresh red raspberries." When we reached our bedrooms during a break in the proceedings, we both found bowls brimming with red raspberries.

We used the knowledge that we were monitored to good negotiating ends as well. One major sticking point was the interest rate the Soviets would pay on the Lend-Lease debts. Interest aside, the two sides were far apart on what was owed. We contended that our aid to the Soviets during the war amounted to $2.6 billion. We had dropped the amount we would accept to $800 million, but the Soviets had to be dragged kicking and screaming just to get them to $300 million. Leonid Brezhnev wagged an angry finger in my face as he told me Americans did not understand that the Soviets had paid not just with rubles but with the far more precious blood of 23 million Russians to defeat the Axis. What was more, interest payments were a capitalist invention that was toxic to all true-blooded Communists.

I decided to put three different and inflated interest figures, ranging from low to high, into separate computer printouts. The highest interest rate I marked "Peterson proposal," the middle "Kissinger authority," the lowest "presidential authority." Then I left all three printouts in my briefcase in my bedroom and suggested that Jim Lynn join me in a walk around the dacha for a little exercise. When we got back we saw the telltale signs—briefed to us by the CIA—that my briefcase had been opened. Much later, when the Lend-Lease agreement finally was reached, we got the interest rate we wanted, and the Soviets mistakenly thought they got a bargain rate lower than Kissinger or I preferred.

Certain other Soviet negotiating habits had to be confronted. One was the Soviet delegation's tendency to lay out the party mantra in endless rhetorical overtures and ideological statements and then start the real talks with a cleared throat and the word "Adnakah," Russian for "however." This was unproductive, and ultimately boring. Finally, I told Patolichev that I would agree up front to everything he had said prior to "Adnakah" if he would stipulate that the real negotiations process began just afterward.

Outside the negotiations, I confirmed with anecdotal evidence the statistics I had developed earlier about the Soviets' lack of productivity, competitiveness, and innovation. The consumer products I knew best were motion picture cameras like those we had produced at Bell & Howell. I visited several Moscow camera shops to make comparisons, and what I saw stunned me. Their models were at least two generations old and would have been impossible to sell in any competitive market. Not only that, but no money was being invested in research and development. This was clear because the cameras I saw had stolen Bell & Howell's old designs and patents.

During the trip, I gained other anecdotal evidence that the Soviet economy was structurally flawed and uncompetitive, a far cry from an economic superpower. I knew that Soviet agriculture consumed enormous resources, especially investment in farm equipment, but tellingly, their agricultural productivity was only 9 percent of ours.

One night at dinner, I sat next to a farm official who was both informed and drunk, having tossed down several too many vodkas. When I told him I had seen Soviet farm equipment sitting in the fields that looked as if it might be "underused," as I gently tried to put it, he produced a stark critique of Communism that would have made any capitalist proud.

As he sloshed more vodka into his glass, he said he had visited the American farm belt. There in the Iowa cornfield he had seen machinery working for hours on end—something Soviet farmers did not do because they could not own land and so had little stake in the productivity of the land they farmed. As far as farm machinery went, Soviet farmers didn't own that either. It could work or not; if not, they didn't try to make it work. They just went home for the day. And there was no dealer organization whose future sales depended on reliability and service, so no one had a stake in keeping the customers, i.e., the farmers, happy. Further, one Soviet ministry was in charge of producing farm equipment, but another ministry was responsible for parts. So farm machinery and its upkeep were not tied to each other, nor to any productivity they could generate in the food supply. These sclerotic arrangements were also tied to a chaotic distribution system, with the result that millions of tons of food products were routinely left rotting in the fields.

Maybe it was the vodka that made my friend speak so candidly. But he confirmed what I already believed—state planning was no match for a competitive, dynamic, fast-moving, innovative, globalized, and market-based economy.

Vodka was so ubiquitous that it seemed to be a component of the Russian character. It not only loosened tongues; it brought out jokes among people whose warm and self-deprecating humor was almost always present. The mayor of Saint Petersburg (then called Leningrad) gave our delegation a lavish lunch one day, during which he downed so much vodka it was hard to believe he could function at all. At the end, he excused himself, saying he had to make a television lecture. "On what subject?" I asked.

"On the great dangers of alcoholism," he answered with a huge burst of laughter.

Russian hospitality included closing the magnificent Hermitage museum in Saint Petersburg on a Sunday for an exclusive tour by our delegation. Its collection was magnificent, traditional and classical. However, they were less eager to show off art outside the mainstream that might be viewed as counterrevolutionary. I had started to collect modern art, and wanted to see a collection of works by the Russian-born painter Wassily Kandinsky in Moscow. But Soviet orthodoxy reviled abstract Russian painters as "revisionists" and refused them any spot in the Soviet art pantheon. The authorities would certainly not lend Kandinsky's works the credibility of being seen by an American diplomat. That was the one, and actually only, request we were denied.

Near the end of our negotiations, we met with Brezhnev at his summer home on the Black Sea near Yalta. It was a handsome place with an Olympic-size swimming pool (by contrast, the pool at Camp David is only twenty feet or so long) that he proclaimed was the "only one like it in the world," both an indoor and an outdoor pool. This was accomplished by massive glass doors, perhaps twenty feet high, that disappeared into the walls at the touch of a button. This struck me as a very capitalist-like swimming pool.

It was here that Brezhnev gave me his finger-wagging lecture about Soviet sacrifice and interest rates. Here, too, he talked excitedly about the Siberian oil and gas development deals that were possible once our commercial ties solidified. This, in effect, told me what I had suspected all along—economically speaking, the Soviets indeed needed us far more than we needed them.

Heading home after our visit to Brezhnev's summer home, our delegation made a stop in Warsaw, Poland. There we found strong differences from what we had experienced in Russia. Poles have always loved their freedom, but for much of their history have suffered from geography—being squeezed between Germany and Russia. The end of World War II freed them from Nazi domination, but the Soviets moved right in and put their boots on Poland's neck. For the long duration of the Cold War, Poles looked longingly to the West. They showed our group this longing in the subtlest of ways, but the signals resonated. In contrast with the Russians who told us ad nauseam that their coffee, tea, and soft drinks were superior to any in the world (as a result of their superior water), the Poles greeted us with—among other offerings— king-size bottles of Coca-Cola. Later, at the dinner reception where we had the customary exchange of gifts, I received a large, modern, avant-garde painting by a Polish artist. I don't know how they had learned of my art experience in Moscow, but they were saying that in Poland art, like so many other things, was not governed by rigid ideology. In other words, "We really are different from those guys."

Landing back in Washington, I knew we had made great progress in our talks. The public would not know the full extent of that progress for a few months, however. In fact, we were greeted on returning by an editorial in *The New York Times* headlined "Failure of a Mission." But as I explained in a forty-two-page briefing document I forwarded to Nixon and Kissinger in San Clemente, and later in person at the Western White House, agreement was firmly within reach on every issue.

Henry had dinner at our house one fall night after he returned to Washington from a meeting with Brezhnev where much of the agenda was about economic matters. He confessed with a smile that he would henceforth not refer to commercial matters as "minor."

Agreement!

Negotiations with the Soviets were swiftly concluded in Washington. We resolved the final issue, the Lend-Lease interest payment, one night in October 1972, and the White House could announce the entire commercial package on a timetable conveniently prior to the election.

I didn't know it at the time, but I still had one unpleasant duty to perform. General Alexander Haig had been delegated by the army to the National Security Council as its senior military advisor, and quickly became one of Kissinger's chief deputies. Haig called with an urgent message the night we reached agreement. He told me that I would now need to explain to Secretary of State Rogers that I had overstepped my bounds by mistakenly and presumptuously handling the Lend-Lease negotiations, which were properly the province of the State Department.

"But Al, that's not true," I said. "You know that I acted on explicit orders from the president and Kissinger."

But he had his orders. "Pete," he said, "we deeply appreciate all you have done and the president wants you to do this one thing more. Remember, the president knew nothing about this. All this was at your own initiative."

Devious did not begin to cover it. I really liked and respected Bill Rogers and had no interest in diminishing him. He had suffered enough of that at the hands of his old friend Richard Nixon and Henry Kissinger. Furthermore, a secretary of state being diminished by a commerce secretary is more humiliation than anyone should endure. But I called Bill Rogers and asked to see him. When we met, I apologized profusely, confessing that it was outrageous that a mere commerce secretary would have had such cheek. I told him I had become so wrapped up in the whole complex process, and so anxious to make a deal, that I had overstepped my authority.

But I had a partial solution. I suggested that we sign the overall agreement at the State Department, with Rogers acting as the chair of the meeting between me and Patolichev. I also suggested that Rogers announce the agreement in front of television cameras at the White House, signaling its importance, and then leave me to answer questions. Bill knew he didn't know the details well enough to explain them to the press, and I was sure he knew he had been frozen out of the negotiations. He also knew certain disingenuous aspects of the Nixon White House were by then part of the job description. But Bill was a decent and honorable man, and he agreed. And who in Washington doesn't like being on television announcing a successful negotiation?

Al was delighted at the result. He said, "Peterson, you have a real future in this town." That did not turn out to be the case.

CHAPTER 10

WASHINGTON, ROUND FOUR (AND OUT)

Strange Victory

The morning after Richard Nixon's historic landslide reelection victory in 1972, the members of the cabinet were summoned to the White House. I assumed, as did the other secretaries, that the president wanted us to share in the celebration. Perhaps he would spell out his vision for what he wanted to accomplish in the second term after the significant achievements of the first.

But soon after we were ushered into the Cabinet Room, I saw Nixon in a pose I recognized. He was slouched as he walked in, his shoulders hunched, his neck thrust forward so that he seemed to be looking out from a dark corner. This was almost always a bad sign.

When we all sat down, the president delivered a brooding monologue, including the observation that this second term would not be like Disraeli's, the British prime minister who served in 1868 and again from 1874 to 1880. It was impossible to know precisely what he meant, for that second term had advanced equality in England and produced treaties reshaping Eastern Europe. What was disorienting was that a day after whipping George McGovern by 18 million popular votes and 520 electoral votes versus 17, the president was in a dark mood when one would have obviously expected just the opposite. Why wasn't he giddy with happiness, especially since this would be his last election and all around him at the table were some of his oldest and most loyal friends and supporters hoping to uncork some champagne and raise a glass to his success?

As this sober so-called celebration—no champagne, no toasts to the future of a winning team—started to break up, Haldeman told us all to wait. He then rushed after the president as he retreated, still slumped, into the Oval Office. Moments later, Haldeman returned to "remind" us that the president expected all of our resignations immediately. The president had issued the same order to the senior staff—but as usual, Nixon had left the unpleasant work to others. In the aftermath, the euphoria of election night gave way to depression, anxiety, and genuine puzzlement. News reports said later it was the first time a president had asked his entire cabinet to resign.

I had been back in my cavernous office in the Commerce Building—someone once likened it to the Hall of Mirrors at Versailles without the mirrors—for only a short time when my secretary told me the president wanted to see me at Camp David the next day. Caspar Weinberger, an old Nixon friend who was then director of the Office of Management and Budget, was the other invitee. Cap, as he was known, had succeeded George Shultz as Director of Management and Budget when Nixon appointed George secretary of the treasury the previous May. Cap also had long California ties to Nixon.

We boarded the marine helicopter at the White House pad the next morning. On the clattering flight out to Camp David in western Maryland, we joked back and forth uneasily about where the trapdoor was in the helicopter floor that would open and suck us through into political oblivion. But we reached Camp David in one piece, and there was no trapdoor for Cap. Nixon offered him secretary of health, education and welfare, a major assignment and a step up career-wise. For me, the trapdoor was camouflaged.

The president ushered me into a rustic Camp David living room—the place had originally been built as a camp for families, then converted to a presidential retreat by Franklin Roosevelt during World War II when German U-boats made the boating vacations he preferred too dangerous. Despite the casual setting, the president wore his usual dark suit, white shirt, and tie. Outside, leaves swirled, but even the fall colors at their peak paled against the purple shades of rhetoric Nixon laid on me. He told me he had read all the stories contending I was the best commerce secretary since Herbert Hoover. They weren't true, he said. I was better than Hoover. There was no comparison. What Henry Kissinger and I had achieved in the integrated commercial and strategic negotiations with the Soviet Union was remarkable. And speaking of Henry, he and George Shultz both held me in genuine respect, something that could not be said of anyone else in the administration. Furthermore, I had total support of the business community. Later developments made me wish I had his very generous words on tape!

As he spoke, my mind raced. Surely he wasn't offering me secretary of state. Henry would certainly get that. Perhaps Treasury, if he had a new assignment for George Shultz. Did he want me to be secretary of defense?

The president moved from my supposedly fine qualities to a new foreign policy initiative he had in mind. In 1972, he had built bridges to our former adversaries, China and the Soviet Union. It was now time to rebuild them to our friends in Europe. He meant for 1973 to be the "Year of Europe," a year in which our relationships with Western Europe, principally Great Britain, Germany, and France, were to be redefined. France, in particular, clung to the Gaullist illusion of its singularity and remained aloof to close transatlantic ties. But Nixon reminded me that I had once advocated integrating negotiations with our principal European allies across a wide front of issues that included trade, defense, and energy. Now was the time to pursue that course, he said, and I was the man.

He proposed to name me the first United States ambassador to Europe. This new post would combine ambassadorships to NATO, the European Economic Community or Common Market, the Organisation for Economic Co-operation and Development, virtually every multinational European based entity. Looking back, it probably wasn't even legal.

I would be headquartered in Brussels, the de facto capital of this emerging Europe. Brussels and its old stone guild houses were not exactly what I had in mind when I was imagining my future. Still, I could see the possibilities. It was a bold concept that offered challenging negotiating opportunities. And the chance to work side by side with both Kissinger and Shultz made the prospect that much sweeter.

I told the president it was intriguing but that I wanted to think it over, partly, I said, to figure out how to do the job effectively. Back in Washington, I checked in with a wise old head and longtime friend, Peter Lisagor, who headed the Washington office of the *Chicago Daily News*.

"It's an interesting offer, Pete," he said. "But you should make sure they aren't just shipping you out to the other end of a telephone that will never ring."

Bureaucratic rosters are full of just such people. Their positions sound lofty and come with all the perquisites—limos, fine offices, diplomatic housing. But for all the appearance of prestige, the jobs are so vaguely defined that measures of performance are difficult if not impossible to make. Ultimately, one wonders if performance was the object in the first place, or just an assignment to tread water, or worse, a way to get someone out of Washington. That, clearly, wasn't what I wanted. But what Nixon had proposed seemed different, a position that offered real possibilities.

Still, I was not entirely convinced. I really didn't want to take the kids out of school in the middle of the year to go to Brussels, another drastic change of their environment. Moreover, to tackle negotiations on such a broad scale would require a lot of planning. I would have to work out a detailed plan of negotiation, and the departmental concerns of Shultz at Treasury, Bill Rogers at State, Melvin Laird at Defense, and, of course, the national security picture under Kissinger would all have to be fully considered. This would take some time here in the United States.

I called John Ehrlichman with a straightforward proposal. I told him I would go to Brussels in six months. During the interim, I would work with Henry, George, Bill, and Mel on a negotiating plan. By next June—1973—when the school year was over, I would move my family to Brussels. Henry and George had told me that made sense to them.

Ehrlichman paused, then said he would have to call me back. He did, within five minutes. No, he said, moving in six months would not be acceptable. Go now, or not at all.

Sobered, I thought of Peter Lisagor's prescient warning. The White House was indeed shipping me off to the far end of a telephone that would rarely ring.

My Big Fat Greek Calves

The shock wore off in time. The truth was, I should not have been surprised. The president had a history of treating even his old friends roughly. He had used me as his beard after he sidelined Bill Rogers in Lend-Lease interest talks with the Soviets. John Volpe, the transportation secretary, had also received the presidential brush-off. Volpe, the three-time governor of Massachusetts who had nominated Nixon at the Republican convention in 1968, was spurned by Nixon as his running mate so that he could pursue his Southern Strategy with Spiro Agnew on the ticket. Later, Volpe would be given three hours to decide whether to be fired or appointed ambassador to Italy, an ultimatum he received for the crime of persistently demanding meetings with the president. The Palace Guard considered this presumptuous for a minor cabinet officer.

The treatment of Agnew was even worse. The administration used him as a sneering anti-liberal accusing the left of "pusillanimous pussyfooting" on law and order and spewing phrases like "nattering nabobs of negativism." This won him political points (and points for alliteration), but within the White House, he was virtually isolated. I never saw him at a single policy meeting. Furthermore, he frequently ate alone in the White House mess, a fact I found astonishing. Nixon and Agnew were longtime political colleagues, yet the Palace Guard had drawn a circle that excluded him.

I had no claim on friendship or closeness with the president. And in fact, after the 1972 election, George Shultz had confided that there was "a sense of unease" about me in the highest levels of the White House.

I could think of any number of reasons for the Palace Guard's "unease." I knew that Sally's distaste for Nixon, expressed frequently, had filtered back to the White House. Even my continuing friendship with my former boss and colleague at Bell & Howell, Senator Chuck Percy, had probably contributed. Chuck was a Republican, but the reactionary Palace Guard considered him a liberal who couldn't be trusted to support their views. As for the president and myself, I never really knew how he felt about me, but I always assumed that he felt equal amounts of respect and distrust.

Further, I think there was resentment on the White House staff about my treatment by the media. Whatever the reason, I had received favorable coverage dating back to my time as the president's assistant for international economic affairs, when *The New York Times* had hyperbolically referred to me as the "economic Kissinger." My power and access had never lived up to that description, but the media had treated me well as commerce secretary, too. A couple of months before the 1972 election, one source ran a long profile calling me a "reshaper of trade policies" and an "innovator." That article, and one in *Time* magazine that followed the election, compared my "clout" to the man whose picture peered down from above my fireplace. I was said to be "the most powerful Secretary of Commerce since Herbert Hoover."

I tried to deflect those comparisons. I told *Time* that I kept Hoover's portrait over the fireplace in my office "to remind me of the hazards of ambition," and joked that a powerful secretary of commerce is an oxymoron. (I made a hobby of collecting oxymorons after that. Before the 2006 elections, my favorite was House Ethics Committee.)

After the *Time* article appeared, a friend of mine on Time Inc.'s board told me a story that he said was unprecedented in his experience. Administrations routinely complain about unfavorable coverage. This time, however, a senior member of the White House staff called to object that the articles about Peterson were too *favorable*.

My deepening estrangement from the White House had come into sharp focus one fall weekend well in advance of the election. Sally and I attended a gathering at Kay Graham's Virginia country home, Glen Welby, with guests that included Clay Felker, the legendary magazine editor, and Richard Holbrooke, who had opened the door to his rising diplomatic stardom by authoring one volume of the Pentagon Papers. I was in the middle of a tennis game when one of Kay's staff interrupted to inform me that a White House operator was on the phone for me. Haldeman had the all-efficient White House switchboard track me down. He had some question on an obscure point that I don't recall, but I do know he wasn't pleased to find me at play in the enemy camp. In Nixonland, it was accepted that the friend of my enemy is my enemy. Early on, I had let them know I felt my social life was really *my* business.

Nor was the president amused. Sometime later, but still before the election, I was briefing him about what I foresaw as a looming energy crisis. I thought OPEC might well inflict a big spike in oil prices or, in the worst case, an embargo, for both political and revenue reasons. I also argued that energy deserved a place at the top of the international agenda along with security and trade issues. But the president seemed to have little interest, and I felt a snide vibe coming from him as I talked. When I finished, he said with a curl of his lip and a sardonic edge in his voice, "Well, Pete, that is an interesting analysis. It might even appeal to your friends in the Georgetown cocktail set."

My number was up, and I should have sensed it from all the signals I was getting. When you get fired from a high-level job in Washington a pink slip doesn't always show up in your mailbox. You have to read the code. I finally knew for certain when George Shultz related the White House's "unease." At that point you just know what you're supposed to do, and you can do it messily or gracefully. I chose gracefully. The going-away parties started in December, a month after the election. One in particular was notable. Tom and Joan Braden had the whole gang at their gracious house in Bethesda: Henry Kissinger, Kay Graham, the Kennedy clan, the Alsops, Bob McNamara, Senator J. William Ful-bright, former ambassador and Paris peace talks envoy David Bruce. If someone had tossed a bomb into the dining room that night, it would have wiped out much of the Georgetown set (and most of whatever fun and wit existed in those days in Washington).

Spirits were high. I rose to offer a toast, one that I had planned ahead of time. "I want to offer a toast to Bob Haldeman," I said. Haldeman was obviously not present.

The guests exchanged uneasy looks, as if they thought I'd had too many drinks.

"As you know, loyalty is very important to this White House," I said, "and with friends like you, one can never be safe." That drew an appreciative laugh of self-recognition. "So I was called in for a loyalty test, which Bob administered. This test includes three criteria. They're the three Ps—political, psychological, and physiological loyalty. I'll tell you in advance, I flunked all three tests. On the political test, Bob asked me, 'Is it true your wife voted for McGovern?'" Everybody laughed at that. "I

told him, 'Bob, there are some things too intimate to be shared even between a husband and a wife.' On the psychological test, Bob wanted me
to describe my friend Chuck Percy in one word. I tried 'Republican.' No.
I tried 'Chicagoan.' 'No,' he said, 'it's "Upchuck."' And I didn't do any
better on the physiological loyalty test, either. I tried my best, I really did."
I added, "But my calves are so fat that I couldn't click my heels.

"So here's to Bob Haldeman," I said with a raised glass. "He was
only right to fire such an abject loyalty test failure as I."

We laughed and talked into the late hours, and Sally and I went
home as happy as possible under the circumstances. The next day the
family and I left for Jamaica on our first vacation in two years. I told my
much valued assistant, a White House fellow named Brandon Sweitzer,
not to contact me unless it was really important.

Brandon called a few days later. It was the day after Christmas.
"Mr. Secretary," he said. "I thought you should know there was a big
story by Sally Quinn about you in *The Washington Post* this morning.
Didn't you say that party at the Bradens' was off the record?"

"I thought it was," I said.

"Well, it's all out there," he said. "Don't worry, it's a positive story,
extremely so. But did you make a joke about Haldeman and your fat
calves?"

I was appalled. Oh, God, I thought, my big, fat, naughty Greek
mouth.

The story, on the front page of the "Style" section, was headlined
"The Trouble with Peterson." It quoted "a very high White House official" as saying, "The trouble with Pete Peterson is that he cared too much
about substance." But it was the fat calves line that everyone remembered. Haldeman, in a measure of revenge, clipped the story and put it
up front in the president's daily news briefing. Versions of it ran everywhere, in Jack Anderson's syndicated newspaper column and in a number of the major magazines. It was the talk of Washington, and it has
happily followed me wherever I have gone for years. In Germany, Helmut
Schmidt, then the defense minister (and later chancellor), greeted me
with questions about the condition of my calves. Thirty years later, Bob
Dole, the former Kansas senator and Senate majority leader, asked me to
pull up my pants leg so he could see for himself how fat my calves were.

The remainder of my term mixed humor and pathos. Nelson Rockefeller, in his final term as New York's governor, his presidential aspirations as a liberal Republican eclipsed by the Southern Strategy, requested an appointment. When I greeted him at my office in the Commerce Building he wrapped an arm around my shoulder and said, "Fella, let me tell you something. You may be feeling rather dumb right now, but long after anybody remembers what you did here at Commerce, they'll remember that line about your fat calves. Everybody knows that the White House gang are a bunch of Nazi bastards, and you were the first to have the guts to say it. Like all great humor, it was very funny but also very true, and people will remember it for years."

Some scenarios even described me as the most prescient of the cabinet officers. Presumably, I alone had a crystal ball that allowed me to anticipate the future impact of Watergate. But that was ridiculous: The unglamorous truth was that I had been fired. I had known literally nothing about the inner workings of the Watergate affair. That inside information was for the Palace Guard, not us outsiders.

Soon after my minidramas, I received the most anomalous invitation I have ever received, or probably ever will, a personal invitation from the president to join him, the vice president, families and close friends, in his box for his second inaugural swearing-in and address. I have always felt that most of us are relative strangers even to our own unconscious. Still, knowing this, I have elsewhere in this book speculated, however presumptuously, on Nixon's complex and, at times, convoluted psyche. However, to this day, I remain totally baffled by this invitation to his inauguration. It is well beyond my capacity to even speculate. (Incidentally, I accepted the president's surprising invitation.)

Letting Go

Meanwhile, the sad postelection carnage of Nixon's cabinet continued. Five of us—James Hodgson at Labor, Mel Laird at Defense, George Romney at Housing and Urban Development, Volpe at Transportation, and me—had been fired and most would be gone before the new year was barely a month old. Attorney General Richard Kleindienst, caught in the undertow of Watergate, would be gone by May. Meanwhile Volpe, given only a few hours to decide on Italy or oblivion, chose Italy.

Sally and I attended a desultory White House Christmas dinner. The president's dour mood injected a Scrooge-like note of "Bah! Humbug!" to the gathering, and then he launched a tirade against *The Washington Post* and *The New York Times*, complaining of their treatment of his administration. At one point he dismissed the waiters and ordered the doors closed, as if they were likely to leak his intemperate comments.

Of course few outside the Palace Guard, and certainly not I, knew then just how deeply Watergate had infected the administration. I could only wonder at the personal vindictiveness of this whole destructive process. Did the president need to create new enemies when the voting public had signaled its widespread support? In some deeply psychological sense, was he lost without enemies? Did he need enemies so badly that he even made them out of his best friends? Whatever the pathology, I was astonished recently to hear the Nixon tapes where he speaks harshly and repeatedly of his enemies in the press, the professors, and even the establishment. To hear him forcefully advocating the bombing of another "enemy," the Brookings Institution, was even more shocking.

I was privy to none of the desperate counterattacks and cover-ups planned inside the White House. I put a foot into the Watergate waters after I heard the staff damning *The Washington Post* and discussing taking away the company's television station licenses in retaliation for the paper's Watergate coverage. I visited Kay Graham in her office and told her I knew nothing and wanted to know nothing about Watergate, but that she should be sure the *Post*'s reporting was accurate. Otherwise, I said, I was sure the administration would try to inflict pain on her business interests, including the *Post*'s television properties. Attorney General John Mitchell had hinted as much the previous summer, when Carl Bernstein asked his reaction to a story the *Post* was about to publish implicating him in spying on the Democrats as part of the president's reelection effort: "Katie Graham's gonna get her tit caught in a big fat wringer if that's published."

Over time, Congress and the public learned of the secret Oval Office tapes. John Dean gave his damning "cancer growing on the presidency" testimony before the Senate early in 1973. Nixon threw Haldeman, Ehrlichman, and Colson overboard. My fat calves made me look better than I may have expected or deserved.

The White House announced that I would be the "personal representative" of the president, visiting with leaders of the free world and helping to plan a negotiation that I came to call the "Year of Our Friends." They also announced I would be leaving the administration in June. This upended *Time* magazine's speculation that I was one of the cabinet members likely to stay on. The Soviets seemed shocked. Brezhnev expressed surprise and sent an emissary with a thoughtful gesture— a personally signed photograph and the inscription, "With respect." The Soviet experts told me such a thing was rarely done.

Had I stayed, what else would I wish I could have done as commerce secretary?

As I reflected on my tenure at the Commerce Department—if I can call thirteen months tenure—there are a few things that I would have focused on in a second term.

I would have wanted to work more with labor unions to minimize the highly adversarial us-versus-management syndrome. In its place, I wondered how one could build a culture and a philosophy of compensation that would focus on creating a bigger pie that, in turn, if fairly shared, meant more pie for all, workers, management, and stockholders. Today, workers' wages have become stagnant, while executive compensation (including golden handcuffs) has become outsized, and is often poorly related to performance. This situation has greatly aggravated the sense of unfairness and adversariness. This is hardly the kind of optimal climate for the competitive imperative, increasing productivity.

I would have also wished to focus more on the growing problem of workers who are victims of creative destruction. In recent years, fears of job losses attributed to globalization (but more often due to technology) have obviously ballooned.

It is ironic that, in the face of these understandable job fears, there are serious shortages in middle-skilled jobs. Furthermore, many of these jobs are less "off-shorable." I am referring to maintenance technicians, not simply for mechanical systems but for electrical and electronic control systems, welders and air traffic controllers to name a few such shortages. These jobs do require skill training that is often not widely available. We obviously need a national skills strategy.

These kinds of "adjustment assistance," which, in effect, focus on protecting the workers rather than protecting the industry, cost but a small fraction of the social and economic benefits of providing the training, skills, and the adjustment assistance for the jobs that will be available.

My Next Career

My net worth had suffered greatly. It was clear to me by then that the real money was made by people who invested in, owned, and built businesses, not by people like lawyers, consultants, and financial advisors who sold their expertise and their brains and bodies by the hour or by the project. I also knew I would not want to focus my business energies on only one or two industries. The best part of my work in Washington, in addition to the large number of contacts and friends I added to my Rolodex, had been its sheer variety—negotiating with the Soviets and the Japanese, and solving problems like dolphins and baby seals. And I liked the international focus of my Washington assignments, and wanted to continue in this area.

Apparently there was some demand for this grab bag of contacts, traits, and preferences. I received many offers as I sent out feelers and interviewed, and I was grateful for them all. I was invited to join over forty boards of directors, and take on several top corporate jobs, including the presidency of American Express working under its legendary CEO, Howard L. Clark.

Increasingly, I focused my attention on Wall Street. I had no experience in the world of finance, but it's a popular Wall Street cliché that the only qualification one needs for Wall Street is a mastery of second grade mathematics. What I didn't know I felt I probably could learn quickly, and there were plenty of people who handled the details like point spreads or premiums for convertible debentures. I had my corporate operating experience and many corporate relationships to offer, and the international experience I had gained during my time in Washington. And the offers for top Wall Street jobs were flattering. Salomon Brothers wanted me on their small executive committee to run their investment banking business. So did First Boston, indeed as CEO. I decided, eventually, on Lehman Brothers, which had as part of its legacy a history of activity in one of my real loves, investing—not just in start-ups but in buying and building businesses. I agreed to come on as vice chairman of this venerable firm starting at the beginning of the summer on June 5, 1973.

Sally always liked New York. The feminist movement was raging, and Sally grabbed the opportunity to find a new identity. She made many new friends, often younger journalists, writers, poets, and, without exception, nonestablishment New York liberals.

Sally also found her new identity in her aspiration to be a psychotherapist. Earlier, in Washington, she had taken a few courses at American University. In New York, she went to New York University where she earned her master's degree in psychology.

But once I had decided to let go of Washington, Washington would not let go of me. Henry Kissinger called me toward the end of May. It was urgent, he said, that we have dinner. When we met, he told me Nixon still wanted me to handle a special assignment—planning for the Year of Europe negotiations. This would not preclude my taking the vice chairmanship of Lehman Brothers, but was something I could handle in addition to it. The president was convinced I was the right person for the job.

I told Henry I was tempted. However, it would take me a few weeks to establish myself at Lehman Brothers. Perhaps then I could take some time off to handle the assignment in Europe. Henry conferred with George Shultz and they agreed that this scenario could work.

Al Haig was now Nixon's chief of staff, replacing Haldeman. He took over discussions about my new Year of Europe assignment, and said that my appointment would simply have to be announced on June 6.

But that's impossible, I said. To start at Lehman Brothers on June 5 and a day later publicly accept an assignment that would take me off to Europe would be impolitic to say the least. I wanted it "perfectly clear," to use a favorite Nixon phrase, that I was committed, first and foremost, to building a career with my new Lehman partners and that would take some time on the job before careening off in new Washington directions.

Haig insisted on June 6. What was more, he said during one early morning phone call as we argued back and forth, the president insisted, to the point of telling me that it was a presidential order.

"Al," I said, "this is the same president who wanted to ship me off to a nonassignment to get me out of the way. Now he *insists* that I take a job on a timetable that will undermine the next phase of my career, and that makes no sense. The answer is no."

I found out later what the president was up to. For months he had virtually been hiding in the White House. Trying to keep the flood of Watergate from rising higher, he had somehow persuaded the canny conservative Mel Laird, who had left the secretary of defense post at the end of January, to rejoin the administration as a presidential counselor. Nixon was to announce the Laird appointment in a Rose Garden ceremony on June 6, and wanted to also name me as a counselor to the president at the same time. It was a transparent ploy, designed to show that he had cleansed the administration of its bad seeds and was ready to begin anew with upright and independent-minded aides. Earlier, in the wagon-circling era of the Palace Guard, I was not to be trusted. Now, amid the wreckage, the president still believed I could be used to shore up his frayed prestige. Consider the symbolism: conservative Laird to the president's right; independent, moderate, "Fat Calves" Peterson to his left. If I had agreed, I would have ended up looking like a fool, appearing to defend the indefensible as the Watergate crimes emerged into full view.

Washington Postscript

Henry Kissinger was one of those in the administration who also stood above the mud of Watergate. In September 1973, after I had been at Lehman Brothers for a few months, Henry called to ask if Sally and I could come to Washington to attend his swearing-in as secretary of state and a private dinner with a few of his best friends.

It was a thrill to see Henry elevated to a position he so clearly coveted and deserved. Afterward, at the White House, there was a receiving line for guests. The president was the host. I debated whether to go through the line, but decided Henry would think it odd if I didn't, and with respect to the president, what was I afraid of?

As I approached Nixon, he saw me and suddenly ordered the Secret Service to stop the line. He had to speak to me, he said, and drew me aside out of earshot of the others. "Pete, I need you back," he said. I could have any major ambassadorship—London, Tokyo, or Moscow.

I mustered all the courtesy at my command, and declined. But as I left the line I thought that this off-the-wall offer was another sign the president was being derailed by the gathering storm of Watergate. I couldn't wait to get back to New York!

The pressure on Nixon clearly was intense. Just how much so, I learned later when the articles of impeachment against the president were drafted. They included the charge that he had solicited political contributions from International Telephone & Telegraph (ITT) to call off the Justice Department in an antitrust action that would have forced ITT to sell Hartford Insurance. As it happened, the president in 1971 had asked me to meet with ITT's CEO, Hal Geneen, and Geneen had come in with charts arguing that the Hartford acquisition was legal.

I didn't know antitrust law, and I referred the material to Arthur Burns, who headed an antitrust task force. I wrote a note to John Ehrlichman telling him what had happened and asking what else, if anything, he wanted me to do. Nothing, Ehrlichman replied, because the president, that very day, had "handled" the matter with Kleindienst (who at the time was deputy attorney general).

Now, more than two years later, reading the ITT charges against the president, I recalled this episode and volunteered to recount my part of it to the Justice Department. When I met with an investigator, I found that my memory was relatively vague about some of the details. I recalled writing the note to Ehrlichman, at which the investigator riffled through his papers and held it up for me to see. "Mr. Peterson, is this what you are referring to?" he asked.

The investigator continued. "Mr. Peterson, we note that you also placed telephone calls to Felix Rohatyn." (Felix was a senior banker at Lazard Frères.)

The statement hung there. Yes, I had placed calls to Felix. He was an old friend. ITT was one of his clients and he was an ITT board member. He was also the executor of the blind trust into which I had placed my investments during my government service. It is illegal for a government employee to discuss trust matters when he is in a position to influence them, thus the blind trust designation. "You weren't talking to Mr. Rohatyn about your blind trust, were you?" the investigator asked.

I certainly didn't think so, and I certainly didn't think we had talked about ITT. But I couldn't remember what we *had* talked about. Only later did I recall that the calls had been about getting his senior partner, André Meyer, invited to a White House meeting. I promptly passed this on to the Justice Department. I vowed that if I ever returned to public service, I would keep far more careful records.

Of course, the most careful records of all were Nixon's secret White House tapes. I could never understand why he had not simply destroyed them when he had the chance. Was it part of his self-destructive pattern? Others speculated that he planned to sell the tapes for a big price. I think he also was torn between wanting to keep a record of his legacy and knowing that that same record could hurt him, but believing that, in any case, his accomplishments would outweigh his defects.

In some ways, they did. I directly experienced his deviousness, paranoia, and character flaws. I also had great respect for his brilliance, boldness, and the sheer range of his mind. Surprisingly, given our mixed personal history, we became rather close after he left office. I still have his handwritten letter from 1977 thanking me for serving "the nation with great dedication and distinction" and adding that the country still needed my "extraordinary ability and wisdom." As chairman of the Economic Club of New York, I arranged his first major post-presidential speech to a black tie dinner that the board warned me would be boycotted. Instead, the three levels of the Waldorf-Astoria ballroom sold out in three days, and Nixon spoke brilliantly for almost forty minutes without a single note, dazzling his audience.

The last time I saw him was in the early 1990s at his office in

Saddle River, New Jersey, where he spent his last years. He opened the door himself when I arrived, having given up protection by the Secret Service. We discussed world affairs for an hour and a half, and I still found his command of events breathtaking. And he once again revealed his tendency toward disparaging his political opposites. He had taken a hard line on some subject and added, "Pete, this won't appeal to your Eastern, elite, liberal friends—you know, those old farts and airheads at the Council on Foreign Relations."

I had at that point been the chairman of the Council on Foreign Relations for several years, a fact he suddenly remembered and threw in a disclaimer. "Not you, of course, Pete," he quickly said.

And then, as I was leaving, he asked out of nowhere if I knew his son-in-law Ed Cox. He wanted a favor. Could I get Eddie into the Council on Foreign Relations? I resisted a temptation to laugh and then to ask, "Along with the young farts and airheads, Mr. President?"

Over the years, nothing has happened to change my opinion of my tenure in Washington. Working for the government, I had some unique experiences and made wonderful, lasting friendships and contacts around the world. I had laid foundation stones for opportunities in business and in major nonprofit institutions. For all of the turmoil, none of these things would have been possible without those thirty months in Washington.

Sally Quinn once asked if it hadn't been a costly experience, particularly in light of what I had given up financially to move from Bell & Howell to Washington.

"Yes, you're right," I said. "It may have been costly, but it was also priceless."

CHAPTER 11

NEW YORK, ROUND ONE

Welcome to New York

New York City and Washington, D.C., are a little over two hundred miles apart. You can drive between them in four hours, ride an Amtrak train in three, or fly the shuttle in an hour. But the cultural and psychic separation is far greater than the length of the commute. Washington is a company town that tends to be obsessed with one thing—politics. New York believes it has much more, or at least much else, on its mind.

That was true even in 1973, when the city was at a low ebb in its civic fortunes—nearly bankrupt, beset by crime, racial tensions, poverty, its infrastructure crumbling, its handsome mayor John Lindsay, a Republican who had defected to the Democrats, distracted by his presidential aspirations. But the city's beat went on regardless, always provoking, always stimulating, often shocking.

What first shocked me in New York was not the carnivorous corporate culture within Lehman Brothers. This would appear all too soon, but that shock was preceded by another rude bump on my personal seismograph—the price of New York real estate, even at what I was told were record low prices. When we moved to Washington, I sold the lakefront house in Winnetka, five bedrooms and baths with a tennis court, for $120,000. Our Washington house on Rock Creek Park also had five bedrooms and baths, a pool, and sauna. It cost $200,000. New York, to me, meant Manhattan; I didn't want to commute from the suburbs, but in Manhattan an apartment large enough to fit my family would cost at least $300,000 to $400,000. That kind of money, given my massive negative cash flow while working for the government, was going to be hard to pull together even after selling the house in Washington. The stringent financial net worth rules enforced by the boards of New York cooperative apartment buildings added to the problem.

Our real estate broker found a prestigious building on the Upper East Side with a large apartment for sale at a price that at first sounded like a steal. Ten Gracie Square was at the east end of 84th Street, with a park across the street, and its front yard was the East River. The apartment had five bedrooms and six baths and was $110,000, within the range of my available cash. And apparently, the co-op board wasn't averse to having a former commerce secretary in the building, even if his net worth was less than they might have liked. The catch was that the apartment badly needed renovating. But it would be a beautiful family home once that was done. I put $90,000 down and agreed to pay the rest within three years. When I tell my children the price today, they think I'm joking. I'm told the Gracie apartment recently sold for $9 million!

So one problem was solved, if incompletely.

Sally and I decided not to scrimp too much on the renovations. I knew that many Wall Streeters migrated each weekend to houses at the east end of Long Island or the wilds of upstate New York or Connecticut, but this luxury was beyond our means, at least at first, and if we were going to be in the city all the time we wanted our new home there to be right. But here again, where would the money come from? I was paying six tuitions now that Sally was at New York University. Michael was of preschool age, and tuition at New York private schools like Dalton and Brearley made Washington's look cheap. Even with my Lehman Brothers salary, I would have to find a separate source of funds to restore the Gracie Square apartment.

Ten years earlier, when we were still in Chicago, I had acquired a few pieces of Surrealist art. My interest in Surrealism grew out of some time I had spent in psychoanalysis. Freudian and Jungian analysis was all the rage in the late 1950s and early 1960s. It was something people, in particular the more "worldly" and "intellectual" crowd, undertook as a route to self-awareness and perhaps to have something to talk about. I don't recall that my decision to go "on the couch," as they say, arose from anything more than curiosity. I certainly didn't see it as a sign of weakness, as some—men especially—seem to interpret it. It seems to me quite the opposite, that self-exploration grows from the confidence that you can handle what you find. As a result, I spent two or three years recalling moments of my childhood, assembling pieces of memory, analyzing my dreams, and trying to fit all this into my current behavior patterns. The psychotherapist was from the classical, nondirective school, meaning that he did very little prompting or intervention, but allowed me to meander across my mental landscape and pick out the scenery that was most meaningful to me. It was a helpful, but not defining, experience.

But I did, indeed, come to understand more about my own behavior. The strategies I had used as a boy to restore my mother's attention and love after my sister, Elaine, died were with me still. I had strived to be perfect in her eyes, stuffing myself with her cooking, carving that alabaster box, getting straight As, and now I sought perfection in my business life. But I was trying too hard to achieve it, wasting time and resources to gain that last incremental measure of perfection, too often on some marginal issue, when I could have used the same time and resources better elsewhere.

Delving into dreams, the unconscious and subconscious self, led me in turn to Surrealist art. A second factor here was *The Lonely Crowd* by David Riesman, a University of Chicago professor I had known and admired. The book, published in 1950, was a landmark study of American character, and it differentiated between the inner-directed and the outer-directed man. The former was led by an inner gyroscope of his own principles and values, while the latter found out who he was by listening to others. Enter Max Ernst and his painting, *M Portrait, or the Letter*.

Ernst had painted it in 1924. It showed a torso with a disembodied head and a long arm with a microphone. The colors were vivid—red, green, and purple. I saw it in Paris in 1963, along with another painting by Ernst and one by Victor Brauner, a Romanian. It was the first Ernst that spoke to me most loudly. The microphone-head seemed to be onstage and, it seemed to me, was listening to the audience to determine who he was—a clear example of the outer-directed man, the man I wished not to be. (I have no idea if Ernst intended this particular interpretation. I once attended a dinner party he was at in Phoenix, Arizona, where he wintered. He told me a story of attending a lecture by a local art professor who sought to interpret the psychological or even the unconscious basis of Ernst's paintings. At first, Ernst chuckled at what the professor had to say, but before long he was laughing out loud. Things got to the point where the professor demanded to know who this person was and what was so funny. The professor was embarrassed to learn it was the artist himself—the one he was so earnestly and presumptuously trying to explain.) Ernst's painting resonated with me, but what he meant I couldn't say, nor could anyone else say. In any case, I bought three paintings for the grand total of $7,000, approximately the after-tax proceeds of my $12,000 bonus that year from Bell & Howell.

Since then, my tastes had evolved to take in a broader expanse of modern art, like the abstractions of Wassily Kandinsky to which the Soviets in Moscow had refused me access. I came to appreciate artists such as Rothko, DeKooning, Gorky, Deibenkorn, Matisse, and Picasso, particularly their drawings.

I suspected that the Ernsts and the Brauner had appreciated in value. I thought they might provide some of the money we needed to have repairs made on the Gracie Square apartment. So I called a Chicago and New York art dealer, Richard Feigen, to have them appraised.

To my astonishment, the appraisal came back far above $300,000. Feigen sold the three paintings privately and I netted $350,000, which more than covered the renovation costs. Next to Blackstone, these paintings were the best investment I have ever made.

Welcome to Wall Street

The Lehman Brothers offices at One William Street, in the narrow, dark canyons of the Wall Street financial district at the southern tip of Manhattan, had no need of physical rehabilitation. The "baroque palazzo," as one newspaper writer called it, had been built in 1907 by another investment bank before Lehman Brothers bought it and made it the firm's headquarters in 1928. It was eleven stories tall, triangular in shape to fit the pattern of the surrounding streets, and it dripped with amenities like the Partners Dining Room, where the partners ate at a long table covered with ornate china and silverware. A large fireplace dominated one side of the dining room, and the walls were hung with portraits of the founders.

The founders—the original Lehman brothers—were three German Jews, Emanuel, Mayer, and Henry Lehman, who were successful cotton traders in Montgomery, Alabama. They formed their partnership in 1850, and opened their first office in New York in 1858. After the Civil War, they shifted their headquarters to New York and gradually expanded from cotton trading to investment banking. During the firm's early years, Lehman helped finance the launch of such American retail giants as Sears, Woolworth, and R. H. Macy.

As the firm grew, the Lehman family became prominent members of New York's aristocracy. The scion of the family from the 1930s through the mid-1950s was Herbert Lehman, a progressive-minded Democrat who served as New York's governor and U.S. senator. Robert "Bobbie" Lehman, a good friend of the Whitneys, the Harrimans, and other prominent New York families, presided over the firm until the late 1960s, winning renown for his ability to spot early promising young enterprises such as Pan American World Airways, Trans World Airlines, and the Radio Corporation of America, which became RCA. When I arrived at Lehman Brothers in June 1973, it was Wall Street's oldest and in some ways most distinguished investment banking partnership.

But, I was to find later, Lehman Brothers was also notorious for its internal fractiousness. Bobbie Lehman, also known as RL, a slightly built and quiet man, had ruled as a kind of Sun King. In those days, the partnership agreement specified that there were two kinds of partners. RL was the only party of the first part, which had all the votes, and all the other partners were of the second part, with virtually no legal power. They were an eclectic collection: Ivy League graduates born to govern; men with drive but little education who had risen from positions such as Wall Street runners; former businessmen and government officials including Eddie Gudeman, Marcel Palmero, Ed Kennedy, and General Lucius Clay (who administered Berlin after World War II and mounted the Berlin Airlift when the Soviets cut off overland access to the city from the West); and a few longtime bankers such as Jim Szold and Frank and Paul Manheim. This mix of cultures, backgrounds, and religions was considered to be one of Lehman's strengths. Prior to the 1970s, Wall Street was largely divided between "Jewish" firms such as Goldman Sachs and Loeb Rhoades and "Gentile" firms such as Morgan Stanley and Eastman Dillon. Lehman and RL himself bridged this divide.

As long as RL was active, he controlled whatever clashes might occur. But as he and his more senior partners aged, the younger men grew more powerful and confident and began to assert themselves.

Bobbie Lehman died in 1969 without designating a successor. This increased the tensions as partners jockeyed for position. General Clay became chairman of the Executive Committee, but the firm was actually run by three other men: Fred Ehrman, widely considered a misanthrope who was later fired by a group that included his own nephew; Joe Thomas, a graduate of Exeter, Yale, and the Harvard Business School, who had started Litton Industries with Roy Ash and Tex Thornton and whose son had entered the firm; and Herman Kahn, a hard-charging banker whose son had also joined Lehman and who had risen from runner to highly successful banker and virtually invented the private placement of corporate loans with insurance companies. There was little chance these three men who had never run anything could together lead a diverse group of talented but independent people to a common cause.

The following year, but before I joined the firm, Lehman Brothers changed from a partnership to a corporation for its various investment and securities trading businesses. The divisions along ethnic lines were then exacerbated by divisions over lines of business. Lew Glucksman's commercial paper—unsecured short-term loans to corporations—business had become an important part of the firm but neither he nor his colleagues had much clout or status. They waited resentfully, poised for their opportunity to strike.

With no real leadership, the divisions festered. Lehman developed a reputation as a dog-eat-dog world in which the traders and the investment bankers, among others, eyed each other with unalloyed suspicion. The traders, including Glucksman's peddlers of commercial paper, considered the investment bankers a bunch of spoiled and rather unproductive Park Avenue brats—white-shoe elites who were more show than real dough. The investment bankers thought the traders were crude and uncultured, and that they gave having money a bad name. These opinions were so ingrained that, according to one frequently repeated story, most of the senior partners had their desks in a single room because none of them trusted the others out of their sight.

There was never a clear path to making partner. Those decisions were made secretly, as were the determinations about partner ownership and compensation. Thus cliques plotted against one another like Byzantine princes, operating independently and hiding information. One staple of the rumor mill had a partner in one group secretly planning a hostile takeover of a Lehman client handled by a partner in a rival clique. Another had a partner persuading another partner to sell him his stock in a mineral company when he knew, as the selling partner did not, that the company was about to strike a rich new mine.

Lehman earned $18 million in 1972, the year before I joined. But despite its profitability, Lehman Brothers needed a rehabilitation of its culture far more desperately than I knew or even suspected.

Why did I wade into this mess when I had my pick of offers? The truth is, I had failed to learn how bad the problem really was. Ending one phase of my life in Washington, I was anxious to get on to the next thing—investing in and building companies—and I simply didn't pay enough attention. Aside from my inadequate due diligence, one big reason I joined Lehman was George Ball, who was one of the partners on the investment banking side. He had served as undersecretary of state in the Kennedy and Johnson administrations and, when *The New York Times* published the Pentagon Papers in 1971, was revealed as a forceful—though unsuccessful—critic of sending American troops to Vietnam. He left the government in 1966, returned in 1968 as ambassador to the United Nations, and was a force in Hubert Humphrey's campaign against Nixon the same year. George and I hit it off from the start, drawn together by a mutual interest in foreign policy and its adjunct, economic policy. Further, he was unfailingly gracious, which proved to be a commodity in all too short supply at Lehman Brothers. During my tenure there, his office was always next to mine.

Another reason I chose Lehman was my affinity for Warren Hellman, the firm's young president. A Californian who had graduated from Berkeley and the Harvard Business School, he was an enthusiastic, even driven, outdoorsman who ran, biked, and skied. Warren and his wife, Chris, herself a former medal-winning World Cup skier, had come to Washington when I was interviewing to recruit me for the firm, and I found Warren to be a very good banker with strong values. His crusty, profane uncle, Frederick L. Ehrman, was then the chairman and CEO of Lehman Brothers. Ehrman had also spent some time with me during the recruiting phase. He seemed eager to have me join the firm, though his standoffish personality made it hard to tell. Another of my favorites among the Lehman partners was General Clay, a straight talker with little tolerance for nonsense.

But there were some serious omissions in my recruiting process, and only later would I come to recognize their significance. Ball, Hellman, and Ehrman formed the recruiting committee. I did not meet Lew Glucksman or James Glanville, both powerful senior partners at the firm, before arriving to take up my duties. It wasn't necessary, I was told. George and Warren, and other senior figures, too, were probably concerned that I might clash with these two partners, and wanted to avoid a demolition derby before I could get off the starting line. They managed only to postpone the demolition.

Into the Maelstrom

I joined Lehman as vice chairman and one of the four-member Executive Committee. The others were Ehrman, Hellman, and Andrew Sage II, with whom I shared the vice chair's title, but who, at that point, had little interest in managing the firm. My actual start date was June 5, and my salary of $300,000 was a marked improvement over my $42,500 government pay. It came with the understanding that I would spend a lot of time on investments. It would take me back to my Bell & Howell days when I would have the fun of buying, building, and restructuring companies.

By now, at forty-seven, I had covered the waterfront of wealth creation. I had seen that professionals like doctors, lawyers, and accountants made a great deal of money but rarely got truly wealthy. Their expertise was highly valued, but there were limits to what they could charge.

Investment banking was more lucrative. But it was still a version of the living made by Sherman McCoy, Tom Wolfe's bond salesman character in *Bonfire of the Vanities*; his wife described it as collecting "golden crumbs" that fell from other people's tables. Given the right information and analysis, I could be pretty good at giving financial and mergers and acquisitions advice. Still, you told other people what to do, and they could take your advice or not.

True wealth, and true satisfaction, to me, came from owning, building, and growing companies. Your decisions accumulated and developed momentum. You could see an idea take form and achieve reality. And the tax code rewarded the risks required, by establishing a big gap between the tax rates on capital gains and earned income. Lehman had a history of building companies through equity participation.

My equity participation in Lehman required that I put some money in the pot. Coming up with the $750,000 or so required of a partner at my level was not going to be easy given my financial status leaving Washington, and I didn't have any more art to sell. First, I won agreement from Fred Ehrman to spread out my payments over several months. But I didn't want to risk a large share of my resources without some financial due diligence. I hired an outside accountant to confirm Lehman's in-house evaluation of the firm's book value. He went over the books and assured me that they were accurate, and I proceeded with my stock purchase based on his report.

As it turned out, this was a very big mistake.

I had not been at Lehman a month when a bombshell fell on the Executive Committee. The firm's chief financial officer, Arthur Fried, walked into the conference room where we were meeting. With one hand clutching a sheaf of papers and his face a sickly gray, he told us in a worried voice that the company's government bond trading business had lost between $15 million and $20 million before taxes.

The bond trading operation was part of Lew Glucksman's domain. These securities were supposed to be marked regularly to the current market prices, but they had not been. Glucksman's people had gambled that interest rates would fall, but they had gone up instead. And up. And up. Since bond prices fall as current interest rates rise, the value of the bonds had crumbled. At the same time, the money borrowed to finance the bond purchases cost more and more, far outstripping the modest return of the government-issued bonds themselves. Given that the firm's equity totaled only about $17 million, those investments had been, in retrospect, a reckless gamble.

News of the bond trading disaster spread quickly throughout One William Street. The reaction, from partners to the support and back-office staff, ranged from anger to near panic. Within days, the New York Stock Exchange put Lehman Brothers on its early warning list of firms whose debt was dangerously overweighted in comparison to capital. Bankruptcy was clearly possible, and many of the partners called for Glucksman's scalp.

The crisis reflected not only upon Glucksman, but also on Fred Ehrman and his leadership as CEO. Discontent among the partners quickly reached a head. On the night of July 19, a group of nine senior partners convened at George Ball's apartment high in the United Nations Plaza at the edge of the East River. The beautiful view of the city lights and of Queens across the river clashed with the hard-edged purpose of the meeting. Warren led things off. He said it was time for a change, but that he did not want the job of chairman and CEO. "The obvious choice, it seems to me, is Pete," he said.

He and George had warned me ahead of time that he would make this argument, but I found myself shocked nonetheless. I had been in the business for only a few weeks at that point. I asked this group of senior partners if they really wanted a Wall Street greenhorn running the whole show. They came back with the reasons I had heard before from Warren: An outsider with my reputation, beholden to neither the bankers nor the traders nor to any of the other cliques, was the kind of leader that was needed to restore the firm's credibility and keep clients from shying away. They wanted to know if I would take on the job. I had misgivings but I recognized, as they did, that there were no other good alternatives within the firm. I said I would.

And truthfully, I had no real choice. I had committed to contribute my equity share and would have a big chunk of my net worth tied up in the firm. It was vital that I do what I could to save it. I was genuinely concerned about my financial solvency.

Now that the plot was afoot, to put it in Shakespearean terms, my first concern was to approach Ehrman with a generous transition offer. Part of heading Lehman, I thought, was to take on its reputation as a place where no partner or group of partners was safe from the predations of another. I had no doubt that Ehrman would put me in the predatory category, but I wanted to handle the announcement and succession plans as graciously as possible.

Several partners told me I didn't have a chance at this. "That SOB doesn't know what gracious or generous means," one of them told me. Still, I persuaded George and Warren to join me in a meeting with Ehrman in his office. It had been less than a week since the initial senior partners' meeting, during which other top partners had signed on to the plan.

I led the conversation. I told Fred that the huge bond trading losses had traumatized the organization. Clients were in danger of defecting. The partners had reached a consensus that a change at the top had to be made, and the firm needed to be restructured to absorb the losses and prevent their recurrence. I hadn't asked for it, but the partners had agreed on me as their choice.

"Here's my proposal, Fred," I said. "You announce immediately that you've decided to step down at the end of the year, in favor of me as your successor. You can say you recruited me yourself, and that it was clear a successor was needed given your age and health concerns." (He was in his late sixties and had suffered two heart attacks.) "For the five months between now and the end of the year, I'll remain vice chairman and do whatever I can to make the company work." I promised that his years of Lehman service would win my generous praise when I took over.

When I finished, I thought I had offered a face-saving way out of a tough situation.

Ehrman listened to my proposal without a change in his usually baleful expression. It must have been clear to him that George, his nephew Warren, and the other senior partners backed this plan all the way. But at the end, to my astonishment, he said, "Fuck you, and no way."

I looked at my companions to see how they were taking this. George, diplomat that he was, was looking at Ehrman and nodding thoughtfully. Warren, as I had learned in my short time at the firm, had the reputation of having an explosive temper (though he never displayed it to me). His nickname was "Hurricane Hellman." But he also feared his often tyrannical Uncle Fred, and now could not look him in the eye. All he could do was stare at his uncle's short, white socks, which had a tendency to sag over the tops of his black shoes.

Ehrman then said he would demand an immediate return of his equity capital if he were forced out. This was not merely a rejection of a graceful change. This was a financial time bomb, because Ehrman was a major stockholder. The firm had a policy that anyone leaving would have their equity returned within one year. But after the huge bond trading losses, only about $11 million in equity remained. More than half of that, about $7 million, was the equity shares of four or five very senior partners. They were all over seventy, and if any of them were to die or decide to retire, the short-term equity drawdown would drive the firm even nearer to bankruptcy than it was already. This early payout of equity was a foolish policy, particularly for such a sophisticated bunch of bankers. Apparently none of them felt that the great Lehman Brothers could possibly fall on hard times. This was the sober reality that I confronted when the board of directors voted to proceed immediately with the transition despite Ehrman's objections. The news broke on July 27 and I took over August 1.

Restructuring

After my elevation to CEO just a few weeks after joining Lehman Brothers, I knew some at the firm were questioning my corporate finance expertise. But I told myself that these were the financial geniuses who had combined a scrawny balance sheet with potential huge and early claims on the firm's limited capital by several septuagenarians. The early payout over only one year was unusual at the time. I knew I had to somehow persuade these senior partners to adopt a plan that included longer payouts to retirees.

Joe Thomas was among the most senior of the partners and the largest equity holder in the firm. In his late sixties, he was a legend. He served on such boards as 20th Century Fox and Black & Decker, had major equity invested in several entities, and owned thoroughbred race horses in Europe. Moreover, he was widely loved. At an earlier time, Joe was the obvious person to have taken the chairmanship and CEO jobs over Fred Ehrman, but he had no interest in managing the firm.

In the current circumstances, Joe's health was of more than passing interest, and I approached him first in my campaign to secure longer payouts. He suggested that we talk at his favorite health club. This delighted me. But instead of giving me an address outside the building, he told me to meet him on the eleventh floor of the One William Street Lehman building. When I got off the elevator, Joe was standing at a door down the hall, waving me in his direction. He greeted me with the warm smile and firm handshake that were signs of the delightful personality everyone had talked about. But the room he ushered me into was like no health club I had ever seen. Indeed, it seemed more like Joe's private in-house bar, which indeed it was.

I noticed immediately that he had the cherry nose of a big drinker. Even more alarming were the tubes entering his nostrils from a nearby oxygen tank on a wheeled cart; Joe had advanced emphysema. On the table in front of him were a water glass full of bourbon whiskey and a bottle in case he wanted more. After he said hello, he produced a large cigar from an inside pocket of his suit and scratched a match to light it. This, I thought with a stab of alarm, was likely to be an explosive first meeting.

But Joe was both engaging personally and astute about the firm's difficulties. He readily agreed to my proposal to change the equity payments from a one-year window to five years to let the company better control its resources. After Joe agreed, we managed to persuade all the senior partners except Ehrman to accept a five-year payout.

This solved one major and immediate problem, but our overall vulnerability remained. To help me address it, I asked for an analysis of where Lehman was and was not making money. A product line profitability and competitive analysis is standard operating procedure in any corporation. I was shocked, however, to learn that Lehman had no real idea of its profit performance in any of its various businesses—investment banking, brokerage, asset management, and so forth. All I could think was that the firm had gone into its various businesses because everyone else was doing it.

We had to fill this informational and analytical void quickly. Without those kinds of analyses, I would have little idea of how to restructure Lehman Brothers most effectively. Turning to outside consultants would, I knew, cost a lot of money and take a lot of time while they familiarized themselves with the business. But we had plenty of under-utilized in-house expertise. Lehman was blessed with an unusual number of very bright MBA colleagues. Putting them on the case would not only save time and money, it would also get them involved in solving the problems the firm faced instead of sitting anxiously on the sidelines and second-guessing.

We set up not one single group, but several task forces to look at the various sectors of Lehman's businesses. Soon some solid analyses and sensible solutions were landing on my doorstep. The great psychological advantage, when we put them into effect, was that they were not simply imposed by me, but grew out of a new team effort.

Part of my role as the new head of Lehman Brothers was to demonstrate my commitment to the firm's survival. Among other things, I needed to show people still getting to know me that I understood that these were hard times at the firm and that I was not a certain Washington or corporate type who needed to be surrounded with lavish perquisites and grand executive trappings. One way of doing that was to reject those trappings. I took a small existing office, only about 150 square feet, which would have been a closet in my office at the Department of Commerce. Instead of ordering new furnishings, I used what was on hand. I hoped the message I was sending would cascade down through the entire firm.

Not that I was spending much time in my office anyway. My schedule was hectic, partly because our competitors tried to steal our clients by pointing out that Lehman was a weakened firm with a thin capital base and even on the brink of bankruptcy. They also told clients our market share was slipping everywhere, for example, that we had once ranked third in underwriting publicly traded equity securities, and by the summer we had slipped to sixth. So I struggled to protect our existing client base and at the same time cut costs by laying off employees. We went through a major downsizing, not simply at the lower levels but at the level of partners who were not really performing. The biggest cuts came in sales, Glucksman's government securities area, and in administrative areas where we found redundancies. By that fall, our payroll was down about 25 percent.

We also had to go on offense. It was vital that we add new clients to those we already had.

The bond trading losses had produced the worst year in Lehman Brothers history. The company lost $8 million for the fiscal year that ended September 30. But by late fall we had staunched the bleeding and the company was making money again—very little. Our debt and capital moved into closer balance and the NYSE took us off its early warning list. Fred Ehrman agreed to a slightly longer payout period and took an interim title as consultant. In November, *The New York Times* reported "The crisis is past" and described the partners as "gung-ho and pulling together." My Washington misfortune, said the story, had made me a "white knight" on Wall Street who had "emerged from a coup d'etat, which he had not planned, as chairman and unifying force."

That first year at Lehman was one of the toughest of my life. But when the close of the fiscal year rolled around, on September 30, 1974, we had managed to return to the black side of the ledger. From the $8 million loss of the year before, we produced a $25 million profit. It seems like petty cash in today's dollars, but at the time it was a thrill.

The partners had received no bonuses the year before, when the company was fighting for survival. In the fall of 1974, we still very much needed capital but the Executive Committee and I agreed that we should pay out some of our earnings as rewards for the year's very hard-earned success. I wanted to show that the top partners were not the only ones involved in the revival. So I put a ceiling on the top bonus, which was mine, at around $450,000. The other five or six Executive Committee members received about $350,000 to $400,000, and one got $425,000.

Now the gamesmanship and petty jealousies emerged again. Men with $300,000 bonus checks in their pockets made it clear, in the form of serious complaints, that they were miffed. The partner who had received $25,000 more than they had was not nearly as capable as they were. The bonus distributions were unfathomable, unfair, unconscionable! This came from people who had gotten nothing one year earlier, when the firm was on the brink.

I was quietly furious. I have always found it difficult to shout, or truly verbalize my anger. Lew Glucksman would have exploded. It might have been healthier for me and the organization had I, too, been more vocal. To myself I was thinking, "What a bunch of spoiled and ungrateful schmucks!"

I had also never been comfortable with the entitlement mentality of these yuppies. I had one of those Depression-baby mentalities. For example, I focused much of my shopping on getting a double discount on Bloomingdale's sales days, when I got both the sales discount and my discount as a director of Federated Department Stores, which owned Bloomingdale's. Even though I had a million or two dollars at the time, I still had a Polish knockoff Burberry raincoat. It wasn't until the latter part of the 1970s that I felt I could buy a real Burberry, and that was only because someone had stolen my Polish knockoff. For years, I have worn the same $34.95 Timex watch, and still do today. I love the big numbers and the fact that the dial lights up.

Alas, though I had steered Lehman Brothers from the brink back to profitability, I had failed to turn its carnivorous personality around. There was much to do.

CHAPTER 12

New York, Round Two

New Directions

We had staved off bankruptcy and returned to bonus-paying profit margins, but much about Lehman Brothers still needed to be changed. One thing we needed badly was additional capital.

Extending the equity payout period for retiring senior partners (or their estates, in case of death) had amounted to sticking a finger in the dike. In order to attract new partners and clients, we needed adequate capital to reassure them that we could run the business on a long-term basis. In the close-knit world of Wall Street, rumors grow and spread like California wildfires fanned by Santa Ana winds. Our brush with bankruptcy had already damaged our reputation, and our competitors wanted to keep the story alive, by unfounded gossip if that was what it took. We had to demonstrate that we had the capital to finance our deals.

Lehman was not alone. Recent changes in government regulations on trading had served notice on the entire industry that all firms needed more capital, thus we would be competing for available funds. I still hungered to have the money to put into investments on our own account, to have the pleasure and excitement of seeking out and owning well-conceived and well-operated businesses and watching them grow.

So where to get more capital?

George Ball and I discussed the matter. We determined that some foreign banks, which at the time were exploring a more active role in the

United States, might appreciate the relationships that Lehman could provide them. George knew Enrico Braggiotti, the general manager of the major Italian bank, Banca Commerciale Italiana, which was headquartered in Milan and had significant operations in Switzerland. We decided to approach him.

First, we put together a new business plan based on our restructuring. The analyses I had asked our in-house teams to put together had produced some new directions. These veered toward business sectors where we might excel and away from ones that weren't working or that required hefty amounts of capital. I did not want to be in areas where we could not excel. Our real estate business, to take but one example, was largely unblemished by success. A significant number of the property deals we had advised fee-paying clients to invest in had gone sour. This caused the company quite a bit of embarrassment around New York, and I determined it was an area we should get out of. Mergers and acquisitions, on the other hand, seemed to be an area where we could grow. It was also an area that did not require capital.

With our business path now clearer, I supervised the production of a major presentation with color charts and all—the full Peterson treatment. It did this old ad man—or I suppose I might say "Mad Man"—proud, but the true test was whether it would sway the Italians. George and I headed to Switzerland on a mission that we both considered vital to the firm's future.

We met in Basel with Braggiotti and two or three of his colleagues. Their Swiss offices were low-key and traditional. They were cordial in a strictly business way, no extravagant hospitality, but they were clearly interested in what we had to say. I took several hours going through the entire business plan, and the meeting ended with handshakes and a promise that they would think it over.

Two days later, back in New York, we got their answer—a $7 million cash infusion in exchange for 15 percent of Lehman's stock plus $2.5 million in preferred stock. It was the best of both worlds for both sides. Preferred stock gave the Italians first call on dividends and assets, but the dividends it paid were low-yielding and, since it was nonvoting stock, it avoided serious dilution of the partners' stock positions and maintained our independence in governing the firm. Everyone was happy.

Somewhat later, we negotiated a merger with Abraham & Company, a quality brokerage house, that brought in $4.9 million more equity capital.

These equity infusions were without question a triumph for the firm. We got not only capital that we desperately needed, but also a huge vote of confidence that rippled through Wall Street and silenced the sniping from our competitors. The Street's rumor mill, with little to chew on concerning Lehman Brothers, moved to other subjects for a time. It even, for a moment, quieted the dissidents among the partners.

With our capital position improved, it was time to pursue some of the new initiatives laid out in our business plan. Mergers and acquisitions loomed as the most promising of these, and I began a major thrust in that direction. It would be hard to shake clients from their traditional underwriting banks, but I believed that my relationships with a broad range of CEOs might help us enlarge our presence as advisors and financiers in M&As.

By now it was 1975. I set up a small group of banking partners, including myself. It was Lehman Brothers' first formal new business program, and it proved to be the right move. Lehman's M&A operation soared; within two years, aided by the talents of my future partner in The Blackstone Group, Stephen Schwarzman, who was then only twenty-eight years old, we would achieve a dead heat for first place with the legendary team of Bruce Wasserstein and Joe Perella at Credit Suisse First Boston. (Of course, we measured our status by the *number* of deals in which we participated, and they measured by the size of the deals, the more traditional yardstick. But we at least had a slight claim on bragging rights.)

Once we had shored up our capital position and established ourselves in areas where we could grow, we now had to make our case before a larger audience. Yet this was risky business, given the unease left over from our problems of two years earlier. The business media approached us incessantly for stories. I never agreed to talk with them before I felt confident that whatever appeared would bolster our image, not hark back to old news and renew the doubts.

When *Business Week* promised a cover story, we decided we should go for it. But I had a condition, a big one. The *Times* had already described me as the "white knight at Lehman Brothers." It was very flattering, but I wanted to erase the impression that a lone figure had ridden in to save the day. We needed to be seen as a team, working with one another and pursuing common, not individual, goals. This, I believed—rather naively, it turned out—might help end the fractiousness that was such a dark spot on Lehman Brothers' image. So I told *Business Week* that it had to put the entire executive committee on the cover.

It was hard for the editors to swallow, but they agreed. In the end, they pulled a slightly fast one. They took a group photo, but positioned me slightly apart from the others, so that when the magazine came out I was on the outside cover and the six other key partners— George Ball, Warren Hellman, Alexander Abraham, Robert S. Rubin, Lew Glucksman, and Jim Glanville—were on an added foldout page. Nevertheless the story, which ran in the issue of November 10, 1975, set off sighs of relief among the partners. Headlined "Back from the Brink Comes Lehman Bros," it was as favorable a piece as we could have hoped for.

But dissension still lurked beneath the surface. And indeed, it was impossible for a mere picture on the cover of a magazine and some positive coverage to quench the rivalries that animated Lehman's partners. They were some of the most talented people on the Street, but they simply did not work well together. Senior Goldman Sachs partners told me they coveted our talent pool. But I knew that Goldman Sachs was a more effective firm, the reason being that its partners worked together, finding creative solutions and obtaining deals that no individual partners could do working solo. Some of Lehman Brothers' so-called partners, despite my efforts to stress teamwork, seemed committed to work against each other.

Organizational consultants refer to a "positive-sum" game, that is, a situation in which the organization as a whole adds up to more than the sum of its parts. By contrast, a well-known Goldman partner once told me, "Pete, I think you are dealing with a negative-sum game." In other words, the firm was less than the sum of its individual parts.

Bonus Babies

When I arrived at Lehman Brothers, the assignment of year-end bonuses was done on an almost arbitrary and secretive basis. This fed the bitter complaints I had witnessed when bonuses were handed out in 1974. The levels of self-absorption and self-dealing took on new heights—or depths—each year at compensation time. I had dealt with compensation issues as the CEO of Bell & Howell, and also served on the compensation committees of several major corporate boards, such as 3M, General Foods, RCA, and Federated Department Stores. I knew that well-tested techniques existed for fair, effective, and performance-based year-end bonus distributions, and I decided to put some of them into place.

Peer reviews and performance metrics were one such technique. In the investment banking area, I selected three of the most well-respected and trusted banking partners, Roger Altman, François de Saint Phalle, and Vincent Mai, to conduct the peer review. In turn, we set up three performance criteria. The bankers' compensation would be judged on the new business they generated, business processed, and finally, their managerial contributions to the well-being of the firm, such as how they worked with others and whether they helped train new employees. (Performance was far easier to measure on the trading side; you looked primarily at the profits that remained after a charge for the use of capital, and compared these numbers with our competitors'.)

We started by listing every piece of new banking business gained during the previous year. The peer review team then interviewed all the bankers on the history of each piece. The aim was to determine who deserved what percentage of the credit for each of these new business clients.

The results were hilarious. A stand-up comic would have introduced the subject by saying, "You can't make this stuff up." A rational person would assume that the credit percentages would add up to 100 percent, or close to it. Instead, the total credit claimed for the average piece of new Lehman Brothers business during the year preceding totaled 450 percent! Obviously, some partners were claiming credit for new business that they had little or nothing to do with.

This happened, particularly egregiously, in the case of International Harvester. Their CEO and I served together on the finance committee of the board of General Foods. One day he called me to say he was unhappy with Morgan Stanley and was turning International Harvester's investment banking business over to us. That was it: end of story. He told me to assign the best bankers to work on the account.

The phone call bringing us this major account had come during a year in which I had been fortunate enough to generate a substantial part of the firm's major new business. But I instructed the peer review committee to exclude me from the numbers on new business. That meant the credit claimed by others for the International Harvester account should have added up to zero. It did not. Seven partners claimed shares of credit amounting to 270 percent!

I was being called a rainmaker. Assuming it were true, I've wondered why I might have achieved that status. I have thought about other genuine rainmakers like Henry Kissinger and James Wolfensohn, former president of the World Bank. To this day, they are remarkably successful in garnering important advisory clients. Part of their success, I'm sure, is the quality of the specific advice they offer. But another part, I'm equally sure, is their public service, their global reputation, and the pleasure it brings prospective clients to be associated with men of Henry's and Jim's quality and status.

I do think my government service, my public crusades, and my nonprofit institutional work have been ingredients in whatever success I have had as a rainmaker. But I do not pretend to have Henry's or Jim's rock star status. I complemented whatever access to senior people I had with a lesson I learned in my McCann-Erickson new business experience: Prospective clients are primarily interested in their own businesses and their own business problems. I rarely made a new business call that was not preceded by a good deal of homework and focused on some specific insights or ideas we had about their particular business.

This is not to say this is the only approach to rainmaking. I know of very successful rainmakers who entertain, golf, socialize, and charm their way to new business. I concluded that was not my comparative advantage.

Better Times at Lehman

By this time, we were in the late 1970s and Lehman Brothers was doing very well. I felt confident enough in the firm's prospects to take on a new public policy assignment, chairing the federal Commission on Executive, Legislative, and Judicial Salaries, at President Gerald Ford's request in 1976. These federal pay commissions convened every four years. The last two had recommended raises but Congress, fearing voter reaction, turned them down. The result: 5 percent raises since 1969 versus 60.5 percent inflation. The government was bleeding talent; no one who wasn't rich or young and untested could afford to work for it. Yet, in the post-Watergate era there were few ideas less popular than paying public officials more.

We decided to focus on what the market might tell us. Judges, we learned, generally took significant pay *cuts* when they joined the government and gained the biggest increases when they left. Congress was the opposite; it was the *only* group that was paid more after joining the government payroll than they had earned before. There was little turnover at the most senior cabinet levels of the executive branch of government or at the Supreme Court. These were positions that paid large "psychic income." (This didn't deter Chief Justice Warren Burger from calling me at my home one night lobbying for higher pay for Supreme Court justices, including himself. I turned him down, making clear that in the post-Watergate malaise we were not proposing pay increases unless they were absolutely necessary.)

Both political logic and the market dictated that we recommend very small pay increases at the highest levels of the executive and judicial branches and substantially more at the lower levels where the turnover was highest. President Ford accepted those recommendations.

Logic did not prevail, but self-interest did when it came to the Congress. Their salaries had been linked to the same level as federal district judges. We argued that the two should be de-linked, as our market study had indicated that the judges should be paid more than the men and women of Congress.

The Congress said no. I thought their grounds were specious and disingenuous: For example, one of their arguments was that the Constitution set out three *equal* branches of government and that went for pay, too.

We thought that establishing a Code of Conduct was needed to restore confidence in government after the Watergate debacle. To take but one plank of our Code of Conduct, we wanted to limit or eliminate the fees that members of Congress could accept for speaking engagements and trips, often from trade associations that had legislative agendas. The potential for conflicts of interest was high, and the other two branches were barred from accepting such honoraria.

I liked President Ford enormously for his decency and humility. I spent an hour and a half talking to him one on one, arguing that he, as a veteran of Congress, would be remembered by history if he curbed lawmakers from accepting cozy speaking fees. I told him he could achieve the same kind of legacy as Ike had in his parting message when he warned against undue influence by the "military-industrial complex."

Alas, Ford was such a product of the Congress that he just couldn't bring himself to inflict this "pain" on his congressional friends. Politics proved itself neither logical, fair, nor "market-oriented" at that point. But we persisted and, after a year or so, were successful in limiting the speaking honoraria that members of Congress could accept.

Back at Lehman, we had further solidified our capital position through a merger with Kuhn, Loeb and Company, an old-line investment bank, in 1977, creating Lehman Brothers, Kuhn, Loeb, Inc. Nevertheless, we remained in need of long-term equity capital, and so even though we would earn about $200 million, I felt we should still put a limit on cash bonuses. Accordingly, I capped my bonus at $1 million and did the same for Lew Glucksman, now very well rehabilitated from his bond trading disaster and serving as the firm's president, replacing Warren Hellman.

It was a sad day for me when Warren quit. He told me he wanted to raise his children in Vermont, where he and Chris had founded the

Stratton Mountain School as a college preparatory academy for Olympic skiers in training. But I knew that skiing was only part of his motivation. I suspected that Warren also felt that working with Glucksman and Jim Glanville was abrasive work that wore through the thickest skin and eventually drew blood.

Despite his drawbacks, Glucksman brought many complementary skills to the table, not to mention profits on our trading businesses. On the surface at least, he and I seemed to work very well together. This was why I had elevated him to president.

But he retained a streak of willfulness that could be disruptive. All the bankers knew that bonuses depended on the performance-based peer review system. Nevertheless, Glucksman walked into my office one day and confessed that he had stepped out of line. He appeared genuinely troubled. He said he had secretly promised Bob Rubin, his close friend and colleague and one of our most brilliant bankers (not the equally brilliant Robert E. Rubin, who served as secretary of the treasury during Bill Clinton's administration), that Bob would get a bonus two-thirds of whatever Lew's was. The Executive Committee agreed that this was much too much given the three performance metrics we had set up. He had, for example, brought in no new business.

Lew promised not to make such unilateral and arbitrary decisions in the future. But the episode bothered me deeply. To make good on Lew's promise meant undermining the whole idea of a meritocracy, of performance-based bonuses. To ask Lew to break his promise was just as difficult. For all of the infighting and self-dealing, Lehman's credo was that we honored our agreements. So, in spite of genuine anger in some quarters, I let Bob Rubin's compensation stand. That, in retrospect, was a mistake. The episode left me depressed and unsatisfied. For all of our success in strengthening the venerable house of Lehman, I still felt the firm lacked a culture of meritocracy, openness, and fairness.

Based on my experience with therapy, I found that Freudian slips of the tongue often reveal a lot about my inner feelings. One day, during yet another fractious experience with year-end bonuses, I found myself slipping and blurting out "fartners." I had obviously meant to say "partners."

Glanville

No one illustrated the persistence of the old ways more than Jim Glanville. He was from Cooper, Texas, northeast of Dallas, and had been a field engineer at Humble Oil before leaving the oil patch for Wall Street, taking an impressive list of oil and energy contacts with him. Many of them developed into major Lehman clients. Jim was a prime example of the talent we had at Lehman Brothers. But that disruptive talent was applied—as it often was—to his own dubious ends.

Early on in my tenure in 1974, when we were undergoing our restructuring, I saw that we needed to beef up our position in the institutional markets—the pension funds, large university endowments, corporations, mutual funds, and the like. To this end, we needed to improve our ability to distribute, that is, to sell, securities to institutions. Strengthening our equity research was essential. The executive committee was unanimous on this, or so I thought.

Mitchell Hutchins was a rapidly growing firm whose record in equity research was excellent. Its CEO, Don Marron, was a very good friend of mine, and he was interested in merging our firms. He wanted, naturally, to feel that they would fit well together, and expected that he would fill a senior position.

Our negotiations were well along when Don called me with disturbing news. "I thought you said everybody was on board with our working out some kind of deal," he said.

"We are," I replied. I told him of the executive committee's unanimous vote.

"That may be," he said. "But I just had a visit from Jim Glanville that he asked me to keep secret, and Peter, you must honor this. He's not on board at all. He had nothing but bad things to say, and he made some snide comments about you, too. I'm sorry to say this, Pete, but I know you can appreciate my reaction. I would never want to join an organization where this kind of disloyalty and destructiveness is going on. And I thought you should know what you're dealing with."

The Mitchell Hutchins merger died, at great cost to our research and ultimately our distribution capacities. I never confronted Glanville afterward, because I had promised Don Marron that I wouldn't. But he had provided a true—and truly senseless—illustration of the infamous Lehman culture.

Glanville did it again over an Amax assignment. Amax, based in Greenwich, Connecticut, was a giant mining company that produced coal and a variety of metals, including iron ore, copper, lead, zinc, nickel, aluminum, and gold. The company was a longtime and closely connected Lehman client. George Ball was on its board of directors, but Glanville was primarily responsible for servicing the account.

In the 1970s, many oil companies had a lot of extra cash and were looking to extend their reach into new fields they viewed as compatible. Metals fit this description. Standard Oil of California (SoCal) had had its eye on Amax for some time. Indeed, in 1975 Glanville had helped engineer a friendly stock swap that gave SoCal a 15.5 percent stake in Amax and Amax a needed cash infusion.

By 1977, however, Amax had new management that looked less kindly on SoCal's continuing overtures. Pierre Gousseland had become Amax's CEO, and he believed SoCal was bent on a total takeover. Gousseland wanted to fend off any SoCal bid, and he enlisted us—for a $1 million advisory fee—to develop a defense strategy. We laid out a series of steps that we believed would keep Amax independent. These were discussed among the executive committee, but I assumed they were, of course, confidential between us and Amax.

Glanville was not only involved with the Amax account, he also had close contacts at SoCal, including its CEO, H. J. "Bill" Haynes. But it was Amax that had retained us to fight off the SoCal offer, and that was where our loyalties lay. Or should have.

One morning in August, George Ball came from his office next door into mine and closed the door. On this occasion his expressive face showed worry and distress. Pierre Gousseland had called, he said. It was imperative that the three of us have lunch that day. He wanted to discuss a development that he had termed "very disturbing."

Picking at his meal in one of the small Lehman dining rooms, Gousseland told us that he had learned from some highly credible sources that Glanville had been leaking some of our defensive tactics to his friends at SoCal. Further, said Gousseland, Glanville was encouraging SoCal to move aggressively against Amax. George and I were both appalled. This struck at the very heart and soul of Lehman Brothers. No first-rate financial firm traffics lightly in matters of integrity, confidentiality, trust, and loyalty to clients. Had news of this double-dealing leaked, it would have severely damaged Lehman's reputation. Fortunately, Gousseland supported both George Ball and Lehman Brothers, and said nothing to outsiders.

I left the lunch with my blood boiling at Glanville's treachery. I ran through in my mind all of his possible rationales, which I knew would come down to the argument that Gousseland didn't know what was right for Amax and Glanville and his friends at SoCal did. Presumably, he could have gotten a big merger fee from SoCal. But that wasn't Glanville's choice to make. We were on retainer with Amax, and it was simply wrong.

I was more troubled than I knew. After the lunch, Gousseland left and I went with George back to his office. The next thing I knew, I was waking up in an ambulance. George Ball, in shirtsleeves, was leaning over me with an emergency medical technician on the other side monitoring my vital signs. "You suffered a seizure," George said. "We're on our way to New York Hospital to get you diagnosed."

A year later in 1978, Glanville added the final straw.

When I got to Lehman Brothers, I had instructed the financial staff never to assume I knew, but to tell me of any possible infraction of either the law or the spirit of partnership rules. One such rule—a fundamental one—was that any investment projects offered by any clients needed to be disclosed and made available to the entire partnership. The logic was simple. Under certain circumstances—if, for example, individual partners provided significant financial services for which they were personally rewarded but not the firm—their personal profits would come at the expense of the firm as a whole.

Lehman's venture investment culture meant that the firm had equity capital invested in certain fully disclosed client stocks. Given the firm's ongoing need for capital, the Executive Committee voted unanimously in 1978 that we should liquidate as many of these investments as we could to increase our cash position.

It wasn't always easy. We had to get approval from the clients, and sometimes the talks were difficult. But the partners cooperated and we eventually cashed out of these client stocks and added the proceeds to the firm's thin capital base. With one exception.

Glanville had argued that we could not sell our holding in our client Freeport-McMoRan, a large copper and gold producer, without seriously jeopardizing the client relationship. But that wasn't the only reason, as I learned when our senior tax professional, Ron Gallatin, asked to meet with me privately and confidentially.

He was obviously nervous. He first reminded me of my strict instruction to be informed of any violation of the partnership rules. Reassured that I was serious and would protect him against any reprisals, he continued.

"Pete," he said, "I know you have been having trouble getting Glanville to sell the Freeport-McMoRan investment. Here's what is going on. In lieu of redeeming that investment, the client has offered him a sweetheart real estate deal. It offers very good returns and is very tax-efficient. Glanville and a few colleagues plan to take it for themselves. He has offered me 5 percent of the deal if I will do all the tax work for free and if I keep it secret. I know he's a powerful guy and it's a great risk for me to tell you this, but I also know that what he's asking me to do is wrong."

I thanked Ron profusely, probably stammering as I vacillated between gratitude and outrage. Then it hit me: Could he prove it? Otherwise, it was his word against Glanville's, and we all knew who would win that battle. "Is this still in the talking stages, or are there papers?" I asked.

Ron produced a folder that contained a full set of papers ready to be signed.

Glanville's audacity was breathtaking. I immediately called the other members of the Executive Committee together. After I had briefed them and shown them the papers, they agreed the action was intolerable and voted unanimously for me to confront Glanville.

I met with him soon afterward and produced the evidence. "Jim, I think you'll agree this is clearly not what a good partner does to his colleagues," I said. "If you actually attempt to complete this deal, it is grounds for dismissal."

He basically just shrugged. A few days later, around the beginning of August, he left for Lazard Frères along with three of his close friends among the partners. Glanville took much of Lehman's energy client portfolio with him, but, at least to me, it was worth the loss to feel some crisp, fresh, untainted air flowing through the building in his absence. The business press treated the matter as a coup by Lazard. As *Fortune* magazine put it, Lazard had "startled the clubby world of New York investment banking by poaching four senior men . . ." We at Lehman knew better, and many of us, on balance, were happy to be poached.

Of course, Glanville did not go as quietly as that. Not long after he left, we were served notice of a lawsuit. He was suing on the grounds that one of the firm's investments, a coal slurry pipeline that he followed, had been improperly valued. The claim was outrageous, given that he sat on the Executive Committee, which regularly and formally approved all valuations.

Worse than the lawsuit was the diatribe he wrote to George Ball. Glanville, George, and I had been the only non-Jews at the senior management level of Lehman Brothers. Now Glanville revealed a dark streak of bias and resentment. His letter essentially accused the Jewish members of the Lehman Executive Committee of consistently taking the side of Israel over the United States and its Arab oil suppliers on such policy questions as the return of land seized in the 1967 war. He also charged that the committee chair had "hidden" his "ethnic persuasion." Since I was the chair, and had frequently and publicly discussed my Greek heritage, this was equally ludicrous.

Most of the Executive Committee members were outraged. Many wanted to sue. I thought this would only prolong and publicize the dispute; an eye for an eye and a tooth for a tooth often leaves both parties disfigured. And as a practical matter, our clients would not want to see their bankers in this kind of tawdry dispute.

I did, however, set up a meeting with Michel David-Weill, the chairman and managing partner of Lazard Frères. He had taken over from André Meyer, a Wall Street legend known both for his acuity and his rough treatment of his colleagues.

"You and I would agree that Wall Street is a tough and competitive place," I said. "No place for the weak or the fainthearted. But I believe we would also agree that questioning your competitors' patriotism goes beyond the pale." I handed him Glanville's troubling letter.

He read it thoroughly. When he looked up, I expected him to agree. Instead, he reached into an inside pocket and brought out a cigar, a very long one for such a small man. He lit it, blew smoke, and waved it away. "Ah," he said, "everyone knows what Glanville is like. But he has a number of important clients."

"And does that excuse him from making blasphemous comments about my Jewish colleagues?"

At this he simply smiled dismissively. It was the smile of a self-satisfied man who feels he is informed about the world, a smile he gives to a man he believes is simple and naive.

I barely contained my anger as I walked away. Once, when I was deeply frustrated at turning Lehman's cultural deficit around, Felix Rohatyn and I had talked about jointly running Lazard Frères' New York office. What a poor move that would have been. The Street's conventional wisdom held that Lehman and Lazard suffered from a similar cultural disease eating at their cores.

Brain Surgery/Shock

Sally and my son Jim got to the hospital following my seizure. I had been examined, admitted, and assigned a private room. Sally and Jim were obviously concerned. So was I, but I couldn't give them any information. I said I had no idea what had hit me. While they were there, my internist's partner walked into the room. He was a study in brusque efficiency as he said, "Mr. Peterson, you are probably wondering what you have."

"As a matter of fact, I am," I said. "I'm not used to waking up in an ambulance without remembering how I got there."

"You have a brain tumor," he said. This blunt announcement set off shock waves, but he wasn't finished. "You probably want to know what kind of tumor, whether it is malignant or benign," he continued.

He didn't wait for me to answer. "The odds are about ninety percent it is malignant."

The whole exchange, if you could call it that, covered less than sixty seconds. He turned and walked out of the room. Sally followed on his heels, demanding more information. Jim looked stunned. I certainly was, as I tried to absorb this hammer blow of news. Was it a death sentence? What was it? When Sally returned, looking pale, she conveyed the grim prognosis. The doctor had told her I probably had six weeks to live. I felt like I was trapped in a bad comedy routine about doctors and their bedside manners.

By then, the New York network had gotten wind of my predicament. My bedside phone started ringing with a flood of sympathetic calls. Henry Kissinger and Averell Harriman were among the callers. They each wanted to know what they could do.

"Get me the best neurologist in the world," I said.

It took less than an hour for them to call back. Consulting with George Ball, they had determined that Dr. Fred Plum, the head of New York Hospital's Department of Neurology, fit the description. When he arrived, he began a diagnosis that started with an hour and a half of intensive questioning, demonstrating right away the difference between the best and the rest. Among his first questions: "Has anything unusual or abnormal happened today, something that might have gotten you upset?"

I told him of the luncheon with Pierre Gousseland and my reaction to the news of Glanville's treachery. Dr. Plum added that information to his notes.

At the end, he apologized for the knee-jerk diagnosis given at the outset. "You should never have been given information like that without some definitive tests," he said. He had scheduled a series of tests for the next morning. "But," he added, "I have studied hundreds of brain tumor cases, and contrary to what you were told, I think the odds may be as good as fifty or sixty percent that your tumor is benign."

The next morning, I readied myself for the battery of tests. Ominously, a surgeon was present. When I asked why, I learned that the tests might indicate a need for emergency surgery. Having had enough bad news over the previous twenty-four hours, I let it rest at that.

There were no MRIs (magnetic resonance imaging) in those days. The procedure was more rudimentary. A technician shot some hot-feeling chemical into the large vein in my groin. Seconds later, a gigantic camera started clicking and taking multiple images of my brain, following the blood flow highlighted by the chemical. It gave me a decidedly eerie feeling. The camera knew what it was seeing, but I did not. And what it saw was a life-or-death secret.

Hours later, Fred Plum came into my room. By now some cards, and several sprays of flowers, had arrived to brighten the dark atmosphere. Sally, who had been there throughout, was sitting in a chair by the window. Dr. Plum was carrying a stack of pictures from the machine. He pointed out one long blood vessel charting a path to a dark mass that looked like a barnacle at the back of my brain. "Malignant brain tumors typically grow too rapidly to permit the growth of such a long blood vessel," he said. "I believe there's an eighty to ninety percent chance that your tumor is benign, what is called a meningioma."

"Having said that," he added with considerable equanimity, "we still have to take it out and do a biopsy to be sure."

The operation the next day lasted seven hours. And sure enough, the biopsy showed the tumor was benign. Ten days later I was released from the hospital feeling fine and immensely grateful to Fred Plum (who became a lifelong friend). In the aftermath of that harrowing episode, I now take an MRI annually to be sure there has been no recurrence of the tumor.

In the months and years following my brain surgery, things returned to normal. My hair grew back over the sutures in my scalp where my skull had been sawed open to give the surgeons access to my brain. I resumed my efforts to try to tame the rogue culture at Lehman Brothers. I got back to golf and tennis, Michael and Holly advanced through their elementary schools, David through Dartmouth, and Jim graduated from Bucknell and went to work at NBC in the finance department. Sally and I went on as before. I was often out at night attending meetings, or dealing with business over weekends on the golf course or elsewhere. This was all a part of my providing for the family, and Sally coped with it. Or so I assumed.

Bad Times at Home

One day in the fall of 1978, I arrived home from work at a relatively normal time. We sat down with Holly and Michael to have dinner, served by our live-in help. After dinner, when the children had returned to television or their homework, Sally said quietly, "I need to talk to you. In private."

We went into the library, a book-lined room at the apartment's southeast corner. The windows looked over the East River and down to the 59th Street Bridge. We were far away from everyone else in the apartment.

"What is it?" I said.

She gathered herself, and looked at me. "There's no easy way to say this, Peter," she said. "I want a divorce."

I didn't think I had heard her correctly. "I'm sorry, say that again," I said.

"I want a divorce."

To say I was stunned doesn't do justice to my feelings at that moment. Disbelief, incomprehension, fear, embarrassment—all came to me in waves. I felt like one of those cartoon characters who run off the edge of a cliff and suddenly realize there's nothing under them but air. My foundation, my security, had suddenly been snatched away.

In retrospect, I should not have been surprised. There had been warning signs. I had always prided myself that Sally was an attractive woman and a good mother, but her urge to rebel had been growing for some time. She had always been the wild card among the cabinet wives in Washington, and even on the Georgetown party circuit, where any enthusiasm for the Nixon administration was limited, her contempt was apparent. Now, six years removed from public life, her rebelliousness had taken other forms. She preferred a crowd that was far younger and more literary than my business and establishment colleagues and their wives. She found them boring. More and more, she had been opting out of events that involved them and going her own way. On nights when I was tied up on business, she was out with her young friends. I had ignored these signs, if indeed I noticed them at all, as preoccupied as I had been with the demands of running Lehman Brothers. I was either too trusting, or too insensitive, or just too naive to contemplate or confront her restlessness.

She wanted to move out as soon as possible. My protests, she told me, were useless. She had been thinking about it for some time. And in the end, I knew trying to fight her would leave both of us more damaged. After a few months of awkward cohabitation, she moved to an apartment I bought her on 72nd Street and took Holly and Michael with her, though we would share custody. The kids were understandably upset. But, as time went on, the kids, as they are inclined to do, seemed to make adjustments in their own lives. But not I.

Now I felt alone in an apartment with five bedrooms and six baths and views of the East River that I was no longer able to appreciate. I stood by those windows in the middle of the night, staring out and trying to find answers as sleep eluded me. When the long, sleepless nights finally ended and I could go to work, I had trouble concentrating. I was clinically depressed. My blood pressure shot up. As my close friends observed my devastation and inability to function, they concluded (quietly) that while I had every reason to be distressed, I was overreacting to the circumstances.

When I finally understood this, I decided I needed to return to psychotherapy. Whereas my previous experience on the couch back in Chicago had been motivated primarily by curiosity, this time I really needed to understand what I was feeling. Therapy had gained no greater level of acceptance in the interim, at least among most of the businessmen I knew. They still acted as if talking about feelings was a sign of weakness, and as if even talking about having psychotherapy was to be avoided. The public image of shrinks has probably contributed to attitudes like this. They're often depicted in the movies and on TV as plenty weird, as they scribble notes and tug on their goatees. Alpha male CEOs are supposed to be able to solve their own problems, not turn them in fits of self-indulgence over to people who supposedly have magical powers to discern the inner workings of the mind. But having been there, I knew what psychotherapy could do and I knew I needed help. I opted to go for an intensive approach.

Intensive, in the context of my problem, meant longer than the usual sessions. This is because, as any of my friends can tell you, I am a talker. And when one is as talkative as I am, one can easily talk around hidden feelings, at least for a time. During the standard therapy session, the patient has fifty minutes. I decided to have not just one, but two consecutive sessions to help me get at the roots of my problem. And indeed, it was during those second hours, after I had talked myself out, when I dug deeper and some of the more profound insights slowly emerged.

Through a combination of free association and analysis of my dreams, I began to understand the roots of my reaction, actually, my overreaction. I had regressed to the time of an earlier abandonment— my mother's withdrawal of affection at the time of my sister Elaine's death. I was acting as if I was still a child, helpless, abandoned, and alone. E. L. Doctorow, the famous novelist, probably phrased it best when he told me once when we were talking at a dinner party that a neurosis is "an obsolete reaction to an earlier experience."

Obsolete, for certain. I had re-created as a fifty-two-year-old adult the feelings of a dependent four-year-old. But I was neither helpless nor dependent. Once I understood this both in my head and, more importantly, in my gut, I began to feel better.

As I became more rational, it was clear that Sally and I had grown apart. Ours was a rather prototypical 1950s marriage contract. I provided well, and certainly brought home the bacon. But I did not deliver well on the emotional front, even by 1950s standards. She took care of the home and kids very well indeed. In the 1960s, Betty Friedan would write *The Feminine Mystique*, a book that laid out the latent depression inherent in these housewives focused solely on home, hearth, and children.

Sally never complained. I wish she had.

The life she wanted was no longer compatible with mine. We were not soul mates. Logic, when I was finally able to embrace it as a result of my double sessions twice a week for several months, told me that it made no sense to cling to a relationship with those toxic ingredients. I finally understood that I could get along without her and that was better for both of us. This understanding did not end my psychotherapy, but it put me at peace as I moved on.

I would learn in time that Sally, at forty-seven, a mother of five, and an aspiring psychotherapist, had fallen in love with Michael Carlisle—a graduate of Andover and Yale, who had grown up with William Styron and Arthur Miller as the closest of family friends—who represented, as a literary agent, more of what she wanted out of life. He was also more than twenty years younger. He was not part of the stuffy old "establishment," and represented more of the literary, unconventional, and bohemian style she was denied in our relationship. While at first, learning of another man represented another blow, in time, it hastened my recovery as it began to illustrate clearly the differences that had grown between Sally and me. Incidentally, Sally's choice proved to be a good one, as she and Michael got married and have been very happy together for the thirty years since.

To a large extent, I had replayed with Sally the marriage of my father and my mother, where his workaholism had always denied her some level of emotional comfort and companionship. Realizing all this, and recognizing that my present strengths bore no relation to my dependent past, I was on the road to recovery.

While I take full responsibility for my actions, or perhaps I should say my inactions, and exaggerated preoccupations, I think it is also fair to say that the American culture in those early days was at a somewhat different place. In the 1950s, most women, about 70 percent, were nonworking and it was seen as their "job" to take care of the home and the kids. To a much greater extent than today, it was felt that the husband, who worked so hard to take care of his wife, home, and kids financially, "deserved" to relax when he came home.

Frankly, I didn't really much want to relax at home. I have never had a martini in my life and I rarely drink even wine. But I did expect Sally to "handle" the children. This division of labor was not the root of our problem. Sally's wanting to lead a new life was the principal cause of our "irreconcilable differences."

Joan

My friends were glad to have me back as I began to emerge from my depression in the spring of 1979. New York society can be not only a great tonic and a distraction from one's troubles, but one of the world's great dating services. Once Sally and I were separated and clearly headed for divorce, my attentions turned to a woman I had met in the late 1960s, who at the time had dazzled me. I was a member of the board of NET in 1968—National Educational Television—when Joan Ganz Cooney presented her plans for the creation of *Sesame Street* through the Children's Television Workshop. The idea for *Sesame Street* was dazzling, too.

Joan, at the time, was married to Timothy J. Cooney, who held the position of civil defense chief in John Lindsay's mayoral administration. They divorced in 1975. After Sally and I split, my interest in Joan rekindled, aided by the keen perceptions and suggestions of our mutual friends. The first of these dating arrangements came at the hands of Mort and Linda Janklow, the topflight literary agent and his art patron wife, who had a dinner party and seated Joan and me together. It wasn't especially subtle, but it worked. Soon afterward, I called and asked her out to dinner.

I impressed Joan mightily on that first date. It was purely a matter of coincidence. We dined at Argenteuil, a clubby cafe with French cuisine in the East 50s (since closed). The conversation, first over drinks and then dinner and wine, dwelled on our marriages, our work, and the kinds of things professional people talk about. My ears perked up when Joan began to tell me about problems she was having with the *National Enquirer*, the sensational supermarket tabloid whose stock in trade was lurid crime and celebrity scandal. Apparently, she said, that included her and the Children's Television Workshop. The *Enquirer* was hotly pursuing allegations that the workshop had misapplied federal grant funds. The claims were minor, a matter of confusing language in the grants, but the paper was prone to pump them up, and she had visions of Big Bird on the front page.

"You can stop worrying," I said.

She looked perplexed. "What do you mean?"

"They won't run the story."

"Why not?"

"They just won't. I can virtually guarantee it."

It had been a long time since I had seen my old college friend Gene Pope, but we had stayed in touch. It was practically a matter of urban legend that he had bought a struggling New York paper, the *New York Enquirer*, and turned it into the *National Enquirer*, building a circulation of over five million. Its lurid headlines beckoned shoppers standing in the checkout lines, promising fare more juicy than the contents of their shopping carts. Gene once told me he got the idea from watching people gawk at auto accidents. He had moved the operation to Florida in 1971 and never left. When I was the secretary of commerce I had appeared, at his request, at a meeting of supermarket executives he wanted to impress. More lately, he had retained me as a financial consultant. I told Joan of my close relationship with Gene Pope, and said I would ask him to consider not covering the *Sesame Street* story, which he did not.

Joan and I were seeing each other regularly. After we had dated several times, I thought it was time to introduce her to the kids. Introducing her to the realities of parenting five children was not the easiest phase of our relationship. Jim was spending a lot of time with his girlfriend at Gracie Square while he worked at NBC. David was still a junior at Dartmouth but during college breaks he and his many friends descended on my East Hampton beach house, a big old fully furnished place I had bought a few years earlier for only $145,000. Holly and Michael were at the Dalton School, living with Sally, but spending many weekends and other nights with me. They were all, to some extent, angry and fearful over our breakup and were tentative at best toward Joan. Michael, the youngest, who at the time was nine, was perhaps the most open to Joan. When he met Joan, this wise young soul gave her the nod of approval by appraising her in one word: "Suitable."

Joan's assets stretched well beyond suitability, as I was finding out on a daily basis once we got serious. Joan had no children of her own. Inevitably, she found my five more than a handful. Holly and David, in particular, tended to act out some of their anger over the divorce. This made for some uncomfortable moments.

On weekends, especially holiday weekends, the kids made the East Hampton house into what Joan called a "kiddie motel." David and his girlfriend, for example, would come in from the beach and simply drop their wet towels on the kitchen floor, setting off alarm bells in Joan, who liked things orderly and neat. Holly later revealed at Joan's sixtieth birthday toast (after they had become close friends) that she would purposely put towels in the swimming pool and leave the wet ones on the deck just to drive her new stepmother insane.

Despite these distractions with the kids, Joan and I were falling in love. She was extremely smart and insightful. We talked for hours at a time about many areas of mutual interest, which included everything from politics, to public policy, to the business world (Joan served on several major corporate boards). We also enjoyed many other activities, including tennis, movies, the theater, and some of the New York social life. Above all, we shared a similar sense of humor, and so our courtship was filled not only with intellectual stimulation, but also laughter and joy.

As things progressed, it was clear to me that I could not ask Joan to live at Ten Gracie Square without creating potentially serious tensions. Joan would feel she was inhabiting Sally's and the children's space, with constant reminders of my previous life.

If I wanted Joan to marry me, which I did, I knew it would help a lot to get a new apartment that Joan liked.

By now it was 1980, and my broker went to work. Soon she invited us to look at a space in the legendary River House, at 52nd Street and the East River. (Movie buffs will know it from the 1937 *Dead End,* starring Humphrey Bogart as a waterfront gangster, Joel McCrea as a do-gooder architect who wanted to transform the waterfront by erecting the apartment building, and a gang of slum kids who used the river as a swimming hole.) River House was built in 1931, but not until the arrival of the United Nations almost twenty years later was the change in the neighborhood complete.

We both liked the River House apartment. Now I began a full-court press for marriage, using negotiating tactics that I now think might have been a little bit aggressive. I told her that if she wanted to participate in the major renovations—"Don't you want to make the space your own?"—now was the time to commit. At one point I said, "I can't tell you how long I'm going to wait for an answer, but it's not forever." Did she, or did she not, want to marry me?

My view, after all, was that ours was an ideal partnership. Moreover, it was obvious that I loved her deeply. Our friend Don Hewitt, the genius behind the long-running CBS hit *60 Minutes*, put it more simply. "It really computes," he said.

It amazes me in retrospect that Joan rarely exhibited the behavior of one of the characters she helped produce—Oscar the Grouch. Though she clearly loved me, she did, however, have momentary "sinking spells," as she called them, contemplating how to endure the Peterson clan.

With my four children in New York, the marital burden sharing was very one-sided. (The only burden she brought were her beloved two cats and a dog who insisted on sleeping with us. After our marriage, we were never fewer than five in our bed.) I never had pets, certainly not dogs. In fact, I rather feared dogs ever since the time at a five-year-old's birthday party for boys and alas girls, too, a white Spitz took a small chunk out of my derrière and the mother pulled down my pants in front of all, including the girls. The humiliation far exceeded the pain.

Nonetheless, given the profound inequality of marital burden sharing, I was very restrained in complaining about the bed-sharing arrangements.

Finally, after many proposals, Joan agreed. When the moment happened, it took a minute before I understood what she was saying. Can the heart of a fifty-three-year-old man leap with joy? Yes, I promise you, it can.

And by that time, early in 1980, the children had softened. While from time to time tensions would develop between Joan and the kids, year by year the relationship steadily improved.

The next step was the wedding. If there had been complications earlier from my children's resentments, they were displaced by a whole new set of hierarchical concerns. Joan had been brought up in the Roman Catholic Church and, as a divorcée, could not remarry in the church. Still, she told me she wanted a religious rather than a civil wedding. She described the Greek Orthodox faith as "a kind of 'religious cousin' to the Catholic Church."

I had not set foot in a Greek Orthodox church for over a quarter of a century. When I discussed our intentions with my family over a dinner we convened to get their thoughts, everyone's jaws dropped simultaneously.

My cousin Anastasia was there that night. She was the granddaughter of my mother's Uncle John Petrow of Fremont, Nebraska. An outspoken feminist, she told Joan, "A priest? I think you ought to get a lawyer." She was suggesting that we forge a prenuptial agreement. A prenup is common practice when marriage brings together two unequal partners, but we never considered such an idea. Joan, after all, had forged a worldwide enterprise without any help from me, and I didn't need to protect my assets from a person with her integrity and capabilities. Besides, I think we both were certain our future together would be permanent.

Joan was adamant, however, that she would have a religious wedding, and her determination won the day.

I called a priest with whom I had worked when I had spoken at a Greek event. Father Alex was an assistant to Archbishop Iakovos, the longtime leader of the Greek Orthodox Diocese of North America, and I thought Father Alex might perform the ceremony. "Oh, no, Peter," he told me. "His Eminence will insist on doing so."

The small, private wedding I had originally imagined was showing signs of turning into a production.

The archbishop was an ageless sixty-nine, with a white beard, dark brows, and wide, lively eyes that reflected both curiosity and compassion for the world around him. He had known every president since Eisenhower, and he walked the walk of committed Christianity. He had, for example, joined the marchers who followed Martin Luther King on the famous Selma-to-Montgomery march for civil rights. He also had a delightful, quiet sense of humor. When we met to discuss plans for the wedding, I told him, "Your Eminence, you look wonderful."

"Peter," he said, smiling, "you will come to understand that there are three age groups in life: young; middle-aged, and 'You look wonderful.'"

We agreed that Archbishop Iakovos would preside, but the wedding would be a small one, held in a chapel in his residence at Madison Avenue and 79th Street.

Once the place and date, April 26, 1980, were set, a single stumbling block remained. This one, however, could not be mediated, stemming as it did from an admonition dating to the days of the apostles. And it was a big one. Saint Paul, in his first letter to the Corinthians, lays down views that are troubling to many in modern, secular society.

They particularly contradict the widely accepted notion of feminist equality. "Christ is the head of every man, and the husband is the head of his wife," he wrote, going on to contend, "Neither was man created for the sake of woman, but woman for the sake of man."

Joan, as the co-founder and CEO of *Sesame Street* and the Children's Television Workshop, with a presence in over one hundred countries around the world, and a recipient of many honorary degrees, had distinctly contrary views about that being read in the ceremony. I found her views not only understandable but reasonable. She first tried negotiation. "Can't we just take that out of the ceremony?" she asked Father Alex.

"No," he said. "But don't worry about it. It will be in Greek and no one will understand it." It sounded to me like the Greek Orthodox equivalent of a papal dispensation, as if Joan could later claim, "Well, I didn't understand the vows."

Such evasions, however, were not part of her makeup. She protested that my cousin Anastasia would be among the wedding guests and that she was not only "the most ardent of feminists" but also spoke and understood Greek. "And I think Pete does, too," she told Father Alex, implying that I might take the words of the ceremony as a guide to managing our relationship.

In the end, it turned out that Saint Paul's retrogressive admonition does not make its way into the Greek ceremony's wedding vows. In fact, there are no vows at all. So Archbishop Iakovos married us, in Greek, in a joyous ceremony attended by my children and some of our closest friends. I could see, at the larger reception afterward, that the people who cared the most about us both were truly happy, that they saw the marriage the way I did, as a loving partnership of mutual interests and profound respect. If Saint Paul would disagree with that as a sound basis for a marriage, I'd like to have a word with him.

Our lives since then have featured dramas created by the conflicting demands of careers, children's marriages, births of grandchildren, moves and renovations. Our family was drawn together as we experienced the tragic illness and death of our beloved thirty-six-year-old daughter-in-law. Michael's wife, Meredith, the devoted mother of then five-year-old Beau and six-year-old Alexander, died from breast cancer on October 17, 2006.

As we have endured John's and Meredith's tragedies and enjoyed our blessings, not a moment has passed that I haven't been enormously grateful for Joan's presence in my life and by my side.

My Children

Among the more gratifying aspects of our relationship, which has now spanned nearly thirty years, is the close relationship Joan enjoys with my children. She is particularly close to the two youngest, Michael and Holly, whom she helped bring up. That meant a big change in Holly's case. She moved on from her early attempts to sabotage my relationship with Joan to become best friends, a bond that deepened when Holly married and had children. Joan adores them.

Indeed, all my children and grandchildren alike love and respect Joan, and she feels the same for them. They recognize, as I do, what a remarkable woman she is—her intelligence, beauty, and fierce integrity. For creating a show that reaches some 235 million children worldwide every week, Joan was awarded the highest honor the nation can bestow on a private citizen, the Presidential Medal of Freedom, by Bill Clinton in 1995. But it is in the personal capacity that I hold her most dear—as a surpassingly great wife and a true supporter and friend to all of my children. They also know she has trouble saying no to them.

In many ways, our five children are so different from one another as to pose a fundamental challenge to genetic theory. On the other hand, Jim, David, Holly, and Michael have one delightfully important thing in common. They, and our nine grandchildren, all live in New York City. This has made birthdays, holidays, vacations, sports, and life in general so much more satisfying. John, of course, remains happy at his school in California.

Thinking of my four younger children, I have come to appreciate some of their common qualities: their smartness and their smarts, their parenting and their integrity, their sense of humor, and also some of the quirks that define them as unique individuals.

My father would love Jim's "economia" and I love his wise brain and deep integrity. If one plays golf with Jim, one has to get used to the idea that even if his ball is down in the middle of the fairway, he will be over in the rough looking for wayward golf balls. I doubt he could ever contemplate shelling out cash for new balls.

David is not only a natural charmer, but is the risk taker. When he was about twelve, I was foolish enough to let him drive the snowmobile in Wisconsin. I sat right behind him, figuring that would be enough control. Instead, he drove so fast around a corner that I was thrown off into a snowbank. My cries for help could not be heard over the roar of the snowmobile, and David sped all the way to our home a mile away before he noticed I was not there. In a similar way, watching David ski was a harrowing experience, and he had several broken bones to show for it.

Holly is not only charismatic, she is also clearly the pushiest of the lot. The rest of the family recoils as Holly successfully negotiates getting a table, tickets, a discount when none is available. As she puts it, "You may not like the process, but you like the outcome."

Michael simply embarrasses the rest of us with how mature, unneurotic, unquirky, and wise he is. With tear-filled eyes and infinite pride, I watched Michael, in an act of extraordinary courage and love, deliver in a strong and unwavering voice an eloquent eulogy to his beloved Meredith at her funeral. Thankfully, Michael is now very happily married to Tara Petus, a wonderful wife and stepmother to Alexander and Beau.

I am humbled when I realize how fortunate I am to have such a loving, supportive, and accomplished wife, and wonderful children and grandchildren. They bring great joy to my life.

Today, and with Joan's great help, I think I have finally begun to get the message about the meaning of a balanced life. We see our children and grandchildren frequently. For example, I play golf with my children and grandchildren more than with others. I have taken my daughter Holly with me on many Council on Foreign Relations trips to countries around the world. We vacation together with the children and grandchildren. In turn, Joan and I also spend much time together; I shall leave it to her to assess its quality.

We now have a friendly relationship with Sally and her charming and interesting husband, Michael. Time will reveal how much net damage was done by the divorce, my earlier preoccupations, and, in turn, my later attempts to revitalize my familial relationships.

CHAPTER 13

NEW YORK, ROUND THREE

Lehman Swan Song

I was approaching my tenth anniversary with Lehman Brothers in the spring of 1983. They had been good years, on balance, despite all of the internal traumas. The last five, in fact, had been extraordinary. Lehman Brothers, Kuhn, Loeb, as the firm had been known since the 1977 merger, was just completing five straight years of record earnings. We enjoyed the highest return on equity in the industry. And after the departure of Jim Glanville, it had been, by and large, uncharacteristically stable. Virtually no one of consequence had left the firm in years.

That spring, Lew Glucksman and I sat down over breakfast with John Whitehead and John Weinberg, who were the co-heads of Goldman Sachs. We ate in one of the private dining rooms at the new Lehman headquarters at 55 Water Street, a fifty-four-story high rise where we had moved in 1980 to gain more space and bring the banking and trading operations under one roof. It wasn't a deal meeting, just a goodwill breakfast at which we discussed business trends in a relaxed and cordial atmosphere. While I remember the details of the meeting only vaguely, I vividly remember—and came to regret—the idea that sprang from it.

Co-CEO arrangements have a spotty record. People who reach the pinnacles of business success, particularly in the hyper-competitive world of Wall Street, tend to have the kinds of egos that don't play well with others. But under Whitehead and Weinberg, Goldman Sachs was thriving. It made me believe that if the egos could be harnessed, a combination of top talents could produce real benefits.

I wondered why Lew and I shouldn't share the CEO post at Lehman. We were the same age. He had been president for a year or so and was making a great contribution. Lew was an expert trader, banker, and hands-on manager who really functioned as the firm's chief operating officer. I occupied the house's corporate side, where I was much more connected to the worlds outside the firm—of business, CEOs, and government. It seemed to me that the way we split these duties—and the expertise we each brought to our side of things—created a natural partnership. For his part, Lew had given me several explicit signs that he very much enjoyed the ways in which we complemented one another. He had sent me a handwritten note telling me how much he appreciated the quality of our relationship. I didn't save it, but given what was to come, I wish I had! At the time, I thought sharing the top spot would be both beneficial to the firm and fair to Lew.

You can rightly call me naive. Joan, whose eye for character flaws in people is sharper than my own, warned, "Give him a fingernail and he's going to take an arm," when I broached the subject with her one night over dinner.

Still thinking it was the fair thing to do, for better or worse, I went ahead. Lew, to no one's surprise, was delighted. We announced the co-CEO arrangement in a joint letter that May that went out to the entire corporate and financial community.

My optimism was temporarily borne out when Lew, at a small party the very next month marking my tenth anniversary with the firm, presented me with a beautiful Henry Moore drawing. The Moore fit well with the modern art that I by then was collecting with a passion. Lew's unusually warm compliments in a generous toast were a perfect fit as well, dovetailing with my vision for a symbiotic partnership at the firm's helm.

My vision, however, proved illusory.

Our co-leadership took the form of informal meetings, held at least once a week in a room near my office at the new headquarters on Water Street. We met over breakfast and worked in shirtsleeves, a pot of coffee on hand, and, for Lew, an ashtray for the cigars he loved to smoke. We were physical opposites; I had largely conquered the addiction to pastries and rich foods I had brought from childhood and was no longer very overweight. Lew was a much heavier man who looked as if he religiously avoided physical activity. We were stylistic opposites as well. I had long ago graduated from Brooks Brothers to well-tailored suits, while Lew dressed as if he didn't really care much what people thought of his appearance. Rumpled was the kindest way to describe him. He frequently wore light-colored suits in defiance of the de facto Wall Street dress code, and when he wore dark suits they often displayed dandruff on the shoulders. None of these things should matter, but in some quarters they do, sending subtle and not so subtle messages to colleagues, competitors, and clients. Nonetheless, we had, or so I thought, an effective working union and that, it seemed to me, was what mattered. At our meetings, we covered all the matters of significance such as personnel issues and new clients. Between meetings, we each focused on our areas of strength, I on the corporate investment banking side of things, Lew on the rest. One of Lew's trusted aides, Jim Boshart, a six-foot, five-inch former college basketball star, shuttled between us with the information we both needed about corporate and personnel developments that we would discuss at the next meeting.

In late June, about six weeks after we had announced our co-CEO arrangement and even less time since Lew had presented me the Henry Moore, he sent word through Jim Boshart that he wanted to meet in a new spot that morning—a small windowless office in his domain near the trading floor. I could think of no reason for this change. By the same token, I saw no reason to consider it significant. I took the elevator down to the trading floor expecting a pleasant meeting. I had, after all, learned earlier that day over breakfast with Bruce Smart, the CEO of the Continental Group, that he had selected Lehman to handle a major M&A assignment. I looked forward to telling Lew about this significant new piece of business.

But that conversation didn't happen. When I sat down, Lew launched into a long soliloquy about what he wanted to do with his life. He talked in circles, about his career thus far, about wanting to be in charge of something, about feeling barred from a position of real leadership. I sensed a tone of resentment in his words, that he felt he was toiling in the trenches running Lehman's operations while I, the firm's

public face, was having fun dining with government and corporate mo-
guls. The new business these meals brought in didn't seem to matter.
Finally, the swirls of this verbal blizzard parted enough for me to see
that what he was talking about, what he really wanted, was to become
the sole CEO. This notwithstanding the awkward reality that only six
weeks earlier, we had told the financial world how happy and proud we
were to be sharing the executive duties. The meeting that I had foreseen
as routine and innocuous went on for several hours.

"This comes as quite a shock, Lew," I told him at last. "I'm going
to need to think about it."

What I thought and what I felt could not be separated. What I felt
was a keen sense of betrayal. I was angry with myself for my naïveté.
Moreover, I was uneasy about how Lew's declaration would affect the
firm. I sensed the old trader versus banker divisions were implicit in his
wish to stand alone at the pinnacle, and I feared that the two groups of
partners would find themselves at war again.

My first call after the meeting was to Joan. "I admit it," I said.

"Admit what?" she asked.

"You have better instincts than I do. Lew wants to be the CEO all
by himself."

"You gave him an arm and he wants your head," she said, escalat-
ing the analogy.

"That's about it."

"Will you fight him?"

"I don't know yet. I'd like to solve it short of that."

I quickly decided that if this odd situation was likely to be solved,
some high-level diplomacy was needed. George Ball, universally liked
and highly experienced, might be able to guide both sides to a solution.
I suggested to Lew that we use George as an intermediary. Lew quickly
agreed.

"I'm shocked!" George exclaimed when I recounted the meeting and
told him what Lew wanted. He was too much of a gentleman to say much
more. And he agreed with diplomatic grace to accept what we both knew
was a most unpleasant assignment. I told him that I had intended to stay
on for two or three more years. Under the new circumstances, my position
was that Lew and I should remain as co-CEOs, at least for a decent in-

terval. I was willing to leave earlier than I had contemplated, but I thought a graceful transition period was in order and very much in the firm's interest, given the recent co-CEO announcement.

George spent several hours with Lew and then called and said he was ready to report. I told him I wanted Joan with me when I heard what he had to say. The three of us met at a little Greek restaurant near River House at First Avenue and 50th Street, where George told us what he'd learned. The short version is that Lew was adamant. He had been at the firm for twenty years, and it was "imperative" that he take over now. He was ready for his close-up and would not be denied. There was no room for compromise.

I pondered George's briefing. The timing was right, from Lew's point of view, since trading profits during that quarter were very high, and it's not a myth that money is power in our business. However, there seemed to be no business reason for this urgency, given the firm's five straight years of record results. What was more, the nine months through June 30 had been the most profitable in the firm's 133-year history.

But business results really weren't the real issue. George confirmed that Lew harbored resentments over slights financial and social. He saw these as directed at himself and the other traders in the firm and itched to shift the balance in their favor. Perhaps another reason lay in the earlier proposal by Peter Solomon, a senior banker and a member of the board, that the firm go public. Maybe Lew sensed, as did others, that his style and manner—his blustery temperament, his rumpled suits, the clouds of smoke and ash that accompanied his cigars—would work against him as the head of a public corporation if that ever came to pass.

I still had the old ad man's instincts that made me sensitive to public relations. Lew's proposed coup, if it occurred so soon after we had announced that we were sharing leadership, would create a public relations nightmare. Beyond that, however, I was not all that averse to leaving Lehman. On too many days, the very tough and greedy culture and environment left me angry and exhausted. The firm's internal problems had earlier led to my very real explorations of moving to Lazard to join Felix Rohatyn. On the personal side, I'd gone through brain surgery and a difficult divorce, the latter event redeemed by my marriage to Joan. Now I wanted to build my still new life with her, and devote less time to herding cats disguised as independent Wall Streeters. I also wanted to pursue my interest in investing. But I certainly did not want to destroy all that had been created at Lehman in the last ten years.

With all this in mind, I kept proposing compromises. I was willing to transfer power to Lew after a reasonable period. Much as I had suggested to Fred Ehrman that he stay on until the end of the year to ease the transition when I first arrived at Lehman, I now told Lew (through George) that I would relinquish my role at the end of 1983. We could even make the announcement now, allowing our clients and the business press to absorb the news. The co-CEO step would then look like a more logical move in that direction, as if we had planned it that way all along.

Furious negotiations took place over a twelve-day period. Lew's answers to my compromise proposals kept coming back "No!" His critics within the firm assumed he was not willing to take a chance on something "going wrong" in the interim, despite the fact that it would be only a few months.

George, Steve Schwarzman, and several others felt that if the matter came to a vote of the partners, I would win. I felt, in any case, that such a victory would be both hollow and Pyrrhic. Lew would take some of his best traders, leaving the firm seriously damaged. The restructuring I had led in the wake of Ehrman's ouster ten years earlier had been traumatic and exhausting. I had zero appetite to go through another implosion.

Still, I continued to explore constructive options. As I did, one day I received a surprise call from Jim Boshart. Despite his allegiance to Lew, Jim recognized how exhaustively I had sought a reasonable compromise.

"Pete," he said, "I've watched how closely you have tried to work with Lew, and I can only imagine how furious you must be. You certainly know from George that he's rejected all your suggestions for a more gradual transition. And I can confirm that he is absolutely adamant. But he also appreciates, as you do, that an open fight would do damage to the firm. For that reason, he is willing to consider a financial settlement of some kind."

I had been so focused on engineering a graceful transition that the idea of such a settlement had not entered my mind. But when I told Joan about Jim's call, we saw the potential for an upside. I remember thinking, "Maybe this lemon has a small lemonade to offer after all."

Joan and I agreed that it would be foolish not to find out what Lew had in mind. I suspected that he wanted to avoid a fight for reasons that were far different from mine. His offer, my friends surmised, was spurred by the fact that he was not sure he'd win. I, in turn, was not interested in a fight whether I "won" or not. I believed that such a fight would produce no winners.

Pursuing Lew's "generosity," Jim and I, with help from my then lawyer, Mort Jencklow, negotiated a package that included $300,000 a year for three years to cover the expenses of a new office I expected to set up, as well as my share of Lehman earnings for that period. Then I threw in a wild card. If Lehman Brothers, Kuhn, Loeb was sold within three years, I would receive a percentage of the sales price equivalent to my ownership share of the business. I felt that I had played a major role in reviving the firm from near bankruptcy to record levels. If the firm were sold, I assumed its price would reflect that revival, and I would feel truly stupid if I were to forsake a share in the proceeds of any sale that occurred in that time. I felt I was giving Lew a freebie. I had every reason to assume that since Lew was so hot to run the business on his own, he could not possibly have any interest in selling. Jim confirmed my assumption. He said that Lew saw no sale on the horizon and would agree to this add-on proposal. Which he did. Lew was so eager to see me leave that he also offered an immediate payout of my equity, not the three-year payout I had adopted when I took over from Fred Ehrman ten years earlier, when capital preservation was vital to the firm's survival. We signed the papers around the end of July.

We announced my departure to the board on July 26 and the announcement hit the papers the next day. As *The New York Times* reported it, "The surprise departure, to go into effect in stages from October to January, came only two months after Mr. Peterson had agreed to share the duties of top executive with a key associate." Some board members were shocked, and I was given to believe that several were upset that they had not been informed of the arrangement. Two days later, another story in the *Times* proved the value of avoiding a big fight. "Gentle Transition at Lehman," read the headline, and one partner was quoted as saying that my leave-taking "was an act of statesmanship."

According to our agreement, I was to step down as CEO on October 1. My term as chairman would extend for three more months, until the end of 1983, and then my career at Lehman would end and I would leave the firm. Lew could easily have agreed to my proposals for a gradual transition (without any financial settlement), since the schedule was not much different from the one I had suggested in the first place.

In December, many of the Lehman banking partners gathered for my departure party. The evening began with drinks at our apartment and moved on to dinner at the River Club, an in-house club. It was a party full of friendly laughs and very funny skits and mutual toasts and roasts. One of the skits mimicked me making a new business presentation, and at the end revealing a chart as I said, "And now the critical strategic issue—*our fee!*" Ninety percent of those who came were banking partners. One trading partner came but hedged his bets, having drinks but leaving before dinner. I felt a mixture of emotions as I spoke and laughed that evening with my colleagues. Many seemed genuinely sorry to see me go, and I was sorry to be leaving them. The fact was, however, that we were all going to be better off—at least in the short term—since we had managed to keep the split cordial, at least in public. The highlight amid a night of highlights—of warmth and real fondness—was when Roger Altman rose to present me a going-away gift "with the admiration and affection of your many friends at Lehman Brothers." It was an original drawing by Willem de Kooning, and this evidence of their regard and acknowledgment of my passion for collecting modern art was almost enough to make me change my mind. But only for a moment. Indeed, during the traumatic months that followed while the Glucksman implosion was playing itself out, I received several feelers, one quite serious, about coming back. I said, "Absolutely not."

The party's glow faded, and was replaced by the Christmas season, always frenetic in New York. It was hardly a merry time for me, troubled as I was by uncertainty about my future. I was feeling restless, anxious to get on to the next thing; this was a trait of mine. In the meantime, Joan and I escaped to Italy. We spent Christmas in Rome, where Mario d'Urso showed us a good time. Mario was another victim of the Glucksman coup, a Lehman partner in international banking whom Lew forced out soon after he took power. From Rome we went on to Venice where we joined a number of friends, including Jason Epstein, one of the founders of *The New York Review of Books*, and novelist Gore Vidal, to celebrate the arrival of the New Year. The holidays in those old-world cities were stately, almost medieval, and I craved that kind of dignity for a change. But wanting, as they say, isn't getting, and when the clock struck midnight, I found myself wincing and wondering what the year ahead would bring.

Even before I left the firm, Lew had rapidly asserted his new power. At times, his actions seemed to be aimed less at effective management than at settling old scores. While I continued reporting to the office, where I worked at maintaining the confidence of unsettled clients, he made a series of what certainly looked like unilateral decisions that some thought should have been submitted to the board. He greatly exacerbated the tensions between the two sides of the house by allocating additional shares and bonus money to the traders, shares and money that he took from the bankers. He allocated a quarter of the entire bonus pool for fiscal 1983—the year ending September 30—to himself and four other partners. He gave himself and his cronies more shares, reversing a trend I had started to increase shares among the firm's brilliant crop of younger partners. He forced out several partners on the banking side. Finally, he elevated his close Lehman friend and collaborator Bob Rubin to president, and, while Bob was a truly gifted and brilliant banker, he was not considered a real manager or leader. So, in effect, the firm had two Mr. Insides and no Mr. Outside to act as its client, public, and new business face. All this created a palpable climate of fear among the partners.

By then I was planning my long-held dream of pursuing merchant banking, the term that describes seeking out promising companies to invest in and help build. It also covers restructuring companies to find cost savings and create new synergies and new directions.

At bottom, my responses to my Lehman exit were neurotic. I had moved too quickly to the next thing. My father would have disapproved of even a moment's "unemployment," and between carrying his workaholic gene and my own obsession with continuing to demonstrate performance, I felt I simply had to get a job right away. Even though I could afford to spend some time mapping my next move, not working was a mortal sin.

So I rushed into an ill-advised partnership with someone I had checked out hurriedly—too hurriedly. My advisor was one well-known Washington friend and a prominent New York lawyer, but I should have vetted my move more carefully with some of my Wall Street friends. It was a truly dumb mistake, and looking back, its sole virtue was that the partnership did not survive for long.

This experience taught me that to rush into a job out of embarrassment, anxiety, or fear is to be governed by the past. Obviously, since one is going to be living and working in the future, the focus should be on what lies ahead.

Whenever anyone talks to me about career advice, particularly in the aftermath of an awkward exit, I urge them to take their time and not to rush into a job that shows critics and former colleagues how employable they are. Long after others stop remembering or caring about the circumstances of that exit, one will be living with the new job. And that is all that will matter.

I learned another lesson, too. To a considerable extent, others judge the seriousness of an inelegant exit by how seriously one takes it. Laughing it off sends a signal that it's not all that devastating. Ken Auletta, one of the journalists covering my departure from Lehman, wrote that some of the partners deemed me "imperious." I referred to this charge one night at a rather large dinner I was chairing. I told the guests that one night when Joan and I were in bed, I asked her, "Darling, do you find me imperious?"

" 'Absolutely not, Mr. Peterson,' she said."

Not long into the New Year that I had anticipated with such trepidation in Venice, word reached me that the Lehman partners were in near revolt. Losses on the trading side had heightened their fears of a capital implosion and plummeting share value. They could see a scenario in which their time, talent, expertise, and net worth would dwindle under Lew's leadership.

What was worse, it was reported to me in November that in May of 1983, the agribusiness firm Conagra had allegedly made a $600 million offer to purchase Lehman. This supposed offer was not presented to me or, to my knowledge, to the rest of the board, but allegedly was squelched by Lew Glucksman. If indeed there was such an offer, his failure to tell the board would have been an obvious violation of corporate governance and a serious breach of fiduciary responsibility in a partnership. The $600 million more than tripled Lehman's share value at the time—$177 million—and the partners would obviously have had a right to know about it.

Lehman began to implode: Discussions emerged into the open about selling the firm both to solidify its capital base and to let the partners realize their share value.

In the end, Lehman Brothers, Kuhn, Loeb was sold in the spring of 1984 to Shearson/American Express for $375 million. Thanks to my settlement agreement, I shared in those proceeds. The sale brought to an end the 134 years of independent partnership started by Emanuel, Mayer, and Henry Lehman before the Civil War. The firm's reputation was still such that Shearson/American Express became Shearson/Lehman.

My personal feelings about the 1984 collapse of Lehman Brothers? A fair amount of ambivalence. Some self-justification that this guy Peterson must have been doing something right; anger that I spent ten years of exhausting and aggravating work to help bring Lehman back from the brink of bankruptcy—way back—just to see all that work essentially wasted; a certain sense of personal betrayal by Lew Glucksman.

On the other hand, gratitude that I was lucky enough to have negotiated my share of what, at the time, seemed like a very improbable sale. And, some substantial sadness. (As to the 2008 Lehman bankruptcy, I also feel some sadness. I shall leave that bankruptcy to the financial historians. The full story has clearly not yet emerged.)

Self-Assessment

Monday morning quarterbacking raises a serious question of how things might have been different had I pushed out one or two of the leading dissidents. Recently, one of Lew Glucksman's former partners in the bond trading area told me not to take the Glucksman coup personally. He reported that when Warren Hellman was named president, Lew and Jim Glanville were plotting on how they could displace him. Oh, how innocent I was! I was too trusting and too eager for temporary peace. I should have been tougher. Getting rid of a few of them might have caused temporary trouble but the firm would have benefited in the long run.

I suppose that the best I can say for myself is that during most of my era, based on years of record earnings and high retention of key employees, the malignancy was in remission. But alas, it was only temporary. The cancer had not been cured.

CHAPTER 14

BLACKSTONE:
THE BEGINNING

Getting Started

It was a driving rainstorm on a late Friday afternoon in Boston and Steve Schwarzman and I were drenched. We had decided to form a boutique investment banking firm, focusing on private equity. But first, we had to raise some money. Getting that money was much tougher than either of us could have imagined.

We were heading to the MIT Endowment Fund. When we got there, we were informed we were to meet with a very junior person. Apparently, the head of the fund found us fledglings too unimportant to meet with. Here I was: a former chairman of Lehman Brothers starting at the bottom all over again. A therapist had once told me that another person cannot humiliate you. You only allow yourself to be humiliated. Whatever the reason, I felt humiliated.

Matters got worse. A junior person, a woman in her late twenties, had not even looked at what we considered a well-tailored placement memorandum and had little idea what we were about, and on top of that, she had zero interest in private equity funds. Why the meeting was set up in the first place was a nagging mystery. We walked out into this still driving rainstorm and spent forty-five minutes trying to hail a cab. Hiring a car to sit and wait for us was out of the question in those days. We already had written more checks than we cared to remember to get set up and we didn't need to be reminded we had de minimis revenues.

So began the most exhausting, frustrating, and, at times, depressing marketing experience in my life. It was two years of hell, begging, and wet shoes.

Steve Schwarzman and I had decided early on that we were natural partners: I, a rather senior figure with broad contacts and relationships, a good deal of business experience, and a history of persuasion; I had always been a pretty good salesman. He, a rising star who had graduated from Yale and the Harvard Business School; he had a unique ability to hammer a deal into place and make it work, and he had important business relationships that were separate from mine.

We had worked together successfully for a decade, employing a range of skills that complemented one another. I brought in a lot of the new M&A business. Therefore, I had to be involved, but personally managing the firm and a large number of deals simply was not possible. Nonetheless, it was important that our clients know that Steve and I agreed on a strategy for dealing with their interests, and for putting that strategy to work. Steve was creative, and an extremely good negotiator. He was also excellent about keeping me informed, and sensitive to clients' needs, knowing almost instinctively when to involve me directly. For my part, it was vital to work with someone I not only respected, but also trusted, and I trusted Steve, both for his abilities and because he knew how to leverage me. We had worked together on some very large acquisitions, including deals involving Bendix and RCA. Of all the client assignments that we worked on jointly, I don't recall a single client who was anything but very impressed with Steve's performance.

But before we could seriously explore working together, we had to extract Steve from Lehman. The standard Shearson/Lehman partnership agreement bound partners to the merged firm for three years before they could take their cash out by redeeming their shares. Steve, however, felt that he had negotiated a deal that allowed his early exit. His close and personal relationship with Peter A. Cohen, the chairman and CEO of Shearson/American Express, had been a big factor in bringing about Lehman's acquisition by the larger company. The two were the same age, and neighbors in the Hamptons. More importantly, Steve had a term sheet spelling out an agreement exempting him from the three-year term. My own agreement with Shearson included an oral understanding that Steve would depart early as part of my agreeing to help Shearson/Lehman maintain various client relationships. Despite these understandings, however, Shearson dug in and refused to honor them and let him depart without further negotiation. Among their fears was the very real concern that Steve's departure would trigger a stampede of partners trying to head for the exits, taking with them a big chunk of clients. But Shearson held the cards and the cash.

Shearson finally agreed to let Steve out at what seemed to us to be an outrageous price. For three years, whenever we advised a client that they alleged to be on the Shearson/Lehman "client" list—which looked like the entire Fortune 500—we would have to pay Shearson half of any advisory fees we earned. It was grand thievery!

But not being in business together was even less attractive, so we agreed. Steve and I sat down, took a deep breath each, and wrote checks for $200,000 apiece from our personal funds to create a partnership stake. We took a small office suite in the Seagram Building on Park Avenue, the sleek tower of dark glass designed by Ludwig Mies van der Rohe that conveyed the prestige that we could only hope for. On its 52nd Street side, it housed the Four Seasons Grill, where the rich and powerful occupied their regular banquettes for power lunches. We hired two assistants, and set about trying to think through and define what the firm we envisioned was about, what we were going to do with it, and how we were going to be different from the others.

One of our first challenges was what to call our fledgling enterprise. Steve suggested "Peterson, Schwarzman," but that did not appeal to me. Another lesson I had brought from the University of Chicago was that one should plan for success as well as failure. With success, we would bring in more senior partners, and presumably they would expect to be part of the firm's name. We would then face the Merrill Lynch syndrome of name creep that had become a joke in the industry: Merrill Lynch, Pierce, Fenner & Beane, and later Merrill Lynch, Pierce, Fenner, Beane & Smith. I could see Peterson, Schwarzman followed by a cavalcade of names that marched endlessly across corporate letterheads.

Steve came back with an inspired idea. "Pete," he said, "*schwarz* is German for 'black,' right? And Peter translated to Greek is *petros*, which means 'stone.' If we put them together we get 'Blackstone.' What do you think?"

I thought it was brilliant. It was worthy of the best professionals in that elusive field called product branding. At the same time, it ingeniously bridged his understandable desire for some personal name recognition with my wish to have a name we could live with happily ever after. Blackstone it was.

Having been in the investment banking business a long time, we were used to working with OPM—other people's money. Wall Street's lesson in this regard is that it is more blessed to receive than to give. Now, we were working with a different kind of OPM—our personal money.

In the beginning, our expenses rapidly outstripped our income, which was approximately zero. We wrote checks to pay the assistants, the rent, and phone, and our travel costs. Neither Steve nor I was taking a salary at that point. As our stake dwindled, we found our check-writing hands stricken with a reluctance verging on real palsy. Our cash on hand dipped to $100,000, then $50,000.

We knew the only way out was to build an advisory business, which could generate much near term revenue. Looking ahead, we knew that if we could establish it, this advisory service would be one of our continuing businesses. So Steve and I put on our salesman's faces. We tried every known form of coaxing and invented a few new ones.

My Rolodex provided some initial contacts. I wrote to about fifty of my best corporate friends stressing how we intended to stand out from the pack. By the 1980s, Wall Street had morphed from long-term and genuine client relationships toward a "the deal comes first" mentality, and this even included deals that were hostile to the interests of long-standing clients. Not only that, these deals, friendly or not, were increasingly being handled in the big firms by younger and less experienced bankers.

Our new firm, Blackstone, was different, I wrote. We would focus on honest advice that did not conflict with our clients' interests, a result of the fact that we weren't doing equity research, underwriting, or trading. Moreover, we would give senior-level attention to each client. The latter wasn't difficult to promise; with just the two of us, we had no junior staff.

Most direct mail campaigns pull in business from less than one percent of the addressees. Of course, they're not targeting friends. We were, and we did quite a bit better, gaining advisory assignments from major companies like Firestone, Inland Steel, Union Carbide, Armco, and Bristol-Myers Squibb. These advisory assignments gave us, for the first time, an income. But some of these companies inevitably overlapped with the so-called Shearson Lehman client list, meaning we were obligated to split our fees with them. Those were some of the hardest checks we ever had to write.

We were angry—and ambivalent. Angry, that our small start-up firm with little revenue would pay blackmail to a firm that had broken its agreement. Ambivalent, because we were relieved that we were no longer part of that Lehman culture.

Some Blackstone Principles

I thought there was room on Wall Street for a new kind of firm, a meritocracy in which the partners and associates were not at one another's throats, but were mutually supportive, congenial, and trusted one another. I wanted to help build such a firm—a successful business, yes, but also a success in terms of its culture, a culture unlike that of Lehman Brothers. I was focused on avoiding another Lehman-type implosion. I foresaw an opportunity to help build a genuine institution, one with values and governance that didn't depend on a single personality like Bobbie Lehman and that would continue to thrive after I retired, whenever that might be.

As we struggled to get our footing, we also were looking ahead. We knew what kind of firm we were trying to build, but how would we get there? Did we need a CEO, and if so which of us should it be? Or should we try to be co-CEOs, the arrangement that had produced such disastrous results when I tried it at Lehman with Lew Glucksman? After all, Steve and I already had signed a founders' partnership agreement in which the two of us had to agree on major issues; that is, we each had veto power over the other.

But the Lehman memories gave me pause. I also remembered the confusion Bell & Howell executives had felt when Chuck Percy had installed me as president and CEO, but in his part-time role as chairman continued to talk with our business colleagues about various operating problems. Chuck had been making a sincere attempt to stay involved and to ease the transition while he monitored my performance. And perhaps he had also been trying to justify his compensation. But the effect was to obscure who was in charge.

This argued for a single CEO. I was fifty-nine and had a lot of managerial experience. Steve was thirty-eight, and while he was a brilliant investment banker, he had spent no time in management. I knew that some people saw him as awfully young and brash to boot. Conventional wisdom, therefore, would have made me the CEO.

But I didn't want to stake Blackstone's future on conventional wisdom. I knew from my nearly twenty years as a CEO that doing an effective job requires intensive focus day and night. It takes a toll on your personal life. Joan had been remarkably understanding during the tumult at Lehman but I now wanted to invest much more of myself to her and to our marriage. And there were the extracurricular and public policy matters I wanted to continue to pursue. I had succeeded David Rockefeller as chair of the Council on Foreign Relations in 1985 and wanted to help revitalize that worthy organization. The Institute for International Economics, which I had helped found in 1981, was doing valuable research on a global scale and I wished to remain an active part of that. I was serving on the board of MoMA, the Museum of Modern Art, and it deserved attention. And I meant to keep on writing and speaking about America's long-term structural and unsustainable promises and the problems it posed for our country's future.

All this argued against my guiding Blackstone as its CEO. In the end, I decided Steve should be president and sole CEO from day one. I would simply be chairman and co-founder. If I saw a problem, I would talk directly and privately to Steve. In a worst-case scenario, where I strongly disagreed with a major management decision, I could rely on my founder's veto power.

Steve and I and Roger Altman, vice chairman, who had followed us over from Lehman, formed an early Management Committee. Ideas about how to build the firm were flooding in from all sides. Since we had now shown our ability to capture significant M&A business, many of our friends and supporters pressed us to expand: become a full-service firm and engage in underwriting, equity research, and trading. It took a clear head to respond to such glimmering visions. I harked back to the business mantra at the heart of the theories of Adam Smith, the patron saint of the University of Chicago Graduate School of Business. Smith suggested that success in business lay in focusing on the things that you do better than others. Or as he put it: Pursue your "comparative advantage." It was advice that had always served me well. There were plenty of quality full-service firms and capacity on Wall Street. If we tried to take them on we would face stiff, well-financed, and expert competition. More importantly, neither Steve nor I was expert in any of these fields, nor did we have any capital. In this respect, we would be at a serious comparative disadvantage. We decided to heed old Adam's considerable wisdom.

Many also argued that Blackstone should pursue the then current craze in the industry—investing in hostile leveraged buyout transactions. In many of such takeovers, the financial leverage came from high-yield or "junk" bonds from Drexel Burnham Lambert, a firm that would crash and burn at the end of the 1980s under the weight of insider trading scandals involving Michael Milken. But as we wrote in our initial sales pitch, we committed to pursuing only friendly investments. To do otherwise would have violated the principle of comparative advantage. We were on friendly terms with many American CEOs and boards of directors and we did not want to attack our friends and weaken our valuable corporate relationships. We might forsake some deals because of it, but we believed this somewhat contrarian position would lead us into lasting and ultimately more beneficial corporate partnerships.

Both of these decisions helped us avoid potentially damaging conflicts of interest. In the first instance, not getting into stock trading and equity research and underwriting removed a major source of potential conflicts. Stock researchers at full service firms naturally tended to want to say good things about the companies they cover, given that those companies either are or might become underwriting clients. Furthermore, their compensation was often tied to those underwriting revenues.

It's no secret that corporate management doesn't like negative equity research reports, and expresses its displeasure by directing underwriting business to firms where the research people find good things to say. Such "fudged" reports skating over negative information that investors could have used were a factor in the Wall Street scandals of early 2000.

In the second case, firms that truly look to build and maintain relationships generally never have trouble looking their clients in the eye. That's not the case when you may be financing an attack on one on behalf of another. Even on Wall Street, where expediency reigns, we felt there was corporate value in old-fashioned concepts like loyalty and trust.

Another of our strategic principles was to structure our business to provide job security for our employees. I had presided over brutal corporate downsizings at Bell & Howell and Lehman Brothers. Even one of those experiences was one too many.

We wanted to minimize the effects of upswings and downturns that would have us frantically head-hunting to increase our professional staff one minute and firing people the next, with all of the personal trauma that entails. The solution was to develop some businesses that were countercyclical. Bull markets and easy credit generally mean that mergers and acquisition business is good, while a weakening economy and tight credit are going to force some companies into bankruptcy and restructuring. But M&A and restructuring professionals are more or less interchangeable; they both know how to maximize a company's assets under varying circumstances. Thus, we started a restructuring advisory business. By covering both bases, we figured we could minimize job cuts and gain a dividend in stability and employee loyalty. Today our reorganization and restructuring component is one of the industry's leaders. We also decided to build a substantial asset management business, which would produce steady fees in good times and bad.

Finding a Toehold

Our biggest early advisory client was Sony. Steve knew the senior U.S. Sony executive, Mickey Schulhof, well, and I had a long and close relationship with Akio Morita, Sony's co-founder and CEO, going back to my days in Washington. Akio was a founding director of the Institute for International Economics. This illustrated the complementary relationship I held with Steve.

The first of our Sony transactions started with a Wall Street rumor. It had Larry Tisch, who with his brother Bob had expanded the Loews theater chain into a diversified corporation with hands in tobacco (Lorillard), watches (Bulova), and insurance (CNA Financial) and revenues in the billions, accumulating a large stake in CBS, which had expanded from its radio and television roots to become something of a media conglomerate. Indeed, by 1986, he had spent $800 million to amass 25 percent of the company's shares and was running it as chairman and CEO. This led to another rumor. Tisch wanted to spin off CBS's music business.

We knew that Sony had a major joint music venture in Japan with CBS Records. Morita had made the original deal with the legendary William S. Paley, who, before retiring, had built CBS from a chain of small radio stations to a communications empire. Akio liked and trusted Paley, but he did not know Larry Tisch. It was clear as Steve and I discussed Tisch's possible ambitions with Morita and Schulhof that Sony was both interested and concerned. From a defensive standpoint, they felt the Japanese joint venture might be damaged if Tisch sold the music business to a new owner they did not know. Switching to offense, they saw advantages to buying the CBS music business, such as significant cost savings and solidifying their relationships with their music clients. After we told Akio the rumors of Tisch's plans to sell the record division, he empathized. He said he wanted to proceed as long as the discussions were completely friendly so as not to jeopardize future relationships.

The Japanese in those days were very sensitive about appearing overly aggressive in their acquisition efforts in the United States. Fear of Japan's industrial might was almost a phobia in many circles as Hondas and Toyotas crowded Fords and Chevys out of American driveways and television watchers spent their evenings glued to Sony and Panasonic TV sets. Akio was very Western-oriented and knew well the potential for political and public relations fallout if large Japanese acquisitions in the

United States were not handled with discretion. Therefore, he did not want us to do a lot of haggling if CBS's price was in "the right ballpark."

So, Steve and I met with Larry Tisch. We strongly emphasized that we were approaching him on a friendly basis. Was it true that he wanted to sell CBS Records, and if so what was his price? Larry was his usual direct self. He had bought and sold many businesses throughout his business life and was acutely aware of market values. A screen near his desk flickered with all the stock market indices and the latest prices. Yes, he said, he was interested, and the price was $1.25 billion.

Preliminary analysis told us this price was easily justified. We saw the clear potential for cost savings and increased sales that would come from combining the CBS and Sony music businesses. Indeed, we felt its value to Sony was considerably higher. We told Sony of our meeting with Tisch and his price. They responded immediately: Go for it.

Elated, we informed Larry that Sony was on board. That's great, he said. He would get the CBS board together and present the offer for what he felt would be simply a formal approval. But a few days later, a very chagrined and surprised Larry Tisch called to say that the board had turned down our deal. Members had questioned the strategic wisdom of disposing of a business that they felt was closely related to the CBS core entertainment product. Thus, they decided that it should not be sold at anything less than a premium price. That price was $2 billion. "And not one penny less," Larry added.

Steve and I were puzzled, a bit angry, and very embarrassed. It had never occurred to us that Larry might not have discussed with his board the prospect of selling such an important asset. In virtually every public corporation I knew anything about, such a decision would never be made otherwise. And most certainly, those board decisions and approvals would be required before a "final" price was given to an outside buyer. Larry was fully capable of representing his 25 percent ownership, but I could certainly understand why the outside CBS directors felt they had a special responsibility to the stockholders who owned the other 75 percent of the company. Larry had often been a control stockholder in his various enterprises where the board approval of his decisions was no doubt often little more than a formality. He was also under fire from the CBS News division, which felt his business decisions were likely to squander its stellar reputation as the "Tiffany network" that Bill Paley had built.

Mickey Schulhof understood the political dynamics at CBS, but I feared that my discussion with Akio Morita could be a very different matter. I told Akio that I understood this turn of events was unprecedented and very "un-Japanese," and that I would understand if he were critical and angry. I had never known Akio to be anything less than a total gentleman, and he was in this case.

We left it to him and Sony to decide whether the CBS Records business was worth what was indeed a premium price. The answer came back quickly to us: "Yes, it is worth $2 billion to us."

Steve and I congratulated each other for the second time. We arranged a private luncheon meeting at CBS with Tisch, Schulhof, and Norio Ohga, the president of Sony who had built Sony's burgeoning music business in Japan. We treated it as a formality and a social opportunity for Ohga to get to know his American counterparts. Once again, it turned out we were naive.

The pothole in the road concerned corporate pensions, some of which are not fully funded. When that happens, the seller of the business typically needs to fund the shortfall unless there is a clear understanding to the contrary. We had every reason to believe that the typical situation would apply. Larry had delegated the final details to a financial staff at CBS, and in our dealings with them, it had been agreed that CBS would make up any underfunding. By the same token, CBS would keep any overfunding. The staff had brought in an outside firm to appraise its pension funding. These independent experts had concluded that the CBS pension plan was underfunded by about $50 million. This was a small percentage—about 2.5 percent—of a fully priced $2 billion deal, and, given our understanding with the financial staff, we naturally assumed that it would be absorbed in the existing deal with CBS making up the shortfall from the proceeds.

We were going over this point when Larry astonished us by jumping up and walking out of the meeting. Ohga, a true gentleman, could only have believed that Larry had been suddenly taken by a bout of stomach flu. The Japanese, courteous to a fault, would never have done such a thing and could hardly have imagined it. Steve and I thought otherwise. When we confronted Larry directly in his next-door office, he was red in the face. He said, "I told you guys not a penny less than $2 billion, and I meant net, net, and net."

Larry was throwing us a curveball and we told him so. We had a clear understanding with his financial staff that CBS would make up any pension-funding shortfall. But Tisch was adamant. He was the decider. So once again I had to explain this embarrassing turn of events to Akio, who once again was a gentleman about it and simply said, "Pete, I trust you."*

This CBS records experience had been a harrowing roller-coaster ride down and around such mercurial business practices. We were naturally a little apprehensive when John Nevins, CEO of the Firestone Tire and Rubber company, came up with a challenging proposal. I'd written to him in our direct mail campaign. He responded saying yes, it was clear he should be looking for a buyer. Going in, he let us know he had done careful analysis and would only reward exceptional performance. "People in your business often get extraordinary fees for getting a perfectly ordinary price," he said. He proposed, instead, a "performance-based" incentive fee arrangement. In other words, the higher the price *above* $60 per share, the higher the fee. At $60 or below, the fee would be relatively small. The stock price had been in the $50 range.

We thought of our business as rather fragile in those days. We felt we were not in a position to turn down a big opportunity like this. Besides, even if it were an unconventional arrangement, John's proposal had the virtue of being fair.

His original perception was on the money. Sixty dollars a share was in the ballpark. Our first offer came from Pirelli, the Italian tire maker. They and their bankers came up with a price of $58 a share. After a series of discussions, we felt we might get them up to $60 but no higher.

Then Bridgestone, Japan's large tire maker, appeared at Firestone's

---

*Later, Akio, anxious as always to be an innovator in all things, asked me to be the first American director of a Japanese corporation. I had to resign from the board of a great American corporation, 3M, because of product overlaps. I still remain very close to Sony as a senior advisor to Howard Stringer, the CEO, and the board. I am proud to say I recruited Howard Stringer.

doorstep. They were extremely interested, subject to price and assurance that their purchase of an old-line American company would not set off political fireworks in Washington.

I headed to Washington to check the political landscape and found it benign. As for price, Bridgestone said they were prepared to offer a figure that they assumed Firestone and its board would agree was more than fair and very friendly. As with Sony, a friendly deal was very important to Bridgestone. Steve and I decided between us that Bridgestone would probably offer $65 a share, which Firestone would have been happy to accept. To our total astonishment and considerable delight, Bridgestone offered $80 a share.

Steve, the consummate negotiator, had never seen an initial offer that he would quickly accept. He suggested $82, which earned him some laughter from the Bridgestone bankers. The price stayed at $80, but when John's performance-based incentives were applied, our fee came to an astonishing $15 million—far greater than Blackstone's total other revenue that year.

We later negotiated Sony's acquisition of Columbia Pictures. These deals all served to put "little ol' Blackstone," less than four years old in 1989, among the leaders in the Japan-U.S. mergers and acquisitions business.

Raising a Buyout Fund

Our deals for Sony and Bridgestone gave us financial breathing room. We wanted and needed that breathing room, but there was a lot more we wanted.

Private equity was a rather small business when we started Blackstone. Henry Kravis, George Roberts, and their partners at Kohlberg Kravis Roberts had been trailblazers in the leveraged buyout business since forming KKR less than ten years earlier, in 1976. Teddy Forstmann of Forstmann Little was another, though unlike Henry, Teddy rejected the use of junk bonds to finance his buyouts. In both cases, the private equity business offered what I had long wanted to achieve—

owning and operating businesses. You're not selling your mind and body making (admittedly high) one-time fees to advise clients on one aspect of business or another or steering a merger or acquisition to completion. The M&A business was profitable, but it was like a greyhound race—once around the track and then you have to start over. In private equity, you could build significant value and wealth over a long period.

Raising a private equity fund, however, was far easier said than done. Steve and I knew where the money was. There was only one small problem. We had no investment track record whatsoever.

The biggest investors, by far, were pension funds, both public and corporate. Pension funds obviously have fiduciary processes that come down in most cases to simple prudence. They hire financial consultants who review a firm's capabilities and most important, one's investment track record. We had little to show them but our smiling faces and a demeanor that could only be described as urgent, if not desperate. The net result: no public pension investors in our first private equity fund.

There was the depressing day we wasted calling on the Delta Air Lines pension fund along the service road of the Atlanta airport. To begin with, we were given the wrong address, resulting in a mile-and-a-half walk carrying suitcases and briefcases. We were getting a bit paranoid at the time and wondered whether it was purposeful humiliation. When we arrived at a dreary reception area, we were kept waiting for an hour drinking some of the worst vending machine coffee in history. Again, they had not read our placement memorandum and they declared they had no interest in private equity funds, at least not ours. After this sobering and humbling experience, I growled, "Schwarzman, one more so-called meeting like this one and I am going to personally hire and pay for your replacement as meeting organizer."

The Delta fiasco was especially galling since I had to rush from the meeting to catch a plane to Washington, where I had been invited by the Business Round Table to join a presentation to President Ronald Reagan about concerns over his large budget and trade deficits, the "Twin Deficits." I made it to the White House with one minute to spare before a lunch that preceded the Cabinet Room presentation.

I remember the presentation vividly. Over lunch, I had stressed the size and the dangers of the unusually high budget and trade deficits with Howard Baker, the former senator from Tennessee who was Reagan's chief of staff, and Jim Baker, the former chief of staff who was secretary of the treasury in Reagan's second term. As we left the White House mess and headed for the Cabinet Room, Jim said, "Pete, it's important that the president hears your concerns straight out. I'm going to walk into the Oval Office now and tell him to ask you a question that gives you an opening to do that. But sometimes he forgets. So when you see we only have about five minutes left, if he hasn't asked the question, look at me and I'll give you a signal."

Reagan opened the meeting in a way that put me off a bit, reading his introduction to the meeting from cards printed with big type. It was utterly perfunctory: "Gentlemen, I welcome those of you from the business community . . ." Then, as the meeting progressed, Jim Baker's contingency plan played out exactly as he'd feared. The president failed to ask me the question. So I took my cue from Jim and directly expressed my concerns about the Twin Deficits. In spite of my blunt, straight talk, the president could not have been more gracious. He turned on his legendary charm, even asking me if I would like my picture taken with him.

Back on the road, we tried to find investors in Japan. Early on, we had the same zero success rate despite a deep well of prospects furnished by some Japanese friends and contacts. Private equity funds were a rarity there at that time. Further, the Japanese were absolutely committed to full consensus and due diligence. They wanted evidence of our capabilities, and when we proposed that our international connections presented opportunities to do business in Japan, North America, and Europe, we were greeted with deep skepticism, particularly given our lack of a track record.

From my personal experience, the Japanese have always been unfailingly courteous, but that was not to be the case among some of the senior members of the audience for my endless series of presentations in Japan. More often than I care to remember, at least one senior member of the audience or more would fall sound asleep during my presentation. I felt like tiptoeing out of the room so as to not to disturb their sleep. On those occasions in Japan when Steve was with me, I would joke: "Schwarzman, this never happens when I handle these presentations alone."

But slowly things began to turn around. By refusing to take no for an answer, we started scratching out a few hits, first singles, then a double or two, and at last a few wonderful home runs.

When I was at Lehman, I had worked with Garnett Keith, Prudential Insurance's vice chairman and the head of their investment activities. We arranged a lunch where we made a presentation, and in keeping with his utter charm, Garnett surprised us afterward with the news that Prudential would invest $100 million in our fund, and would be our lead investor. This was huge; Prudential was the biggest in this business, and also a big force in Japan, and being our lead investor meant they would help on the underwriting and let other investors know of their support. Then my good friend, gregarious and gifted Jack Welch of General Electric, took me aside at a seventieth birthday bash for Katharine Graham in Washington and said, "Pete, why haven't I heard from you?" Steve and I had begged GE and I told him so. "Call me in the morning," he said. That call brought us another $35 million.

From Japan, the slow process of building a consensus finally concluded in our favor during a two-week (it felt like two years) trip that included calls on Japan's two largest investment and securities firms, the Nomura Group and Nikko Securities. Nomura hardly knew who we were, but Nikko's deputy president Yasuo Kanzaki was friendly to us and Nikko was looking for a mergers and acquisitions partner in the United States. We were on our way to the airport when the car phone rang. I took the call. It was Kanzaki, who said Nikko had decided to proceed. This set off a flurry of scribbling in the back seat as Steve and I compared notes (silently) on how much to ask for. I wrote "$50 or $100 million?" on a memo pad. Steve pointed to "$100 million." I relayed the latter figure to Kanzaki. He agreed instantly, prompting Steve to snap his fingers and whisper, "Damn, I knew we should have asked for $150 million." In the end, Nikko's investment eventually totaled $200 million, split between an investment in our private equity fund, badly needed capital for the firm itself, and a joint venture for Japan-U.S. mergers and acquisitions.

Later, some old friends would come through for us as we moved further into capital raising for our additional private equity funds. One vote of confidence I was particularly honored by came from Singapore's legendary longtime prime minister, Lee Kuan Yew, the man who was responsible for the transformation of Singapore from poverty to economic miracle in a single generation—and who, incidentally, presided over one of the most rigorous, future-oriented, and successful pension savings programs ever created anywhere in the world. A fellow director of the Institute for International Economics, Prime Minister Lee had invited me to give the Singapore Lecture. This was an annual talk on a major subject in the field of economics, delivered to senior officials, ministers, and professional staff of the wealthy island city-state at the tip of the Malay Peninsula; I had talked about America's economic outlook and its meaning to the global economy. The prime minister invited me back, along with Steve and Dan Burstein, a Blackstone colleague, to discuss U.S. economic and foreign policies, at a dinner at their equivalent of the White House to which he invited his major cabinet ministers. Shortly after these credibility-raising events, two Singapore government investment funds put $80 million into a subsequent Blackstone private equity fund.

At the outset, I had set $200 million as the level of funding I thought that we could work with for our first fund. By the fall of 1987, with Steve fortunately pushing me hard to think bigger and go beyond my original goal, we had $840 million—the largest first-time buyout fund ever assembled: Blackstone Capital Partners.

Blackstone Capital Partners

This first Blackstone Capital Partners Fund closed just in time. We missed Black Monday, the stock market crash of October 19, 1987, by only a few days. The Dow Jones Industrial Average dropped 508 points that day—22.6 percent. It was then the largest one-day percentage drop in history. The Federal Reserve came to the rescue, and the Dow bottomed out the next day without falling much more. Still, had we attempted to close one week later, some of our investors might have departed. Dumb luck, yet again.

We worried about the market crash, but we also had cause for celebration. Managing to raise the buyout fund was a personal vindication. It meant that we must be pretty damn good marketers, which boded well for our future efforts. It also reduced any lingering worry that I had been indelibly stained by the Lehman affair. In fact, some of our investments came from friends who knew the Lehman dynamic and invested as a means of showing their personal support. It was a clear signal that we—and I especially—could look ahead and not back over our shoulders.

So ended two years of hell, not just for Steve and me but for my family and particularly Joan. Steve and I had kept a bruising schedule of meetings and travel, both domestic and around the world. Yet again, I had not been home a lot and Joan and my children had been on their own too long. She had had far more than enough of my global Willy Loman routine.

Transitions

Life did not stand still during the two years it took us to raise our buyout fund. I turned sixty in June 1986—a rather melancholy birthday I found—a passage marked by a small party appropriate to the fact that I was still trying to reinvent my life. My father died less than two months later, on July 30, and his death hurtled me back into the past.

He died at a local hospital in Kearney, and it came as no surprise. He was ninety-three and in a wheelchair. Congestive heart failure had robbed him of the strength to walk, and the world he knew had faded behind curtains of dementia. My mother had cared for him, aided by a parade of my Greek relatives in and out offering any help she needed. But I wondered what he remembered of her, the house I had grown up in, my brother, John, and me on our occasional visits, our wives, his grandchildren who were now young adults. He would have appreciated the turnout at his funeral and the words of gratitude for his many charitable contributions. It would have confirmed his belief in the opportunity he had made the most of, the opportunity for which he so often and so fervently expressed thanks with his favorite phrase: "God Bless America."

My mother took it stoically when Papa died. Since she was now alone in Kearney, I told her I would be glad to move her to New York where she could be close to the grandchildren she loved so much and had so thoroughly enjoyed. "Oh, I'll be all right," she would sigh, sounding a bit like a Greek tragedian.

But in the months following his death, a profound change came over her. She was happy. She was more relaxed. She laughed more. She became more active, and took up charitable work. It was only then that she told me the story from their long-ago honeymoon, of him making her walk on the other side of the street after exploding at the boldness she displayed in taking pictures without asking him. I looked back on her life with my strict and straitlaced father and saw instance after instance where he had stifled her. But she had loved him, and was dedicated to him, I was sure of that.

After I had moved to New York from Washington, I took the entire family out to Kearney for their fiftieth wedding anniversary celebration. There was a big dinner, and my father got up and gave a lengthy toast, distinguished by the depressing fact that he never once mentioned my mother. This speech was no oversight; he had written it all out beforehand. I was aghast. He spent most of his remarks talking about me, praising the fact that I had been the first Greek cabinet officer and adding his habitual "God Bless America." Then he went on to implicitly insult my brother, recalling, "We used to say Peter got all the brains and John got all the hair."

This was too much. I got up and did my best to smooth things over, speaking effusively about both John and my mother. The next morning, when I went to their house, I remonstrated with my father about his failing to account for John's many warm friendships and other admirable human qualities that I frankly envied. I was not about to remind him that he had ignored his wife of fifty years in his wedding anniversary toast, particularly while she was sitting in the room intent on our conversation. But instead of taking my side, my mother jumped all over me. She blamed me for "attacking" my father and said

I hadn't needed to defend John because "we always liked him better." In more troubled times, this might have been enough to put me back on the therapist couch.

But if my mother was comfortable with her life then, and said she wanted no disruptions to the way things were, her new attitude after my father died told a different story. I saw her become transformed, and for the first time recognized the person that my older relatives remembered from Greece. They had always described her as a girl who had been full of life and curiosity and laughter. Now I saw those qualities emerge, and they would stay with her for the years that remained to her. My children, who adored her, detected this new spirit too, and they grew closer than ever with YiaYia, the Greek for "grandmother" and their pet name for her. She would live happily for almost six more years until she died in her sleep at home on February 24, 1992. She was eighty-nine. We buried her next to my father, but had there been a choice in the matter—there wasn't, because there wasn't any room—I wonder if she would have chosen to lie next to my sister, Elaine, whose death had shattered her so long ago.

Off the Ground

We immediately started to look at transactions for our new fund. In the fall of 1986, Carl Icahn, the famous corporate raider, started to pile up shares of USX, the new name of the venerable United States Steel Corporation. The name change signified a change in emphasis; USX still made steel, but it was now a company heavily into energy production, including Marathon Oil and Texas Oil and Gas. At the time, its steel unit was in trouble owing to overcapacity, old plants, intense foreign competition, and a strike over long-standing labor issues that had gone on for three months.

In addition to energy and steel, USX's other prime component was a transportation business that included railroads, tugboats, ships, and barges. For several weeks in September and October 1986, USX shares were the most heavily traded on the New York Stock Exchange, as

Icahn accumulated shares and tried to prevent the company from pulling off a stock buyback proposal. USX chairman David Roderick tried to fend him off.

It seemed likely that the Icahn intrusion could end up being a greenmail situation, the financial version of blackmail in which the raider's objective is to wrest money from his target. Icahn wasn't interested in running a huge steel, energy, and transportation conglomerate. But buying off Icahn would require a large amount of cash, a commodity then in short supply at USX. This was to be in the form of a one-time, special dividend to stockholders, of which he was the largest.

To get the cash, USX decided to sell 51 percent of their transportation business. This percentage just over half would permit any debt in the spinoff to come off the balance sheet of the USX parent company. We were anxious to buy it. We felt it was vital that USX sell to a friendly partner, since the company depended heavily on this transportation business to ship raw materials like coal and iron ore as well as their finished products. An unfriendly 51 percent profit partner could wreak havoc on the operations and ultimately the profits of the USX steel business and on the parent company.

We decided to emphasize our willingness to look at the transaction from the operating viewpoint of USX, and in the context of a friendly, long-term business relationship. We tried to think through the kinds of decisions that could create disharmony and dysfunction in the partnership and in the steel business. How, for example, would shipping rates be set? How could USX be assured that we would continue to invest adequately in new equipment and rail beds to assure that our venture would continue to provide speedy, safe, and efficient transportation? And suppose Blackstone wanted to sell its 51 percent interest? How would that be handled in a way that protected USX's business and financial interests? Those and many more operating questions would inevitably arise.

So to differentiate Blackstone from other bidders, we decided to move price to the back burner. In our first meeting with USX, we laid out the ways we would focus these governance and operating issues from the outset. We argued that doing so would improve the odds of a long and happy relationship. We could tell from their reaction that other bidders had not stressed this approach. Naturally, it resonated with the USX management who would be running the steel business.

Blackstone's $500 million purchase of 51 percent of Transtar, our name for the new spun-off company, was announced in the financial press on June 21, 1988.

The structure of the Transtar deal bears looking at. It helps explain what is a mystery to many and a reason to criticize for some. The question is how private equity firms like Blackstone make money. Critics say, "You don't make anything. Why should you be so highly paid?" But we do make something. We make opportunities for businesses to grow and change, which creates more opportunities all up and down the line. At the same time, I would certainly admit some investments are far more difficult than others. Transtar was not one of them.

Here's how it worked in the case of Transtar, which turned out to be an extraordinary investment, made possible by the characteristics of Transtar as a company and the benign financial conditions that existed during our period of ownership.

Its cash flows were solid and steady, owing to many long-term contracts. The equipment was relatively new and well maintained so that little new capital would be required, and depreciation was high. All this made it possible to buy Transtar in a highly leveraged deal, meaning much of the purchase price was borrowed, 95 percent, in fact. And because we were willing to be flexible and creative about overseeing and operating the new company, we got it at an excellent price.

The equity put into the deal totaled only $25 million, or 5 percent of the purchase price. Of that, 51 percent was Blackstone's—$13,421,000. The remaining 49 percent investment came from USX. With the solid cash flows, large in relation to the business, we were able to benefit from a virtually assured and steady flow of dividend payments as well as recapitalizations and other realized proceeds while at the same time paying off the loans.

During the last phase of this investment, we agreed to split Transtar in two. USX took back 100 percent ownership of the company's properties that served its major plants, while Blackstone took 100 percent of the properties that were less central to USX's ongoing operations. That gave us the freedom to hire new management, build those businesses, and eventually sell them at a very good price with a minimum effect on USX operations, which reflected the friendly approach we had promoted from the very beginning.

In 1999, twelve years after the original purchase, when we sold the part of the business that we had retained, we realized proceeds totaling $344,601,000 and our annual return on our investment was a stunning 129.9 percent, or 26 times our original investment. Blackstone's carried interest gains, as they're termed, amounted to something over $60 million.

Before I seem too self-congratulatory about this success, I should add a caveat: Conditions in the 1990s were so favorable to the private equity business that, with reasonable prudence, one would often have had to be rather inept *not* to do well. Economic growth was robust during much of the decade. Ample financial capital was available to fund debt at low interest rates. Private equity competition was far less intense than it is today. Finally, and very important, price-earnings ratios rose substantially during much of the 1990s. At the start of the decade, the average price-earnings multiple of a Standard & Poor's 500 company was 15.1 times net earnings. By 1999, that ratio had more than doubled to 33.8 times. That meant you could sell the same company, without any improvements in operations, at roughly twice the price paid in 1990.

Today, private equity firms have to make their money by aggressively improving operations, reconfiguring static or moribund companies and their management (about which more later). But in the case of Transtar, we made much of our profits through financial engineering with a company that was so solid that it made a highly leveraged transaction possible.

The profit from the Transtar deal was, of course, important. But more important in the long run was the signal that our relationship with USX and our governance of Transtar sent to the corporate world. It backed up our claim that we were committed to friendly-only private equity investing.

Blackstone has now set up about thirty-five such friendly corporate partnerships, and leads the field in this area by a wide margin.

CHAPTER 15

BECOMING A FORCE

Branching Out

By 1988, the year Blackstone made the Transtar purchase, the firm had grown from the original four to sixty-two employees. We had moved from the Seagram Building to larger offices a few blocks away, then a year later moved to 345 Park Avenue, a high rise between the Seagram Building on the north and Saint Bartholomew's Church on the south, where we would stay. With our first private equity purchase under our belts, Steve and I were looking for new challenges.

To grow into a private equity player had required two years of beating the bushes for investors. To grow beyond that, we would have to apply another of our founding principles. We wanted to expand into new business areas by finding apt strategic affiliations. Linkups with affiliates who knew what we didn't would give us entry into fields that offered opportunities that we were not equipped to exploit on our own. We decided that we would find the very best talent, and sell them on working with us for both parties' mutual benefit.

Where would we find these experts? We reasoned that there were gifted, entrepreneurial professionals working in large firms who, like ourselves, would prefer a sense of ownership, not only in their business but by owning a share of Blackstone's profits as well, and a chance to operate "their" business in a smaller setting. We also, based on our experience in the fractured Lehman culture, thought that many of these same talents would want to escape the politicized, bureaucratic, and Balkanized environments that existed at some of the big firms. Many would not, for any number of reasons, want to tackle the uncertainty of setting out entirely on their own. But as our affiliates, such people would benefit from the infrastructure we had built. We thought there could be some cross-fertilization of clients, relationships, projects, and intellectual capital between their business and other Blackstone businesses. We could also offer them help in raising funds and give them access to administrative services in areas such as back-office functions and compliance. Increasingly, ours was a credible brand that would open doors for them. And we believed they would enjoy some general camaraderie, since we knew from our early experience that very small firms could sometimes get lonely.

The idea of such affiliate arrangements appealed to both of us, but we had to be certain we were forming relationships with the right people. I have always believed that the ethical tone of an institution is set at the top, and ethics and integrity had been paramount at Blackstone from day one. We stressed with potential affiliates that the same standards applied to them and we thought that the best people would like the emphasis. Later, in the wake of the Enron and WorldCom scandals, we added a provision to our strict code that every partner and employee must sign annually. It includes the clear understanding that it is not enough to avoid misconduct themselves. They also have the affirmative responsibility to report any improper behavior. Not to do so is grounds for dismissal. Enron and WorldCom were brought down by scandals that grew to major proportions because employees who knew of the malfeasance were afraid to report it for fear of retaliation against them as whistleblowers. The affiliates carry our brand name. We were determined to avoid improprieties that could damage the Blackstone brand and, therefore, the entire firm.

Beyond extending our strict ethics standards to Blackstone affiliates, Steve and I determined that we would never set up an affiliate, however promising the business area, unless the head of the group and his team were tops in their field. Poor results in one affiliate, we knew, could affect the reputation of the entire firm. We didn't want to worry about how or what they would do. Quite the opposite, we would need to have enough confidence in the team to invest a significant amount of our own and the firm's capital in their operation, which, in turn, would help the affiliate in raising funds.

Our first affiliate, and among our most successful, was the Blackstone Financial Management Group, which gave us a fixed income asset management component. Larry Fink had been at First Boston and Ralph Schlosstein had worked at Lehman and later in the Jimmy Carter White House when they joined us as partners in 1988. They were major and complementary first-rate talents who wanted to be significant owners of their own business and they proceeded to take their operation to extraordinary heights. Along the way, it acquired the name BlackRock, a name that was an obvious play on Blackstone. Its success ultimately led to a desire by Fink and Schlosstein to ally themselves with a firm with a much larger capital base than we had at the time, and we sold BlackRock to the Pittsburgh National Corporation (PNC) in a deal that closed in 1995.

Our inability to keep BlackRock in the family was our costliest mishap by far. I knew we had to respect Larry's and Ralph's wishes. They delivered their message at a breakfast. I normally had a cappuccino, which didn't taste very good that morning. Today, BlackRock has a stunning $1.43 trillion under management and a $20 billion market capitalization. What a combination BlackRock and Blackstone would have made over the long haul! But we at least made a handsome capital gain of $75 million on this sale, from a very small investment.

Blackstone Alternative Asset Management

In 1990, Blackstone's partners saw that much of their and the firm's capital would be tied up in private equity investments. By their nature, private equity investments are both long-term and illiquid. Cash is not only tied up, but value tends to tick up and down with the stock and bond markets. We realized—indeed, our commitment to corporate stability demanded—that we also needed to invest in funds that, unlike private equity, were liquid, weren't correlated to conventional stocks and bonds (thus the name Alternative Assets) and that offered down-side protection from the stock market's high-risk, high-reward volatility. The theory of the case is quite straightforward. Executing it was any-thing but straightforward.

Thus the creation of BAAM—Blackstone Alternative Asset Man-agement, or our fund-of-hedge-funds business. In the early stages of BAAM, the funds invested were largely our own and the firm's capital. This made us doubly sensitive to downside risk, and so we crawled be-fore we walked or ran. We had the Nikko equity capital of $100 million, which was available for whatever investments we wished to make. But we wanted to be sure that we really built the know-how and had the right team of professionals to manage a big and complex business before we took any further steps and Blackstone's name became publicly in-volved. This self-education process took several years of learning from experience, and sometimes the experience was painful.

In the first instance, it was painful in a financial sense—we lost 8 percent in one early year. And recall that these funds were largely our own and the firm's money.

It was also painful in the sense that we made a series of personnel choices that were simply mistakes. And the melancholy reality was that there were too many of these kinds of mistakes throughout the firm. We started to be known for our high turnover. That reputation, in turn, began to harm our ability to recruit new personnel.

I have often pondered why we made these early mistakes. I think that perhaps we were so anxious—some might say too anxious—to grow without taking the time to develop our own crop of talent. Hiring from the outside is inherently more risky than developing your own talent. Also, it is often hard to know the real reason someone is available. Many people are adept at rationalizing their limitations by blaming others for them. One also knows that firms typically try hard to hang on to their top talent, so when so-called top people are on the market you have to look hard for the real reasons they are available.

We at Blackstone have learned our lesson. We now put major em-phasis on thoroughly vetting prospective employees, particularly those being considered for senior positions. G. H. Smart is the crack manage-ment assessment firm we hire to guide our interviews with top-level professionals. From their intensive due diligence, we learn up front the candidates' reported strengths and weaknesses as well as the sometimes elusive reasons they left, or indeed were let go, from other positions. Today, thankfully, our turnover is very low.

J. Tomlinson "Tom" Hill, who had vast experience as the former co-CEO of Lehman and was a longtime personal friend, took direct charge of BAAM in 2000. Tom is also Blackstone's vice chairman.

Today, we have nineteen different strategies and another nineteen customized vehicles, often tailored to meet the specific needs of very large institutional investors. Today, BAAM funds under management total over $33 billion, a far cry from the $53 million in our original fund in 1990.

We have had a strong wind at our backs in building our BAAM business. Originally, our major investors were high-net-worth individuals. After some downside events from the late 1990s into the 2000s, the really big investors, in particular public and corporate pension plans, sharpened their appetite for the fund-of-funds' downside protection.

In the early 1990s the total investment in such funds was about $40 billion. Today, the total of such investments has grown exponentially to about $2.5 trillion. The management fees they pay us provide Blackstone with a regular, large source of income and the stability that accompanies it.

Real Estate

Our search for a real estate affiliate coincided with the savings and loan crisis that began when S&Ls, formerly tightly regulated, began to operate under looser rules in the late 1980s. These lifted the ceilings on interest rates they could charge and also allowed them to engage in more speculative lending and investing. Chasing high interest rates in a real estate boom, many of them made risky loans that came back to bite them. Several high-profile failures resulted and these led to a huge federal taxpayer bailout in the range of $200 billion in the form of the Resolution Trust Corporation, created by Congress in 1989.

By 1991, Steve and I thought the Resolution Trust's real estate properties, taken over from the investment portfolios of failed S&Ls, represented some unusual opportunities. We weren't real estate people. But we could see that the world of commercial real estate had been turned upside down by the S&L crisis. There was excessive supply that forced prices downward, and a lack of debt and equity funding. It was also clear that the federal government, having been forced into the real estate business, would want to get out as soon as possible. Having been in government and observed the background and talents of many federal officials, I doubted that many of them had the savvy to price the Resolution Trust properties aggressively or even accurately. And, in those early days, there were relatively few bidders. In other words, it was a good time to buy.

We used a variety of sources of capital, including our own personal funds and those of the firm. We envisioned those early purchases as what one might call "demonstration investments." They were designed in part to give us the experience and credibility to raise a large real estate fund, which we didn't see running ourselves but would place it in an affiliate dedicated solely to real estate and run by people far more expert than we were.

As it happened, I was on the board of Rockefeller Center Properties, which Claude Ballard chaired. He had headed Goldman Sachs's real estate investment operation, and as a result he knew everyone in the field worth knowing. One day at a meeting, I asked Claude if he could help us out.

"Who's the best person you know in real estate?" I asked. "And how can we get him (or her) to come to work with Blackstone?"

"John Schreiber in Chicago is the best." (Claude was right.) "But you'll never get him." (Claude was wrong.)

Taking no for an answer was not what had produced our first buyout fund, and it wasn't going to give us the topflight team we wanted to head a Blackstone real estate affiliate. Maybe we had an offer he couldn't (or wouldn't) refuse.

Steve made the first contact, which John later described as "out of the blue." I'm not sure if he deliberately employed a stealth strategy or if it just worked out that way, but he told John he was looking for references on a couple of people we were looking at to get us into real estate.

Two weeks later, Steve called him back and said, "You're the guy we're looking for."

John was intrigued, but wary. He wanted ownership and autonomy, but he didn't want to move to New York and he didn't want to work full-time. We struck an agreement that allowed him to stick his toe in the water. He would help us launch our real estate operation and commit to working only forty days a year. Forty days later, in October 1992, he had already worked forty days and I think in that time had absorbed the attractions of both the Blackstone affiliation and our insistence on friendly corporate partnerships. He abandoned the forty-day limit and said, "Let's make it full-time." In the process he became a significant owner of Blackstone Real Estate Properties (BREP) without having to absorb the expenses of creating a new firm. It was a situation made to order for what we had envisioned as our affiliate relationships.

With John at the helm, by December 1993 we had made a total of five real estate purchases requiring a total equity investment of $141 million. We still had no significant real estate fund; much of the money came from Blackstone and its partners, including John.

John immediately lived up to his lofty reputation, putting in place a team that produced 42.7 percent investment returns annually on these early deals, a stunningly successful record.

John's leadership also gave us the credibility we needed to raise money for our first dedicated real estate fund. This brought us in contact with Steve Myers, the investment officer who directed the very successful South Dakota state retirement fund.

Steve Myers happened to be an ardent admirer of the work of The Concord Coalition, an organization I co-founded that focused on fiscal responsibility. He came to New York to check us out, after which we went to Sioux Falls for a long presentation meeting with his board of directors. With his board's approval, Steve honored the great team we had put together by agreeing to fund an unprecedented 50 percent of our initial real estate fund.

But like almost any prudent investor, he wanted to be certain he wasn't rushing in alone. He stipulated that we would have to find another major investor for at least 20 percent of the fund.

Steve Myers's challenge led us to Hank Greenberg and the American International Group (AIG), at that time, a very large and credible investor. Hank and I had gotten to know each other well at the Council on Foreign Relations. By now I had been chairing the Council for nine years, with Hank as the vice chairman and very much a senior partner. When we approached Hank, he invited Steve Schwarzman and me to AIG for lunch and, in his usual decisive fashion, agreed at that same lunch to back 20 percent of the real estate fund, meeting Steve Myers's stipulation.

Blackstone Real Estate Properties was off and running in 1994 with a $344 million fund, not at all bad for that period when billion-dollar real estate funds were very rare. Some of our most successful early deals embodied the Blackstone signature form of friendly corporate real estate partnerships with IBM and Standard Oil of Indiana.

BREP grew rapidly. One of our most visible deals was Blackstone's 1998 partnership with Los Angeles–based Colony Capital, which bought London's Savoy Group of famous super-luxury London hotels, including The Berkeley, Claridge's, The Connaught, The Savoy, and the Lygon Arms in the Cotswolds, for $866 million. Five years later, after investing in upgrades to the hotels and their restaurants, we sold the operation to Dublin-based Quinlan Private for $1.37 billion. The annual financial return was a modest 11 percent, but the psychic return to the Blackstone brand around Europe and to us as individuals was very high indeed.

Blackstone now owns hotel groups including Boca Resorts, Wyndham International, and La Quinta Inns, and with the purchase of Hilton, we are now the largest owners of hotels in the world (615,000 rooms in total). Blackstone is also the country's biggest office landlord.

Since its inception in 1992, Blackstone Real Estate Properties has realized gross annual returns averaging 39.2 percent through 2007. John's role, as he puts it modestly, is to let BREP partners run the business day to day while he acts "as third base coach to these young capable guys." These consummate professionals include Jon Gray, who runs our U.S. real estate investments and, at age thirty-eight, is one of the most talented young executives in the financial services industry.

Finding Value in Private Equity: A Case Study

In many ways, the 1990s were the best of times for private equity, with robust economic growth, plenty of capital available at low interest rates, price-earnings ratios that doubled during the decade, and a benign regulatory attitude in Washington.

The situation began to change around 2000, and by 2007, began feeling like the worst of times. Price-earnings ratios have fallen by half, from 33.8 times earnings in 1999 to 17.2 times earnings in 2008. Economic growth has slowed considerably with the recession, and the result of the housing, energy, and subprime mortgage crises. Readily available capital at low interest rates is the lifeblood of this highly leveraged business, and given the subprime and credit crisis problems, from the middle of 2007 through 2008 there was a drought of it. Blackstone made no significant private equity investments in the first two quarters of 2008.

But you can't run and hide during business downturns. Business cycles affect nearly all businesses, and some of the best buying opportunities often occur at low points in the cycle. Undervalued and underappreciated companies frequently offer the best opportunities for improvement, and for profit. The new decade simply demands a far more proactive operating approach, rather than simply financial engineering, to realizing value from the companies we owned.

One such company is Nielsen (formerly VNU), the world's largest research and information business, which we acquired in 2006 as part of a consortium of six private equity partners. It was what the industry calls a "club deal" because the cost, $11.5 billion requiring $4.1 billion in equity, was too much for any one private equity fund.

As in any such deal, solo or otherwise, we and the others—Carlyle, Kohlberg Kravis Roberts, Hellman & Friedman (co-owned by my former Lehman colleague Warren Hellman), Thomas Lee, and Alpinvest— devoted months prior to the purchase analyzing the possibilities. Our due diligence persuaded us that we could significantly lower costs and make other changes post-acquisition that would much improve productivity, grow revenues and profits, and increase value.

Once we made the purchase, the head of our Portfolio Operating Group, James Quella, helped lead a group of Blackstone operating experts to lay out a preliminary plan in this direction. The first step was to find a senior management team, and most importantly a CEO, that could plan and execute a strategic vision to improve results. The search led us to David Calhoun, vice chairman at General Electric and, by wide acknowledgment, one of the best executives in America. He came on board in 2006 and put in place a topflight team.

David could have had his pick of top positions; he led lists of CEO candidates at companies much larger than Nielsen. Recently, I asked him what persuaded him to take our offer. "Pete, being private, we don't have to obsess over quarterly earnings, stockholders, and equity analysts. We can concentrate on long-term performance improvements. I also don't have to put up with bureaucratic impediments and delays that are often an inevitable part of big companies. I also wanted to run my own business and invest a meaningful amount of my own money." Dave and his team invested $89.5 million at the same price as Blackstone.

David and his team focused early on internal operations. Right away, they identified cost savings that in our third year of ownership will hit about $500 million annually. One source of savings is the bargaining power Blackstone obtains from its portfolio of companies, economies of scale that drive down the costs of health care, insurance, travel, telecommunications, and the like.

By also selling previously unproductive assets and reinvesting in high-growth businesses serving new media, David now projects that annual earnings growth over the next five years will go from 3 percent to 5 percent prior to our purchase to 15 percent to 20 percent. Nielsen's value is now estimated to have increased by a stunning $13 billion.

This is much harder work than realizing value from a company like Transtar. But it is good work, and increasing value in the case of a company like Nielsen is good for the investors and the economy.

Taken together, Blackstone's private equity portfolio companies have aggregated revenues of $112 billion, 645,640 employees, and pretax profits of $22.7 billion. This aggregation would make the Blackstone portfolio one of the fifteen largest companies in America.

Fun at Blackstone

In spite of the intense activity around the firm, the new funds, the new affiliates, the relentless drive for new investors and new clients, there was always time for fun. And it was equal opportunity fun. Mostly roasts. And for reasons that elude me, I emerged as the favorite roastee. Perhaps it was the only safe outlet for suppressed hostility. I never admitted that I rather enjoyed the attention.

One year, at the annual Christmas party, the young associates played the Johnny Carson "Karnak" game: "Here are the answers. What are the questions?" (My books on the federal deficit, not exactly beach favorites, were a favorite target.) One year the answers were: 1,000,000, 999,999, 1, and 0. What were the questions? First, how many books did Peterson print? Second, how many did he sign and give away? Third, how many were bought? And finally, how many were read?

My surprise sixty-fifth birthday, years earlier orchestrated by a brilliant producer, my wife, was another occasion, and a high-talent occasion it was, for still more roasts. Gifted movie director Mike Nichols said, "Pete Peterson is a combination of Spencer Tracy and Mr. Magoo." Ted Sorensen, President Kennedy's remarkably talented speechwriter, delivered the only long, tortured, circular convoluted sentence he had ever written. It was followed by, "Joan, I told you I could get Pete Peterson and the word humble in the same sentence."

I felt my Blackstone colleagues also performed very well against this world-class talent. Schwarzman, dressed in a Japanese kimono, and with a remarkably good Japanese accent, played the lead role as head of a large Japanese investment fund that I was pitching. Roger Altman played me.

The script went like this: "Oh, Honorable Peterson, what a privilege it is to greet such a distinguished American. How can I help you?"

"Sir, thank you. I am here to solicit your interest in investing in the Blackstone Private Equity Fund."

"Oh, Honorable Peterson, could what I have heard possibly be true—that you have no investment track record?"

"Oh, Honorable Sir, as someone with your remarkably broad experience knows, there is so much more to life than a track record."

"What then, Mr. Peterson, are you offering?"

"We will be very international and make investments in Japan, America, and Europe."

"Oh, Honorable Peterson, now I understand. Trilateral Fund. Lose money all over the world!"

Then, there was the Blackstone skit roasting my notoriously sloppy eating habits. Julian Niccolini, the infamous maître d' at the Four Seasons Grill, playing himself, asked: "Mr. Chairman, do you want to spill the iced tea on your tie, or would you like me to do it?" Roger Altman, playing me, said, "Go ahead. You do it." And Julian did. I applauded my Blackstone colleagues for such an effective sight gag.

As in all really good roasts, there was far more than an ounce of truth in all this.

Going Public

Early in 2007, Steve reported to me that he and Hamilton "Tony" James, Blackstone's very able president and chief operating officer, who had joined the firm from Credit Suisse First Boston in 2002, had been thinking through the pros and cons of taking Blackstone public. He asked what I thought.

The irony did not escape me that a private equity firm, which emphasized why their private companies did better over the longer term, should be going public.

There were obvious pluses to a public offering. If the firm offered around 10 percent of its stock for public sale, which was the range being discussed, the partners, then numbering fifty-seven among an employee roster that had grown to 819 (now 1,336), could liquidate some of their holdings. It would greatly increase the firm's capital base and give us a much larger source of funds for investing. Use of the firm's capital for investment in transactions would return 100 percent of the profits to the firm rather than the maximum of 20 percent that can be earned in leveraged transactions investing other people's money. It also would give us capital to invest in our funds. At the time, the entire equity capital of the firm was less than $200 million, petty cash in today's world, and we simply did not have the capital or the currency to make significant acquisitions that we very much wanted to make.

But there were minuses as well. I told Steve that from my experience as the CEO of a public firm, I had found it a very different world. There would be endless meetings with equity analysts, the release of quarterly public earnings estimates, across-the-board disclosures ranging from executive compensation to successes and failures both personal and financial, board meetings, annual stockholder meetings, and on and on. If we decided to go ahead, I thought we should try to restructure the governance arrangements typical of a public company. As a result, our team spent a great deal of time structuring the transaction in ways to preserve as much as possible of the kind of governance that we had as a private firm.

And I told him that he would be the public focal point. He might get too much of the credit, but often too much of the blame. Blackstone already had a rising public profile as the result of the ongoing bidding war with Vornado Realty starting in late 2006 to acquire Equity Office Properties, and when Blackstone won, it proved to be the largest leveraged buyout ever at $39 billion. With that kind of money being talked about, it was inevitable that attention would focus on the people in charge. Steve would receive a level of scrutiny he had never experienced before. I told him both his business life and his personal life would be under the media's microscope, and he had to be prepared.

I did not take a position. He was the CEO and had guided Blackstone to the point where an IPO was even reasonable to talk about. It was a long-term decision. It was February of 2007 and I would be eighty-one in a few months. I was feeling strong and involved but still looking at a retirement date at the end of 2008 after which I wanted to focus on my major public policy passions. Our partnership agreement gave me veto power, but given my age and my plans, it would have been inappropriate for me to use it. I told Steve that if he had thought through all the issues, I would support his decision, whatever it was.

And of course, the decision was to go ahead.

By then it was March of 2007, and my forecast about an uncommon level of public and personal scrutiny of Steve had already come true, far sooner and more harshly than I would have predicted. Steve was born on Valentine's Day, and February 14, 2007, marked his sixtieth birthday, one of those milestone moments people often celebrate in style. Lavish parties thrown by people who can afford them have always been fodder for populist media coverage. Steve's plans were second to none, and the press got wind of them early. Stories focused on the huge Park Avenue armory that would be the venue, the guest list of celebrities and financiers, and the news that singer Rod Stewart would headline the entertainment, plus several other stars, including the comedian Martin Short, the composer Marvin Hamlisch (*A Chorus Line*), singer Patti LaBelle, and the Abyssinian Baptist Choir.

I was at the same table as Jack Welch and Liz Smith. Though they said little, their eyes said a lot. We just knew it was one of the most expensive parties we had ever been to. Yet I don't think any of us anticipated the press firestorm that followed.

Despite Steve's many charitable contributions and gifts, especially to the arts, and the New York Public Library, he was emerging, as an article by James B. Stewart in *The New Yorker* put it, as "an easy target for critics of Wall Street greed and conspicuous consumption."

Today, I am sorry to say that when people think about Steve, the sixtieth birthday party often detracts from his many accomplishments. I think of his rapid growth from a gifted young M&A advisor to a very effective CEO. He is also a great marketer, and a fine strategist.

A few days before the party, Blackstone closed the Equity Office Properties deal, creating a perfect storm of publicity. The buyout exceeded the total price of Henry Kravis's biggest deal and Steve was crowned "the new king of Wall Street" by *Fortune* magazine. That only focused more attention on the party and its cost.

As the date for our IPO moved closer, the valuations placed on Blackstone added new fuel to the perfect storm. I had done some checking to see how other public firms were valued. Bear Stearns, then a successful full service firm with 15,500 employees (before its collapse in the subprime mortgage crisis), carried a value of $21 billion. Evercore Partners and Greenhill and Co., two boutique advisory and investment firms, were valued at $988 million and $1.86 billion, respectively. The great Lazard, with 2,200 employees, was valued at $10.5 billion. The market valued Lehman Brothers, which had 29,000 employees, at $42.2 billion.

I was simply astonished when the underwriters, led by Morgan Stanley and Citigroup, valued Blackstone at $31 billion. Nevertheless, the underwriters defended their valuation by citing Blackstone's growth record and its diversified set of promising businesses. These, they said, deserved a much higher price-earnings ratio than many other firms in anticipation of significantly faster and more secure future growth.

We assumed there would be no vesting requirements for Steve and me, since, as co-founders, we already owned our shares outright. Nonetheless, as the underwriters pointed out, potential buyers would be focused on Steve's incentive to stay on as CEO for a substantial period, as the perception of Blackstone's value was tied closely to his continued leadership. They thought that most of his holdings should be vested over a three-year period. My situation was quite different. I was much older, of course, and had announced that I would retire no later than the end of 2008.

On June 18, 2007, the day of the IPO came. A piece of me didn't believe it would really happen. So I called the bank to be sure that the wire transfer of proceeds from my sale of Blackstone shares had gone through. The bank's verbal assurance was not enough. I asked for written assurance. When that came in a minute later, my mind raced back to the *Blazing Saddles* character played by Madeline Kahn who said in her Germanic lisp, "It's twoo, it's twoo!" I was an instant billionaire! The wire transfer was for a stunning $1.85 billion. By the time I paid capital gains taxes (given our initial $400,000 investment in Blackstone, it was, of course, 99.999 percent capital gains), and provided for some trusts and other commitments, I had netted a bit over $1 billion.*

------

* History has placed my arrangements in a somewhat harsher light. Blackstone's IPO was priced at $31 a share, the price for which I sold. After rising to a high around $38 in the days after the offering, the stock fell, along with many financial industry stocks in the subprime mortgage crisis, and as I write this, is trading at around $6. This has caused me to be treated by some like a horse trader that got a high price for a horse he knew was lame. Others have praised me for my market prescience and even for anticipating the subprime credit crunch. Nonsense.

I called Joan and we had some rare champagne for dinner. How I wish I could have called my father. It might have pleased and impressed him as much as my being the first Greek cabinet officer.

As a kid growing up in the 1930s, I heard all this talk about millionaires like John D. Rockefeller and Andrew Carnegie. When I was younger, I once asked how many zeros were in a million. Six zeros! It seemed out of sight. A billion is nine zeros, 1,000 million dollars. Imagine a millionaire, which I never expected to be, one thousand times over.

Only the government dealt in billions. And the famous line of Senator Everett Dirksen about the federal budget, "A billion here, a billion there, pretty soon it adds up to real money."

What would I do with $1 billion of my own?

I knew deep down in my psyche that I would much prefer giving most of it away rather than spending it. I'm not one that really enjoys living large. I have no desire to be a conspicuous consumer. When I see a thirty-something hedge funder loudly revving up his red Ferrari convertible in the Hamptons, I feel much more contempt than envy.

I always remember that to my father, the ultimate pejorative was "big spender." And my father's watchful eye still hangs over me. Buying a huge yacht is out of the question. So is a big plane. Most of the time, I take the shuttle to Washington.

I didn't feel I really needed anything. Still, I had always fantasized about one thing—a Fifth Avenue apartment with a terrace. I love to read outdoors. Joan had always vetoed it on the grounds that it was a bit unseemly and even a bit immoral that the mother of Big Bird, educator of poor children in America and around the world, would be ostentatiously splurging.

This apartment dialogue (actually a one-way dialogue) had gone on for years. One day on the way home from a funeral, Joan mused

---

My main focus was to fund a major philanthropic effort. Tony James knew this and proposed that I be allowed to sell 60 percent of my Blackstone shares. To be fair to my Blackstone colleagues who did not enjoy this level of liquidity, Tony proposed that I give up 15 percent of my total shares. I agreed. I had no crystal ball or magic tea leaves. It is also worth noting, with regard to Blackstone's stock price, that its partners and employees still hold some 74 percent of Blackstone stock and I still hold about 4 percent.

about what I would be feeling and doing on the way home from her funeral. She said, "Darling, you are incapable of living alone. Coming home from my funeral, you would be calling some woman for a date." I said, "Joan, that is unfair, but I would be calling a real estate agent."

This started a real two-way dialogue. She said, "You are serious about a new apartment, aren't you?" "Yes dear, I am very serious." And so, we now have a new Fifth Avenue apartment with a terrace. I revel in it. As a matter of fact, as I write this, I am sitting on that glorious terrace.

The clouds of the populist storm swirled and deepened and, in the wake of our public offering and the now famous public sixtieth birthday party, came down on the private equity industry in Washington. At issue is a proposal to more than double the tax on gains made from carried interest, the term used to describe the share—generally amounting to 20 percent—of any profits that private equity managers realize, above some fertile or minimum annual rate of return of 8 percent to 9 percent. For reasons that strike me as unfair, and bad tax policy, the tax increase would not apply to thousands of real estate, oil and gas, resource and family partnerships that are identical in structure to the private equity partnerships. Whatever the outcome, it will prove to be a difficult, defining political battle.

Given the huge inequality of incomes in America, I can certainly understand the argument that a genuine fat cat such as myself should pay more taxes. The question is, What is the right way to go about it?

I also have great empathy for the middle-class anxieties and underlying realities that animate the outcry. Stagnating real incomes, metastasizing health care costs, ballooning food and energy costs, globalization, job fears, housing price worries, foreclosures, collapsing retirement savings, and so forth have caused financial nightmares for wage earners. The middle working class, labor unions, and their friends note a stunning disparity of incomes: The percentage of total income going to the upper one percent has ballooned since 1980 from 10 percent to 23 percent.

Put in even starker terms, the top tenth of that one percent, which also includes me, makes as much money as the bottom 50 percent combined. Such inequality, Alan Greenspan has said, "is where the capitalist system is most vulnerable. You can't have the capitalist system if an increasing number of people think it is unjust." I have no trouble accepting both the fact that we Wall Streeters are the new folk enemy, and why we have achieved that unique recognition.

My position on the need to increase revenues, including increasing marginal taxes on us fat cats, ideally in conjunction with spending restraints, is greeted with very restrained enthusiasm by my Wall Street and Republican friends. Still, I believe our gargantuan unfunded liabilities and promises—and the profound need to convince essential foreign lenders that we are getting our fiscal house in order—require that everything must be on the table, including more taxes.

I certainly hope I am wrong, but I foresee over the short to midterm a radically restructured financial services sector with substantially less leverage and liquidity—a very tough fund-raising environment, as investors cope with the sharp falloff in financial asset values, much more regulation, and higher taxes. These forces would obviously greatly complicate the outlook and the management of private equity firms.

The shape and slope of these forces are obviously far beyond Blackstone's ability to predict or control. What Blackstone can do is to respond as proactively and imaginatively as possible. I firmly believe this management team can do just that.

Beyond our status as the largest alternative asset firm (securities other than conventional stocks and bonds), we also have acquired or built a variety of businesses in other fields of finance (such as GSO, a credit-focused firm that is a leader in leveraged finance, and led by the very able Bennett Goodman, and Park Hill, an idea initiated by Ken Whitney and a firm that has helped clients raise more than $65 billion). These have helped make Blackstone the most diversified and, I would argue, the most balanced firm in the business.

Would I ever have thought that I would be very grateful to Lew Glucksman for his "coup"? Whatever we might have achieved at Lehman, it could not compare to the thrill and success of helping build Blackstone to what it is today. Still, it was time for me to move on, yet again. But where, and how?

CHAPTER 16

My Idea of Fun

I've always felt I could do or should be doing something more than just business. Another of the carryovers from my childhood was that spending my time primarily focused on only one thing was about as sinful as doing nothing at all.

New York, anything but a one-company town, provided a unique outlet for some of my diverse passions, in particular: foreign policy, foreign economic policy, and the big one, U.S. fiscal responsibility and generational equity. Thankfully, I've been able to arrange my business and private lives to take advantage of the wonderful opportunities New York has provided me to enjoy these passions.

Foreign Policy: The Council on Foreign Relations

Richard Nixon may have thought of the Council on Foreign Relations as a bunch of "old farts and airheads." In fact, it is increasingly one of the strongest independent voices raised on American foreign policy. The Council itself does not take policy positions, befitting an organization whose members range from Madeleine Albright to Dick Cheney. But its scholars and members are free to speak (and write) their minds, and the result is a running commentary from across the

308

political spectrum on the challenges and opportunities we face around the world. This open, free, and highly informed exchange was not always the case, and I am proud to say that I helped the Council change from a lever of foreign policy behind the scenes to a public forum of ideas.

As a board member of the Council, I had done a good deal of fundraising, which I always assumed was a principal reason I was chosen to be chairman. Since many seem to be turned off, if not a bit frightened, by the thought of raising money for charities, I'm sometimes asked why it isn't hard for me to be such a persevering fundraiser. I suppose my father influenced me more than a little. As children, my brother and I wished he had given away less so that we could have more. But as I got older, I remembered the joy it gave not only the less fortunate recipients, but also my father. I suppose I said to myself, "What is wrong with asking for money if it ultimately seems to give so much pleasure to everyone, the receivers as well as the givers?"

I was no longer young when David Rockefeller asked me to chair the Council in 1985, but I became a wide-eyed boy again. That I, the son of Greek immigrants from a small, rural town in Nebraska, could follow David was a rare privilege. The chairman's shoes would have to be filled with skill, generosity, and great humility, to say nothing of a sense of humor. Pomposity can sometimes creep into high-minded endeavors such as the Council on Foreign Relations. I felt it must be resisted at all costs, and humor was one of my antidotes.

David's "retirement" dinner when he stepped down as the Council's chair was an occasion that seriously risked getting bogged down in earnestness and becoming too saccharine. I approached David's delightful wife, Peggy, with an idea that I thought would lighten things up. Peggy raised prize bulls at her farm outside New York, and I asked her if she had a picture of her favorite, whose name was Keep It Clean. The Council had commissioned a portrait of David, and I asked Peggy if she would unveil the photograph of Keep It Clean in front of David and the dinner guests and introduce it as "the portrait of the male she loves as much as any male in the world." She found a picture of Keep It Clean that worked just right, and when Peggy undraped the portrait of her favorite "male," a bovine face stared out at the crowd. David was stunned at first, and then joined the crowd in uproarious laughter.

As chair of the Council, one of the things I wanted badly to do, besides making the Council membership younger and more diverse, was to change the branding of the Council. We would have more impact as a centrist organization if we were not still seen as liberal elites. I didn't have much hope of changing opinions on the lunatic fringe of the far right, where the John Birch Society had accused David Rockefeller and me of having Communist leanings. But I still tried. I was doing a guest appearance on a right-wing radio program when someone from a Montana militia group called in. He demanded that I admit the existence of the Council's vast secret army jointly controlled by the United Nations. No one knows what spurs these kinds of crackpot theories, given the thoroughly capitalist and Republican résumés David and I and so many other Council members bring to the table. I reminded the caller that our board members included noted conservatives such as Jeane Kirkpatrick (who was vice chair at the time), Dick Cheney, George Shultz, Brent Scowcroft, and Henry Kissinger, and on and on. Were they, too, members of this far-left conspiracy of world domination? And, by the way, where was the large secret army hidden? The caller hung up.

In 1986, the members told pollster Daniel Yankelovich in a board-commissioned survey that they wanted the Council to have more public impact. What followed was an award-winning Web site, on-the-record meetings, and bipartisan task forces on major issues, with the findings presented at well-attended news conferences.

On another front, the economic rise of China and India have increased the importance of the integration of economics into foreign policy; the Council responded by setting up the Maurice R. Greenberg Center for Geoeconomic Studies in 2000 to focus on issues including energy, trade, and immigration.

Foreign Affairs, the Council's magazine with four foreign editions under the leadership of gifted editor Jim Hoge, also reflects the new dynamic of more public outreach. This public profile would have shocked the founders of this once rather secretive Council.

Encounters Around the World

In early 1987, Council members visited the Soviet Union. It was a tense time. Ronald Reagan had pressed the case against Soviet totalitarianism, calling it "the evil empire." Mikhail Gorbachev had taken over as general secretary of the Communist Party and as de facto Soviet leader two years earlier. The nuclear arms control summit in Reykjavik, Iceland, the previous October had collapsed over Reagan's "Star Wars" missile defense plan. The Cold War was still pretty cold as we approached our two-hour meeting with Gorbachev, the first he had granted to American outsiders.

My friend David Rockefeller was unable to join us on this trip, but our delegation was packed with high-powered people. They included Cyrus Vance and Harold Brown, who had been President Carter's secretary of state and secretary of defense, respectively; Henry Kissinger; former United Nations ambassador Jeane Kirkpatrick; former Chairman of the Joint Chiefs of Staff General David C. Jones; Republican senator Charles Mathias of Maryland; and Peter Tarnoff, who was then the Council's president.

Gorbachev's mood could not have been improved by our deciding to meet the day before with Andrei Sakharov, the dissident Soviet physicist who had recently returned to Moscow from internal exile in Gorky. Indeed, our session in Gorbachev's Moscow office started out as frosty as the Russian winter. He bypassed the usual diplomatic foreplay and took potshots at virtually every one of our group. Which Henry Kissinger and Jeane Kirkpatrick were there? he asked rhetorically. Was it the ones who had made hostile remarks—he had quotes—about the Soviet Union, or some other, new and different persons?

"Is this as bad as I think?" I asked Cy Vance in a hastily scribbled note.

He wrote a one-word answer: "Yes."

I had escaped Gorbachev's sniping, probably because he had no idea who I was. This allowed me to venture a badly needed change of subject. "Mr. General Secretary," I said, "we can continue these discussions on this track or we can try a different one. Let me suggest another possibility." (I knew from my earlier discussions with Brezhnev that the Soviets knew their Achilles' heel was a persistently weak economy.) "It seems to me that both of us are living in a far more competitive global economy," I continued. "We must each, in our own ways, confront new competitive economic challenges. Might we discuss how each of us, both collectively and individually, can respond to these challenges?"

Gorbachev seemed to brighten as he considered the question. Then he smiled and said, "Now, that is a subject worth talking about!"

With that, the meeting stretched from two hours to three, and received front-page treatment in top newspapers for Gorbachev's call for improved Soviet-American relations. But Reagan kept the pressure on, famously calling on Gorbachev in 1988 to "tear down this wall" dividing East from West Berlin. Less than a year later, George H. W. Bush took office and with his secretary of state, Jim Baker, engineered a measured and highly successful transition from the Cold War to the post-Soviet era with a united Germany.

Two years after we met with Gorbachev in Moscow, the Council made a trip that I remember for its sheer emotional impact in 1989. This time we were in Poland, which I had last visited as secretary of commerce. Our itinerary took in Auschwitz and the Holocaust Museum at the former Nazi death camp near Kraków in southwestern Poland. Included in our delegation was Seweryn Bialer, a Holocaust survivor who had been imprisoned at Auschwitz as a teenager. A professor at Columbia, he accompanied us as an advisor.

Emotions run high for anyone who sets foot in Auschwitz. The air is charged with outrage at the methodical inhumanity of genocide that is on stark display—the photographs of newly arrived inmates, tumbled piles of luggage, thousands of eyeglasses, mounds of human hair used to make textiles and fabrics and stuff pillows—to say nothing of the gas chambers and crematoriums. Seweryn had survived with luck and courage, propping himself up with hidden sticks of wood to appear strong for work details (the alternative was the gas chamber when one was weak with dysentery). Seweryn eventually escaped by hiding himself in a large garbage shipment that was sent out into Poland, where he joined the anti-Nazi underground.

This was the background as we walked into the Holocaust Museum.

Suddenly Seweryn screamed and rushed forward to embrace one of the museum staff. The two clung together, tears streaming down their faces. The rest of us watched, hushed and in awe. When he had regained his composure, Seweryn introduced the man who had been one of his partners in his escape from Auschwitz. They had not seen each other since. There were twenty-one of us along on that trip, including Kay Graham, publisher of *The Washington Post,* David and Peggy Rockefeller, former Deputy Secretary of State John Whitehead and his new wife, Nancy Dickerson, the pioneer broadcast journalist (it was their honeymoon), and my daughter, Holly. There was not a dry eye among us as we shook Seweryn's friend's hand. I have never witnessed a more moving scene.

Holly came with the Council again the next year, when we visited the Persian Gulf. David and Kay Graham were back again as well, and real estate mogul and publisher Mort Zuckerman, Pamela Harriman, former ambassador to France, and Jim Burke, CEO of Johnson & Johnson, were also among the twenty-two-member delegation. A third of our group were women, which caused a problem when we reached Saudi Arabia, the focal point in an itinerary that also included Kuwait and Oman.

King Fahd, in whose country women still are not allowed to drive, sent word that he would be more comfortable if the women were excluded from our meeting with him. I replied that this was totally unacceptable to us. Moreover, I told his foreign minister, I foresaw serious public relations problems for them unless the king relented. One could only imagine how *The Washington Post,* among others, would have reacted if Kay Graham were excluded. The king relented.

King Fahd had odd sleeping and work habits. We arrived at the palace for our audience after midnight. This was apparently typical for his important meetings. I gave David the seat of honor on the king's right, and I took the seat on David's right. David returned the favor by insisting that I ask the first question. In our previous meetings in the Kingdom, the various ministers and members of the royal family had recounted the past goals and achievements of the 1980s. I asked if His Majesty could lay out the Kingdom's goals and programs for the decade of the 1990s that lay ahead.

The king nodded, and then proceeded to speak nonstop for nearly two hours, reviewing yet again the achievements of the 1980s and saying nothing whatever of his plans for the 1990s. The clock ticked ever so slowly past two-thirty in the morning. My seat behind David (from the king's perspective) gave me at least a little respite. Holly said later she feared I'd suffer whiplash from repeatedly jerking my head up after my chin fell to my chest. David had no such relief. He had to stay awake with his eyes open. Moreover, as he told me later, he had to resist the growing pressure on his bladder. (One did not interrupt the king to take a bathroom break!) I finally kept myself awake by counting the numbers of times David crossed and uncrossed his legs, looking rather like a man performing a physical therapy routine.

When we finally returned to our hotel in the wee hours of the morning, my companions brought me the results of a hasty straw poll: Peterson was no longer to ask the first question.

All of our Council trips tended to be a bit overscheduled and often left too little time for the frolics I enjoy. (Kay Graham once said I have a high school sense of humor without ever indicating whether it was at least a good high school sense of humor.)

So I instituted a tradition of setting aside a part of one evening as a roast party. My favorite roastee was Lally Weymouth, daughter of Kay Graham and a reporter for *The Washington Post*. Everyone else's favorite roastee was, of course, me.

My most provocative roaster was Mimi Haas, a friend from San Francisco and a big supporter of the Council on Foreign Relations. I shall give equal time to one of my roasts of Lally and one of Mimi's roasts of me. I have admitted I am a talker, and Mimi never lets me forget it. Other than King Fahd, the only person to outtalk me on one of our trips was Fidel Castro. So Mimi gave me a large badge, showing me dressed and looking like Fidel with the caption "Gray Yawn," a roast of my book on global aging, *Gray Dawn*. To add impact to her efforts, Mimi had printed hundreds of these badges, which she has distributed nationally and far more widely than I would have preferred. The other day I went to the Four Seasons Grill for lunch to be greeted by Julian Niccolini, the naughtiest of all maître d's, wearing the Fidel Castro badge. These have become Mimi's version of a weapon of mass destruction.

Lally Weymouth, a devout Reaganite, was a vociferously outspoken critic of the Communists. One day in Moscow, we met with the chairman of the Soviet Communist Party. I took him aside to explain that Weymouth was a very important journalist whose favorable comment about him could be enormously important to his gaining a more positive perception in the United States. Thus, I thought it might be worth some extra effort for him to give her an unusually warm embrace. The photographer was, of course, ready, and the result was one resembling two old lovers. I then showed this photograph to the board of the Council and sent it to her important colleagues at *The Washington Post*. The effect on Lally was everything I could have hoped for.

Kay Graham is obviously right about my high school sense of humor. I also note my humor has never been referred to as "dry."

David and I led many other trips under Council auspices to places such as China and Vietnam, South Africa, Russia and Kazakhstan, Turkey and Israel, Mexico and Cuba (Fidel Castro outdid King Fahd; Fidel didn't stop talking until four-thirty in the morning), Libya, Egypt, and India. But it was the trip of a foreign president to New York that brought a tsunami of controversy down upon the Council and my leadership.

The president was Mahmoud Ahmadinejad. The Iranian's obscene threats against Israel's survival and his denial of the Holocaust had made him a pariah among Western nations. When he was due in New York on a United Nations visit in September 2006, Iran's ambassador to the United Nations proposed to us an appearance before a top-level Council group.

Even the suggestion of a meeting with him was controversial. Secretary of State Condoleezza Rice called it "a bad idea—a really, really bad idea." Council member Abraham Foxman, head of the Jewish Anti-Defamation League, said he and others were considering quitting the Council "to make it clear how offensive this is." Elie Wiesel, the Holocaust survivor and Nobel Peace Prize winner whose prolific writings amount to a collective Jewish voice, talked of a mass resignation of Jewish leaders who were Council members. The Israeli ambassador to the United States published a letter calling a meeting with Ahmadinejad a "terrible mistake."

These were powerful voices. But I felt the Council had to resist political correctness. We had met with offensive characters before, including Castro, Yasir Arafat of the Palestine Liberation Organization, Zimbabwe's president cum dictator Robert Mugabe, and Gerry Adams of Sinn Fein, the political wing of the Irish Republican Army. Indeed, our national leaders, including Richard Nixon and Ronald Reagan, have met with our nominal enemies including China and the Soviet Union if there appeared to be a chance to advance stability and peace.

Iran was (and is) such a hotbed of pathologies, including its bizarre Holocaust denial, its nuclear program, its support for Hezbollah and Hamas and other terrorist groups, its interference in Iraq, and its threats to destroy Israel, that I felt we had no choice but to talk with him. It would most certainly not be an endorsement, but a way of learning more firsthand about his nature and his message. Richard Haass, the Council's president, who was the State Department's director of policy planning during George W. Bush's first term, said of the Ahmadinejad meeting that talking is "a tool, and I'm confident that if used right, it can advance our interests."

We knew Ahmadinejad would not be an easy subject. Brent Scowcroft, the national security advisor under Presidents Gerald Ford and George H. W. Bush, had called him a "master of counterpunch, deception, and circumlocution." He responded to questions with more aggressive questions of his own. I had seen enough of him on television to conclude that he was a natural demagogue and, like a lot of demagogues, was in love with his own voice and rock star status and was liable to make wild, credibility-destroying statements. We approached the meeting, held at the hotel where he was staying, determined not to pull our punches. (Indeed, I had made sure that each of the major issues would be covered by members of our delegation who were expert in those areas.)

And we didn't. Ahmadinejad bobbed and weaved in keeping with his reputation. He could have taught Muhammad Ali the rope-a-dope. I told him most Americans accepted and were horrified by the Holocaust and asked him by what conceivable evidence he justified calling it a myth. He responded by saying he had not seen any studies of American attitudes that justified my statement and asked what qualified me to speak for the American people. When I told him his outrageous statements made constructive engagement with Iran much more difficult, he said that I didn't speak for America. He said he was willing to consider an "objective" study of the Holocaust issue by recognized "experts." One could only imagine how objective his experts would be.

His most effective opponent on his Holocaust statements was my good friend Hank Greenberg, the former head of AIG. He told Ahmadinejad he didn't have to rely on objective studies or secondhand information. He had seen the Holocaust firsthand as an infantry officer who had helped liberate the concentration camp at Dachau at the end of World War II. The Iranian's bearded jaw dropped and he asked Hank how old he was. "Eighty-one," Hank answered. For once, there was nothing Ahmadinejad could say.

But in the end there were no surprises, and no Council resignations. I came away from the meeting with my two earlier feelings confirmed. He may have mastered an arsenal of rhetorical tricks, but for all his vaunted cleverness, the president of Iran was nothing but a loathsome bigot and we were right to have the meeting.

My involvement with the Council on Foreign Relations has been one of my greatest privileges. My longtime partner and close friend, Les Gelb, president emeritus as well as senior board fellow at the Council on Foreign Relations, made my chairmanship so much more productive and fun. Then, Richard Haass, president of the Council, has done such a good job, and Carla Hills and Robert E. Rubin were such obvious replacements as co-chairmen of the Council that I felt totally comfortable stepping down from my chairmanship in 2007 after an unusually long stretch of twenty-two years.

Foreign Economic Policy: The Peterson Institute for International Economics

In 1981, George Shultz and I were approached to chair this much needed think tank proposed by the German Marshall Fund as a gesture of thanks for the Marshall Plan. Fred Bergsten, my close colleague in the

Nixon White House, was to be its director. Fred asked George Shultz and me if either of us was willing to be chairman.

With Democrat Jimmy Carter in the White House, George was then back in private life heading the Bechtel Corporation, and shuttling between San Francisco and Washington did not appeal to him. Persuasive statesman that he was, he agreed to serve on the board if I would take on the chairman's duties. I said I would. The board has a remarkable collection of global economic and financial legends and the Institute, in my view, houses the brightest aggregation of economic talent at any think tank anywhere. Recently, a University of Pennsylvania study of 5,465 think tanks rated the Institute and the Brookings Institution (which has a budget six times larger than ours) tied as the two top think tanks in the world.

Some think tanks focus on the here and now, and by the time they've studied an issue it has often come and gone or the government is already deeply embedded in it. The obverse is looking five to ten years into the future. Following my White House experience, I believed strongly that the Institute for International Economics, as it was originally called, should look at issues one to three years out, so they might be dealt with during a presidential term.

Fast-forward to today and the dizzying pace of globalization makes clear how important it is to chart a clear path through a minefield of international economic developments. We in the United States now confront massive global imbalances stemming from our addictive tendencies to consume more than we produce and save less than any developed country. As a result, we have unprecedented trade deficits and the huge and unsustainable levels of foreign borrowing that accompany these deficits. Once the world's largest creditor, we are now the world's largest debtor.

The Institute has done a series of sophisticated projections that indicate what America's foreign debt load might look like in 2020 and 2030 if we continue to rely on what I consider to be these dangerous levels of foreign borrowing. The answer: In some scenarios, America would have a foreign debt load similar to that of certain *developing countries*. And aside from the huge economic and financial risks of such dependence on foreign sources of capital, have we forgotten the critical links between our economic security and our national security, and our sovereignty,* and our ability to play a desperately needed, if admittedly smaller, role in global leadership?

Existing global institutions such as the International Monetary Fund (IMF) and the World Trade Organization (WTO) need constant evaluation to guide or goad them to peak effectiveness. New institutions may be required.

As countries grow ever more fearful of their economic outlook in the face of what I agree is the "greatest economic crisis since the Great Depression," there is a growing need to fight protectionism and to encourage new and open trade agreements at international, regional, and bilateral levels. Increasingly, as countries react to today's shocks, shutdowns, and breakdowns in global capital markets, there are also the early signs of what we might call financial protectionism. Like all forms of protectionism, these too would likely end up being destructive of the global financial system.

The benefits of worldwide open trade are certainly not apparent to everyone, especially workers in industries that downsize or close altogether as their jobs go elsewhere. Thus it is the subject of ongoing and often angry debates in the United States and around the world. The Institute has played a central role in these debates. It has provided the only quantitative analysis of the impact of globalization on the U.S. economy, estimating that our country is $1 trillion richer *per year* as the result of the last sixty years of trade expansion. The same analysis suggests that we would gain another $500 billion a year if the remaining barriers to trade

---

*When America was the leading creditor nation, it on occasion used its financial and economic clout to achieve its geopolitical goals. For example, in the Eisenhower period, Great Britain and France sent troops into the Suez Canal confrontation, directly contrary to U.S. policy. The United States applied several economic and financial sanctions, including putting double pressure on the declining British pound by threatening to dump its British and French securities and restricting oil shipments to Western Europe. Given their weakened economic state and their dependence on the U.S., the British and French quickly withdrew their troops. To take a current possibility, there is no reason the Chinese could not use their $1.3 trillion—and rapidly growing—stock of Treasury bills in similar ways. Already, China is asking for the guarantees of their vast U.S. Treasury holdings.

could be eliminated. When U.S. trade representatives and secretaries of the treasury, corporate leaders, and the media make the case for globalization, these are the Institute figures that they often quote.

The Institute also clearly recognizes that there are losers as well as winners from globalization in the United States, and has proposed specific steps to deal with the fallout. For example, our existing unemployment insurance (UI) program, which was created in 1935, is seriously out of date. The shortcomings of the existing program are captured in three statistics:

- Only one-third of unemployed workers actually receive UI.
- Average payments replace only one-third of workers' previous earnings.
- One-third of recipients exhaust their payments before finding a new job.

The Institute has proposed a program of "wage insurance" whereby workers who have lost their job are incentivized to get a new job by being compensated for some substantial portion of the difference in wages between the old and new jobs for a period up to two years. Another program focuses on making health care insurance more portable. Recall that 90 percent of the people receiving health insurance are covered through their employers.

The Institute has also recommended that adjustment assistance should be expanded to include communities that have been severely damaged when a major plant is closed and moved elsewhere.

Clarence Darrow, the famed criminal defense lawyer, once won a case and saved the life of one of his clients. The defendant's family rushed up to Darrow to ask how they could possibly express the depth of their feeling and emotion. Darrow responded rather dryly, "I have yet to experience the emotion that could not be expressed in terms of money."

I have been happy to be able to express financially my depth of feeling for the Institute and, in turn, in 2005 the Executive Committee expressed its feelings by honoring me with its decision to name the Institute the Peter G. Peterson Institute for International Economics.

Karl Otto Pohl, former president of Deutsche Bundesbank, called it "the most qualified Institute of this kind in the world." Fred Bergsten, a triple-threat star of the nonprofit world, deserves much of the credit.

Fiscal Responsibility and Generational Equity

My desire to help shape public policy continued to intensify after I left Washington. But it was not until 1981 and the beginning of Ronald Reagan's presidency that I felt the call, as an evangelist might put it.

My revelation on the road to Damascus came about by happenstance. Joan and I had our eye on a house near East Hampton on Georgica Pond, a lagoon just behind the ocean beach. It was owned by a friend of ours. We knew she wanted to downsize and had even set a price, but, so far, we hadn't been able to persuade her to actually sell the house.

She was Maria Vernicos Carras Rolfe. Like me, she had Greek parents, but she had been born in Egypt, grown up in London, and gone on to work in international business, investing, and philanthropy. Maria's late husband, Sidney Rolfe, was a well-known international economist with whom I had sometimes shared ideas. After he died in 1976, Maria had stayed involved with business and economics, working to bring women into the top ranks of recognized authorities in those professions, partly by simply making them visible to their peers, both male and female. That meant, among other things, including them in forums for discussion, which led her to create the Women's Economic Round Table.

She had the Round Table up and running as a full-fledged forum for education and networking by 1981. It was then that she approached me to speak at its inaugural luncheon. "I am determined that you speak to us," she said.

I was equally determined to buy her house.

Relentless negotiator that I am, I said, "Maria, I'll make you a simple proposal. I will pay the asking price for your house. If you accept, I will speak at your luncheon." Maria had not come as far as she had without developing some negotiating skills of her own. "Okay, but on one condition," she came back. "You will speak about the Reagan budget. I want a serious analysis, wherever your analysis takes you."

We shook hands, and I called my real estate broker that same afternoon to put our East Hampton house on the market. Then, to honor my agreement with Maria, I plunged into a serious examination of the Reagan budget.

I had voted for Ronald Reagan, partly because I felt that Jimmy Carter, a man of admirable intentions, was hapless as president. Interest rates had soared on his watch, and I was growing increasingly insecure about the economic and, in particular, the inflation outlook. I had assumed that Reagan, a social conservative, was also a fiscal conservative in the manner of old-line Republicans.

But what I found astonished me. The assumptions of Reaganomics, as the president's budget proposals were being called, were optimistic to the point of caricature.

Reagan had proposed huge tax cuts, which were supposed to spur the economy into a growth spurt. But at the same time, he was proposing a huge military buildup that would significantly increase spending, without compensating cuts elsewhere in the budget. There were some spending cuts, but they were at such a general level and so unspecified as to be highly unconvincing. Missing from the mix entirely were any cuts at all to the elephants in the room—the vast entitlement programs such as Social Security and Medicare. But Reaganomics claimed that the massive tax cuts would fuel such economic growth as to cause a net budget surplus by 1984 even in the face of the big spending increases and tax cuts. Reagan's opponent for the Republican nomination, George H. W. Bush, had called this "voodoo economics" before he lost and signed on as Reagan's vice presidential candidate. Voodoo economics was exactly what it was.

The speech I gave was highly critical. I didn't see long-term budget cuts anywhere on the horizon that were going to compensate for the loss of tax revenues and the additional military spending. I simply did not believe that lower tax rates would yield such huge projected increases in revenue. As a result, the prospective deficits were huge and stretched "as far as the eye can see." I thought deficits matter (I still do), particularly the long-term structural deficits, and I said so.

The business press, including *The Wall Street Journal*, covered the speech. As one might imagine, reaction in some corporate and political quarters was unfavorable. The outspoken Henry Ford Jr., among others, called in hopes of opening my eyes. "Pete," he said, "we Republicans have waited for years to get our president. How can you be carping, particularly at this early stage?"

"Henry, have you reviewed this budget?" I asked.

No, he hadn't. Nevertheless, he had bought into Reagan's sunny optimism.

The *Journal*'s editorial board also sought to bring me around. I received a call suggesting that I would find a discussion of supply side Reaganomics "illuminating." The discussion—more like a religious mantra chanted over and over as if repetition would make it so—took place over lunch among the high priests of the supply side. I thought of them as priests because their convictions seemed animated not by serious analysis, history, or evidence, but by faith. They told me I was stuck in the past. I did not understand the new world of "expectational economics," in which huge tax cuts would provide major productivity and growth incentives. As productivity rose, chasing the carrot of expectation, the economy would grow at far faster rates and therefore produce far greater federal tax revenues. This was why, by 1984, only three years away, we would have the budget and trade surpluses predicted in the Reagan budget.

I didn't drink the Kool-Aid. Indeed, my sense of right and wrong was now involved. I had concluded not only that Reaganomics was not good for the country, but that if the trend continued, things would get worse. Much worse. By late in 1982, I had convinced five former secretaries of the treasury to join with me in creating the Bi-Partisan Budget Appeal. Three were Republicans—John Connally, my Washington "friend" (who switched parties in 1973), Bill Simon, and me; and three were Democratic treasury secretaries—Mike Blumenthal, Douglas Dillon, and Henry Fowler. A few hundred CEOs, mostly Republicans, joined us. In addition, I also reached out to enlist prominent lawyers, academics, and former senior government officials in our effort to promote the need for fiscal responsibility. The Budget Appeal's double-page advertisements in major newspapers attracted some major attention, including highly publicized press conferences and television appearances. The Reagan administration didn't like it at all.

It wasn't just the Reagan administration that needed convincing. Many Republicans seemed to never see a tax cut or a military program that they didn't like, but the Democrats in Congress viewed protecting or enhancing the entitlement programs with similar enthusiasm.

I was deeply concerned about our system of entitlement programs in particular. Social Security, created by President Franklin Roosevelt in 1935 as an antidote to old-age poverty during the Depression, had acquired the force of holy writ. There was no doubt that Social Security had alleviated the financial stress that truly needy seniors experienced in their later years and continued to do so. But in its early days, there were many more workers than retirees, meaning that Social Security was taking in far more money from workers and employers than it spent on Social Security benefits to seniors. Soon the Social Security surpluses became too big to resist. Instead of keeping them separate, as was originally planned in a real trust fund, our political representatives began to use the trust fund as a piggy bank to finance other, non–Social Security programs. Meanwhile, rapidly growing numbers of retirees and longer life spans, combined with many increases in benefits and a comparatively smaller cohort of workers, pointed to an actuarial long-term nightmare. There was no means testing, which meant that retirees got Social Security checks whether they needed them or not. And benefits were indexed to both the cost of living and average wage increases, so benefits were adjusted upward constantly.

It was nearly impossible to get anyone to take this ultimate train wreck seriously, because among other reasons, Social Security would continue to run annual surpluses for a while and also had one of the most forceful lobbies in Washington on its side. AARP, the American Association of Retired Persons, listed a total of 38 million dues-paying members. There wasn't a politician in Washington who wasn't paralyzed in the face of the AARP and other organizations of senior citizens, whose motivated members wrote untold millions of letters to Congress and voted in high numbers.

When Reagan reacted to the initial criticism of his budget, he scaled back his tax cuts by a small percentage and later was forced to increase taxes. He also proposed a six-month deferral of the cost of living raises in Social Security. But when he tried to cut Social Security benefits by an additional $46 billion over five years, he got slapped down. In 1983, a bipartisan Social Security commission chaired by Alan Greenspan proposed a few reforms that Reagan and Tip O'Neill, the Democratic Speaker of the House, agreed to, in an all-too-rare example of bipartisan compromise on a sensitive entitlement issue.

Nevertheless, as I looked at the initial Reagan budget and the nation's hands-off policy toward reining in significant entitlements, I felt that I needed to act like Paul Revere and sound the alarm. The result was a two-part piece in *The New York Review of Books* that appeared in December of 1982. I pointed out that Social Security spending had grown from one percent of the federal budget in 1950 to 26 percent—in only thirty years! Its spending exceeded the combined net investment in plant, equipment, research, and development of all the private companies in the United States. America's machinery for creating wealth was being starved of fuel. This was going to seriously affect future generations, for one thing, with much higher payroll taxes. And when the baby boom generation, 78 million strong or twice the size of the crop of 1980s elderly, started retiring after the turn of the century, ballooning the ranks of retirees, I foresaw the system crumbling if something was not done.

In the article, I proposed a five-part program of reform: temporarily freeze and thereafter limit cost of living adjustments; tax benefits that are received in excess of one's contributions; lower initial benefits for higher income recipients; gradually raise the retirement age by at least three years; bring federal civil servants into Social Security, both to add their contributions and to eliminate the more expensive federal retirement system.

As far as sheer readership, my jeremiad in *The New York Review*, with its liberal circulation, was a spectacular success. My friend Jason Epstein, the *Review*'s co-founder who had encouraged me to do the piece in the first place, said he had rarely seen such a response to any single article. The response was thoughtful, but much of it did not heap me with excessive praise! Rather, I was accused of being an alarmist. The outcry resulted in yet another issue of *The New York Review* focusing on Social Security. Headlined "Peterson Responds to His Critics," this issue featured articles critical of my arguments, as well as my response to this criticism.

I thought I held my own against this onslaught. In reaction to my proposal to reduce benefits for the well off, my Democratic critics pulled out their old saw: "Programs for the poor are poor programs." In other words, they in effect argued that one had to bribe the rich to help the poor. "But if everyone is on the wagon, who will pull it?" I responded. I addressed the problem of deficits and entitlements in other articles, including one that appeared in *The New York Times Sunday Magazine*, and two cover pieces in *The Atlantic Monthly*. The first, a treatment of Reaganomics entitled "The Morning After," in the October 1987 issue, to my great surprise won the National Magazine Award for best public policy article.

Now that I had my hands around the megaphone, I was determined to keep up the pressure. Sounding alarms about the Reagan deficits and the looming Social Security and Medicare shortfalls was enough of a challenge to keep an army of bell ringers busy. It could have occupied me full-time from the early 1980s on. But I also had some other things I wanted to accomplish.

Diane Sawyer, a close friend from our White House days, calls me a "relentless crusader." The Reagan White House took irritated note of the fact that so many of their Republican business friends signed on to our Bi-Partisan Budget Appeal. Nancy Reagan took a similar irritated note. I sat near her at a State Department lunch. Normally, and later on, she was charming. That day, she said nothing and simply glared at me. If my crusading were to have any effect, it would not be with any help from that White House.

The Concord Coalition

By the end of the 1980s, the huge Reagan deficits, the doubling of federal public debt as a percentage of the GDP from 23 percent to 45 percent, and a looming recession seemed to focus the public mind a bit on fiscal responsibility. I felt the time was right for a new grass-roots campaign to address these issues. As I watched Democratic presidential candidate Paul Tsongas in the 1992 election preach the sacraments about generational equity and long-term fiscal responsibility I knew he would make a great general. Warren Rudman, father of the Gramm-Rudman budget deficit reduction legislation, was a natural Republican counterpart. Thus the forming of The Concord Coalition.

The Concord Coalition was originally co-chaired by former senators Paul Tsongas and Warren Rudman and myself as founding president. After Paul's death in 1997, former Democratic senator Sam Nunn became co-chair, and today former senator Bob Kerrey, also a Democrat, has taken his place as the co-chair alongside Warren, a Republican, to keep its bipartisan leadership intact. Bob Rubin is vice chair.

Concord made some progress early on, enough so that in 1993, *60 Minutes* called me to do a story. Lesley Stahl, charming devil that she is, thought it would be "good television" if I were to confront a group of about a hundred senior citizens at a meeting in a New York suburb for their reactions to some of my entitlement reforms. I could certainly see it would be good for television; it was far less clear that it would be good for Pete Peterson. Still, it was part of the deal, and *60 Minutes* had a huge audience. At the meeting, I was not my usual assured self. In fact, I was as nervous as I had ever been in a public session. Would they throw rotten rhetorical tomatoes at me with tens of millions watching?

At this televised meeting, I laid out not only the basic facts about our unsustainable entitlement programs for the elderly, but some possible reforms or, to put it more plainly, some benefit cuts. For example, I asked the question, "Which is responsible and more fair, to slip the hidden huge check to our own kids, or to have us well off, like many of us in the room, and certainly myself, be subject to what I call an 'affluence test'?" To my surprise and delight, a substantial majority voted for this benefit cut.

This left me with the feeling that if we could just talk directly to the American people, rather than letting special interests talk for them, we would have a real chance for reform.

The Concord Coalition gives an annual "Economic Patriot" award to economic and political luminaries who are not afraid to attack our deficit-ridden status quo. Recipients have included Alan Greenspan, Paul Volcker, Bob Rubin, John McCain, Sam Nunn, and Bill Clinton.

Not long ago, we launched a "Fiscal Wake Up" tour and have, to date, traveled to over three dozen major cities. We have joined forces with the left-of-center Brookings Institution and the very conservative Heritage Foundation to spread our message and increase our credibility and bipartisanship. And we help sponsor the giant debt clock owned by the Durst family in New York's Times Square to remind Americans just how fast our public debt is growing. David Walker, then the U.S. comptroller general, and Bob Bixby, our able executive director, have become rock stars in the major film documentary *I.O.U.S.A.*, which features this Fiscal Wake Up tour.

Overall, The Concord Coalition has produced mixed results since its founding in 1992. One the one hand, we are generally recognized as a leading nonpartisan source of objective information on fiscal matters. I would also say that while we have consistently received quiet encouragement from the leaders of both parties, publicly almost no political leader has been prepared to endorse proposals such as structural reforms of Medicare and federal retirement programs including Social Security. Such steps are both "absolutely necessary" and "not yet politically possible," or "they are 'inevitable' but also 'unmentionable.'" Politicians, like other animals, give first thought to their own survival.

The Clinton Years

The Clinton-Rubin era gave me some hope, and at times new frustrations.

President Clinton must have seen our Concord Coalition ads in the newspapers while he was in office and, whenever I saw him, he always seemed interested in what I was writing. When my second cover article in the May 1996 edition of *The Atlantic Monthly*, "Social Insecurity," appeared, White House friends told me he had not only read it and underlined it, but distributed it to staff.

But Clinton was not always completely forthright and consistent with the American people on these issues. One year, I heard that at a Renaissance holiday "weekend" meeting, he had told the audience that the Social Security Trust Fund would keep the system solvent for forty years or so. In other words, no problem.

Sometime after that Renaissance weekend, he appeared at a New York Public Library event that I attended, and afterward he asked me to meet with him one on one right there at the library. The subject was entitlements. The breadth and depth of his knowledge was simply extraordinary. I said, "Mr. President, you aren't buying this Social Security Trust Fund business, are you?" "Oh, God no, Pete. As you have written and as I know, the Trust Fund is a fiction. It is a cash in, cash out, pay as you go system," he said. I replied, "Yes, Mr. President. I call the Trust Fund an oxymoron. It shouldn't be trusted and it is not funded. The money has already been spent on other programs." He laughed and agreed.

After that meeting, chief of staff Leon Panetta called to say the president was setting up the Bipartisan Commission on Entitlement and Tax Reform, co-chaired by two great public servants, Republican senator John Danforth and Democratic senator Bob Kerrey. Would I join? I of course said yes.

The early days of the Commission were promising. We agreed on a bipartisan staff: We didn't want any argument about the facts. And the brute facts were overpowering.

In one of the Commission hearings, the representative from the AARP took the Commission through their usual litany of *new* benefits that they were recommending. In those days, these types of unreasonable AARP proposals were not unexpected. (Today, I am happy to say that Bill Novelli, president and CEO of AARP, is far more understanding of the problems we face.) A partner of mine on this commission was Alan Simpson, the delightful Republican senator from Wyoming, who whispered to me, "Pete, you hit them high, I will hit them low."

We did. Believing that adding to the benefits was a preposterous notion, I said, "Sir, by a vote of 31–1, every one of the congressional and Senate members have called the current entitlement programs 'unsustainable' and pointed out that by 2025, entitlements and interest payments would consume the entire budget. What are you proposing to cut? How are you proposing to pay for your added benefits?" He demurred with something to the effect that they would welcome the opportunity "to work with the Commission." Unrelenting, I said something to the effect, "Well, here we are. Work with us." His weak response confirmed my point.

Though Clinton showed early signs of trying to make progress on this issue, he was not very consistent in his support. In 1998, Clinton asked the AARP and our Concord Coalition to sponsor some "town hall" meetings on entitlements across the country that the President himself would attend. The AARP said they would be more "comfortable" if someone other than myself represented the Coalition. Martha Phillips, executive director of The Concord Coalition, took my place. (After the Bipartisan Entitlement commission meetings, I was not one of AARP's folk heroes; perhaps they might have even thought of me as a folk enemy.)

In the first town hall meeting, in Kansas City, Missouri, Bill Clinton shocked us all. Obviously knowing better, he kicked off the meeting with a chart showing that the Trust Fund would keep the Social Security system solvent for decades. I was utterly incredulous. Could I have heard the president wrong? After the hearing, I called Martha Phillips and asked if I had heard him correctly. She assured me I had. Still, I wasn't of the mind to take on the president of the United States.

In the end, despite the Presidential Bi-partisan Entitlements Commission having called the entitlements "unsustainable," the congressional members failed to approve a single reform. And finally, Bill Clinton, confronting Monicagate, effectively deserted his own Bi-partisan Entitlement Commission effort.

I just sighed to myself: "That's politics."

The 2000s brought us the George W. Bush Social Security private account proposals, which were actually intended eventually to supplant the Social Security system to some extent. There is a strong case for such private accounts if—and it is a very big *if*—these are *added on* to a solvent Social Security system (which I consider an essential social safety net), and if we actually save more to finance these accounts. He deserves at least some credit for daring to bring up this toxic subject. But to borrow additional trillions for such private accounts was, to me, a travesty.

Allow me to share with you some of my current concerns:

That The Concord Coalition and other deficit crusaders including the Peterson Foundation, which I founded in 2008, have much more work to do is revealed by the fact that as I was putting the finishing touches on this book amid the worst economic crisis to hit our country in four generations, the debt clock ran out of room. Think about it. It has a capacity of thirteen numbers plus a dollar sign, enough to show $9,999,999,999,999. But when our public debt hit $10 trillion in October 2008—that's $10,000,000,000,000—the clock's keepers had to drop the lighted dollar sign and ordered a new clock with more space.

The truth is that the $10 trillion is but a small fraction of our true liabilities and unfunded promises.

The disclosure and transparency we so often and glibly talk about is seriously missing from the federal budget. Today, the $10 trillion public debt we so decry is less than one-fifth of the total future federal liabilities and unfunded benefit promises, of which Social Security accounts for $7 trillion and Medicare $34 trillion of what, in total, is over $56 trillion. The current $56 trillion financial hole is about four times the size of the entire economy. These kinds of debts would be unfinanceable. A much expanded debt clock will be needed, unless we change our ways.

The congressional hypocrisy is also overwhelming. The politicians tell us the middle class must have tax cuts. Why don't they also tell us that if we leave Social Security and Medicare intact, payroll taxes, which fall heavily on the middle class, would have to double, well within the lifetimes of our children. Those kinds of tax increases would obviously be unthinkable.

To add to the hypocrisy, Congress passed the Sarbanes-Oxley Act in a fury of disdain over corporate scandals and the limited financial disclosure of the corporate sector. Yet, if the Congress were to follow the same Sarbanes-Oxley corporate requirements for the annual funding of government retirement benefits, it would add over $1.5 trillion a year to the budget whose deficit is, of course, already in the trillions. If Congress were senior officers of a public corporation, they would be jailed for financial disclosure high jinks.

As we think about feeding this entitlement monster, we might want to listen to the unison of respected voices imploring Americans, and America, to save more and invest more in our future. Since we obviously have been ignoring this imperative, we might also want to remind ourselves of the immutable equation between consumption, on the one hand, and savings and investments in the future on the other. Try as we might, we have failed to invent a way to consume and save the same dollars. So, the more we consume, the less we save.

Entitlement benefits going to us old fogies is about as pure a form of consumption as I know of and has as little to do with the future as any expenditure I can think of. So, for those of us who say to ourselves we are devoted to reenergizing America's future, we might ask ourselves how we reconcile this imperative with feeding this entitlement consumption monster with its gargantuan appetite.

While I was writing this, I was greeted by my two-month-old grandniece, Vivian, who screamed the moment she saw me. Perhaps it was my guilty conscience but I found myself hallucinating that she had just learned that her federal "birthday" present, if you will, of $175,000 of well-hidden obligations, in current dollars, was her share of the deep financial hole she was inheriting.

Today, given America's preoccupation with living in the moment and, in that spirit, today's massive economic crisis, it is widely believed that this is a most unlikely moment to contemplate actual entitlement reform. Instead, we see President Obama, Treasury Secretary Geithner, and several congressional leaders all urging us to tame the entitlement monster, our so-called "structural" deficit. Why? One of my theories: We now glibly talk of the $2 trillion annual budget deficit to cover the various grant stimulus programs. At the same time, other countries, which have been funding our deficits, are launching their own unprecedented stimulus programs. The question arises: Who is going to lend us this $2 trillion? And on what terms? This, then, raises the additional question: If we are concerned about borrowing these trillions, how on earth will we be able to fund the $42 trillion of unfunded entitlement obligations and promises? The answer: We'd better give these lenders the confidence that we are indeed getting our act together. So perhaps a fiscal lemonade can be made out of our fiscal lemon, today's giant crisis.

In question-and-answer periods to my speeches, I am bombarded with simplistic, painless solutions to these problems that disingenuous political candidates have led the public to accept.

"Mr. Peterson: Why don't we get rid of those damn earmarks? I am told that would solve our deficit and debt problems." And someone else would say, "If we could only get rid of those damn Bush tax cuts—for you fat cats that is—I've been assured that would do it," and finally, "It would also take care of the problem if we could just get out of Iraq."

The melancholy truth: If we did *all* of those three things, including eliminating *all* of the Bush tax cuts, it would only cover 15 percent of our deep financial hole.

Of these long-term obligations, health care is obviously the biggest elephant in the room. Growing health care costs not only threaten our competitiveness but threaten to bankrupt the entire economy. We spend twice as much per capita as the rest of the developed world with no appreciable differences in health outcomes. And we still have 45 million Americans uninsured. We have the world's only open-ended cost-plus system, with no health care budget and a perverse system of cost incentives. In some cases there is a total lack of cost incentives or cost consciousness. This perverse system actually encourages unnecessary but costly medical procedures. And our clogged, egregiously costly litigation system is like nothing in the world.

Permit me to take but one example—my back problems. I have stenosis, or a form of arthritis. A well-known orthopedic surgeon looked at my MRI (incidentally, we have over ten times as many MRI units per capita as some other developed countries). "Pete, you need back surgery." I decided to talk with a back specialist who does not do back surgery. "Pete, the studies on this type of surgery indicate about fifty to sixty percent success. Did the surgeon tell you about epidural shots of cortisone?" "No, he didn't. What is the downside of epidural shots?" I asked. "There are none and these shots are much cheaper and much less painful, and their effects far less prolonged than back surgery. A program of epidurals and exercise often helps with your kind of back trouble." Happily, I chose the latter course and my back is fine.

What are the perverse cost incentives that I referred to? The cost of the back surgery, $14,000. The office visit for cortisone shots cost about $250. The financial incentive to do surgery is obvious. (To further anecdotalize the perversity of our health care system, my real need was not for back surgery but for a hip replacement, which worked out beautifully and solved my back problems.)

This perverse system results in inexplicable variations in medical procedures across the country. There are, for example, six times more back operations or prostate removal operations in some areas than in others. I know we have Red States and Blue States, but are we seriously asked to believe that we really have Bad Back States and Bad Prostate States? Clearly, this is the kind of bizarre outcome we can expect when we have the world's only open-ended cost-plus system and the perverse cost incentives that go with it.

We also spend about a fourth to a third of our vast Medicare costs (Medicare has about five times bigger unfunded liabilities and promises than Social Security) in the last months of life, far more than the rest of the world. Yet, remember Terri Schiavo. Clearly, such long-term medical procedures raise not just serious cost issues, but equally serious ethical, cultural issues, literally life-and-death issues.

After visiting the New York Hospital Intensive Care Unit where I was to see a surprisingly large number of octogenarians in what seemed comalike conditions getting very expensive, heroic life support, I asked the head of the neurology department at that time, my friend Dr. Fred Plum, how, for example, Great Britain would handle the same kind of cases. "Pete," Dr. Plum said, "for many of these stroke cases, where the prognosis is very dim, the British neurologist would turn the case over to the patient's general practitioner, who would send them home where the patient would die the so-called old man's death from pneumonia, as they often did." Can one imagine an American political candidate taking this position?

In this depressing litany of unsustainables, I should also mention our prodigious propensity to consume and our dismal or zero personal savings rate. The resulting mushrooming and dangerous foreign debt gives other countries "a financial guillotine" that an unfriendly country could use to do huge economic damage to the United States, as well as geopolitical damage to our strategic interests around the world. We simply must save more, as a country and as a people.

And then, of course, there is our energy gluttony, which endangers the environment, greatly increases our foreign borrowing, and again leaves us vulnerable to unfriendly suppliers. Also on the list is the low math and science scores of our students in an increasingly technological and competitive world economy.

I could add to this list of unsustainables, but I think you get the point, and I'd like you to keep reading.

In fact, my harping on the matter of our long-term fiscal irresponsibility, our generational inequity, our looming Social Security and Medicare deficits has become a theme and a source of humor for some of my friends. Ted Sorensen, President Kennedy's famous speechwriter, has been one of the most gifted roasters. Regarding one of my prior books, he said, "About Pete's new book . . . Once you put it down, you won't be able to pick it up."

He has also told the following joke: As he tells the story, the two of us are on a plane to the Middle East. Before it lands, terrorists take over the plane and announce they are going to assassinate me and Ted as two former United States officials on a bipartisan basis, one Republican, one Democrat. We are asked: Do the two of you have any last requests?

"Yes," I say. "I have one last speech I want to give to the people on the plane about the relationship between the U.S. budget deficits and the death of the American Dream."

"And you, Sorensen," they say, "What is your last request?"

"Well, I've heard that speech by Peterson," he says. "And my last request is that you shoot me first."

My homes are all well furnished, but people who know me politely suggest that my favorite piece of furniture is not an antique table or an heirloom chest but my trusty soapbox. On these various unsustainables, after all, I've been climbing up on it for years and delivering my opinions, solicited or not. As you will learn in the next chapter, I have no intention of getting down from that soapbox.

CHAPTER 17

THE FUTURE

What would I do with that pile of Blackstone IPO money? I could try to take it with me, but that seemed a most unlikely prospect. I could count it and try to make it grow (a very popular option). But I found that prospect a very empty one and, frankly, boring.

As I pondered not only what to do with this pile of money but what to do with myself and my future, I had to remember that I would also be retiring from Blackstone on December 31, 2008. As with the Council on Foreign Relations, I was to be named chairman emeritus and co-founder to boot. One thing I knew. I had no intention of becoming Peter G. Emeritus in life.

The rational side of me knew the time to leave Blackstone had come. The emotional and perhaps irrational side of me was another matter. One day, one of my young Blackstone friends ran into me in the elevator and said, "Hi, Pete. Are you still coming to work?" It was a sobering question.

I found myself thinking about my earlier and admittedly hectic background as CEO of Lehman Brothers for ten years and my twenty-three years at Blackstone. My typical Lehman day went something like this. Some colleagues would ride to work with me, either to brief me or decide an issue. A breakfast with a client for a new business prospect awaited me at the office. Of course, a business lunch. Introducing a foreign leader at the Council on Foreign Relations in the late afternoon. Even trying to write speeches in the dentist's chair. On the receiving

336

end of twenty-five to thirty telephone calls. An equal number of outgoing calls. Hundreds of letters to sign to the CEOs of the Bi-Partisan Budget Appeal, for example. Five or ten meetings during the day and often some kind of dinner meeting. Several assistants going full speed all day. And then, on the weekends, writing magazine articles and books. I'm not sure hectic quite describes it.

My Blackstone years were less frenzied but still very full. In addition to a jam-packed schedule, almost no day went by in which I wasn't engaged in some Council affair or business. And then there was often something having to do with the Institute for International Economics, The Concord Coalition, and weekly New York Fed telephone meetings and monthly board meetings.

From the time in June 2007, when I had stepped down from the chairmanship of the Council on Foreign Relations, and I had announced, as part of the Blackstone IPO, that I would be retiring no later than the end of 2008, the phones seemed to stop ringing. There were fewer and fewer faxes. People wrote much less. My schedule was often a blank page. Bliss! I was liberated. I was free.

Yet I was miserable. Indeed, I was depressed. I had trouble sleeping. I felt joyless. Humor came less easily. I found it difficult to focus for any period of time or to read anything of any length. Socializing lost much of its normal appeal. Much more often than in times past, friends would ask if I was feeling well. Most of my friends were supportive and were kind enough to listen to my long melancholy and, I'm sure, boring monologues. A few, particularly those whose enthusiasm for psychotherapy is restrained, reminded me I had "nothing" to be depressed about. After all, I had a great wife and family, plenty of money, an interesting life, and generally was in good health. Their simple—and to me simplistic—message: Just snap out of it.

What was I if I wasn't defined by my work? As the months passed, I came to feel hollow. Why, I asked myself, was I so "vaguely discontented" as the song "It Might as Well Be Spring" goes, and why couldn't I enjoy all the free time and money to do whatever I wished?

It was a fertile field for therapy, as well as, I was to find, for psychopharmacology. As a lifetime overachiever, I was to find that I felt my new world of growing inactivity was a kind of metaphor for my declining years, for my heading downhill or, in a sense, slowly dying. A few added nonterminal health issues, all related to aging, and two bad falls, each requiring surgery, added to that anxiety and feeling of melancholia. I suppose we all fear death in one way or another.

I came to understand what others have found; that major transitions in careers, particularly for an active octogenarian, can be far more difficult and, in ways, more painful than I would have ever thought.

I then started looking at the lives of other billionaires. Virtually all the ones I really admired were major philanthropists. Men like David Rockefeller, my role model in so many ways, Mike Bloomberg, George Soros, Eli Broad—each is passionate about his own passion to do good. I decided that was what I wanted to do.

But do good about what?

I was also moved by the discipline of gratitude. I am so grateful and lucky that I have so fully lived the American Dream. Had I been born in a different country, at a different time and with different parents, I could not imagine being where I am today. Yet I feel that, on our current course, the American Dream is imperiled and, indeed, so is America's future.

Sadly, for the first time in my memory, the majority of the American people join me in believing that, on our current course, our children will not do better than we have done. In fact, a majority believe their children will do less well. That, of course, strikes at the heart of the American Dream.

Earlier, I spoke of the undeniable, unsustainable, and untouchable, politically speaking, challenges America confronts—the tens of trillions of dollars of unfunded entitlements, the dangerous dependence on foreign capital, our pitiful level of savings, the metastasizing health care costs, our energy gluttony. In the words of the iconic Paul Volcker, former chairman of the Federal Reserve Bank, "Altogether the circumstances seem to me as dangerous and intractable as any I can remember, and I can remember quite a lot."

Every expert I know believes that these various structural deficits are unsustainable. Herb Stein was the Nixon humorist, if you will forgive the oxymoron, in the White House in which I served (he was also the chairman of the Council of Economic Advisors). He once observed, "If something's unsustainable, it tends to stop." He also said: "If your horse dies, I suggest you dismount."

And yet, we keep trying to ride this horse.

Underlying these unsustainable and untouchable challenges is a broken political system, and the problem runs far deeper than the bitter partisanship.

It is certainly a very different political system than our founders ever envisioned, one in which our political representatives would consider their much shorter congressional sessions as a temporary assignment to achieve certain specific objectives. Then they would go home again to resume being farmers or lawyers or merchants—what we might call self-imposed term limits. Today, our representatives see their jobs not as temporary, but as a career. They would much rather keep their jobs than tell us the truth.

As a result, our political leaders are focused not on the next generation, but on the next election. And when the long-term problems are large and real, our politicians anesthetize us, mislead us, divert us—anything other than clearly and honestly spelling out these long-term challenges, proposing solutions and leading us to confront them. They assume we have become such an indulgent, instant gratification society that we want it all. We want it now. And that we don't want to give up or pay for anything. So too often our political leaders are not leaders at all but enablers, co-conspirators joining us in a state of denial, in a kind of disingenuous and greedy silence.

Margaret Thatcher is the only leader of a developed country who has successfully reformed a social security system. I once asked her why it was that the leaders of the other large G7 developed countries have not been similarly successful. What was in their minds and experience? She crisply explained, their attitude is: "Why should I take the pain for somebody else's gain?" In our U.S. democracy, this difficulty of taking steps that have short-term costs but long-term gains is referred to as NIMTOF, that is, any gains from the reforms are "not in my term of office."

Today, Washington is also overwhelmed with special interests, which typically have one mantra: We want more. And if this means slipping the huge and hidden debt and tax bill to our kids and grandkids, so be it. It is a gross example of taxation without representation. If not unconstitutional, it should certainly be declared immoral.

Our children are unrepresented. The future is unrepresented. Obviously, we need a new kind of special interest. A special interest of the future. A special interest on behalf of our children and grandchildren.

Sadly for the politicians and most certainly for the rest of us, there are no easy answers to these challenges. Yet answers simply must be found. And they all require the S-word, sacrifice, which at least in recent times has been the least popular word in the American political dialogue.

Still, we are too prone to blame politicians for not having the courage to lead us to a better future. We the people also need to be leading followers: that means you and me. If it is true that politicians can't get too far ahead of the voters, we the people must make it safer for them to do the right thing. We must change the political equation. We must make it at least as politically painful to do nothing as it is to do something about these unsustainables.

I am also deeply concerned about America's character and our national mind-set. I see an indulgent country living almost entirely in the moment, afflicted with an aggravated case of myopia, and a sense of entitlement, one of my least favorite words.

I found myself wondering whether America had ever overcome what at the time must have also seemed "unsustainable." What could history teach us?

Over fifty years ago, Americans paid off the debt of the most costly (in every sense of the word) war in history, and launched the G.I. Bill, the Marshall Plan, and a very extensive infrastructure project, the Interstate Highway System. At the time of the Vietnam War, President Lyndon Johnson was severely criticized for giving the country "guns and butter"; in other words, fighting a costly war and at the same time launching the Great Society and the War on Poverty as well as huge unfunded domestic spending initiatives like Medicare. I joined a meeting of businessmen in the Oval Office during that period. The tortured president couldn't seem to stop talking, defending and rationalizing. Today, we are trying to do LBJ one better. We are told we can have guns, butter, *and* tax cuts. What a contrast from the good old days when

America offered its people the stark choice of guns *or* butter, at least unpaid-for butter.

Going back further, George Washington did not want to pass on the debts that were run up to finance the Revolutionary War. It would, he said, be "ungenerously throwing upon posterity the burden we ourselves ought to bear." President Eisenhower said much the same thing in his 1961 Farewell Address: "As we peer into society's future, we—you and I, and our government—must avoid the impulse to live only for today, plundering, for our own ease and convenience, the precious resources of tomorrow. We cannot mortgage the material assets of our grandchildren without risking the loss also of their political and spiritual heritage. We want democracy to survive for all generations to come, not to become the insolvent phantom of tomorrow."

We had done it before. Why could we not do it again? I simply refused to believe that we parents and grandparents have become so selfish and self-absorbed that we do not care about the imperiled future we are endowing to our children and grandchildren.

I was inspired by wisdom from the anti-Nazi theologian Dietrich Bonhoeffer: "The ultimate test of a moral society is the kind of world it leaves to its children." I felt that I could no longer duck the moral question of slipping our own kids and grandkids the huge and hidden check for our free lunch. I felt it was long past the time we become moral and worthy ancestors.

I decided that educating, motivating, and activating the American people to do something about these and other unsustainables was where this old warrior would make his stand. As I did the planning, I started to feel better.

So I set up a special kind of foundation. It would focus on America's key sustainability challenges that threaten the future of America and American families. There is no shortage of foundations focusing on the important here-and-now needs. It would not be another foundation of the think tank variety. The truth is that, for most of these challenges, there already are workable proposals. The problem is not a lack of proposals, not thinking about these problems. The problem is doing something about them.

It would be a decisive, fast-acting, un-bureaucratic foundation. As you have read in this book, I have studied foundations a bit. They all do very worthwhile work, but given concerns about governance of public foundations, I have found more than a few encumbered by slow-moving and bureaucratic decision-making processes.

However, public foundations have defining tax advantages. The donor gets a major charitable deduction, which can be made with the type of Blackstone stock units that I hold. A private foundation would provide me none of these tax advantages, but it has less demanding governance requirements. I opted for the private formation structure. My wife, Joan Ganz Cooney, my very able son Michael, and I are the only board members.

The next question was: How much would I contribute to this foundation? I knew the mission was daunting and that all too little had been invested in fighting the seemingly untouchable, intractable unsustainability challenges.

As I reflected on the "how much?" question, two experiences came to mind. The great novelist Kurt Vonnegut once told a story that seemed to capture the situation perfectly. He and Joseph Heller were at a party given by a wealthy hedge fund manager (that used to be a redundancy before the financial crunch of 2007 and 2008) at his majestic beach house in the Hamptons, the summer playground on Long Island where the rich and famous congregate. Kurt and Joe both had made their marks by satirizing life's absurdities—Kurt with best-selling novels like *Slaughterhouse 5* and *Breakfast of Champions*, Joe with the incomparable *Catch-22*. During the course of the party, Kurt looked around at his surroundings and asked Heller: "Joe, doesn't it bother you that this guy makes more in a day than you ever made from the worldwide sales of *Catch-22*?"

Joe thought for a moment and then said, "No, not really. I have something that he doesn't have."

"What could you possibly have that he doesn't have?" Kurt asked.

"I know the meaning of enough."

My father tried to teach me the meaning of enough. When I asked about why we didn't have a new car, or why I couldn't replace my old bike, he said, "My son, we have more than enough, and others need it far more than we." I'm confident he never read the poet and artist William Blake, who wrote "You never know what is enough unless you know more than enough." Yet, somehow, the twentieth-century Greek immigrant and the eighteenth-century English mystic shared an intuitive understanding of something we could all learn more about. At the time when I was a boy I felt I didn't have enough. Today, I realize that even before Blackstone went public I had much more than enough.

I decided I would commit $1 billion, the great bulk of my net proceeds from the Blackstone public offering. I assumed that big a commitment might make a difference not only in potential impact but in attracting an absolutely top leader of this effort, a must from my standpoint.

This strategy turned out to be the right one. We managed to attract the man that I thought then, and I know now, is the best person in the country to lead this foundation: David Walker, then comptroller general of the United States, the chief watchdog of the national cash flow and an impassioned crusader for fiscal sustainability. After hearing him speak, my wife, Joan, said, "This man is an oxymoron. He is a charismatic accountant."

In making this big a commitment, I knew I would have some doubters. Wasn't I being presumptuous and even worse, foolhardy? Didn't I realize how formidable the obstacles are? Yes, I thought I did. I do appreciate that the odds of success are daunting indeed. And yet, the words of my friend and a former professor at the University of Chicago, George Stigler, ring in my ears: "If one has no alternative, one has no problem." I asked myself: Could there be a worse feeling than not having tried and waking up ten to twenty years from now to find that we are living in a weakened America that has lost its American Dream and its leadership to affect events around the world? Not trying was no alternative at all.

We want to create a movement with special emphasis on the young. The young are a part of the true silent majority of Americans. The lack of youth involvement in public affairs is too often characterized by the old joke in which the philosophy professor asks the class: "Which is worse, ignorance or apathy?" A sleepy kid from the back of the class mumbled, "I don't know and I don't care."

In fairness to the young, they have no memories of truly bad economic times. My generation, of course, experienced the Great Depression. My generation also had reasons to have faith in both their public and private sector leaders. Could we blame the young of today if many have so little faith? Still, it is, after all, their future that is imperiled. How do we educate the youth to the crises they will face if things are not changed and, most important, how do we motivate them to do something about them? I have a dream—some would say a fantasy—of a movement that includes 50,000 or 100,000 young people, or more, their parents and grandparents marching on Washington and, in the spirit of the movie *Network,* chanting, "I'm as mad as hell and I'm not going to take it anymore."

But first, we must take responsibility for helping to educate the young on the future they confront. So, how do we educate and activate the true silent majority of America, the young, their parents and grandparents?

We will go where the young people are: new media, bloggers, YouTube, Facebook, MySpace, social networks, video games, and Web sites that have not even been invented. We have approved a major MTV program aimed at hundreds of colleges in the United States. We will have youth summits to get young leaders engaged.

We will recruit business leaders to commit themselves to join the cause. Thomas Friedman of the *New York Times* has rightly called us MIAs (missing in action), from the fight for our future.

We are experimenting with advocacy advertising—not widely used in the foundation world as an educational tool, like the full-page ad we have run in the *New York Times* and the *Washington Post* (see page 345).

We will sponsor the production of films that educate people about the perils that America faces. I was very impressed with what Al Gore accomplished with *An Inconvenient Truth* to dramatize the effects of global warming. The foundation's entry in the film sweepstakes is *I.O.U.S.A.,* a critically acclaimed, award-winning look at our debt problems.

Beyond a more informed and motivated youth, the public and the business community, nothing is as important as the leadership of a committed and trusted president in what must be a bipartisan effort. President Barack Obama's very encouraging commitment to reform entitlements is a most welcome development.

Today's economic crisis is just the tip of the iceberg.

$56 TRILLION

$483,000 per U.S. household

We must also focus on a much larger yet less visible threat: the $56 trillion in liabilities and unfunded retirement and health care obligations (that's $483,000 per U.S. household), and the dangerous reliance on foreign lenders, that threaten our ship of state.

Fortunately, the Obama Administration and a growing number of Congressional leaders recognize the urgent need to address these challenges with entitlement, budget, spending, and tax reforms. We believe a credible approach is necessary: an action-oriented bipartisan commission that would engage the American people, consider all options, and make sensible recommendations that would be guaranteed to be put to a vote in Congress. Endorsing such a commission would be an excellent objective for the President's Fiscal Responsibility Summit.

Meeting today's challenges is very important, but addressing these structural challenges is critical to navigating a better future for our children and grandchildren.

Learn more at www.pgpf.org

Peter G. Peterson
Foundation
Our America. Our Future.

One of the foundation's first group meetings dealt with the balance of payments and savings deficits and the resulting mushrooming foreign debt. The Peterson Institute for International Economics prepared a series of papers to review. We invited Paul Volcker, Bob Rubin, former secretary of the treasury under Bill Clinton; George Shultz, a former secretary of state, treasury, and labor; Martin Feldstein, former chairman of the Council of Economic Advisors; George Soros, a global financier and philanthropist; and Alan Greenspan, among others. They all accepted and participated actively. The press raved about our "convening power." I demurred, telling them that this was an indication of the bipartisan unanimity that these long-term challenges truly are both undeniable and unsustainable. I felt reaffirmed about what I was trying to do. This has in turn motivated me to do more and confirmed to me we are on the right track.

Affirmation of one's work is great therapy.

As I look back on my education as an American dreamer, I realize it certainly allowed me to hit some singles, doubles, and even a few home runs, but also it didn't prevent me from making more than my share of mistakes, particularly in my personal life.

I've also had more than my share of plain old dumb luck. I also know that the best piece of luck was in my choice of parents. I certainly didn't appreciate them as a child. As a youth, in fact, I'm sorry to say that I often resented them. I figured they didn't know what America and being American were all about. It turned out they knew far more than I did.

They knew that realizing the opportunities this uniquely blessed country offered one to become an American dreamer was more than hard work: That was a given. It meant taking responsibility for one's future. It meant investing in that future. It meant saving for it, for education, for one's retirement. They didn't feel entitled to anything more than the opportunity to earn a good future. In sum, they taught me that tomorrow was even more important than today.

And because they knew that the differences in outcomes are often a matter of luck, giving back was an imperative. And besides, it brought the giver genuine and lasting pleasure.

Granted, my way of giving back is a more modern, intellectually charged version than that of my parents. But this version suits me because it uses my natural inclination toward vigorously analyzing every situation and problem. I truly enjoy doing that kind of work. I like to think I'm quite good at it. But the point is, it was my parents' example that turned me into a philanthropic crusader, and yes, a relentless one.

After all, as a young boy of eight years old, I'd stand by the door of our restaurant wide-eyed as I watched my own father as he faced down bigots and told them what being a real American was all about.

A crusade is, by its nature, a battle or a series of public battles, and one builds bonds a bit like those between the fellow soldiers in a war. In the course of these battles over time, taking up common cause with those whose beliefs and goals you share, you forge friendships and develop relationships that are different from normal business relationships. They are often deeper. There is a different level of trust. I have built on many of these relationships in my career. And feeling that connection with colleagues or partners or anyone I worked alongside has been one of the great and constructive pleasures of my business life.

So at the age of eighty-three, I have started a whole new crusade in creating this foundation, I am giving back a lot of my resources and myself to try, in my very small way, to give my children's and grandchildren's generations the same opportunities to share in this American Dream and to become American dreamers.

And, although I am an octogenarian, I don't want to retire. In short, I want the phone to keep ringing. An occasional golf game is refreshing. But I find a daily golf game boring. My daughter jokes that when I do pass on, it will be at my desk with my head hunched over a speech explaining why the Social Security Trust Fund is an insolvent oxymoron. (I hope she's right and that it has lots of PowerPoint charts.) In other words, that big wire after the Blackstone IPO didn't stop me from wanting to be in the game.

Now that I am back in the fray with my foundation, I love working again, and I have no apologies for it! I was made for work, just like my mother and father. And by recognizing how much like them I had become, I realized how very American I am.

CODA

SOME LESSONS LEARNED

I have joked that an honest title of most autobiographical writings would be "How to Be More like Me." Not this one. But people often do ask me about my careers in both business and public policy, as if my experience might contain some nuggets of guidance.

On the business side, the question that many find intriguing is how and why I managed to achieve top positions in such seemingly disparate fields as advertising, manufacturing, and Wall Street while still in my thirties and forties. And maybe there's an implicit question lurking in the shadows: How does one make a billion dollars?

As to my public policy career, if it's fair to call my passionate public interests my second career, I've been asked how I managed to find the time to do it without losing my day job.

My first (and uncharacteristically modest) answer has been to chalk some of my success up to dumb luck, and I certainly have had some very good luck. But my editor found this much too facile. He said it begs the question: Why was I offered so many senior-level opportunities at such a young age? And it fails to address the question of what one does about the opportunities that come one's way, no matter how or why they arrive. For me, George Washington Plunkitt, a famous Tammany Hall boss, had it right when he said, "I seen my opportunities and I took 'em."

Lest this section verge on career advice, let me add a caveat. We are all so different in our interests, our passions, our abilities, our resources, and our strengths, and, yes, our weaknesses, that a standard "how to" career planning approach, at least for me, makes little sense. I emphasize that I have never had a long-term career formula for myself and, most certainly, I don't have one for you. All I could suggest is that you read these themes or principles as connective tissue between my various careers and ask yourself: Does any of this relate to me, my interests, my abilities, my passions?

Perhaps the first lesson—No. 1—I have learned is this: Don't get seduced by a job because it pays a bit more or you have a bigger office and better perks or it is better located. Focus on how it plays to your strengths so you can exercise your comparative advantages. My very first job, the one in retailing, focused on my comparative disadvantages and it was a genuine failure. After that, I learned to avoid job options, however seductive, that do not. Ultimately, I found that how well my career did depended upon how good I was on the job and that, in turn, meant capitalizing on my strengths. Students of Adam Smith will remember that it was one of his seminal teachings for countries: Focus on your comparative advantages. I have found it applies to people and jobs as well.

Once I put my comparative advantages into play, I learned my second important lesson, No. 2: Don't be intellectually lazy. Think about what your institution, or your industry, or, indeed, the overall economy is really about.

In advertising, it was simply not enough to be called a wunderkind. I wanted to define not just what advertising was, but what it could and should be.

In both business and my various public policy interests, I found myself attracted not just to the micro issues—the specific things that one must do well day by day—but to the macro—the conceptual. I liked the small plus the large, the concrete plus the larger and more abstract.

I was also never content to simply know what I knew or what I thought I knew. I wanted to write about it, to speak of it, even to teach others. And, as I did that, I met smart or smarter and involved people, who not only refined but enlarged my thinking. And, in the course of all those writings, speeches, and teachings, I came to feel that for me at least, it was not enough to think and write great thoughts.

That was lesson No. 3: What was really important to me was to pitch in to try to *do something* about things. That means trying to enhance or advance situations that I see as worthwhile, as well as trying to change things that I feel need to be changed. That is why I have spent so much time trying to work with or to start various institutions and organizations. These have substantially widened my circle of people who share my intellectual passions. I have been involved in civil rights, in fiscal responsibility and generational equity, in a code of conduct for the Congress, in reform of charitable foundations, in longer-term, performance-based executive compensation.

And so at key moments in my life, I often found that people had thought of me for a board position, either corporate or nonprofit, or had given my firm some new business, because they had fought alongside me in one of these battles and, apparently, they had trusted my sensibilities and judgment. A prime example was the Bi-Partisan Budget Appeal in the 1980s in which I joined with five secretaries of the treasury and a few hundred corporate CEOs to call for fiscal responsibility in government.

It had simply not occurred to me that these outside activities would contribute so much to my business success. One part of this lesson is not to get involved outside of work only because you think it will help you at work. I did it because I loved it. The rest followed.

Lesson No. 4: Pick your battles carefully, with an eye to personal satisfaction. When nonprofit opportunities came my way, and there were a surprising number, I had some tough choices to make. Should I accept all or most of them or should I select a chosen few? While I am intellectually restless and like to think about and work on quite a variety of issues that interest me, I learned that these multiple interests could lead to being scattered, to trying to do too much—to jumping from thing to thing, job to job. So I chose very few, and one principal criterion was awfully simple. I decided to follow my passion or, as the philosopher Joseph Campbell put it, "Follow Your Bliss." What a pleasure it is to work hard in an area you love! It was, at times, very seductive to join the board of a prestigious institution in order to make good connections. But if it was not one of my passions, I learned to just say no.

Because I was so passionate about certain issues, and could spend the time on them, I was happy to get involved not only in the substantive work of the institution, but also in its governance and, very important, its fundraising.

Again, I found a very unexpected outcome. I was occasionally asked to be the chairman, one of whose key roles often is to raise money. That, in turn, led to many more close relationships with some of America's most important leaders in both business and government.

Much is said about unintended consequences, and it mostly has to do with negative effects. But as I was to learn, there are also unintended, surprising, and positive effects, where my work in one area, such as promoting more fiscal responsibility, led to major benefits in other areas, such as more business for our firm, or, very important, a new crop of interesting friends.

The next lesson, No. 5, is a really big one. It has to do with the way you conduct your entire life.

My parents taught me how terribly important it is to be true to one's principles, to one's self, and to one's moral compass. Because of their mentoring, I was urged to say no to those who did not deserve a yes. And while these no's might involve some obvious short-term cost, there would nearly always be long-term gain.

I wish I could say that I have always lived by these principles, but there were at least two instances when I did not. One was at MIT, when I recycled Roy Cohn's paper. My excuse was lame: I whined that this country boy from Nebraska finally deserved to focus on an exhilarating and newfound New York social life, and I engaged in the disingenuous rationalization that I hadn't "really" copied his paper because I had added "so much" of my own. I had vowed to be honest not only with others, but with myself. This clearly violated that principle and I paid the price. And it was a heavy one.

Another was at Lehman Brothers, where I accepted some unacceptable behavior by a few partners for much too long because I was concerned with "keeping the peace" and maintaining short-term profits.

In both of these cases, there was some short-term gain and pleasure or at least the avoidance of some short-term pain, but it was achieved at the expense of serious long-term pain or cost.

But on those occasions when I kept my promise to myself and followed my principles, even if it was harder in the short run, the long-term benefits were real. I can think of no exceptions to this in my life.

At a series of important junctures in my life I just said no. I felt I had good reasons for saying no, either ethical reasons or an instinctive sense of the lack of character or soundness of a major directive or a person trying to do the directing and deciding. I have never regretted any of those no's.

At McCann-Erickson, for example, there was the boss who jeopardized the pension fund, disregarded prudence to buy an oversized company plane, stole my writings, and tried to seduce me into taking the company's presidency at a ridiculously young age. I quit before lining up my next job, a hard short-term decision but one I've never regretted.

In the Nixon administration, I insisted on maintaining an independent personal life and refused to be used by the political animals around the president. This, too, may have cost me some exciting short-term assignments, but it got me out of Washington before Watergate descended.

I agonized at the time about the choices I was making. I feared that sticking to my principles would lead to a downfall. There was job uncertainty and even temporary public embarrassment. But I still had my reputation for integrity, to say nothing of the much larger job opportunities that emerged.

In other words, at the time, my "Nixon no's" seemed to have led to my undoing. But they didn't really. They were the making of me.

I observed in the Nixon White House that the baggage of working with people with whom one did not share basic values is much heavier than I would have thought. Now I have learned to advocate "traveling light"—that is, avoid accumulating baggage in your work situation that keeps you from acting independently and ethically. For example, the young staffers around H. R. Haldeman in the Nixon White House carried the heavy baggage of his rigid ideology and ethical lapses, and it kept them from acting on their own and, ultimately, put some of them in jail.

Traveling light was sometimes harder to do than I expected. But over the longer term, I learned it was the right thing to do.

Then, there's Lesson No. 6: achieving a healthy and happy balance between one's business or professional life and one's personal life. Alas, in this particular respect, much of my life has been a negative example: a case study in imbalance. I had been through two divorces because I didn't seem to value much beyond working and achieving.

In some cases, it is true that rebalancing one's life may mean that the upward curve of one's business career may be flattened. In my case, I knew my decision not to be CEO of Blackstone would ultimately mean less compensation. However, it would also mean that I could devote more time to Joan, my children, my friends, and my various public causes and crusades. And I have done just that.

The specific adjustments we make are not as important as the basic principle that for many of us, the balanced life will not come about without some serious thought, self-analysis, ultimately prioritizing, and, yes, even some sacrifice. Questions like these need to be answered. What do each of us mean by a balanced life, and how are we spending our time now that creates an imbalance? And what are we willing to change or give up?

Finally, there's Lesson No. 7, which is, perhaps, career advice. Hard experience has taught me not to be seduced by a job opportunity without thoroughly checking it out first. You're not simply trying to find a niche that caters to your comparative advantages, you're looking for flaws and fractures in the corporate culture that can act like land mines and blow up your career. Careful due diligence on prospective employers can pay huge dividends and avoid serious risks. Had I conducted such due diligence in the case of Lehman Brothers, I probably would have opted out.

There is also much to be said for an intensive due diligence process when you're being recruited for a senior position. These kinds of questions are usually appropriate: What are the goals and values of the firm? How political is the climate and in what ways and what areas of the business? Have you interviewed not only their superiors but also some of your likely peers? How do they view your job and having you aboard? What is the firm's reputation for executive turnover? If high, what is the explanation? What do they expect you to do and how realistic are their expectations? How financially solid and stable is the organization? Are there any lingering and substantial legal or regulatory issues?

Looking back, many of my opportunities turned out to be a career choice between short-term versus long-term advantage. I have concluded it should always be about the longer term.

ACKNOWLEDGMENTS

This book would not be what it is without the help of many people, a few of whom I would like to thank here.

About eighteen months ago, I first talked about writing my memoirs with my agent and friend, Andrew Wylie. He gave me his usual wise and much valued counsel. Along the way, at every stage, I had consistent and valuable help from Nick Taylor with editing and polishing my rough drafts. I shall always be very grateful to him.

At that point Jonathan Karp, the gifted editor of Twelve, publisher of this book, entered the scene. His many suggestions were invaluable; I only hope what I wrote in response is adequate. At Twelve, Cary Goldstein and Colin Shepherd have been very helpful collaborators.

Most recently, two of my beloved children, Holly and Michael, gave what I had done still another serious fresh and important edit. I trust our relationship has survived their vigorous interventions. The same could be said of Laurie Carlson, Christine Hadlow, Emile Busi, Mark Doty, and Javed Masood, who teamed up to process what must have seemed like endless redrafts.

During this process, my brother John, cousin Mando, Dan Burstein, Jason Epstein, Harry Evans, Laura Landro, Jackie Leo, Peggy Noonan, Alice Peterson, Tara Peters, and Joel Schumacher were kind enough to read and comment.

All stressed this is not one of my public policy books. It is a memoir. They advised that I simply had to animate whatever points I was trying to make with stories and situations. I only hope my memories are reasonably accurate, relevant, and interesting.

Most of all, I thank my wife, Joan, for her many contributions and for putting up with my fractured life in general and, in particular, my preoccupation over the last year and a half with writing this book. I am sure she is looking forward to this long personal nightmare being over.

INDEX

ABOUT TWELVE

TWELVE was established in August 2005 with the objective of publishing no more than one book per month. We strive to publish the singular book, by authors who have a unique perspective and compelling authority. Works that explain our culture; that illuminate, inspire, provoke, and entertain. We seek to establish communities of conversation surrounding our books. Talented authors deserve attention not only from publishers, but from readers as well. To sell the book is only the beginning of our mission. To build avid audiences of readers who are enriched by these works—that is our ultimate purpose.

For more information about forthcoming TWELVE books, please go to www.twelvebooks.com.